HOW HITCHENS CAN SAVE THE LEFT

HOW HITCHENS CAN SAVE THE LEFT

*Rediscovering Fearless Liberalism
in an Age of Counter-Enlightenment*

Matt Johnson

PITCHSTONE PUBLISHING
DURHAM, NORTH CAROLINA

Pitchstone Publishing
www.pitchstonebooks.com

Library of Congress Cataloging-in-Publication Data

Names: Johnson, Matt (Journalist), author.
Title: How Hitchens can save the left : rediscovering fearless liberalism
   in an age of counter-enlightenment / Matt Johnson.
Description: Durham, North Carolina : Pitchstone Publishing, [2023] |
   Includes bibliographical references and index. | Summary: "Christopher Hitchens
   was for many years considered one of the fiercest and most eloquent left-wing
   polemicists in the world. But on much of today's left, he's remembered as a defector,
   a warmonger, and a sellout-a supporter of the wars in Afghanistan and Iraq who
   traded his left-wing principles for neoconservatism after the September 11 attacks. In
   How Hitchens Can Save the Left, Matt Johnson argues that this easy narrative gets
   Hitchens exactly wrong. Hitchens was a lifelong champion of free inquiry, humanism,
   and universal liberal values. He was an internationalist who believed all people should
   have the liberty to speak and write openly, to be free of authoritarian domination,
   and to escape the arbitrary constraints of tribe, faith, and nation. He was a figure of
   the Enlightenment and a man of the left until the very end, and his example has never
   been more important. Over the past several years, the liberal foundations of democratic societies have been showing signs of structural decay. On the right, nationalism
   and authoritarianism have been revived on both sides of the Atlantic. On the left,
   many activists and intellectuals have become obsessed with a reductive and censorious
   brand of identity politics, as well as the conviction that their own liberal democratic
   societies are institutionally racist, exploitative, and imperialistic. Across the democratic
   world, free speech, individual rights, and other basic liberal values are losing their
   power to inspire. Hitchens's case for universal Enlightenment principles won't just
   help genuine liberals mount a resistance to the emerging illiberal orthodoxies on the
   left and the right. It will also remind us how to think and speak fearlessly in defense
   of those principles"— Provided by publisher.
Identifiers: LCCN 2022026615 | ISBN 9781634312349 (paperback) | ISBN
   9781634312356 (ebook)
Subjects: LCSH: Hitchens, Christopher—Political and social views. |
   Hitchens, Christopher—Influence. | Liberalism—United States. | Right
   and left (Political science)—United States. | BISAC: POLITICAL SCIENCE
   / Political Ideologies / Democracy | BIOGRAPHY & AUTOBIOGRAPHY /
   Editors, Journalists, Publishers
Classification: LCC CT275.H62575 J64 2023 | DDC 320.51092
   [B]—dc23/eng/20220722
LC record available at lccn.loc.gov/2022026615

Cover photo by Kathy deWitt / Alamy

Contents

Introduction

First Principles

In the introduction to his 1993 collection of essays *For the Sake of Argument*, Christopher Hitchens affirmed his commitment to the left: "Everyone has to descend or degenerate from some species of tradition," he wrote, "and this is mine."[1] Hitchens's political trajectory is often presented as a story of left-wing degeneration. His career was "something unique in natural history," as former Labour MP George Galloway put it: "The first ever metamorphosis from a butterfly back into a slug."[2] After Hitchens abandoned socialism and all other formal political allegiances, his critics say he became a fulminating reactionary, a neocon warmonger, and a dreary cliché: the defector, the sellout, the predictable left-wing apostate.

The standard left-wing narrative about Hitchens is that he exchanged his socialism for some species of neoconservatism. After many years as a left-wing dissident in Washington, DC, he took the side of the U.S. government when it launched the most maligned war since Vietnam. Sure, he said a few sensible things about the excesses and contradictions of capitalism in his days as a Marxist, established himself as the most lacerating critic of U.S. foreign policy in the American media, and did more to put an asterisk next to Henry Kissinger's reputation than just about any other writer. But this long radical resume is now just a footnote in what many on the left view as a chronicle of moral and political derangement—the once-great left-wing polemicist becoming an apologist for the American empire. On this view, if the left has anything to learn from Hitchens, it's strictly cautionary.

From socialist to neocon. It was an irresistible headline[3] because it's a story that has been told over and over again—according to many authorities on the left, butterflies have been morphing back into slugs since the dawn of natural history. The novelist Julian Barnes called this phenomenon the "ritual shuffle to the right."[4] Richard Seymour, who wrote a book-length attack on Hitchens, says his subject belongs to a "recognisable type: a left-wing defector with a soft spot for empire."[5] Irving Kristol's famous description of a neoconservative is a liberal who has been "mugged by reality,"[6] which implies a reluctant and grudging transition from idealism to safe and boring pragmatism. By presenting Hitchens as a tedious archetype, hobbling away from radicalism and toward some inevitable reactionary terminus, his opponents didn't have to contend with his arguments or confront the potentially destabilizing fact that some of his principles called their own into question.

Hitchens didn't make it easy on the apostate hunters. To many, he was a "coarser version of Norman Podhoretz"[7] when he talked about Iraq and a radical humanist truth-teller when he went on Fox News to lambaste the Christian right: "If you gave Falwell an enema," he told Sean Hannity the day after Jerry Falwell's death, "he could be buried in a matchbox."[8] Then he gave Islam the same treatment, and he was suddenly a drooling neocon again. He called for the removal of Saddam Hussein and the arrest of Kissinger at the same time. He endorsed the War on Terror but condemned waterboarding[9] and signed his name to an American Civil Liberties Union (ACLU) lawsuit against the National Security Agency (NSA) for warrantless wiretapping.[10] He defied easy categorization: a socialist who spurned ideology, an internationalist who became a patriot, a man of the left who was reviled by the left.

The left isn't a single amorphous entity—it's a vast constellation of (often conflicting) ideas and principles. Hitchens's style of left-wing radicalism is now out of fashion, but it has a long and venerable history: George Orwell's unwavering opposition to totalitarianism and censorship, Bayard Rustin's advocacy for universal civil rights without appealing to tribalism and identity politics, the post-communist anti-totalitarianism that emerged on the European left in the second half of the twentieth century. Hitchens described himself as a "First Amendment absolutist," an echo of historic left-wing struggles for free expression—from Eugene V. Debs's assertion of his right to dissent during World War I to the Berkeley Free Speech Movement. Hitchens argued that unfettered free speech and inquiry would always make civil society stronger. When he wrote the introduction to *For the Sake of Argument* in 1993, he had a specific left-wing tradition in mind: the left of Orwell and Victor Serge and C.L.R. James, which simultaneously opposed Stalinism, fascism, and imperialism in the twentieth century, and which stood for "individual and collective emancipation, self-determination and internationalism."

Hitchens believed "politics is division by definition," but his most fundamental political and moral conviction was universalism. He loathed nationalism and argued that the international system should be built around a "common standard for justice and ethics"—a standard that should apply to Kissinger just as it should apply to Slobodan Milošević and Saddam Hussein. He believed in the concept of global citizenship, which is why he firmly supported international institutions like the European Union. He didn't just despise religion because he regarded it as a form of totalitarianism—he also recognized that it's an infinitely replenishable wellspring of tribal hatred. He opposed identity politics because he didn't think our social and civic lives should be reduced to rigid categories based on melanin, X chromosomes, and sexuality. He recognized that the Enlightenment values of individual rights, freedom of expression and conscience, humanism, pluralism, and democracy are universal—they provide the most stable, just, and rational foundation for any civil society, whether they're observed in America or Europe or Iraq. And yes, he argued that these values are for export.

Hitchens believed in universal human rights. This is why, at a time when his comrades were still manning the barricades against the "imperial" West after the Cold War, he argued that the North Atlantic Treaty Organization should intervene to stop a genocidal assault on Bosnia. It's why he argued that American power could be used to defend human rights and promote democracy. As many on the Western left built their politics around incessant condemnations of their own societies as racist, exploitative, oligarchic, and imperialistic, Hitchens recognized the difference between self-criticism and self-flagellation.

One of the reasons Orwell accumulated many left-wing enemies was the fact that his criticisms of his own "side" were grounded in authentic left-wing principles. When he argued that many socialists had no connection to or understanding of the actual working class in Britain,[11] the observation stung because it was true. Orwell's arguments continue to sting today. In his 1945 essay "Notes on Nationalism," Orwell criticized the left-wing intellectuals who enjoy "seeing their own country humiliated" and "follow the principle that any faction backed by Britain must be in the wrong."[12] Among some of these intellectuals, Orwell wrote: "One finds that they do not by any means express impartial disapproval but are directed almost entirely against Britain and the United States. Moreover they do not as a rule condemn violence as such, but only violence used in defence of the western countries."

Hitchens observed that many on today's left are motivated by the same principle: "Nothing will make us fight against an evil if that fight forces us to go to the same corner as our own government."[13] This is a predictable manifestation of what the American political theorist Michael Walzer calls the "default position" of the left: a purportedly "anti-imperialist and anti-militarist" position inclined toward the view that "everything that goes wrong in the world is America's fault."[14] As we'll see throughout this book, the tendency to ignore and rationalize even the most egregious violence and authoritarianism abroad in favor of an obsessive emphasis on the crimes and blunders of Western governments has become a reflex on the left.

Much of the left has been captured by a strange mix of sectarian and authoritarian impulses: a myopic emphasis on identitarianism and group rights over the individual; an orientation toward subjectivity and tribalism over objectivity and universalism; and demands for political orthodoxy enforced by repressive tactics like the suppression of speech. These left-wing pathologies are particularly corrosive today because they give right-wing nationalists and populists on both sides of the Atlantic—whose rise over the past several years has been characterized by hostility to democratic norms and institutions, rampant xenophobia, and other forms of illiberalism—an opportunity to claim that those who oppose them are the true authoritarians.

Hitchens was prescient about the ascendance of right-wing populism in the West, from the emergence of demagogues who exploit cultural grievances and racial resentments to the bitter parochialism of "America First" nationalism. And he understood that the left could only defeat these noxious political forces by rediscovering its best traditions: support for free expression, pluralism, and universalism—the values of the Enlightenment.

The final two decades of Hitchens's career are regarded as a gross aberration by many of his former political allies—a perception he did little to correct as he became increasingly averse to the direction of the left. He no longer cared what his left-wing contemporaries thought of him or what superficial labels they used to describe his politics. Hitchens closes *Why Orwell Matters* with the following observation: "What he [Orwell] illustrates, by his commitment to language as the partner of truth, is that 'views' do not really count; that it matters not what you think, but *how* you think; and that politics are relatively unimportant, while principles have a way of enduring, as do the few irreducible individuals who maintain allegiance to them."[15] This is a book about how Hitchens thought—and what today's left can learn from him.

1 First Amendment Absolutism

Hitchens on Free Expression

In his original introduction to *Animal Farm* (which remained unpublished until 1972), Orwell discussed the pervasive self-censorship in wartime England: "The sinister fact about literary censorship in England is that it is largely voluntary. Unpopular ideas can be silenced, and inconvenient facts kept dark, without the need for any official ban."[1] The rest of Orwell's essay was a study of the attitudes and habits that gave rise to this phenomenon: unthinking political loyalty, intellectual cowardice, and the refusal to trespass on certain orthodoxies.

"If I had to choose a text to justify myself," Orwell wrote, "I should choose the line from Milton: 'By the known rules of ancient liberty.' . . . The word ancient emphasizes the fact that intellectual freedom is a deep-rooted tradition without which our characteristic Western culture could only doubtfully exist." Hitchens often noted Orwell's affinity for this line from John Milton because he shared the view that intellectual freedom—as well as its corollary, free expression—was the guarantor of all other freedoms. As he explained, "The only thing that should be upheld at all costs and without qualification is the right of free expression, because if that goes, then so do all other claims of right as well."[2]

Despite the fact that Orwell often faced overt censorship, his introduction to *Animal Farm* was more relevant to the threats to free expression in liberal democracies today. Orwell observed that the "uncritical admiration of Soviet Russia" among British intellectuals was "spontaneous" and "not due to the action of any pressure group." He explained that his essay was about the "kind of censorship that the English literary intelligentsia voluntarily impose upon themselves." Orwell is most commonly associated with his attacks on totalitarianism in its purest and most excessive forms (from Stalinism to Big Brother), but he was acutely aware of subtler and more pernicious forms of authoritarianism and censorship.

Orwell understood how orthodoxy could corrupt thought, and he didn't just see this phenomenon at work among Soviet sympathizers. In a July 1944 column for *Tribune*, he discussed the "voluntary reticence" of the British press in general: "One of the most extraordinary things about England is that there is almost no official censorship, and yet nothing that is actually offensive to the governing class gets into print, at least in any place where large numbers of people are likely to read it."[3] Near the end of the essay, Orwell offered his mordant assessment of the state of British journalism: "Circus dogs jump when the trainer cracks his whip, but the really well-trained dog is the one that turns his somersault when there is no whip." Self-censorship is a natural byproduct of groupthink. Whether it was British papers refusing to report on issues that were "offensive to the governing class" (Orwell's example was "the business of the Abdication") or communists turning somersault after somersault whenever the Soviet party line shifted, Orwell could see that the most powerful censors were often a writer's own fears and loyalties.

Every year, the Dennis & Victoria Ross Foundation awards the Hitchens Prize to an "author or journalist whose work reflects a commitment to free expression and inquiry." After receiving the prize in

2019, the essayist George Packer explained why the current intellectual atmosphere would be inhospitable to a career like Hitchens's. In his acceptance speech, he asked, "What are the enemies of writing today?" and his first answer was the fact that writers now "have every incentive to do their work as easily identifiable, fully paid-up members of a community."[4] Instead of making judgments and arguments independently, they sculpt their views to conform to the demands of their groups. This doesn't just mean committing to the group's dogmas—it also means refusing to say anything that might contradict those dogmas.

Packer believes fear is the second enemy of writing. "I don't mean that editors and writers live in terror of being sent to prison," he explained. "The fear is more subtle and, in a way, more crippling. It's the fear of moral judgment, public shaming, social ridicule, and ostracism." Packer echoed Orwell, who thought "intellectual cowardice is the worst enemy a writer or journalist has to face"[5] in a country like Britain, as suppression and coercion from the state are minimal (a point that's even more true today). Orwell didn't just argue that fear led to self-censorship—he believed it led to bad writing. As he put it in his 1946 essay "The Prevention of Literature," "To write in plain, vigorous language one has to think fearlessly, and if one thinks fearlessly one cannot be politically orthodox."[6]

One of the reasons Hitchens thought fearlessly and wrote freely was his wariness of political orthodoxy. As he put it, "You mustn't become, or try and become, a party-liner—however good the party may be—as a writer. That's a betrayal."[7] Although he was a socialist for most of his career, he jettisoned his formal political commitments by the beginning of the twenty-first century. The word "solidarity" was always an essential part of his political lexicon, but the concept evolved in his mind over time—from solidarity with a political movement to solidarity with anyone who embodied or expressed a certain set of ideas and principles. As he explains in *Letters to a Young Contrarian*, "I don't think that the solidarity of belonging is much of a prize. I appreciate that it can bestow some pride, and that it can lead to mutual aid and even brother- and sisterhood, but it has too many suffocating qualities."[8] These qualities include the pressure to think and write in a certain way.

In his 1946 essay "Why I Write," Orwell told his readers: "I knew that I had a facility with words and a power of facing unpleasant facts."[9] Hitchens wanted to call his book about Orwell (*Why Orwell Matters* in the United States and *Orwell's Victory* in Britain) *A Power of Facing*, a suggestion he said was vetoed by his publisher. Hitchens faced many unpleasant facts in his career. After dropping socialism, he claimed to miss his old political allegiances "as if they were an amputated limb."[10] After decades as a ferocious critic of U.S. foreign policy, he came to believe that American power was the only effective instrument to secure human rights and defend vulnerable populations from the Slobodan Miloševićs and Saddam Husseins of the world. However difficult changing his mind on these issues may have been, Hitchens welcomed the barrage of criticism he received for doing so. As his friend the novelist Martin Amis observed: "Christopher's always taken up unpopular positions; he likes the battle, the argument, the smell of cordite."[11]

"In our time," Orwell wrote in his 1946 essay "Politics and the English Language," "it is broadly true that political writing is bad writing. Where it is not true, it will generally be found that the writer is some kind of rebel, expressing his private opinions, and not a 'party line.'"[12] Hitchens made a conscious effort to avoid regurgitating a party line— instead of turning intellectual somersaults to placate some political party or faction, he wrote and thought for himself.

* * *

When the Ayatollah Khomeini called for the murder of Salman Rushdie and those associated with the publication and distribution of *The Satanic Verses* in February 1989, Hitchens was shocked at how quickly many in the West were willing to temper or abandon their professed commitment to free speech. A few weeks after the fatwa was issued, he wrote, "I have seen important figures in the liberal culture employing the excuses of tolerance and pluralism in order to euphemize the intolerant and whitewash the enemies of pluralism."[13] He cited freshly published articles in the *New York Times*, *Washington Post*, and *Washington Monthly* that emphasized the importance of respecting religious sensibilities over free speech.

Hitchens noticed that the left was particularly eager to rationalize or even excuse the fatwa as an expression of legitimate religious grievances: "Nothing is more ironic," he wrote, "than to hear certain liberals and leftists identify Islam and the muezzin with the cry of the oppressed and with anti-imperialism."[14] In this case, the self-appointed representative of Islam and voice of the oppressed was the head of a theocratic state who had just waged war against Iraq with human-wave assaults and used children as minesweepers.[15, 16] Hitchens denounced the "distinguished 'intellectuals' and noise-makers, many of whom quite obviously found Rushdie's book more 'offensive' than the Ayatollah's lethal anathema, or at least no less so. Faced with that astonishing reaction, boring old Voltairean precepts seemed less stale and over-rehearsed."[17] After the Rushdie fatwa, Hitchens discovered that many on the left had the "intellectual itch to change the subject away from free speech versus religious absolutism."[18]

The response to the Rushdie fatwa was an early reification of what would soon become Hitchens's most pressing concerns about the trajectory of the contemporary left. First, there was the refusal to defend liberal principles in the face of an overt totalitarian challenge: "This is an all-out confrontation between the ironic and the literal mind," he wrote, "between every kind of commissar and inquisitor and bureaucrat and those who know that whatever the role of social and political forces, ideas and books have to be formulated and written by individuals."[19] Second, there were the abject allowances made for violence and coercion under an insipid and self-abnegating form of multiculturalism. This was partly a consequence of the creeping influence of postmodernism on the left (which we'll examine in the next chapter): "In the mind of many socialists," Hitchens observed, "cultural relativism has become such an anchor of certainty and principle that it would be physically painful to haul it in."[20] And finally, the fatwa exposed what Hitchens would later describe as a "masochistic cultural cringe" in liberal democratic societies,[21] especially when it comes to theocratic intimidation and any critique that could be construed as anti-imperialist or antiracist.

In a March 1989 article titled "Rushdie's Book Is an Insult," former U.S. President Jimmy Carter complained that "Ayatollah Khomeini's offer of paradise to Rushdie's assassin has caused writers and public officials in Western nations to become almost exclusively preoccupied with the author's rights."[22] While Carter offered the perfunctory acknowledgment that "First Amendment freedoms are important," he was more concerned about the fact that "we have tended to promote him [Rushdie] and his book with little acknowledgment that it is a direct insult to those millions of Moslems whose sacred beliefs have been violated."[23] In other words, Carter believed one of the world's great monotheisms shouldn't be subject to certain forms of artistic reimagining if doing so could cause offense, despite the fact that many of the protesters and rioters who were most incensed by the book couldn't have read it, as it hadn't been translated into their languages. As Hitchens argued, the publication of a novel isn't a violation of anyone's beliefs or rights—the imposition of a death sentence is.

The fatwa was a galvanizing event for Hitchens. It synthesized and exposed many of the deepest problems with what he saw as complacent Western liberalism: its susceptibility to theocratic bullying under the cloak of multiculturalism; its unwillingness to take a firm position even when the two "sides" couldn't be clearer; and most of all, its touch-and-go commitment to free speech. Days after Khomeini issued the fatwa against Rushdie, major bookselling chains—Waldenbooks, Barnes & Noble, and B. Dalton, which accounted for between 20 and 30 percent of all U.S. book sales at the time—announced that they would remove *The Satanic Verses* from their shelves.[24] The CEO of B. Dalton, Leonard Riggio, admitted that his company was allowing fear to cancel free expression: "It is regrettable that a foreign government has been able to hold hostage our most sacred First Amendment principle," he said.[25] Hitchens had nothing but contempt for willing hostages like Riggio:

> Tomorrow, the shopping malls of the United States, which contain now one-third of the book outlets in this country, will of their own volition not sell that book because they're scared of a foreign despot. Now, in my opinion, for that to happen in this country . . . to be scared of a crazy foreign tyrant in this way, is a really serious challenge to what we think of as the safe assumption of free speech and free inquiry, free expression and the necessity to defend it. And in a way, though I find all this very depressing, I welcome it because maybe we need every generation or so to remind ourselves that it's not a free ride to have free expression—not a free ride to have a free society.[26]

The threat of violence was real. When *The Satanic Verses* was banned in India in October 1988, Rushdie told an Indian journalist, "It would be absurd to think that a book can cause riots."[27] In an open letter to Indian Prime Minister Rajiv Gandhi in the *New York Times* published the same month, he argued: "The right to freedom of expression is at the foundation of any democratic society, and at present, all over the world, Indian democracy is becoming something of a laughing-stock."[28] The world wouldn't be laughing just a few months later.

On February 24, 1989, around a dozen people were killed and 40 were wounded when police in Mumbai (then Bombay, where Rushdie was born) opened fire on Muslims who were rioting in response to the publication of *The Satanic Verses*. According to the *New York Times*, the firefight led to a "three-hour battle, with rioters spilling across the crowded streets of South Bombay, burning cars, buses, motorcycles and even torching the small police station."[29] The battle took place after at least three people were killed and more than a hundred were wounded during riots in Kashmir earlier that month.[30] In Islamabad, six people were killed and more than 80 were wounded when police fired on protesters gathered outside an American information center to demand that the book be banned.[31] Syed Abdullah Bukhari, the top cleric at the largest mosque in New Delhi, endorsed the call for Rushdie's assassination.[32]

The bloodshed would continue for years. In July 1991, the Japanese translator of *The Satanic Verses*, Hitoshi Igarashi, was stabbed to death in the hallway outside his office at Tsukuba University northeast of Tokyo.[33] A little over a week earlier, an Italian translator of the book, Ettore Capriolo, was stabbed in his Milan apartment (the attacker demanded to know where Rushdie was hiding).[34] In October 1993, the book's Norwegian publisher, William Nygaard, was shot three times outside his home in a suburb of Oslo.[35] He survived. And in August 2022, a man jumped onto a stage where Rushdie was preparing to speak and repeatedly plunged a knife into his face, neck, and abdomen. The would-be assassin was born almost a decade after *The Satanic Verses* was published.

In his memoir *Hitch-22*, Hitchens recalls his immediate feeling when the fatwa was issued against Rushdie: "It was, if I can phrase it like this, a matter of everything I hated versus everything I loved. In the hate column: dictatorship, religion, stupidity, demagogy, censorship, bullying, and intimidation. In the love column: literature, irony, humor, the individual, and the defense of free expression."[36] He continues:

> To re-state the premise of the argument again: the theocratic head of a foreign despotism offers money in his own name in order to suborn the murder of a civilian citizen of another country, for the offense of writing a work of fiction. No more root-and-branch challenge to the values of the Enlightenment (on the bicentennial of the fall of the Bastille) or to the First Amendment to the Constitution, could be imagined. President George H.W. Bush, when asked to comment, could only say grudgingly that, as far as he could see, no American interests were involved.[37]

Meanwhile, many writers and intellectuals viewed this outright attack on their society's most basic universal principles through the lens of their parochial political concerns. The "whole phalanx of neoconservatives," Hitchens writes, "from Norman Podhoretz to A.M. Rosenthal and Charles Krauthammer, turned their ire on Salman and not on Khomeini, and appeared to relish the fact that this radical Indian friend of Nicaragua and the Palestinians had become a victim of 'terrorism' in his turn."[38] Hitchens was even more furious with the left-wing writers and intellectuals who "took almost exactly the same tone," albeit with a different political inflection:

> Germaine Greer, always reliably terrible about such matters, again came to the fore, noisily defending the rights of bookburners. "The Rushdie affair," wrote the Marxist critic John Berger within a few days of the *fatwah*, "has already cost several human lives and threatens to cost many, many more." And "the Rushdie affair," wrote Professor Michael Dummett of All Souls [Oxford], "has done untold damage. It has intensified the alienation of Muslims here.... Racist hostility towards them has been inflamed."[39]

Hitchens accused these critics of transferring blame from the theocrats, violent mobs, and book burners to Rushdie: "you will notice the displacement tactic used by Berger and Dummett and the multi-culti Left, which blamed the mayhem on an abstract construct—'the Rushdie affair.' I dimly understood at the time that this kind of postmodern 'Left,' somehow in league with political Islam, was something new, if not exactly New Left. That this *trahison* would take a partly 'multicultural' form was also something that was slowly ceasing to surprise me."[40] Hitchens noticed that those on the left who were quickest to offer solemn lectures about alienation and racism were also those who couldn't be relied upon to defend free speech—a phenomenon that became increasingly conspicuous in the years that followed.

Hitchens witnessed another battle between his loves and hates after the Danish newspaper *Jyllands-Posten* published a collection of cartoons depicting the Prophet Muhammad in 2005, sparking an international conflagration that left scores of people dead and again tested the West's commitment to free expression. A month after the cartoons were published, ambassadors and representatives from Turkey, Saudi Arabia, Iran, Pakistan, Egypt, Indonesia, Algeria, Bosnia and Herzegovina, Libya, Morocco, and Palestine sent a letter to Danish Prime Minister Anders Fogh Rasmussen which argued that the "Danish press and public representatives should not be allowed to abuse Islam in the name of democracy, freedom of expression and human rights, the values that we all share."[41] Permitting *Jyllands-Posten* to publish "demeaning caricatures of Holy Prophet Muhammad," the representatives wrote, "goes against the spirit of Danish values of tolerance and civil society."[42] The letter closed with a call for the Danish government to "take all those responsible to task under [the] law of the land in the interest of inter-faith harmony."[43]

In arguing that the prime minister could and should silence the press to facilitate "inter-faith harmony," the representatives demonstrated a fundamental misunderstanding of the role of the Danish government. As Rasmussen explained in his response to the letter: "The freedom of expression is the very foundation of Danish democracy. The freedom of expression has a wide scope and the Danish government has no means of influencing the press."[44] This episode mirrored what Hitchens described as the "mobilization of foreign embassies to intervene in our internal affairs" after the Rushdie fatwa:

> All of a sudden, accredited diplomats of supposedly sovereign nations like Pakistan and Quatar were involving themselves in matters that were none of their concern, such as the publication or distribution or even paperback printing of works of fiction. And this unheard-of arrogation was none too subtly "meshed" and synchronized with the cruder potency of the threat, as if to say in a silky tone that you might prefer to deal with us, the envoys of a foreign power, rather than with the regrettably violent elements over whom we have, needless to say, no control.[45]

The letter to Rasmussen ominously noted that his government's failure to censor *Jyllands-Posten* could "cause reactions in Muslim countries and among Muslim communities in Europe."[46] These reactions included: violent mobs setting the Danish and Norwegian embassies on fire (and attempting to attack the French embassy) in Damascus in early February 2006;[47] a similar assault on the Danish consulate in Beirut;[48] rioting across the Middle East, Asia, and Africa that led to the deaths of more than a hundred people;[49] an axe-wielding Somali man attempting to murder Kurt Westergaard (whose cartoon of the Prophet Muhammad with a bomb in his turban was published in *Jyllands-Posten*);[50] and a series of assassination plots and attempts directed at editors and newspapers that printed the cartoons.[51] Hitchens again lambasted those who cared more about placating the mob than standing up for free expression:

> Nobody in authority can be found to state the obvious and the necessary—that we stand with the Danes against this defamation and blackmail and sabotage. Instead, all compassion and concern is apparently to be expended upon those who lit the powder trail, and who yell and scream for joy as the embassies of democracies are put to the torch in the capital cities of miserable, fly-blown dictatorships. Let's be sure we haven't hurt the vandals' *feelings*.[52]

Major media institutions in the United States were terrified by the possibility of violence, but they used the language of cultural sensitivity to justify their decisions to deny readers and viewers the ability to see the cartoons. According to Robert Christie, a spokesman for Dow Jones & Company, the *Wall Street Journal* didn't print the cartoons because "We didn't want to publish anything that can be perceived as inflammatory to our readers' culture when it didn't add anything to the story."[53] The managing editor of the *Chicago Tribune*, James O'Shea, issued a similar statement: "We can communicate to our readers what this is about without running it."[54] But as Hitchens often insisted, the images *were* the story. Despite the fact that the American media is "totally dominated by images," Hitchens observed, editors told readers:

> . . . here's a story that's all about the fight over some pictures, but we're not going to show you what the pictures are. . . . In the United States of America in 2006, there wasn't a single member of our profession in a position to make a decision who would stand up for one day to outright blackmail.[55]

Most American media outlets refused to publish the cartoons. When Hitchens appeared on CNN to discuss the controversy with Ahmed Younis (then the national director of the Muslim Public Affairs Council), he opened the segment by criticizing the network's decision to pixelate images of the cartoons: "I know as well as you do that you have not done that in order to avoid sparing the hurt feelings of my fellow guest. You've done it because you're afraid of retaliation and of intimidation."[56] The host admitted that he was right. Just as retailers refused to stock *The Satanic Verses* a decade and a half earlier, the majority of the U.S. media decided that standing up for free expression wasn't worth the risk.

* * *

In March 2007, a French court rejected a demand from several Muslim groups (including the Union of French Islamic Organizations and the Grand Mosque of Paris) to prevent a small satirical French magazine from reprinting all twelve of the *Jyllands-Posten* cartoons.[57] Despite the fact that the magazine's offices and several members of its staff had to be placed under police protection for publishing the cartoons, its then publisher said, "It's good news for those who believe in freedom of expression and for Muslims who are secular and support the ideals of the republic."[58] The publisher was Philippe Val, and the magazine was *Charlie Hebdo*.

On January 7, 2015, two gunmen forced their way into *Charlie Heb-*

do's Paris office and opened fire on the staff during an editorial meeting. After killing police bodyguard Franck Brinsolaro, the attackers called for *Charlie Hebdo* editor-in-chief Stéphane Charbonnier by name, along with cartoonists Jean Cabut, Philippe Honoré, Bernard Verlhac, and Georges Wolinski. They were all murdered, along with three other staff members, a maintenance worker, a visitor, and a responding police officer.[59] Several others were wounded during the attack. As the attackers sprayed gunfire, they shouted, "We have avenged the Prophet Muhammad" and "Allahu Akbar."[60] Al-Qaeda on the Arabian Peninsula (AQAP) claimed responsibility for the attack, describing it as "vengeance for the messenger of Allah."[61]

AQAP's English-language magazine *Inspire* had listed Charbonnier as one of its top targets in 2013 for publishing cartoons of Muhammad. Days after he was murdered, an image of the list of targets resurfaced online with Charbonnier's picture crossed out.[62] Under a heading that read "Wanted dead or alive for crimes against Islam," other targets were listed along with their pictures. These included Kurt Westergaard, the women's rights activist and author Ayaan Hirsi Ali, former *Jyllands-Posten* foreign editor Flemming Rose, and, of course, Rushdie.[63] Two days after the *Charlie Hebdo* rampage, Amedy Coulibaly (a friend of the attackers) massacred four people and took hostages at a kosher supermarket in Paris.[64] And in November 2015, an Islamic State killing spree across the city left 130 people dead and wounded hundreds more.[65]

After the attack on *Charlie Hebdo*, there was an international wave of sympathy for the slain journalists and cartoonists. More than one and a half million people took to the streets of Paris to march in solidarity with *Charlie Hebdo*,[66] while millions more protested across France and around the world. The expression "Je suis Charlie" ("I am Charlie") became ubiquitous, protesters held pencils in the air and waved flags that read "Liberté de la Presse" ("Freedom of the Press"), and for a few days the capitulations over the *Jyllands-Posten* riots and *Satanic Verses* fatwa seemed like they belonged to a different era. The feeling didn't last.

In March 2015, PEN America announced that *Charlie Hebdo* would receive its Toni and James C. Goodale Freedom of Expression Courage Award.[67] A month later, 242 writers and members of PEN signed an open letter to the organization protesting this decision: "It is clear and inarguable that the murder of a dozen people in the *Charlie Hebdo* offices is sickening and tragic," the letter stated. "What is neither clear nor inarguable is the decision to confer an award for courageous freedom of expression on *Charlie Hebdo*, or what criteria, exactly, were used to make that decision."[68] Recall that one of the victims of the attack on *Charlie Hebdo* was police officer Franck Brinsolaro, who had been assigned to protect Charbonnier. Members of *Charlie Hebdo*'s staff had spent years under threat for their willingness to satirize and criticize Islam, but they continued to publish anyway. It would be difficult to come up with any clearer criteria for the conferment of a "Freedom of Expression Courage Award."

The signatories of the letter included eminent writers like Joyce Carol Oates, Teju Cole, and Junot Díaz, and they accused PEN of "valorizing selectively offensive material: material that intensifies the anti-Islamic, anti-Maghreb, anti-Arab sentiments already prevalent in the Western world."[69] The letter observed that French Muslims are "marginalized, embattled, and victimized," which meant "*Charlie Hebdo*'s cartoons of the Prophet must be seen as being intended to cause further humiliation and suffering."[70] The authors didn't explain how they knew what the magazine's cartoonists *intended* to do with their work, and they either didn't notice or care that *Charlie Hebdo* attacked all religions and defended the rights of persecuted minorities within Muslim countries and communities.

All the international outrage and grief after the *Charlie Hebdo* massacre didn't change the fact that defending the "right for caricature and satire" (in Philippe Val's words)[71] still poses a lethal risk to those courageous enough to do it. This is because there simply aren't enough writers, editors, and intellectuals willing to challenge a taboo enforced at gunpoint. In his remarks to PEN, *Charlie Hebdo* editor-in-chief Gérard Biard explained: "We can't be the only ones to symbolize values that belong to everyone. . . . It's dangerous for us, because we are in the front line, and it's dangerous for democracy."[72] Rushdie made a similar point about the *Jyllands-Posten* cartoons at a PEN America event with Hitchens in May 2010:

> What happens when the subject of violence arises? . . . The subject is no longer about whether you should publish or not publish these things, but about how do you respond to violence? Do you respond to it with cowardice or courage? At that point, it seems to me that every newspaper in the world should publish the Danish cartoons. Not because they like them, and not actually because they particularly want to insult Islam. But just to make the point that you don't give in to threats.[73]

A quarter of a century earlier, when Hitchens was considering ways to defend Rushdie and encourage other writers to do the same, he recalled that Khomeini had condemned everyone "responsible for the publication" of *The Satanic Verses* when he issued the fatwa. This gave Hitchens the idea of circulating a petition that declared all the signatories "co-responsible" for the book's publication, which was signed by several authors (including Norman Mailer and Don DeLillo) at an event organized by Susan Sontag, and later published in the *Times Literary Supplement* with many more names added to the list.[74] If this principle was generalized—for example, if bookstores had agreed to stock *The Satanic Verses* or if media outlets around the world had published the Danish cartoons—Rushdie, *Charlie Hebdo*, and other defenders of free speech would no longer have to be on the "front line," because they would no longer stand alone.

This doesn't just apply to editors at subversive newspapers—it also applies to dissidents in Muslim countries and apostates who take the risk of publicly criticizing the faith. Ayaan Hirsi Ali has spent many years writing and speaking in defiance of theocratic ghouls who hate and fear what she represents: the emancipation of women, secularism, humanism, and most of all, a powerful female voice that exposes the backwardness and cruelty of Islamic fundamentalism—a voice that can't be silenced with threats of violence. When Hirsi Ali's collaborator Theo van Gogh (with whom she produced the short film *Submission* in 2004) was murdered, his assassin stabbed a note into his stomach threatening to kill her next. And yet, since the publication of her autobiography *Infidel* in 2006,[75] a ubiquitous trope in critical reviews and essays about her work is the idea that her criticism of Islam makes *her* a fundamentalist, just like the fanatics who have marked her for death. Hitchens had no patience for this sort of wincing sophistry:

> In her book, Ayaan Hirsi Ali says the following: "I left the world of faith, of genital cutting and forced marriage for the world of reason and sexual emancipation. After making this voyage I know that one of these two worlds is simply better than the other. Not for its gaudy gadgetry, but for its fundamental values." This is a fairly representative quotation. She has her criticisms of the West, but she prefers it to a society where women are subordinate, censorship is pervasive, and violence is officially preached against unbelievers. As an African victim of, and escapee from, this system, she feels she has acquired the right to say so. What is "fundamentalist" about that?[76]

In response to a *Newsweek* headline that described Hirsi Ali as a "bomb-thrower,"[77] Hitchens again noted the tendency to redirect blame for theocratic violence:

> The subject of this absurd headline is a woman who has been threatened with horrific violence, by Muslims varying from moderate to extreme, ever since she was a little girl. She has more recently had to see a Dutch friend butchered in the street, been told that she is next, and now has to live with bodyguards in Washington, D.C. She has never used or advocated violence. Yet to whom does *Newsweek* refer as the "Bombthrower"? It's always the same with these bogus equivalences: They start by pretending loftily to find no difference between aggressor

and victim, and they end up by saying that it's the victim of violence who is "really" inciting it.[78]

To be fair, the word "bombthrower" is commonly used in the American media to describe controversial figures, but Hitchens was reacting to the broader narrative about Hirsi Ali—that she's a strident and dangerous "Islamophobe" (a word he always despised, as it's often deployed by cynical obscurantists who present any critical evaluation of Islamic doctrine and practice as prejudice against Muslims). He could have mentioned Rushdie or *Jyllands-Posten*, but he didn't need to. The same cultural and political deformations that make politicians, journalists, and intellectuals queasy about defending the right to free expression for novelists and newspaper editors are vivid in Hirsi Ali's case.

There's the cultural cringe associated with any criticism of Islam, which liberals invariably conflate with bigotry. There's the cultural condescension that regards the most extreme and reactionary Muslims as the only genuine representatives of the faith. And there's the anxiety about defending the right to free expression even when it's under sustained assault—partly due to a contorted and instrumentalized form of cultural sensitivity, and partly due to fear.

Openly discussing the tenets and practices of Islam is more than taboo—it's an immediate mortal threat to journalists, authors, artists, and publishers, even in the West. Everyone knows criticizing or satirizing Islam can lead to what Hitchens described as a "simultaneous death sentence and life sentence"[79]—even if the theocratic death squads aren't successful, a life in hiding is its own trauma and punishment. So in most cases, intellectuals and publishers just don't take the risk of discussing Islam openly. As Kenan Malik explains in his 2009 book *From Fatwa to Jihad: The Rushdie Affair and Its Aftermath*: "Nearly two decades on from *The Satanic Verses*, Western liberals had become much more attuned to Islamist sensitivities and less willing to challenge them. They had, in the post-Rushdie world, effectively internalized the fatwa."[80] This process can only be reversed by openly expressing solidarity with those willing to defy taboos and censorship—and more importantly, by defying them yourself.

Hitchens was struck by how difficult it was for many intellectuals—who spend a lot of time congratulating one another on their courage—to assimilate this point. There's no clearer attack on the principle of free expression than offering a ransom for the assassination of a novelist, burning down an embassy to protest a cartoon, or massacring journalists and artists for what they publish. But in each of these cases, there were always intellectuals on hand to shift attention from the violence, censorship, and intimidation to some other concern which had nothing to do with the protection of free speech. For example, the PEN signatories were preoccupied with what they described as a power imbalance between the staff of *Charlie Hebdo* and French Muslims: "Power and prestige are elements that must be recognized in considering almost any form of discourse, including satire. The inequities between the person holding the pen and the subject fixed on paper by that pen cannot, and must not, be ignored."[81] This was a strange position to take months after the people holding pens had been slaughtered by people holding automatic weapons. "It took some nerve," George Packer later observed, "to argue that the balance of power between the heavily armed jihadists and the defenseless cartoonists was with the latter."[82]

It made sense for Packer to discuss *Charlie Hebdo* in a speech about Hitchens's commitment to free expression. The attack on a small French magazine dedicated to secularism and satire was yet another battle between his loves and hates. It's easy to imagine the contempt Hitchens would have had for writers and intellectuals who, upon witnessing yet another frontal assault on free expression, immediately emphasized the victims' alleged transgressions. He almost certainly would've responded as Rushdie did: "If PEN as a free speech organization can't defend and celebrate people who have been murdered for drawing pictures, then frankly the organization is not worth the name."[83] PEN ultimately upheld its decision to honor *Charlie Hebdo*, but the controversy revealed several powerful currents against what seemed like a tide of support for free expression after the attack.

Self-censorship and external censorship are inseparable—writers and intellectuals refuse to say certain things because they fear the social and political consequences of doing so. Yet those who urge silence in the name of political expediency or social cohesion or "inter-faith harmony" often express their "support" for free expression in the same breath. The letter which demanded that Prime Minister Rasmussen muzzle the Danish press extolled "democracy, freedom of expression and human rights, the values that we all share." In their letter to PEN, the authors critical of *Charlie Hebdo* insisted that "We do not believe in censoring expression."[84] Of course, their protest wasn't a form of censorship in itself. But by accusing *Charlie Hebdo* of bigotry, the signatories were attempting to narrow the range of acceptable opinion. As Packer put it: "Theocratic Islam should be off-limits to satirists, the PEN writers argued, because French Muslims belonged to a 'marginalized, embattled, and victimized' group."[85]

In September 2020, a trial for accomplices in the January 2015 jihadist attacks in Paris, including the one on *Charlie Hebdo,* began.[86] *Charlie Hebdo* marked the occasion by republishing the cartoons of Muhammad on its front page, arguing that the magazine had a "duty of information that requires that these documents, which have both historical and criminal value, be brought to the attention of the public."[87] The editors asked: "Do we want to live in a country that prides itself on being a great free and modern democracy, and that, at the same time, gives up on asserting its deepest convictions?"[88]

A few weeks after *Charlie Hebdo* republished the cartoons, a man attacked two people with a meat cleaver in front of the magazine's offices.[89] The assailant, Zaher Hassan Mahmood, told investigators that he wanted to set the building on fire in retaliation for the cartoons.[90] Meanwhile, *Charlie Hebdo's* head of human resources, Marika Bret, was forced to leave her home after receiving "precise and detailed threats," according to the BBC.[91] Bret has been living under police protection since 2015,[92] and she said the magazine's staff faced an "unprecedented level of tension. . . . Since the start of the trial and with the republication of the cartoons, we have received all kinds of horrors, including threats from Al Qaeda and calls to finish the work of the Kouachi brothers" (the pair who attacked *Charlie Hebdo* in 2015).[93] A month later, in October 2020, a French teacher named Samuel Paty was decapitated in a suburb north of Paris after showing his students cartoons of the Prophet Muhammad during a lesson on free speech.[94] The father of one of Paty's students had started an online campaign against the teacher, which chief French anti-terrorism prosecutor Jean-François Ricard said had a "direct causal link" to the attack.[95]

Hitchens maintained that the "argument with faith is the foundation and origin of all arguments,"[96] and he was especially interested in having those arguments about the fastest-growing religion on the planet[97]—a religion which, as he often put it, makes "unusually large claims for itself."[98] He argued that anyone in a free society should be able to challenge, evaluate, and satirize a system of belief that purports to be a source of universal truth, law, and morality. Open inquiry is all the more important when debates and discussions about this system are regularly and ruthlessly silenced. The Virginia Statute for Religious Freedom, which laid the foundation for the First Amendment, states that everyone "shall be free to profess, and by argument to maintain, their opinions in matters of religion."[99] You are not free to profess your opinions in matters of religion if doing so will invite machine gun and knife-wielding theocrats to your doorstep. Nor are you free to practice or abjure religious faith if you live in a theocratic state with official policies and punishments dictating what citizens can and can't believe.

* * *

Because Hitchens focused so much of his work on criticizing Islam (though many of his most caustic attacks on religion were directed at Christianity and Judaism as well), he was constantly accused of "Islamophobia" and other forms of bigotry. But there's another way to interpret his arguments about free speech and Islam: he believed a civil society could only function if it observed a set of universal laws and principles. Beyond the obvious prohibitions against, say, expressing your religious grievances at gunpoint, Hitchens believed citizens of liberal democracies should be committed to pluralism, regardless of their religious beliefs. The rules they impose on themselves regarding apostasy, blasphemy, etc. cannot supplant the laws of their countries. Democratic societies should have the self-confidence to embrace multiculturalism while refusing to tolerate encroachments on liberal values and institutions in its name. This balance will simultaneously protect those values and institutions while creating the conditions for multiculturalism to flourish without descending into cultural relativism and authoritarianism.

Hitchens described himself as a Protestant atheist—he admired the "long struggle to have the Bible rendered into the vernacular," which ended the "priestly monopoly" on its interpretation.[100] "However, the impressive fact remains," he writes in *God Is Not Great: How Religion Poisons Everything*, "that all religions have staunchly resisted any attempt to translate their sacred texts into languages 'understanded of the people,' as the Cranmer prayer book phrases it."[101] However, he acknowledges that the "spell of the clerical class has been broken" in Christianity.[102] He continues: "Only in Islam has there been no reformation, and to this day any vernacular version of the Koran must still be printed with an Arabic parallel text. This ought to arouse suspicion even in the slowest mind."[103] Hitchens's attitude toward religious suppression and provincialism was informed by his commitment to open inquiry—all ideas, especially the ones promulgated by supposedly holy texts, should be as widely accessible and debatable as possible. He recognized that the demand for linguistic purity has long been used by religious authorities to silence dissent, and he found it logically, practically, and morally difficult to accept the "absurd and potentially dangerous conclusion that god was a monoglot."[104] As always, Hitchens embraced universalism over tribalism.

"A religiously neutral state," Hitchens wrote, "is the chief guarantee of religious pluralism."[105] He emphasized the humanism and secularism of America's Founders, which led them to create a system capable of protecting this fundamental right: "It became a point of principle as well as of practice to maintain that liberty of conscience and the freedom of the individual were quite incompatible with any compulsion in religion, just as they would be incompatible with any repression of belief."[106] This is why the First Amendment protects free expression and the free exercise of religion—issues that remain inseparable today. In a 2006 article, Hitchens's friend and the former foreign editor of *Jyllands-Posten*, Flemming Rose, reframed the debate over the Danish cartoons in terms that would have been intelligible to the Founders:

> We have a tradition of satire when dealing with the royal family and other public figures, and that was reflected in the cartoons. The cartoonists treated Islam the same way they treat Christianity, Buddhism, Hinduism and other religions. And by treating Muslims in Denmark as equals they made a point: We are integrating you into the Danish tradition of satire because you are part of our society, not strangers. . . . it is becoming clear that this is not a debate between "them" and "us," but between those committed to democracy in Denmark and those who are not.[107]

This is the essential debate everywhere. Hitchens often emphasized the struggle for political, intellectual, and artistic freedom in what's reductively referred to as the "Muslim world." When he discussed the threat to free expression that arises from Islamist violence, he explained that excuses for the theocratic suppression of speech frequently come "dressed up in the guise of good manners and multiculturalism. One must not wound the religious feelings of others, many of whom are poor immigrants in our own societies."[108] To expose the hollowness of this degrading argument, Hitchens cited a 1994 book titled *For Rushdie: Essays by Arab and Muslim Writers in Defense of Free Speech*: "Among its contributors," he wrote, "is almost every writer worthy of the name in the Arab and Muslim world, ranging from the Syrian poet Adonis to the Syrian-Kurdish author Salim Barakat, to the late national bard of the Palestinians, Mahmoud Darwish, to the celebrated Turkish writers Murat Belge and Orhan Pamuk. . . . In other words, the situation is the exact reverse of what the condescending multiculturalists say it is."[109]

Hitchens was particularly impressed by the 127 Iranian writers, artists, and intellectuals who condemned the fatwa against Rushdie, decried the "systematic denial of the rights of man in Iran," and argued that domestic repression emboldened the regime to "export outside the Islamic Republic . . . its terroristic methods which destroy freedom."[110] Hitchens argued: "To indulge the idea of religious censorship by the threat of violence is to insult and undermine precisely those in the Muslim world who are its intellectual cream, and who want to testify for their own liberty—and for ours. It is also to make the patronizing assumption that the leaders of mobs and the inciters of goons are the authentic representatives of Muslim opinion. What could be more 'offensive' than that?"[111] Like Rose, Hitchens believed the fight is between those who are committed to democracy in the "Muslim world" and those who are not.

When a news network pixelates an image of Muhammad or a publishing house surrenders to the howls of a fundamentalist mob, it's a grotesque insult to say these are efforts to placate *Muslims* or the *Muslim world* or the *Muslim community*. Unlike many of the Western intellectuals who present themselves as defenders of Muslim sensibilities, Hitchens didn't treat Muslims as if they're permanently condemned to live in backward theocracies or under ancient dogmas.

What sounded to many ears like "Islamophobia" was actually Hitchens's refusal to engage with Muslims as if they're somehow less than rational, autonomous human beings. His argument for the inviolability of free expression was informed by his belief in the universality of certain principles and methods of discourse—he had no tolerance for the view that some ideas should be inexpressible because they might offend Muslims or any other vulnerable group. This form of censorship, endorsed and enforced by condescending multiculturalists, doesn't just block the free exchange of ideas in open societies—it also empowers authoritarians by giving them a veto over what can be published, shown, and said. This is what Hitchens meant when he said liberal intellectuals in Muslim countries testified for their own liberty and for ours. These intellectuals are willing to take grave risks to defend the basic political principles that are viewed as a birthright in Western countries, and they're doing so at a time when many in the West can't be relied upon to take even the mildest risks to affirm those same principles.

In a 2006 debate on free speech and the right to offend, Shashi Tharoor observed: "There are societies in different stages of cultural consciousness or sophistication—not everyone is a Christopher Hitchens."[112] Tharoor said he "pitied" the most reactionary members of these societies, but he also argued that newspapers and publishers should give in to their threats of violence and refuse to print material that could inflame them. Hitchens didn't just regard this as an intolerable submission to religious intimidation in his own society—he also believed members of other societies shouldn't be bound by the dictates of self-appointed religious authorities:

> It used to be, before the Enlightenment really crested, that it was left to communities to do this. In other words, that the Jewish community in Amsterdam is the one that sentenced Baruch Spinoza to death—not the Christians—for his heresy. They thought, "We'll leave it to the Jews to punish their own heretics." . . . They [Christians] praised the Amsterdam synagogue for uttering the great curse on Spinoza and expelling and excommunicating the most talented Jew in the Netherlands at the time. Are we really wanting to go back to that, where every community is its own tyranny, everyone's ghettoized? . . . No, I really think we have to have a bill of rights that applies to everybody, and to

which any citizen of any stripe or religion can appeal if they've been oppressed by the wider community or by their own.[113]

These comments captured Hitchens's foundational principles: his belief in the universality of human rights and responsibilities, his insistence that the international system should be shaped to promote and protect liberal values, and his view that unfettered free expression is the most important value of all. If the citizens of "sophisticated" liberal democracies can't be relied upon to uphold and defend free speech in their own countries, they'll be of little use to the dissidents in closed societies who appeal to them for support.

* * *

After George Floyd was killed by Minneapolis police officer Derek Chauvin in May 2020, mass protests and civil unrest swept the United States.[114] In June of that year, the *New York Times* printed an op-ed by Arkansas Sen. Tom Cotton, which argued that the government should deploy the military to prevent rioting and looting across the country.[115]

Cotton's op-ed ignited a frenzy of outrage and condemnation. After approvingly quoting the reporter Laura Rozen, who described the article as "fascist propaganda,"[116] Joyce Carol Oates (one of the most prominent signatories of the anti–*Charlie Hebdo* letter) declared: "It's one thing to air diverse opinions. But when people are actually being killed, maimed & terrorized by lawless law enforcement, such 'bothsiderism' begins to seem obscene. Surely the NYTimes wouldn't present both sides of the Holocaust?"[117] It's curious that Cotton's op-ed made Oates think of fascism and the Holocaust, whereas the murder of journalists and cartoonists by heavily armed anti-Semitic theocrats prompted her to change the subject from the brutal suppression of free speech to the good or bad taste of the cartoons.

While the op-ed was denounced in many American media outlets, the most significant resistance came from within the *New York Times* itself. More than a thousand staffers signed a letter protesting its publication and demanding a commitment that the article "not appear in any future print edition."[118, 119] Many tweeted some version of this statement: "Running this puts Black @nytimes staff in danger."[120] In response, *New York Times* editorial page editor James Bennet wrote an essay which pointed out that he opposed Cotton's argument and emphasized all the paper's opinion pieces "calling for the police to be defunded, praising the power of protest to bring about necessary change and urging prosecutors to get tough with abusive police."[121] But he defended the decision to print the op-ed:

> We published Cotton's argument in part because we've committed to *Times* readers to provide a debate on important questions like this. It would undermine the integrity and independence of *The New York Times* if we only published views that editors like me agreed with, and it would betray what I think of as our fundamental purpose—not to tell you what to think, but to help you think for yourself.[122]

In a memo to employees, *New York Times* publisher A.G. Sulzberger declared his support for the "principle of openness to a range of opinions, even those we may disagree with," and observed that Cotton's article was "published in that spirit."[123] How quickly principles of openness and diversity of thought can be discarded. For Bennet, helping readers think for themselves was suddenly a trivial concern once the question of violence was raised (however spuriously): "In the face of the fear that lives are at stake, arguments . . . about the principles of *Times Opinion* must sound particularly fatuous," he wrote.[124] The day after Sulzberger sent his memo, an editor's note was affixed to Cotton's op-ed, declaring that it "fell short of our standards and should not have been published."[125] Two days later, Bennet resigned.[126]

When deputy editorial page editor Kathleen Kingsbury took over from Bennet, she sent an email to opinion staff urging them to police their colleagues: "Any piece of Opinion journalism—including headlines or social posts or photos or you name it—that gives you the slightest pause, please call or text me immediately."[127] It's no surprise that Kingsbury expressed cringing deference to anyone who may have been even *slightly* offended by something the paper was planning to publish—firings and public defenestrations were taking place across the media industry. For example, the executive editor of the *Philadelphia Inquirer*, Stan Wischnowski, announced on June 6 that he was leaving the paper after it published a column by Inga Saffron titled "Buildings Matter, Too,"[128] which outraged dozens of staffers who believed she was trivializing the Black Lives Matter movement.[129] Many more staff revolts and controversies would churn editors and reporters out of their posts in the months to come.[130]

Shortly after Bennet left the *New York Times*, 150 prominent journalists, authors, and academics signed an open letter in *Harper's Magazine* (a longtime publisher of Hitchens) which argued that the "free exchange of information and ideas, the lifeblood of a liberal society, is daily becoming more constricted" and called for a recommitment to open debate and dialogue.[131] The letter proved to be far more incendiary than some of the signatories anticipated.[132] It was variously described as an attempt to "fetishize civil disagreement"; an "elegantly written affirmation of elitism and privilege"; and an effort to silence "Black, brown, and LGBTQ+ people—particularly Black and trans people."[133, 134, 135]

Why was an anodyne statement in favor of free speech, which was signed by a diverse group of writers and intellectuals (from Cornel West to David Frum to J.K. Rowling to Malcolm Gladwell), interpreted by so many to be some kind of racist, homophobic, transphobic screed? Many on the left were incensed that the *Harper's* letter appeared to be a reaction to events like the furor over the Cotton op-ed, which they regarded as just and necessary. During the largest national protests for racial equality in decades, they argued, who cared if a few editors and reporters lost their jobs? This was a reckoning, after all—structures had to be dismantled, habits had to be abandoned, gatekeepers had to be removed.

To these critics, Twitter mobbings and firings actually represent a form of progress—it's not censorship, it's accountability. The debate isn't being constricted; it's being expanded to encompass marginalized voices.

Many Americans don't agree. In March 2022, the *New York Times* published an editorial titled "America Has a Free Speech Problem."[136] The article cited a survey commissioned by the paper in conjunction with Siena College, which found that 84 percent of Americans believe it's a "'very serious' or 'somewhat serious' problem that some Americans do not speak freely in everyday situations because of fear of retaliation or harsh criticism."[137]

When Hitchens was a student at the University of Oxford, he took part in an effort to deplatform British Foreign Secretary Michael Stewart over the government's support for the Vietnam War as it expanded into Cambodia.[138] After delivering his own remarks onstage at the Oxford Union, Hitchens says he "deserted the other guests, and went to sit with, and shout with, the mob"—a mob he helped to organize. He continues: "At a given signal when Stewart rose to speak, a phalanx also rose and simply and repetitively yelled the one word 'murderer' in his face. . . . The official Minute Book of our little parliament still records that: 'For the first time in the 147 years of the Society's existence, the House voted to stand adjourned *sine die* on account of riot.'"[139] Despite his rationalizations at the time (which were similar to the ones offered by those who seek to suppress voices they don't agree with today), Hitchens wasn't proud of his role in this outcome:

> We had, in our own opinion, not 'silenced' Mr. Stewart, whose views were well known and could easily be broadcast, so much as we had voiced the outrage that should properly be felt at the destruction of Cambodian society. I remember arguing with dexterous casuistry that we had compelled the Establishment press to take notice and had thus, in a way, actually succeeded in *enlarging* the area of free speech. A nice try, I hope you will admit. But however one phrased the case, the only reason for mentioning free speech in the first place was that,

however one looked at it, we had in fact shut down a public debate by force.[140]

This episode of authoritarian bullying demonstrates how easily a mob, when convinced of the righteousness of its cause, can resort to illiberal tactics (amid screams of "Murderer!" a protester in the balcony above Stewart dropped a noose over his head).[141] Such tactics have been deployed frequently over the past several years, especially on campus. When students shouted down Christina Hoff Sommers—then a scholar at the American Enterprise Institute and a despised figure on much of the left for her criticisms of third-wave feminism—at Lewis & Clark College in March 2018, they chanted: "Which side are you on, friends? Which side are you on? No platform for fascists, no platform at all."[142] It's easier to justify the suppression of speech once you've convinced yourself that by storming the beaches of a private liberal arts school in Portland, you're heroically holding the line against the forces of racist totalitarianism.

Hitchens believed the right to free expression should extend to everyone, including *actual* fascists (whose ranks don't, in fact, include Christina Hoff Sommers). In *Hitch-22*, he recalls the "considerable nuisance from fascist and neo-Nazi groups in Britain" in the 1970s: "It was one of one's standard duties as a leftist to turn out on weekends and block the efforts of this rabble to stage a march or to put up a platform in a street market. Stones and fists would fly, posters would be ripped down: it was all part of a storied socialist tradition that went back to street combat with the Blackshirts in the 1930s."[143] So when Hitchens discovered that the American Nazi Party was planning to march through Skokie, Illinois, in 1978, he was surprised that the ACLU was contesting a local ban on the event. But that was before he "read an excellent defense of the ACLU by its director, Aryeh Neier, himself a refugee from Nazism":

The First Amendment to the Constitution, he [Neier] said, enshrined the right of all citizens to free expression and to free assembly. If this protection was withdrawn from anybody, perhaps especially somebody repulsively unpopular, then it would be weakened or diluted in general.[144]

This lesson would stay with Hitchens for the rest of his life. He recognized that free expression wasn't a value to be modified or discarded depending on the circumstances, which is why he didn't accept the argument that marginalized groups need special protection from speech (the American Nazi Party chose Skokie because a large number of Jewish refugees lived there). Hitchens believed the right to free expression itself is what needs special protection, particularly when it's exercised by marginal or hated figures—including figures considerably more objectionable than Tom Cotton. In 2005, the notorious Holocaust denier and historian David Irving was sentenced to three years in prison by an Austrian court for claiming that there were no gas chambers at Auschwitz during a pair of speeches he delivered in Austria more than a decade and a half earlier.[145] He was released after thirteen months. Hitchens argued that his imprisonment was a "disgrace" and a "state punishment for a crime—that of expression and argument and publication—that is not a legal offense in Mr. Irving's country of birth and that could not be an offense under the First Amendment."[146]

Hitchens noted that he had been "writing in defense of Mr. Irving for several years," specifically mentioning a June 1996 *Vanity Fair* article in which he attacked St. Martin's Press for pulling Irving's biography of Joseph Goebbels right before it was due to be published.[147] In that article, he mentioned a conversation he had with Raul Hilberg, author of one of the most influential histories of the Holocaust: *The Destruction of the European Jews* (originally published in 1961, but reissued many times since).[148] Hilberg didn't believe Irving should be silenced: "If these people want to speak, let them. . . . I am not for taboos and I am not for repression."[149] Hilberg made this comment almost a decade before Irving was thrown in an Austrian prison, so his use of the word "repression" turned out to be apt. After Irving was released, the historian Deborah Lipstadt said, "I don't believe that history should be adjudicated in a courtroom," adding that the Austrian authorities had unwittingly made Irving a "martyr to free speech."[150] This was especially perverse given the fact that Irving unsuccessfully sued Lipstadt for libel in the late 1990s after she accurately accused him of denying the scope and depravity of the Holocaust.[151] Beyond questions of repression and martyrdom, Hitchens simply believed readers should be able to make up their own minds about Irving's work: "The dispute between Mr. Irving and myself and many others can be left to adults and scholars to resolve."[152]

In a debate at the University of Toronto on the motion "freedom of speech includes the freedom to hate," Hitchens described John Milton's *Areopagitica*, the introduction to Thomas Paine's *The Age of Reason*, and John Stuart Mill's *On Liberty* as the "classic texts" on free expression in the West.[153] One of the essential themes linking these works, Hitchens argued, is the idea that "It's not just the right of the person who speaks to be heard. It is the right of everyone in the audience to listen and to hear. And every time you silence somebody, you make yourself a prisoner of your own action."[154] In *On Liberty*, Mill made four central points about the rights of the audience and the practical necessity of free speech: (1) silenced opinions might be true, and suppressing them assumes "our own infallibility"; (2) even erroneous opinions can contain elements of truth; (3) when the truth isn't "vigorously and earnestly contested," those who hold it will do so superficially and "in the manner of a prejudice"; and (4) the truth will become a dogma if people aren't free to openly challenge it.[155]

In his article about why he published the cartoons of Muhammad, Flemming Rose explained: "The idea wasn't to provoke gratuitously—and we certainly didn't intend to trigger violent demonstrations throughout the Muslim world. Our goal was simply to push back self-imposed limits on expression that seemed to be closing in tighter."[156] This is the attitude Mill believed was necessary for open inquiry and rational debate—ideas had to be vigorously and earnestly contested as a matter of course. As Hitchens puts it, argument is "valuable, indeed essential, *for its own sake.*"[157] But as Packer observed in his speech about Hitchens, this principle is increasingly met with resistance: "If an editorial assistant points out that a line in a draft article will probably detonate an explosion on social media, what is her supervisor going to do—risk the blowup, or kill the sentence? Probably the latter. The notion of keeping the sentence *because* of the risk, to defy the risk, to push the boundaries of free expression just a few millimeters further out—that notion now seems quaint."[158] Editors like Rose and Charbonnier weren't just willing to risk *metaphorical* explosions, either.

Critics of those who advocate unrestricted free speech point to the harm speech can cause—wasn't it horrifying for the Jewish residents of Skokie to see neo-Nazis parading through their neighborhoods? Isn't it hurtful for French Muslims—who may already feel like strangers in their own society—to see their faith caricatured? But there's a limitless number of ways for speech to be harmful, and efforts to limit this harm with the blunt instrument of censorship are invariably inconsistent and repressive. This is why Hitchens recognized that any attempt to police speech on behalf of vulnerable groups is as unworkable as it is insulting. He believed "only an open conflict of ideas and principles can produce any clarity. Conflict may be painful, but the painless solution does not exist in any case and the pursuit of it leads to the painful outcome of mindlessness and pointlessness; the apotheosis of the ostrich."[159]

* * *

The First Amendment is one of the forces that pulled Hitchens to the United States—he was naturally drawn to a country where suffocating laws like Britain's Official Secrets Act (which prevents many forms of government information from being published) would be flatly unconstitutional. He was a founding signatory of Charter 88,[160] which called for the establishment of a written constitution in Britain—including the right to peaceful assembly, freedom of association, and free expression.[161] One of the reasons Hitchens had such deep reverence for the First Amendment was the fact that he came from a country without one.

"In modern mass society," Hitchens writes in *Letters to a Young Contrarian*, "the dissenting type is unlikely to be faced with the gibbet or the prison cell, or even with the threat of unemployment or starvation."[162] This is especially true in the United States, which is why he was disturbed that many Americans are willing to yield their Constitutional right to speak and read freely. He cited Mark Twain's famous epigram about the self-imposed limits on free expression in the United States: "It is by the goodness of God that in our country we have those three unspeakably precious things: freedom of speech, freedom of conscience, and the prudence never to practice either of them."[163, 164] In a 1943 article in *Tribune*,[165] Orwell cited a few lines from Humbert Wolfe (mistakenly attributing them to Hilaire Belloc) which made a similar point:

> You cannot hope
> to bribe or twist.
> Thank God! the
> British journalist.
>
> But seeing what
> the man will do
> unbribed, there's
> no occasion to.[166]

Hitchens witnessed and experienced the violent suppression of speech many times in his career—he once received a warning from the U.S. State Department that there was a credible threat to his life after hosting Rushdie,[167] and he was assaulted by goons from the neo-fascist Syrian Social Nationalist Party when he was in the process of scrawling "Fuck the SSNP" on one of their posters in Beirut in 2009.[168] But he recognized that the tightest constraints on free speech in twenty-first-century Western societies are the cultural and political taboos that prevent people from writing and saying what they really think. As he explained during his debate with Tharoor, "In the present situation, the main threat to free expression comes from public opinion"—a threat he described as the "hardest to resist."[169] He pointed out that writers in liberal democracies today aren't likely to be censored by the state, but by editors who are concerned about outrage and condemnation from members of the community. "To me," he continued, "part of growing up is saying the community can go to hell, as far as that's concerned. I don't care about the community. I don't care about the crowd. I don't care about public opinion."[170] He reminds us that "many are the works of genius now in public libraries that would have been incinerated if a roll of opinion had been called."[171]

The gulf between this attitude and the incapacitating fear of public and professional censure expressed by Sulzberger, Kingsbury, and many other publishers and editors is wide. While it's true that the publisher of the *New York Times* has to be more cognizant of various communities' concerns than an independent author like Hitchens, Sulzberger acknowledged in his own internal memo that he believed publishing Cotton's op-ed was the right thing to do. What's particularly disconcerting today is the fact that so many editors, journalists, and activists appear to think the threat posed by speech which was once well within the bounds of normal discourse is now so dangerous that it should be silenced and punished. And those who don't share this belief are often too petrified to say so. Like Orwell, Mill was particularly concerned with what he described as the "moral coercion of public opinion"[172]—a form of coercion that can censor speech surreptitiously. It's impossible to know how much self-censorship is taking place at any given time, and we have every reason to believe the phenomenon is widespread today. "Any fool can lampoon a king or a bishop or a billionaire," Hitchens writes. "A trifle more grit is required to face down a mob, or even a studio audience, that has decided it knows what it wants and is entitled to get it. And the fact that kings and bishops and billionaires often have more say than most in forming the appetites and emotions of the crowd is not irrelevant, either."[173]

Hitchens was just as suspicious of populism as he was of top-down authority. He understood how easily consensus can harden into orthodoxy, and he thought writers and intellectuals have a special responsibility to challenge these orthodoxies. This is why he grew tired of ledes and introductions that referred to him with panting incredulity as the author who dared to go after, say, Mother Teresa—as if doing so could only be the act of an opportunist or a contrarian. Hitchens criticized Mother Teresa because she was strangely indulgent toward dictators (like the Duvaliers in Haiti)[174] and conmen (like Charles Keating)[175] because they made the right pious noises. She was a religious zealot who argued that abortion was the "greatest destroyer of peace today"[176] and believed the poor shouldn't have access to family planning.[177] Hitchens's case against Mother Teresa is now regarded as some kind of impish experiment in funhouse iconoclasm—the title of his book, *The Missionary Position: Mother Teresa in Theory and Practice*,[178] doesn't help—but it was thoroughly imbued with his humanism.

Hitchens attacked exalted figures because he knew doing so would expose herd-like devotion to those figures. If he'd written a more generic tract against Catholic fundamentalism, the evidence for one of his central claims—that the pressures of conformity and consensus are among the tightest constrictors of independent thought—would have been less visible. "The search for security and majority," Hitchens observes, "is not always the same as solidarity; it can be another name for consensus and tyranny and tribalism."[179] As always, Hitchens insisted on the primacy of the individual: the dissident against the complacent and coercive majority; the novelist against the snarling torch-lit mob; individual human beings in all their diversity and complexity against the "fanatical classifiers" (the French philosopher Pascal Brucker's term)[180] whose addiction to tribal categorization is a negation of humanism and equality and solidarity.

Hitchens points out that "invitations to passivity or acquiescence" can sometimes be "sly, some of them making an appeal to modesty. Who are you to be the judge? Who asked you? Anyway, is this the propitious time to be making a stand? Perhaps one should await a more favorable moment? And—aha!—is there some danger of giving ammunition to the enemy?"[181] Hitchens cites Orwell's 1945 essay "Through a Glass, Rosily" as the finest repudiation of these anemic evasions and appeals to the virtues of self-censorship. Orwell wrote:

> Whenever A and B are in opposition to one another, anyone who attacks or criticizes A is accused of aiding and abetting B. And it is often true, objectively and on a short-term analysis, that he *is* making things easier for B. Therefore, say the supporters of A, shut up and don't criticize: or at least criticize "constructively," which in practice always means favourably. And from this it is only a short step to arguing that the suppression and distortion of known facts is the highest duty of a journalist.[182]

On university campuses, the suppression and distortion of certain facts and ideas is increasingly viewed as an unalloyed moral good. According to a 2021 survey published by the Foundation for Individual Rights in Education (FIRE), two-thirds of college students say it's acceptable to prevent people from speaking on campus by shouting them down, while almost a quarter believe violence is permissible to stop a speech.[183] Considering the increasingly common conviction that "harmful" speech is *literally violence*,[184] these attitudes aren't surprising, but the implications for the future of public discourse are dire. The principle outlined so lucidly by the ACLU's Aryeh Neier as neo-Nazis descended on Skokie—that a civil society must be willing to tolerate even grotesque forms of speech to uphold its most fundamental values—is clearly no longer in vogue. An earlier FIRE survey found that less than half of college students know hate speech is protected by the First Amendment, while almost two-thirds believe it shouldn't be.[185]

The collision between identity politics and free expression on the left allows right-wing demagogues to present themselves as defenders of free speech, even when this claim is transparently hypocritical and opportunistic. President Donald Trump threatened to imprison and revoke the citizenship of Americans who burn the flag,[186, 187] declared that NFL players shouldn't be free to protest racial inequality,[188] and wanted to strengthen libel laws while demanding that books critical of him be pulled from the shelves.[189] Yet the authoritarian attitudes toward free speech on campus emboldened him to sign an executive order in 2019 to "ensure institutions that receive Federal research or education grants promote free inquiry, including through compliance with all applicable Federal laws, regulations, and policies."[190] Here's how he described the impetus for the order: "We're delivering a clear message to the professors and power structures trying to suppress dissent and keep young Americans . . . from challenging rigid far-left ideology."[191]

Debates over free expression don't have to break along tribal or party lines—you can be a supporter of protests for racial justice and still acknowledge that *New York Times* staffers were wrong to declare that an article they disliked was a form of violence that needed to be squelched. You can resist bigotry against Muslims and any other marginalized group without yielding an inch on the right to publish satire and criticism. As Hitchens demonstrates, if you're opposed to laws against blasphemy, you can also be opposed to laws against Holocaust denial. You can fight censorship from the left and the right at the same time. The real test of your adherence to a principle is whether you affirm it in the tough cases—when other values are at stake and the pressure to make an exception is strongest. If you abandon the principle in those cases, to what extent did you believe in it at all?

* * *

Whenever a repressive government arrests journalists and enforces laws against free expression, there are plenty of nongovernmental organizations (NGOs) and petitions that call attention to these clear violations of citizens' rights. As the PEN America protesters noted in their letter, the Freedom of Expression Courage Award could have been conferred "upon any of a number of journalists and whistleblowers."[192] Had PEN honored one of *those* writers, its 2015 Literary Gala would have been packed with all the usual attendees, no angry letters would have been written, and there wouldn't have been what Packer described as an "incredibly tense" atmosphere at the awards ceremony, "with riot police and bomb-sniffing dogs all around the Museum of Natural History."[193]

But PEN didn't surrender to the censure of its members or the specter of violence—it chose to push the boundaries of acceptable speech out a little further instead of letting those boundaries encroach on the free exercise of the organization's founding principle. Hitchens often pointed out how relieved he was that Susan Sontag was president of PEN when the fatwa was issued against Rushdie: "She stood up proudly where everyone could see her and denounced the hirelings of the Ayatollah. She nagged everybody on her mailing list and shamed them, if they needed to be shamed, into either signing or showing up. 'A bit of civic fortitude,' as she put it in that gravelly voice that she could summon so well, 'is what is required here.'"[194] Civic fortitude is exactly what PEN displayed in 1989 and 2015.

The *Satanic Verses* fatwa and the *Jyllands-Posten* controversy were brazen authoritarian intrusions on civil society. Hitchens was friends with Rushdie, Rose, Hirsi Ali, and several others who live under the constant threat of violence merely for what they have written, published, and said. He was particularly concerned about what the reactions to these intrusions revealed about the political and intellectual culture in liberal democracies: "I felt then as I feel now," Hitchens writes, "that this was a test."[195] It would be hard to argue that our civil society passed. Major American retailers stopped selling *The Satanic Verses*. Almost the entirety of the U.S. media refused to reprint images of the Danish cartoons, and when Yale University Press published a book about the controversy (*The Cartoons That Shook the World* by Jytte Klausen) in 2009,[196] it chose not to print the cartoons or other images of Muhammad that the author wanted to include. In a statement about this decision, Yale University Press declared that it is "deeply committed to freedom of speech and expression,"[197] but the threat of violence immediately exposed the hollowness of that commitment.

When Hitchens was in Cuba in 1968, he asked the filmmaker Santiago Álvarez what it was like working in a state that had "official policies on the aesthetic."[198] As he recalls in *Hitch-22*, Álvarez explained that "artistic and intellectual liberty was untrammeled"[199] in the country—except for any criticism of Fidel Castro, of course. Hitchens responded with the "mere observation that if the most salient figure in the state and society was immune from critical comment, then all the rest was detail."[200] While the prohibition on discussing Castro in Cuba is a stricter form of repression and censorship than what anyone will encounter in a liberal democracy, Hitchens applied the same logic to open democratic societies: if the citizens of those societies are willing to drop their commitment to free speech at the first sign of trouble or controversy—or if that commitment is always subordinate to some other value whenever a conflict arises—all the rest is detail. What will happen when there's another test of this commitment, as there's bound to be? And another?

"Why is a career like that of Christopher Hitchens not only unlikely," Packer asked, "but almost unimaginable?"[201] His answer: the pressures of belonging and fear. These were appropriate themes for a speech in memory of Hitchens—it would be difficult to find a writer who was more independent or unafraid of challenging political and cultural orthodoxies. After noting that he couldn't usually find a "seconder" when he defended Irving's right to speak, Hitchens said: "My own opinion is enough for me, and I claim the right to have it defended against any consensus, any majority, anywhere, anyplace, anytime. And anyone who disagrees with this can pick a number, get in line, and kiss my ass."[202]

Hitchens explained that any debate about limitations on free expression "goes to the core of what I do and what I am. The First Amendment doesn't just provide me with a living, the First Amendment is my life."[203] It would be difficult to find a public intellectual more closely associated with the major controversies around free expression in the late twentieth and early twenty-first centuries. He consistently resisted all the threats to free expression we've considered in this chapter—from theocratic assaults on authors and journalists to the ever-present pressure to self-censor in the face of the dogmas generated and guarded by public opinion. Unlike the journalists, intellectuals, and activists who think free expression is only useful insofar as it secures their political aims, Hitchens argued that it's the "essential liberty, without which all the other freedoms are either impossible to imagine or impossible to put into practice."[204]

Thomas Jefferson argued in the Virginia Statute for Religious Freedom that there's no need for censorship in a free society: "Truth is great and will prevail if left to herself. . . . she is the proper and sufficient antagonist to error, and has nothing to fear from the conflict unless by human interposition disarmed of her natural weapons, free argument and debate."[205] This is why Hitchens always urged his readers to keep the natural weapons of truth within reach: "Seek out argument and disputation for their own sake; the grave will supply plenty of time for silence."[206]

2 Sinister Bullshit

Hitchens on Identity Politics

When I started graduate school, I attended a training course for new graduate teaching assistants. Near the end of our first session, a student (and soon-to-be teacher) stood up and announced that she's a "firm believer in the one step forward, one step back principle." When this declaration was met with a few bewildered looks and a bit of uneasy chair shuffling, she explained: "If you're a privileged student—if you have one step forward in life—then you should take a step back and let others speak in the classroom." Steps forward included whiteness, maleness, straightness, etc., which meant I was pretty much starting at the finish line (it's unclear what we were all supposed to be stepping toward). The instructor thanked her and changed the subject.

This was almost a decade ago—before the Ferguson, Missouri unrest in late 2014 and early 2015, before the Black Lives Matter movement went mainstream, before Trumpism, and before "critical race theory" became a household term and a political bludgeon. In the decade after Hitchens's death, the academy, journalism, and the wider culture moved

toward a form of politics that places identity—typically the most reductionistic forms of identity, such as race and gender—at the center of
analysis and action. College students now insist that academic departments and entire universities are afflicted by white supremacy. Corporate
boards declare that they're doing everything they can in the struggle
against racism with anti-bias training and other diversity, equity, and
inclusion initiatives. The *New York Times'* 1619 Project has reframed the
story of America as the story of racial oppression.[1]

Many of these efforts are laudable—the legacies of slavery and segregation penetrate the present in countless ways, while questions about
representation (or a lack thereof) are well worth asking and addressing. However, many on today's left don't just recognize that race, gender,
sexuality, and other elements of identity have an impact on a person's
economic circumstances, social and political influence, and so on. They
believe some voices should be amplified to compensate for historic and
institutional injustices, while others should be suppressed for ostensibly
perpetuating and profiting from those injustices. Those who hold this
view argue that harsh measures are necessary to address the most odious
inequities in our society—measures which place zero-sum identitarian
conflict at the center of our moral, political, and social lives. Despite
the mounting evidence to the contrary, they believe the stratification of
our society into narrower and narrower identity subgroups will lead to
greater harmony and justice.

"Beware of identity politics," Hitchens writes in *Letters to a Young
Contrarian*. "I'll rephrase that: have nothing to do with identity politics."[2] In the late 1960s and early 1970s, as the revolutionary euphoria
of 1968 began to wane, Hitchens noticed a shift in left-wing discourse:
"People began to intone the words 'The Personal Is Political,'" he writes
in *Hitch-22*. "At the instant I first heard this deadly expression, I knew
as one does from the utterance of any sinister bullshit that it was—cliché
is arguably forgivable here—very bad news."[3] He was witnessing the
emergence of identity politics as a significant force on the left:

From now on, it would be enough to be a member of a sex or gender, or epidermal subdivision, or even erotic "preference," to qualify as a revolutionary. In order to begin a speech or to ask a question from the floor, all that would be necessary by way of preface would be the words: "Speaking as a . . ." Then could follow any self-loving description. I will have to say this much for the old "hard" Left: we earned our claim to speak and intervene by right of experience and sacrifice and work. It would never have done for any of us to stand up and say that our sex or sexuality or pigmentation or disability were qualifications in themselves. There are many ways of dating the moment when the Left lost or—I would prefer to say—discarded its moral advantage, but this was the first time that I was to see the sellout conducted so cheaply.[4]

Hitchens believed the shift toward identitarianism on the left was a renunciation of its most basic and precious principle: universalism. He thought the left should avoid all forms of tribalism and emphasize rights and values that are intelligible and accessible to everyone. It should embrace universal Enlightenment concepts like the primacy of the individual and unconstrained rational inquiry—no voice should be silenced or promoted on the basis of some crude characteristic like skin color or gender or sexuality. While Hitchens recognized that political mobilization on behalf of marginalized groups was necessary—he supported reparations for black Americans,[5] took part in protests for racial equality, and once delivered a "speech at a street rally against an apartheid-era South African cricket team, which led the British police to grab and hold me on a charge of incitement to riot"[6]—he also believed these campaigns should be built upon a foundation of universal rights and responsibilities.

This attitude is falling out of favor, especially on the left and in academia. Identity-based claims to authority are often elevated above appeals to reason that can be universally understood and debated. Consider this definition of "standpoint theory"—a popular concept among scholars who study gender, sexuality, race, postcolonialism, and other identity-focused disciplines—from the *Stanford Encyclopedia of Philosophy*:

"Standpoint theories usually claim that the perspectives of subordinated social groups have an epistemic advantage regarding politically contested topics related to their subordination, relative to the perspectives of the groups that dominate them."[7] This is why many scholars and activists believe the people who speak as members of those groups deserve special consideration on the basis of their subjective experience alone. While it's true that personal encounters with bigotry and other forms of marginalization add valuable context to discussions about many social and political issues, Hitchens believed a liberal society shouldn't tolerate the idea that race, national origin, or any other superficial characteristic should give anyone a special platform in the public square.

This view has a long and distinguished history on the left, particularly among socialists and civil rights leaders like Bayard Rustin, who Hitchens regarded as the "true genius of the civil-rights and democratic-socialist movements."[8] It's no wonder Hitchens was influenced by Rustin, a principal organizer of the March on Washington in 1963 and one of the most important figures in the Civil Rights Movement. Rustin always opposed the militant black nationalist politics of figures like Stokely Carmichael—his political identity was formed by his socialism and humanism, not the color of his skin. He opposed any form of Affirmative Action that required organizations to meet racial quotas[9] and criticized black studies departments at universities, which he believed put black Americans at a disadvantage by compartmentalizing their educational experiences and separating them from the main currents of American intellectual and industrial life.[10] He viewed universalism as a moral and tactical imperative—while the Black Power movement and other forms of separatism would alienate Americans and turn them against large-scale federal spending on alleviating inequality, an inclusive approach would gain more political traction. This strategy was borne out again and again during the Civil Rights era.

To Hitchens, Rustin represented the old left at its best—a radical in every sense of the word who was practical enough to recognize that change doesn't happen without broad and inclusive political mobilization. As a gay black man who was persecuted for his sexuality—Harlem Rep. Adam Clayton Powell threatened to spread the slander that Rustin and Martin Luther King, Jr. were having an affair if King didn't call off marches on the 1960 Democratic Convention in New York, which Powell believed were an encroachment on his political territory[11]—Rustin knew what bigotry felt like. But he focused his efforts on expanding the gains of the Civil Rights Movement with legislation that would secure jobs, healthcare, and other forms of support for all Americans, whether they were members of oppressed groups or not. Rustin argued in February 1965 that the the "legal foundations of racism in America were destroyed" between 1954 and 1964 with school desegregation and the passage of the Civil Rights Act,[12] and he made the case that it was time to push for sweeping structural change: "No longer were Negroes satisfied with integrating lunch counters. They now sought advances in employment, housing, school integration, police protection, and so forth."[13]

As he fought for these policies, Rustin's emphasis on universalism was ever-present: he observed that the struggle for civil rights "may have done more to democratize life for whites than for Negroes" by igniting anti-McCarthyite political activism on campuses, placing the importance of high-quality public education at the center of the national discourse, and focusing unprecedented attention on poverty.[14] He observed that massive public investment was necessary to train unskilled and semi-skilled black workers to fully participate in the economy, arguing that "'Preferential treatment' cannot help them."[15] Rustin urged his fellow activists and voters to forge multiracial political coalitions to push for expansive progressive legislation. He acknowledged that "there are those who argue that a coalition strategy would force the Negro to surrender his political independence to white liberals," but he concluded that "motion must begin in the larger society, for there is a limit to what Negroes can do alone."[16]

Rustin's inclusive principles are increasingly anachronistic in the third decade of the twenty-first century. Books like Robin DiAngelo's *White Fragility: Why It's So Hard for White People to Talk About Racism* and Ibram X. Kendi's *How to Be an Antiracist*, which share the essential conviction that racism is still ubiquitous and race must be placed at the center of social and political analysis and activism, have become defining texts on race in America.[17,18] The message of these books is often explicitly anti-universal—as DiAngelo writes: "Perhaps you've heard someone say, 'I was taught to treat everyone the same' or 'People just need to be taught to respect one another, and that begins at home.' These statements . . . are unconvincing to most people of color and only invalidate their experiences."[19]

Hitchens believed the myopic focus on race, gender, and other demographic categories makes politics even more schismatic and irrational than it would otherwise be. "People who think with their epidermis or their genitalia or their clan are the problem to begin with," he wrote in 2008. "One does not banish this specter by invoking it."[20] In fact, Hitchens believed the entire concept of race should be scrapped as a pointless and arbitrary tribal marker—an argument made personally and powerfully in Thomas Chatterton Williams's 2019 memoir *Self-Portrait in Black and White: Unlearning Race.*[21] However, none of this is to say writers, activists, and scholars shouldn't work to address racism, misogyny, homophobia, and the economic and social issues that lead to unequal outcomes for members of minority groups. As Hitchens explained in a November 2001 debate on reparations:

> In my hometown of Washington, DC, there's hardly one official brick piled on another that wasn't piled there by unpaid labor under the whip. And that dead labor becomes dead capital and dead souls—dead money. And it's piled, actually, in the Treasury Department and the federal financial system, who took that free labor, those dead souls, and turned it into capital. And it's back pay, and it's owed, and it's overdue.[22]

Rustin didn't agree, arguing that "reparations is a ridiculous idea. If my great-grandfather picked cotton for 50 years, then he may deserve some money, but he's dead and gone and nobody owes me anything."[23] Still, Hitchens and Rustin both recognized that there was only one way to have this debate (or any debate) in an open liberal society: by making a case to their fellow citizens with reasons that are intelligible to everyone. Neither of them accepted the idea that "Speaking as a . . ." should be a special qualification—members of marginalized groups can testify to what oppression and inequality feel like, but ideas about addressing these problems have to be universally accessible and assessed without prejudice. The quality of your arguments has nothing to do with your identity. If there's one Enlightenment value that underlies all the rest, it's the idea that reason is the starting point for civilization—arguments in favor of philosophical principles and public policies have to amount to more than personal and subjective statements. They have to offer reasons for a course of action beyond assertions of identity-based authority.

This is a point Rustin and Hitchens instinctively understood. Throughout American history, the most important and successful political movements—from abolitionism to Civil Rights—have appealed to what Abraham Lincoln called the "better angels of our nature."[24] The "our" in that statement doesn't refer to one group in particular—it refers to all Americans and, in principle, all of humanity.

* * *

Hitchens saw the early stirrings of identitarianism half a century ago: "It began as a sort of reaction to the defeats and downturns that followed 1968," he writes in *Letters to a Young Contrarian*, "a consolation prize, as you might say, for people who had missed that year."[25] In *Hitch-22*, he describes a feeling of "anticlimax" in the years following 1968, a period when some on the left began to channel their unspent revolutionary energy into identity politics.[26] In their 2020 book *Cynical Theories: How Ac-*

tivist Scholarship Made Everything About Race, Gender, and Identity—and Why This Harms Everybody, Helen Pluckrose and James Lindsay observe that the emergence of postmodernism—which they argue was the intellectual precursor to the academic theories that inform identity politics as it exists today—was a consequence of the growing disillusionment with Marxism and other political upheavals during this period.[27]

Pluckrose and Lindsay identify several elements of postmodernism (articulated and refined by figures such as Michel Foucault, Jacques Derrida, and Jean-Francois Lyotard) that built the foundation of contemporary identitarianism: skepticism about objective reality, the perception of language as the constructor and locus of knowledge, and the central role of power in all of the above. Hitchens could see the emergence of these concepts in the academy, writing in 2005:

> The study of literature as a tradition, let alone as a "canon," has in many places been deposed by an emphasis on deconstruction, postmodernism and the nouveau roman. The concept of authorship itself has come under scornful scrutiny, with the production of "texts" viewed more as a matter of social construct than as the work of autonomous individuals. Not surprisingly, the related notions of objective truth or value-free inquiry are also sternly disputed; even denied. A new language or "discourse" is often considered necessary for this pursuit, and has been supplied in part by Foucault and Derrida.[28]

Postmodernism has been particularly influential in postcolonial studies, a field which was shaped by Hitchens's friend Edward Said. In a 2003 essay, Hitchens argued that Said's 1978 book *Orientalism*[29] "characterized Western scholarship about the East as a conscious handmaiden of power and subordination. Explorers, missionaries, archaeologists, linguists—all had been part of a colonial enterprise."[30] Pluckrose and Lindsay discuss Foucault's influence on Said—particularly his ideas about the power of language to shape knowledge.[31] For example, Said wrote: "My contention is that without examining Orientalism as a discourse one cannot possibly understand the enormously systematic discipline by which European culture was able to manage—and even produce—the Orient politically, sociologically, militarily, ideologically, scientifically, and imaginatively during the post-Enlightenment period."[32] As Hitchens noted, "'Produce,' as in 'cultural production,' has become one of the key words of the post-Foucault academy."[33]

Hitchens continued: "In [Said's] analysis, every instance of European curiosity about the East, from Flaubert to Marx, was part of a grand design to exploit and remake what Westerners saw as a passive, rich, but ultimately contemptible 'Oriental' sphere."[34] He recognized Said's influence on the development of postcolonial theory in the United States: "To the extent that American academics now speak about the 'appropriation' of other cultures, and seldom fail to put ordinary words such as 'the Other' between portentous quotation marks, and contest the very notion of objective inquiry, they are paying what they imagine is a debt to Edward Said's work."[35]

On the general concept of Orientalism, Hitchens acknowledged: "That there is undeniable truth to this it would be idle to dispute.... Lord Macaulay was a near perfect illustration of the sentence (which occurs in Disraeli's novel *Tancred*) 'The East is a career.' He viewed the region both as a barbarous source of potential riches and as a huge tract in pressing need of civilization."[36] Hitchens knew this attitude represented a long history of imperialist ravings about "civilizing missions" that were, in fact, vicious and rapacious assaults on subjugated populations. Despite the high-minded pretensions of imperialism, its most trenchant critics have always recognized how thin these rationalizations are. Hitchens admired Orwell's clear-eyed condemnation of the imperial system he spent years serving—an experience which only strengthened his conviction that this system was irredeemable: "The truth is that no modern man, in his heart of hearts," Orwell wrote, "believes that it is right to invade a foreign country and hold the population down by force."[37]

In *Hitch-22*, Hitchens writes: "I at first thought Edward's *Oriental-*

ism was a very just and necessary book in that it forced Westerners to confront their own assumptions about the Levant and indeed the whole of the Orient."[38] But he would later observe that the influence of *Orientalism* led to the creation of a "faction in the academy that now regards the acquisition of knowledge about 'the East' as an essentially imperialist project, amounting to an 'appropriation' and 'subordination' of another culture."[39]

This cynical, zero-sum view of cultural education and exchange has moved well beyond the academy. The charge of "cultural appropriation," for instance, is now made with dizzying frequency. Novelists are told they have no business writing about other races or cultures.[40] In 2018, an online mob assailed an 18-year-old girl for wearing a Chinese dress to prom.[41] Chefs and restaurant owners are regularly accused of hijacking and exploiting other cultures if they don't have the right ethnic background.[42] While we can debate which allegations of cultural appropriation are reasonable and which ones aren't, the trend is clearly toward cordoning different cultures off from one another and condemning those who transgress these boundaries. Students and professors want to "decolonize" their universities. Charges of cultural theft and imperialism are commonplace on campus and in the media. Rather than recognize the inevitable (and desirable) fluidity and intertwinement of cultures—especially in a large and diverse country like the United States—many on the left want to freeze these cultures in time and place.

"Cultural-political interaction," Hitchens wrote, "must be construed as dialectical. Edward Said was in a prime position to be a 'negotiator' here. In retrospect, however, it can be argued that he chose a one-sided approach and employed rather a broad brush."[43] In the same essay, Hitchens argued that there's "every hope of cultural and political cross-pollination between the Levant, the Orient, the Near East, the Middle East, Western Asia (whatever name you may choose to give it), and the citizens of the Occident, the North, the metropole."[44] But many of today's postcolonial scholars—as well as scholars in other fields, such as anthropology—are quick to accuse their institutions and colleagues of perpetuating racism and imperialism for making this point. The idea that universities are contaminated by Orientalist prejudice has spurred campaigns to "decolonize" faculties and curricula, which means getting rid of white professors and trimming "dead white males" (David Hume or Shakespeare or Goethe, for instance) from reading lists.

A *New York Times* essay published in early 2021 features Princeton classics professor Dan-el Padilla Peralta, who argues that the "production of whiteness" can be found "in the very marrows of classics."[45] The title of the essay announces that Padilla "wants to save classics from whiteness," which is why he believes classics professors have a responsibility to "explode the canon" and "overhaul the discipline from nuts to bolts."[46] Padilla's campaign against the classics contains all the hallmarks of a thoroughly postmodern project, from the idea that "whiteness" has been "produced" in the discipline's "discourses" to his insistence that he had to "actively engage in the decolonization of my mind" to his focus on the mechanics of social, cultural, and political power. These ideas also inform Padilla's activism. In June 2020, he joined several colleagues in writing a letter to the leadership at Princeton, which declared that racism is "rampant in even our most 'progressive' communities" and "plays a powerful role at institutions like Princeton."[47]

The letter, which was signed by 300 faculty, issued almost 50 demands, including "immediately and exponentially" hiring more faculty of color and creating a committee that would "oversee the investigation and discipline of racist behaviors, incidents, research, and publication."[48] When Padilla's colleagues worried that this demand could threaten open inquiry and free expression at Princeton,[49] he responded, "I don't see things like free speech or the exchange of ideas as ends in themselves. I have to be honest about that. I see them as a means to the end of human flourishing."[50] But universities don't exist to rubber stamp one man's idea of human flourishing. They exist because free speech and the exchange of ideas are, in fact, ends in themselves—prerequisites for determining what human flourishing is and how to work toward it. This was a point Hitchens made at every available opportunity (see chapter 1).

In one of his essays about Said, Hitchens argued that "one must be ready to oppose any analysis that even slightly licenses the idea that 'outsiders' are not welcome to study other cultures."[51] He didn't believe skin color, national origin, religion, etc. should count as qualifications for scholars. Hitchens admired Said's appreciation for and understanding of Western literature, but this only added to his dismay at the academic field his friend helped to create. Said provided a set of organizing principles and a language—a discourse, if you insist—for scholars and activists who believe literary criticism and academic inquiry should be identitarian battlefields upon which some works and figures must be vanquished while others must be victorious. In contrast to this cramped and stultifying attitude, Hitchens celebrated the universalism of intellectuals like Rustin and the Trinidadian Marxist C.L.R. James—a black man who was intimately familiar with the horrors of racism and imperialism, but who never allowed his hostility to these malignant forces to displace his humanism. As Hitchens writes in his memoir:

> He [James] had schooled himself in classical literature and regarded the canon of English as something with which every literate person of any culture should become acquainted. He had a particular love for Thackeray, and it was said that he could recite chapters of *Vanity Fair* by heart. This commitment was important then and was to become much more so as the 1960s fashion turned against "Eurocentrism."[52]

Why did Hitchens argue that James's commitment to English literature was important at a time when left-wing intellectuals were becoming increasingly hostile toward what they regarded as Eurocentrism (a phenomenon they saw just about everywhere they looked)? Because he understood that literature—even literature produced and celebrated by cultures with a long history of imperialism—transcends its social, cultural, and political context. In a 1966 lecture, James said, "I denounce

European colonialist scholarship. But I respect the learning and the profound discoveries of Western civilisation."[53] At a time when the Enlightenment has been "redefined as 'white' and 'oppressive,'" as Hitchens put it,[54] intellectuals like James remind us that this crude essentialism is toxic and regressive. One theme of this chapter is the idea that it's possible to confront the cruelty and prejudice that have always been in the marrow (as Padilla might put it) of Western civilization while embracing and building upon the achievements of that civilization—universal achievements that are shared by all.

* * *

In the twentieth century, postmodernism was politically inert—from its radical assertions about the subjectivity of knowledge to its obsession with power dynamics at every level of society, it wasn't especially actionable on a political level. When Foucault argued that the vicissitudes of language rendered scientific knowledge and value-free inquiry dubious, power permeated every level of society, etc., he was generally making descriptive claims about how he believed the world worked. It wasn't until decades later that these ideas would gain traction politically—a shift we're now witnessing.

After Hitchens discarded Marxism as an organizing framework for his politics, he still claimed to "think like a Marxist"[55]—which is one of the reasons he was opposed to postmodernism. Consider Pluckrose and Lindsay's summary of the difference between Marxist and postmodern conceptions of power: "In Marxist thought," they write, "power is like a weight, pressing down on the proletariat. For Foucault, power operated more like a grid, running through all layers of society and determining what people held to be true and, consequently, how they spoke about it."[56] It's not much of a leap from this view to the idea that people should constantly "check their privilege" and monitor their interactions for "microaggressions" or any other signs of prejudice—social and political demands that have become increasingly common over the past decade. Recall the PEN authors' preoccupation with power when they condemned *Charlie Hebdo*.

Pluckrose and Lindsay argue that many prominent identitarian scholars—such as Patricia Williams, Angela Harris, and Kimberlé Crenshaw—analyze the causes and effects of oppression and marginalization through the filter of postmodernism: "By looking at multiple systems of power and privilege and situating experience as a source of knowledge within them, they moved away from materialist analysis and towards the postmodern."[57] Crenshaw has been particularly influential as a scholar of critical race theory and intersectionality. The former is an academic concept and discipline which began as a method of critiquing legal issues through the lens of race, but which has expanded to encompass many areas outside of law.[58] The latter provides a framework for understanding how various forms of discrimination and oppression interact with one another.[59]

These ideas have driven a significant shift in how many journalists, scholars, and activists view liberal principles like equality and individualism. Pluckrose and Lindsay cite Crenshaw's 1991 essay "Mapping the Margins: Intersectionality, Identity Politics, and Violence against Women of Color"[60] as the catalyst for decades of work by identitarian intellectuals and activists.[61] They observe that Crenshaw was "openly advocating identity politics over liberal universalism, which had sought to remove the social significance of identity categories and treat people equally regardless of identity. Identity politics restores the social significance of identity categories in order to valorize them as sources of empowerment and community."[62] Postmodernism challenges and seeks to replace many of the fundamental tenets of the Enlightenment, which is why it ultimately spawned anti-Enlightenment political movements.

In "Mapping the Margins," Crenshaw observed that a "strong case can be made that the most critical resistance strategy for disempowered groups is to occupy and defend a politics of social location rather than to vacate and destroy it."[63] "Social location" refers to how various elements of a person's identity determine their position in society.[64] Crenshaw argued against the idea that moving past identity categories would lead to social and political progress, reinforcing her point with a discussion of Anita Hill's accusations of sexual harassment against Supreme Court Justice Clarence Thomas in 1991.[65] According to Crenshaw, Hill was "rhetorically disempowered in part because she fell between the dominant interpretations of feminism and antiracism. Caught between the competing narrative tropes of rape (advanced by feminists) on the one hand and lynching (advanced by Thomas and his antiracist supporters) on the other, the race and gender dimensions of her position could not be told."[66] Crenshaw continued:

> If, as this analysis asserts, history and context determine the utility of identity politics, how then do we understand identity politics today, especially in light of our recognition of multiple dimensions of identity? More specifically, what does it mean to argue that gender identities have been obscured in antiracist discourses, just as race identities have been obscured in feminist discourses? Does that mean we cannot talk about identity? Or instead, that any discourse about identity has to acknowledge how our identities are constructed through the intersection of multiple dimensions?[67]

The answer to the clashing forms of identity politics on display during the Anita Hill hearings was, for Crenshaw, more identity politics—only with a greater awareness of intersectionality. According to Crenshaw, the "organized identity groups in which we find ourselves in are in fact coalitions, or at least potential coalitions waiting to be formed.... intersectionality provides a basis for reconceptualizing race as a coalition between men and women of color."[68] It's difficult to see exactly what Crenshaw was calling for in the context of the fraught hearings—a coalition in support of Hill merely because she was a black woman caught between "competing narrative tropes"? Wasn't the real question whether or not she was telling the truth about the harassment?

Hitchens observed that the Hill hearings weren't an auspicious occasion for sober political reflection: "Everyone was slightly out of their skull that week," he wrote in a 1997 review of Hill's memoir of the ordeal, *Speaking Truth to Power*.[69,70] He recognized the same tropes as Crenshaw, but this didn't lead him to conclude that a recommitment to identitarianism was needed—instead, it was a reminder that identitarianism could be exploited by unscrupulous opportunists to hijack and distort political discourse: "The cynics of the Bush White House could do brinkmanship with the pseudo-liberals and say, in effect, we back our lynched black man against your abused woman. Wanna play? 'Identity politics' was used at the highest level to degrade the whole American democracy."[71] In *Letters to a Young Contrarian*, Hitchens argues that the Hill hearings exposed identity politics as a regressive phenomenon: "From a way of being radical it very swiftly became a way of being reactionary."[72]

When Hitchens first encountered identity politics on the left, he "knew in my bones that a truly Bad Idea had entered the discourse. Nor was I wrong. People began to stand up at meetings and orate about how they *felt*, not about what or how they thought, and about who they were rather than what (if anything) they had done or stood for."[73] Though he didn't use the word "intersectionality," he saw how quickly the concept could devolve into absurdity—identity politics, he argued, "became the replication in even less interesting form of the narcissism of the small difference, because each identity group begat its subgroups and 'specificities.' This tendency has often been satirised—the overweight caucus of the Cherokee transgender disabled lesbian faction demands a hearing on its needs—but never satirised enough."[74]

While this may not have been a fair representation of intersectionality—which does, after all, make a sound point about interlocking forms of oppression and their real-world consequences—many activists have used theories like Crenshaw's to argue that all social and political action should be segmented on the basis of identity. Even Crenshaw acknowledges that "Some people look to intersectionality as a grand theory of everything, but that's not my intention."[75] Regardless of her intentions, the effect of her work has been to convert postmodern identitarian concepts into concrete political realities.

* * *

"If I would not vote against someone on the grounds of 'race' or 'gender' alone," Hitchens wrote in 2008, "then by the exact same token I would not cast a vote in his or her favor for the identical reason."[76] The left increasingly interprets such affirmations of basic liberal universalism as threats to marginalized communities—or even evidence of prejudice.

In the early days of the 2020 Democratic primary, Sen. Bernie Sanders went on Vermont Public Radio and said, "We have got to look at candidates, you know, not by the color of their skin, not by their sexual orientation or their gender and not by their age. I mean, I think we have got to try to move . . . toward a nondiscriminatory society, which looks at people based on their abilities, based on what they stand for."[77] This sentiment wasn't well-received on the left. For example, Neera Tanden, who would later become a senior advisor to President Joe Biden, regarded it as an offensive dismissal of threatened groups: "At a time where folks feel under attack because of who they are, saying race or gender or sexual orientation or identity doesn't matter is not off, it's simply wrong."[78] A flood of other critical articles and statements made the same point.

Like Hitchens and Rustin, Sanders is more concerned with class and economic issues than identity politics. When reparations became a surprise issue in the 2020 primary, he argued that poverty should be a more relevant variable for government assistance than race: "I think what we have got to do is pay attention to distressed communities: black communities, Latino communities and white communities, and as president, I pledge to do that."[79] In an interview with the *New York Times* editorial board, he said, "the federal government must substantially increase funding for distressed communities that have long-term poverty rates. Often, not always, African-American communities."[80]

This orientation toward public policies that address the needs of all Americans—which will have disproportionate benefits for marginalized communities by default, as they're generally in greater need of assistance—would have been regarded as progressive just a few decades ago. It's suggestive that Sanders's observation about judging candidates on the basis of their policies and principles, which easily could have been made by King or Rustin, is now considered offensively retrograde by a significant share of the mainstream left.

Anytime Democratic politicians in the United States attempt to move the discourse toward a more universal conception of civic responsibilities, they're derided as ignorant reactionaries who are hopelessly out of step with the mainstream left. When Pete Buttigieg broached the subject during a May 2019 speech, shortly after launching his 2020 presidential campaign, he was careful to provide a litany of caveats: "I may be a part of the LGBTQ community. But being a gay man doesn't even tell me what it's like to be a trans woman of color in that same community, let alone an undocumented mother of four or a disabled veteran or a displaced autoworker."[81] He acknowledged that he wasn't "pretending that there are equivalencies between the different patterns of exclusion in this country."[82] But he also called for a "new form of American solidarity" that would deemphasize identitarianism and the "politics of social location" advocated by Crenshaw: "It is true that each of us can see in our own identity all the reasons we're misunderstood and then say: 'You don't understand me because you haven't walked in my shoes.' Something that is true, as far as it goes. But it doesn't get us very far."[83]

Buttigieg was immediately attacked for this remark. Al Sharpton called it "insulting."[84] Former NAACP president William Brooks wondered why Buttigieg was discussing left-wing identity politics in the era of Trump[85] (Brooks ignored the fact that Trump repeatedly instrumentalized identitarian excesses on the left to discredit his political opponents). The *Hill's* Jonathan Easley described the speech as a "gamble" and reported that it "struck a nerve on the left."[86] At *NBC News*, Josh Lederman said it was "risky."[87] The speech offered a rebuke of identity politics so mild that it would have gone unremarked just a decade or two ago, but any suggestion that identitarianism can be a political obstacle is now anathema on the left.

* * *

In an article published half a decade before Donald Trump declared that he was running for president, Hitchens argued that the changing demographics of the United States—particularly the fact that white Americans would no longer outnumber nonwhite Americans—would lead to political instability. "One crucial element of the American subconscious," he wrote, "is about to become salient and explicit and highly volatile." [88] Hitchens was writing at a time when the Tea Party—the populist forebear to Trumpism—was reaching its zenith in American politics. Conservative commentator Glenn Beck had just hosted a rally with tens of thousands of attendees on the National Mall, an event that took place on the same day King delivered his "I Have a Dream" speech almost half a century earlier.

Beyond the "smarmy tactic" of trying to appropriate the moral prestige of the Civil Rights Movement for a resentment-fueled carnival of self-pitying nativism, Hitchens observed that many Tea Party Republicans were driven by the fear that they were losing their cultural and political influence.[89] There was plenty of evidence for this claim—from their focus on immigration to the prevalence of "birtherism," a conspiracy theory which held that President Obama wasn't born in the United States. Hitchens summarized the events that led up to Beck's march:

> This summer, then, has been the perfect register of the new anxiety,
> beginning with the fracas over Arizona's immigration law, gaining in
> intensity with the proposal by some Republicans to amend the 14th

Amendment so as to de-naturalize "anchor babies," cresting with the continuing row over the so-called "Ground Zero" mosque, and culminating, at least symbolically, with a quasi-educated Mormon broadcaster calling for a Christian religious revival from the steps of the Lincoln Memorial.[90]

Just as Trump would partly build his campaign on racial resentments, the progenitors of the Tea Party movement understood—along with so many populists before them—that nativism and identity politics are among the most powerful forces for political mobilization. "It is increasingly common," Hitchens wrote in 2010, "to hear allegations that Obama is either foreign-born or a Muslim. And these insinuations are perfectly emblematic of the two main fears of the old majority: that it will be submerged by an influx from beyond the borders and that it will be challenged in its traditional ways and faiths by an alien and largely Third World religion."[91] One of the loudest voices screaming that Obama was foreign-born—and therefore ineligible to be president—was Trump, who would later exploit xenophobic grievances and rally his supporters with a crudely exclusionary brand of nationalism that scapegoated Muslims, immigrants, foreign workers, and even allies.

"In a rather curious and confused way," Hitchens wrote, "some white people are starting almost to think like a minority, even like a persecuted one."[92] Of Beck's rally, he observed that the "overall effect was large, vague, moist, and undirected: the *Waterworld* of white self-pity."[93] But he recognized that there was something more insidious and potentially aggressive under the surface of this pathetic spectacle: "Saturday's rally was quite largely confined to expressions of pathos and insecurity, voiced in a sickly and pious tone. The emotions that underlay it, however, may not be uttered that way indefinitely."[94] Within a few years, the American right would adopt its own malignant brand of identitarianism—a form of identity politics that was belligerent and arrogant rather than insecure and insipid.

Identity politics was among the most powerful forces that propelled

Trump to the White House and maintained his immovable support among roughly 40 percent of Americans.[95] When he attacked NFL players for kneeling during the National Anthem to highlight racial injustice, he claimed to represent the true patriots who were appalled by what was actually a dignified and restrained form of protest. He appealed to the same narrow nationalist sentiment when he threatened to imprison anyone who burned the American flag. After a statue of Caesar Rodney was removed from a square in Wilmington, Delaware, Trump declared, "if you demolish a statue without permission, you immediately get 10 years in prison"[96] (the Rodney statue was legally removed by local officials).[97] Just as Hitchens anticipated, Trump relentlessly slandered and attacked Muslims, claiming that he witnessed them celebrating on September 11 and promising to create a Muslim registry, ban Muslims from the country, and spy on mosques.[98, 99, 100, 101]

Hitchens distrusted what he described in a 1989 *Harper's* essay as "racial populism" on the left and the right.[102] With Trump, this form of populism was particularly ugly and divisive, as it often degenerated into outright bigotry. Trump argued that the United States shouldn't accept immigrants from Haiti and "shithole countries" in Africa.[103] In 2019, he told Reps. Alexandria Ocasio-Cortez, Ilhan Omar, Rashida Tlaib, and Ayanna Pressley that they should "go back and help fix the totally broken and crime infested places from which they came,"[104] as if they aren't every bit as American as Trump. This wasn't the self-pity Hitchens witnessed on the populist right a decade earlier—it was unapologetic, high-decibel nativist authoritarianism emanating from the highest office in the land.

Hitchens saw it coming. "Beck's '9/12 Project,'" he wrote in December 2010, "is canalizing old racist and clerical toxic-waste material that a healthy society had mostly flushed out of its system more than a generation ago, and injecting it right back in again."[105] He made this argument in response to moderate conservatives like Ross Douthat, who believed the Tea Party was animated by the innocuous "conviction that the Republicans as much as the Democrats have been an accessory to the growth of spending and deficits, and that the Republican establishment needs to be punished for straying from fiscal rectitude."[106] Douthat argued that the Tea Party was in the process of being co-opted by "Republican politics as usual," and even believed this "would be unfortunate. Their eccentric elements notwithstanding, the Tea Parties have something vital to offer the country: a vocal, activist constituency for spending cuts at a time when politicians desperately need to have their spines stiffened on the issue."[107]

If the Tea Party had been captured by Republican politics as usual, the country may have been spared Trump. But as Hitchens recognized, once the dump valves of embittered identitarianism and conspiracy mongering are flung wide open, it's difficult to shut them. He saw this process of radicalization taking place as early as the 1990s—despite his contempt for President Bill Clinton, he was alarmed when he went on the radio stations of the "paranoid right"[108] and discovered that their criticisms of Clinton had become completely unmoored from reality:

> Didn't I understand that Clinton and his wife had murdered Vince Foster and were, even as I spoke, preparing to take advantage of the Y2K millennium crisis—remember that?—in order to seize power for life and become the Nicolae and Elena Ceausescu of our day? These people were not interested in the president's actual transgressions. They were looking to populate their fantasy world with new and more lurid characters.[109]

After Trump took office, the paranoid right became a reeking swamp of febrile conspiracy theories about deep-state takeovers, Satanic rituals, cannibalism, and child sex rings (all elements of the QAnon cult).[110] Hitchens witnessed the emergence of political and cultural tendencies that would lead to an era of rampant tribalism, conspiracism, and disinformation. Some of the characters have even remained the same—the man who opened fire on a Washington, DC pizza parlor in 2016 was motivated by a conspiracy theory which held that Hillary Clinton was connected to a child sex trafficking operation taking place there.[111]

It's no coincidence that the rise of massively influential conservative talk radio behemoths like Rush Limbaugh occurred in the 1990s—a period when political polarization in the United States (inaugurated by the Gingrich Revolution in 1994) started to surge.[112] Polarization leads to extremism, particularly at a time when people are uneasy about political and demographic change. "Most epochs are defined by one or another anxiety," Hitchens observed. "More important, though, is the form which that anxiety takes. Millions of Americans are currently worried about two things that are, in their minds, emotionally related. The first of these is the prospect that white people will no longer be the majority in this country, and the second is that the United States will be just one among many world powers."[113] The populist forces that emerged in response to these developments, Hitchens wrote, "need and want to sublimate the anxiety into hysteria and paranoia. The president is a Kenyan. The president is a secret Muslim."[114]

Hitchens acknowledged that the Tea Party could be susceptible to moderation in the short term, but he could also see that the ugly and paranoid elements of the movement weren't going anywhere: "A large, volatile constituency has been created that believes darkly in betrayal and conspiracy," he wrote.[115] Within five years, the GOP would be captured by Trumpism—a movement that abandoned what Douthat described as "Republican politics as usual" in favor of the most acrid form of nationalist identitarianism and isolationism that has ever held power in the United States. Instead of resisting this movement with an appeal to our common citizenship and humanity—as well as the universal liberal democratic norms and values Trump trampled for four years—many of Trump's opponents asserted that the only way to resist identity politics on the right was to embrace identity politics on the left.

* * *

When Hitchens discussed Beck's march, he emphasized the "symptoms of white unease and the additionally uneasy forms that its expression is beginning to take"[116]—an argument that might even sound like a version of DiAngelo's *White Fragility*. But there's a vast gulf between these positions—DiAngelo writes that it's difficult for white people to appreciate their cultural and political status "because of two key Western ideologies: individualism and objectivity. Briefly, individualism holds that we are each unique and stand apart from others, even those within our social groups. Objectivity tells us that it is possible to be free of all bias."[117]

In fact, these "Western ideologies" comprise the philosophical and political bedrock of liberal democracy everywhere in the world. The insistence that concepts as basic and universal as individualism and objectivity are somehow "Western" is one of the many ways identitarian scholars feed the very prejudices they claim to oppose. Hitchens explained what's wrong with regarding Enlightenment principles and methods of inquiry as products of "the West" (an ill-defined historical concept to begin with):

> I'm uncomfortable with the idea of Western values and I never use the term.... I don't think there's any geographical location for these values, and I think there's always the danger of ethnocentrism when one suggests that there is.... What I would prefer to say was that there are Enlightenment values, some of them deriving from Greece, some of them from Italy, some of them from Scotland, many of them from Germany and England and Spain, and indeed many of them from the Muslim world, which kept the Greek libraries and texts alive when they'd been lost to the Christian world and brought them back to our attention through the cultural fusion in Andalusia in southern Spain.... These values of free inquiry, the scientific method, the central importance of the individual, and so forth are, I think, what I would define as the core of the Enlightenment cause.[118]

DiAngelo writes: "According to the ideology of individualism, race is irrelevant."[119] But this is a caricature of the individualism that Hitchens and many other liberals embrace. The claim that "race is irrelevant" is self-evidently absurd. With Jim Crow in living memory; the ever-present legacies of centuries of slavery; and massive racial disparities in education, income, health, and incarceration rates, only the most rabid reactionaries would claim that race doesn't matter. Hitchens believed the social and political implications of slavery and racial prejudice are so enormous that it's impossible to fully appreciate or quantify them.[120]

But these facts don't undercut the importance of individualism. "Whatever the role of social and political forces," Hitchens reminded readers after the Rushdie fatwa, "ideas and books have to be formulated and written by individuals."[121] This wasn't just how he understood literature. It was also an affirmation of his belief that the commitment to individualism is the most basic moral and political requirement of a liberal society—a central tenet of the Enlightenment. In the foreword to *Unacknowledged Legislation: Writers in the Public Sphere*, he observes "how often, when all parties in the state were agreed on a matter, it was individual pens which created the moral space for a true argument."[122] Individualism facilitates the open exchange of ideas, including ideas that are considered blasphemous and dangerous by would-be tyrannical majorities—or what DiAngelo describes as "our social groups." Hitchens noted that the individual pens of abolitionist intellectuals like Frederick Douglass and William Lloyd Garrison fatally undermined the rationalizations and scriptural justifications for slavery.[123] History is replete with examples of individuals rejecting the prejudices of their social groups to fight for universal principles—does anyone believe the abolitionist revolutionary John Brown felt constrained by *his* social group?

What DiAngelo dismisses as the "ideology of individualism" is, in fact, the most compelling rejoinder to prejudice of all kinds. Hitchens opposed identitarianism for the same reason he abhorred racism and every form of sectarianism: he refused to wedge people into rigid demographic categories instead of treating them like individual human beings. He often noted that "discrimination" is a strange word to describe bigotry in practice, as bigots actually fail to discriminate between individual members of the groups they despise.[124] He rejected any political argument or movement which insists that our debates should be reduced to interminable squabbles over the pigmentation or reproductive organs or sexuality of the participants. When Hitchens hoped for a post-racial future, he wasn't claiming that the government and society should ignore gross racial inequality and injustice—he was making the case that reason and solidarity should continue to erode the tribal barriers that generate pointless animosity between human beings. Race will remain relevant for many years to come, but the hope is for it to become less and less relevant.

DiAngelo argues that "we don't see the world from the universal human perspective but from the perspective of a particular kind of human."[125] This is a truism—nobody can escape the environment and circumstances that shape them. But DiAngelo's prescription for addressing racial inequality goes far beyond acknowledging bias and working to mitigate disparities—she demands a sweeping political and social reorientation toward race. Don't bother trying to see the world from a universal human perspective, she argues; instead, view every interaction through the lens of racial power dynamics. "Interrupting the forces of racism is ongoing, lifelong work," DiAngelo writes, "because the forces conditioning us into racist frameworks are always at play; our learning will never be finished."[126] In other words, the goal of a post-racial society is a pernicious fantasy. It doesn't matter how much socioeconomic conditions improve for marginalized Americans or how thoroughly our society rejects prejudice—race will necessarily remain at the center of our political and social lives forever.

Hitchens was aligned with DiAngelo in some ways—he described the Tea Party's march on Washington as a flood of racial insecurity, and he knew the undercurrent of bigotry was strong on the populist right. He saw how unscrupulous politicians and media demagogues could channel white anxiety into white rage. But these are the reasons Hitchens's anti-identitarianism was clearly a good-faith argument in favor of universalism over tribalism. His position raises a question about today's peddlers of identity politics: what are they adding to our understanding of racism and inequality? Hitchens demonstrated that it's possible to be a proponent of radical measures to address the consequences of slavery, racism, and the systemic issues that deepen entrenched inequalities without becoming ensnared in identity politics. Yet the merchants of racial division continue to insist that this is impossible.

This isn't just wrong in principle—it's also a strategic mistake that energizes the populist right. It would be unfair to describe Trumpism merely as an expression of white identity politics; in the 2020 election, many analysts were shocked when Trump saw his support among Hispanics increase in 78 percent of Hispanic-majority counties.[127] However, when an interviewer asked Rep. Alexandria Ocasio-Cortez if anything surprised her about the results of the election, she said: "The share of white support for Trump. I thought the polling was off, but just seeing it, there was that feeling of realizing what work we have to do. We need to do a lot of anti-racist, deep canvassing in this country."[128] Trumpism is simultaneously a manufacturer and product of cultural warfare, and the view that millions of American voters urgently need to be educated out of their racism is one of Trump's most powerful political weapons. Meanwhile, journalists and activists who shouted "abolish the police!" after the George Floyd killing and defended violence and looting as legitimate forms of political expression allowed Trump to present the left-wing fringe as the mainstream. This is why President Biden explicitly denounced the *abolish/defund the police* movement during his 2022 State of the Union address.[129]

Similarly, "critical race theory" is today a major focus for many Republican campaigns. While breathless right-wing rhetoric about the perils of "CRT" in schools is often overblown—and attempts by GOP-led state legislatures to ban it from classrooms[130] set a dangerous precedent and pose a clear threat to academic freedom—it's also true that some CRT-based curricula and training programs emphasize collective guilt and racial essentialism. As the linguist and cultural critic John McWhorter explains, these programs argue that it's "appropriate to ascribe certain traits to races, rather than individuals, and that education must 'center' the battle against power differentials between groups and the subtle perceptions that they condition."[131] Terms like "antiracist," concepts like critical race theory, and ideas like *abolish the police* aren't helping Democrats build larger political coalitions or win elections—they're shackling the left to identity politics and giving the populist right a political advantage.

While it's true that racial animus fueled Trump's rise, it's also true that many of his white supporters have legitimate grievances. In the years leading up to the 2016 election, white Americans (especially those without a four-year degree, who comprise 38 percent of the working-age population)[132] suffered a significant increase in deaths caused by drugs, alcohol, and suicide—a phenomenon documented in Anne Case and Angus Deaton's 2020 book *Deaths of Despair and the Future of Capitalism*.[133] Incessantly describing white Trump voters as racists and beneficiaries of white privilege is insulting and counterproductive, as it alienates them and trivializes the real problems they face.

Hitchens believed the United States should confront its racist past honestly. But there's no reason this acknowledgment has to be freighted with identitarianism or illiberal academic ideas about what human beings can and can't understand or say on the basis of their race, sex, etc. DiAngelo's argument hinges on the idea that an emphasis on individualism and objectivity will lead people to ignore the clear advantages and disadvantages associated with race, but Hitchens demonstrates that this isn't the case. It's possible to be fully cognizant of racial realities while recognizing the moral and practical necessity of treating each person as an individual and developing a universalist ethic.

* * *

Hitchens argued that identity politics "keeps us anchored in the past."[134] Beyond the atavistic infatuation with race and other forms of tribalism, there's another way in which contemporary manifestations of identity politics look backward instead of forward. Because identitarian scholars, activists, and journalists frequently make the argument that their societies are fundamentally and inescapably oppressive, they have a bleak view of history—one which essentializes the horrors of the past but diminishes the achievements.

For example, instead of acknowledging the radical nature of the American political experiment and remembering that the United States is a "'written' country, based on a number of founding documents that are subject to continuous revision and interpretation," as Hitchens put it,[135] there's the insistence that something rotten will always be at the core of this experiment. Consider this claim from the Pulitzer Prize–winning lead essay of the *New York Times'* 1619 Project by Nikole Hannah-Jones: "Conveniently left out of our founding mythology is the fact that one of the primary reasons some of the colonists decided to declare their independence from Britain was because they wanted to protect the institution of slavery."[136]

The original description on the 1619 Project's website described it as a "major initiative from the *New York Times* observing the 400th anniversary of the beginning of American slavery. It aims to reframe the country's history, understanding 1619 as our true founding."[137, 138] (1619 was the year the first slaves were unloaded at Point Comfort in Virginia.) Thus, American history isn't a story about the creation and development of a revolutionary, yet deeply imperfect and contradictory, constitutional republic—it's a story about slavery and hypocrisy. "Some might argue," Hannah-Jones wrote, "that this nation was founded not as a democracy but as a slavocracy."[139] She later claimed that right-wing critics had misrepresented the 1619 Project, which "does not argue that 1619 is our true founding. We know this nation marks its founding at 1776."[140] But she explicitly and repeatedly stated otherwise.[141] The *New York Times* also edited the project's website to delete the claim about the United States' "true founding."[142]

It's impossible to dispute the idea that slavery and racism are central elements of American history, nor should anyone want to do so. But these realities can exist alongside the fact that the Founders created a democratic system capable of self-correcting—a process that has been uneven, brutal, slow, and undeniable. The fact of progress is spurned by many academics today: "The biggest obstacle to teaching slavery effectively in America," according to David W. Blight, a historian at Yale University, "is the deep, abiding American need to conceive of and understand our history as 'progress.'"[143] Is Blight arguing that the United States hasn't, in fact, made progress on race? Perhaps unintentionally, Hannah-Jones made an observation that starkly challenges this view: "They had not seen this type of demand for a print product of the *New York Times*," she said of the 1619 Project, "since 2008, when people wanted copies of Obama's historic presidency edition."[144]

There's no contradiction in acknowledging the progress on race in America—as well as the features of the political system that have made that progress possible—and the vicious resistance to racial equality that has accompanied every halting and incremental step forward. "Anti-black racism runs in the very DNA of this country,"[145] Hannah-Jones tells us. "For the most part, black Americans fought back alone"[146]—a statement that ignores major abolitionist figures like Benjamin Rush, William Lloyd Garrison, and John Brown, as well as the Americans of all races who marched on Washington in 1963 and spent decades fighting for civil rights. Although Martin Luther King, Jr. repeatedly criticized "white moderates" in his "Letter from Birmingham Jail,"[147] he also expressed gratitude that "some of our white brothers in the South have grasped the meaning of this social revolution and committed themselves to it."[148] King observed that these white protesters had "marched with us down nameless streets of the South";[149] "languished in filthy roach infested jails";[150] and "recognized the urgency of the moment and sensed the need for powerful 'action' antidotes to combat the disease of segregation."[151]

Hannah-Jones has to downplay the multiracial efforts to secure racial equality in the United States to make reductionistic statements like this: "For as much as white people tried to pretend, black people were not chattel."[152] When the country increasingly embraced black culture, Hannah-Jones saw only theft: "We forged this nation's most significant original culture. In turn, 'mainstream' society has coveted our style, our slang and our song, seeking to appropriate the one truly American culture as its own."[153] Just as postcolonial scholars regard the study of other cultures as a process of subjugation and appropriation, many of our most prominent public intellectuals view cultural integration in the same way.

Cultural critics like Hannah-Jones ignore or disown the politics of universality advocated by Rustin and the other organizers of the March on Washington, who welcomed Americans of all races and backgrounds into their movement. They prefer to incite zero-sum racial conflict. The central message of Hannah-Jones's essay is that American democracy has been "borne on the backs of black resistance,"[154] while Americans of other races have ceaselessy tried to suppress this resistance. As Adam Serwer observed in the *Atlantic*, this view contrasts with the "vision of American history as a slow, uncertain march toward a more perfect union. The 1619 Project, and Hannah-Jones's introductory essay in particular, offer a darker vision of the nation, in which Americans have made less progress than they think, and in which black people continue to struggle indefinitely for rights they may never fully realize."[155] In September 2020, President Trump declared that the 1619 Project "rewrites American history to teach our children that we were founded on the principle of oppression, not freedom."[156] In the same speech, Trump announced that he would sign an executive order "establishing a national commission to promote patriotic education. It will be called the '1776 Commission.'"[157]

Hitchens wrote books about two of America's Founding Fathers:

Thomas Jefferson and Thomas Paine. The latter's pamphlet *Common Sense* was a significant force in galvanizing public opinion among the colonists in favor of independence. Paine certainly didn't connect the cause of American self-determination to the maintenance of slavery, as he was a staunch abolitionist. Benjamin Rush is one of the most influential abolitionists in American history, and he urged Paine to make the case for independence (he also suggested the title *Common Sense*).[158] Although Paine rarely spoke publicly about slavery, he urged Jefferson not to expand it into Louisiana[159] and made his abhorrence of the institution plain. He also may have written anonymously about the subject. As Hitchens notes in *Thomas Paine's Rights of Man*: "Throughout 1775, Paine used a number of pseudonyms—'Atlanticus' and 'Amicus'—to produce a stream of articles. By no means starry-eyed about his new homeland, he was swift in his denunciation of the slave trade, which maintained an open market in human beings in Philadelphia itself."[160] The authorship of the anti-slavery essays attributed to Paine isn't clear, but his abolitionism isn't in doubt.

In a 2005 essay about John Brown, Hitchens observed that "Harpers Ferry was the first defeat, as it was also the seminal victory, of a triumphant cause, precisely because it sounded a trumpet that could never call retreat."[161] Unlike Hannah-Jones, he emphasized other examples of radical opposition to slavery in the early United States, as well as the hostility to the institution among large numbers of ordinary Americans:

> Not content with preserving their own domain in its southeastern redoubt, the future Confederates insisted on extending their chattel system into new territories, and on implicating the entire Union in their system. The special symbol of this hubris was the Fugitive Slave Act, which legalized the recovery of human property from "free" states. The idea of secession or separation first arose among abolitionists confronted with this monstrous imposition. Men like William Lloyd Garrison took their text from the Book of Isaiah, describing the U.S. Constitution as a "covenant with death and an agreement with hell," and exhorting their supporters to "come out now and be separate."[162]

Again, Hannah-Jones's words—". . . black Americans fought back alone . . ."—dangle in the air. Of course, this doesn't change the fact that many of America's greatest heroes did more than compromise with slavery—they actively took part in it. In *Thomas Jefferson: Author of America*, Hitchens is unsparing both in his admiration and criticism of the third president: "At the end, his capitulation to a slave power that he half-abominated was both self-interested and a menace to the survival of the republic. This surrender, by a man of the Enlightenment and a man of truly revolutionary and democratic temperament, is another reminder that history is a tragedy and not a morality tale."[163] With these caveats fixed in his mind, Hitchens summarized the significance of the American Revolution:

> The French Revolution destroyed itself in Jefferson's own lifetime. More modern revolutions have destroyed themselves and others. If the American Revolution, with its secularism, its separation of powers, its Bill of Rights, and its gradual enfranchisement of those excluded or worse at its founding, has often betrayed itself at home and abroad, it nevertheless remains the only revolution that still retains any power to inspire.[164]

It's this power to inspire that so many academics and journalists seem intent on diminishing. The 1619 Project was conceived to disabuse Americans of their optimistic notions about what Hannah-Jones calls their "founding mythology." While the project certainly helps Americans understand elements of their history they should confront more often, it's not as if other historians have failed to challenge orthodoxies about the Founding Fathers or discuss the centrality of slavery in American history. In the acknowledgments in *Thomas Jefferson: Author of America*, Hitchens writes, "It was a fair wind that brought me, some years ago, into contact with Professor Annette Gordon Reed. . . . Her pursuit of truth in the study of Jefferson is a model of historical objectivity, forensic scruple, and moral sense."[165] Gordon-Reed's books *Thomas*

Jefferson and Sally Hemings: An American Controversy and *The Hemingses of Monticello: An American Family* had a singular role in illuminating the nature of Jefferson's relationship with Hemings.[166, 167] Gordon-Reed has never shied from the terrible contradictions of American history, which the story of Jefferson and Hemings encapsulates.

Hitchens observes that the Preamble to the Declaration of Independence "established the concept of human rights, for the first time in history, as the basis for a republic."[168] But he had no illusions about its author: "Jefferson did not embody contradiction," he writes. "Jefferson *was* a contradiction."[169] In a passage that was struck from the Declaration, Jefferson argued that King George had "waged cruel war against human nature itself, violating it's [sic] most sacred rights of life and liberty in the persons of a distant people who never offended him, captivating & carrying them into slavery in another hemisphere, or to incur miserable death in their transportation thither."[170] This was when he famously referred to slavery as an "execrable commerce" and an "assemblage of horrors."[171]

Hitchens notes that it's "possible, at one level, to read the omitted passage and to grieve at the fact that America declared its independence without repudiating its 'original sin.'"[172] However, he points out that it was "absurd, at that time or any other, to put the blame for the slave trade entirely on King George. The American interest in the business, and the profits from it, were much too widely distributed to justify that assertion."[173] As Hitchens's argument for reparations demonstrated, he recognized that these contaminated profits—as well as the monumental injuries that were inflicted to make them—have also been distributed across the centuries. "We can't make up for the Middle Passage," he said, "for the uncounted millions of people who were captured and raped and tortured before they even made it across the Atlantic to be other people's property. We can't undo that. But we can refuse—we can decline—to forget it."[174] He likely would have applauded the 1619 Project for redirecting Americans' attention to the fact that the legacies of slavery are all around them. He referred to "the incised lines that commemorate Sir Christopher Wren at St. Paul's" to describe Jefferson: "Reader, if you seek his monument, look around you."[175] The same could be said of his failure.

In this sense, we *should* remain anchored in the past: the recognition that the socioeconomic chasms we see between black and white Americans are the result of centuries of oppression and marginalization is vital to building a fairer and more just society. But there's no reason why an acknowledgment of America's failure to embody its universal ideals should call those ideals themselves into question, or the revolutionary political experiment that codified them for the first time in history. While the 1619 Project deepens our understanding of racial injustice, it also undermines the foundations of our political system and society. And to what end? How does referring to the United States of America as a "slavocracy" empower citizens to work harder for racial justice? How does telling Americans that racism is in their DNA encourage them to oppose racism? Of course Americans shouldn't be complacent when there are still so many inequities right in front of them, but the relentless insistence that the real progress the United States has made on race actually isn't progress at all is pointlessly deflating and fatalistic.

Gordon-Reed and Hitchens were friends. The subtitle of the tribute she wrote after his death was "How Christopher Hitchens came to love Thomas Jefferson."[176] She said it "meant a great deal to me when he got the Jefferson bug (much to his delight, he and the Sage shared a birth date), and I was able to talk to him about a subject that was to become my life's work."[177] But it was more than mutual interest that drew Hitchens and Gordon-Reed to Jefferson. In 2019, Gordon-Reed challenged the establishment of "1619, rather than 1776, as the nation's founding year": "I dissent from this part. The United States of America was founded in 1776, or when the Americans could definitely hold the territory."[178] She added that "1619 is an extremely important date to remember. It begins the Anglo American experience with slavery. Everyone, children and adults, should know about that."[179] She expanded on these points in a July 4, 2021 interview, highlighting the "dilemma" and "paradox" of the idea that "all men are created equal in a society in which a good number of the people are enslaved."[180] However, she observed that "There is no paradox or dilemma in 1619. . . . The English at that time are not saying things about 'all men are created equal,' or anything of that nature. It becomes an issue when the United States breaks away on the basis of a document that proclaims this universal ideal."[181]

The appreciation for the persistent force of America's universal ideal is what connects Hitchens, Gordon-Reed, and anyone else who recognizes that you don't need to deify the Framers to be grateful that they built the foundation for the most powerful democratic republic on earth. "The idea that government arose from the people," Hitchens writes, "and was not a gift to them or an imposition upon them, was perhaps the most radical element in the Declaration."[182] He always used words like "radical" to describe the American experiment. A recurring theme in his work, particularly in his later years, was his understanding that many of the ideas and institutions Americans take for granted are actually revolutionary and progressive by any objective historical standard. Instead of endlessly dismissing and distorting this fact, the left should embrace it.

Acknowledging the generational consequences of racism and slavery wasn't just a rhetorical exercise for Hitchens. He didn't do so to clear his throat before getting to the main points about the hazards of identity politics. He understood that the American story simply can't be told as a morality tale. But he also recognized that this story is more than a tragedy.

In *Letters to a Young Contrarian*, Hitchens suggests "really deciding to learn from history rather than invoking or sloganising it."[183] This means attempting to meet our obligations to the people in our society who still feel the consequences of the United States' founding injustice every day, as well as honestly confronting all the other ways America has betrayed its principles. But it also means remembering that the greatest successes in this effort have been delivered and defended by those who appealed to what unites us rather than those who obsessed over the differences that have always ripped us apart.

* * *

In a 1986 debate, Hitchens opened by asking: "What is it . . . to be a socialist?"[184] He eventually got around to the "principle of from each according to his ability or her ability, and to each according to his or her need,"[185] but his definition of socialism began with an emphasis on universal solidarity and humanism: "It is necessary to hold, firstly, that all divisions of class, nation, race, and sex are, in the last resort, man-made—and can be man-unmade—are in no sense part of a divine or natural ordinance, and that we are members, like it or no, of one race, the human race."[186] This radical egalitarian view wouldn't win much support on the left today.

Like Hitchens's socialism, his resistance to identity politics arose from his universalism. He believed all human beings, regardless of which identity categories they happen to find themselves in, deserve to be treated as individuals—an idea that traces its intellectual lineage to the foundational thinkers of the Enlightenment. "Never forget," he writes, "even if there are 'masses' to be invoked, or 'the people' to be praised, they and it must by definition be composed of individuals."[187] This is why Hitchens was always contemptuous of demagogues who claim the right to speak for "the people." He was immediately wary of any effort to present human beings as constituents of some shapeless whole, and he was especially suspicious of efforts to do so on the basis of race or any other immutable characteristic. In a 1970 essay titled "The Failure of Black Separatism," Rustin argued against the "notion of the undifferentiated black community" and pointed out that this notion is politically useful to opportunists who "illegitimately claim to speak for the majority" and "liberals as well as racists to whom all Negroes are the same."[188]

At a time when the phrase "all lives matter" has been annexed by right-wing demagogues and arguments in favor of assessing politicians "based on their abilities" and "what they stand for" are regarded as intolerably reactionary by much of the left, it's easy to see why genuine appeals to universalism are regarded with suspicion. But this cynicism overlooks the example of figures like Rustin and Hitchens, and it ignores a political and philosophical tradition that stands against nationalism, racism, xenophobia, and religious dogmatism. In *Letters to a Young Contrarian*, Hitchens argues that tribalism of any sort is a meager substitute for humanism:

> We still inhabit the prehistory of our race, and have not caught up with the immense discoveries about our own nature and about the nature of the universe. The unspooling of the skein of the genome has effectively abolished racism and creationism, and the amazing findings of Hubble and Hawking have allowed us to guess at the origins of the cosmos. But how much more addictive is the familiar old garbage about tribe and nation and faith.[189]

When Hitchens says the mapping of the human genome "abolished" racism, he means it destroyed the claim that there's some sort of genetic hierarchy governing the races. "To be opposed to racism in the postgenome universe," he writes, "is to be opposed to the concept."[190] He makes a similar argument in *God Is Not Great*:

> If you examine the beauty and symmetry of the double helix, and then go on to have your own genome sequence fully analyzed, you will be at once impressed that such a near-perfect phenomenon is at the core of your being, and reassured (I hope) that you have so much in common with other tribes of the human species—"race" having gone, along with "creation" into the ashcan—and further fascinated to learn how much you are a part of the animal kingdom as well.[191]

These scientific discoveries coincide with the fact that, as Peter Singer explains in *The Expanding Circle: Ethics, Evolution, and Moral Progress*, our sphere of ethical concern has steadily grown to encompass larger and larger communities over the millennia: from family to tribe to nation to the whole of humanity.[192] Inspiring as this is, Hitchens also recognized that the "sorts of things that make people quarrel and make them stupid are the same everywhere. The two worst things, as one can work out without leaving home, are racism and religion."[193] His meditation on the implications of the Human Genome Project is accompanied by a discussion of the chaos and suffering caused by arbitrary distinctions between human beings:

> Freud was brilliantly right when he wrote about "the narcissism of the small difference": distinctions that seem trivial to the visitor are the obsessive concern of the local and the provincial minds. You can, if you spend enough time there, learn to guess by instinct who is Protestant and who is Catholic in Belfast or who is Tamil and who is Sinhalese in Sri Lanka. And when you hear the bigots talk about the "other," it's always in the same tones as their colonial bosses used to employ to talk about them.[194]

Hitchens wrote extensively about the ill effects of national partition. From the Greek-Turkish division of Cyprus to the nuclear-armed confrontation between India and Pakistan over Kashmir, he decried the "waste of life and energy that has been involved in maintaining" these borders, as well as the "sheer baseness of the resulting mentality."[195] The ugly history of partition is instructive because it demonstrates how quickly tribalism can generate pointless hatred and how long that hatred often lasts. Hitchens was struck by the fact that the victims of decades-old partitions have descendants who seem just as bitter and tribal as those who suffered the immediate consequences.[196] In fact, with the accumulated injuries (real and imagined) inflicted by both sides over time, these hatreds can become all the more entrenched.

Tribalism is an ineradicable part of being human, which is why it can be inflamed and exploited so easily—one of the many reasons Hitchens despised religion is the fact that it's a social and cultural wedge that often makes conflicts intractable. This is a point today's identitarian scholars and activists should remember: when they compulsively emphasize differences between people, they exacerbate the problems they're trying to address. In a discussion which took place a few years after the fall of the Berlin Wall and a year into the war in Bosnia, Hitchens explained that his hostility to identitarianism was inseparable from his internationalism:

> Everywhere you look in the world at the moment, whether it might be Bosnia or Haiti or the former Soviet Union or West Germany . . . you can see there are always basically two kinds of people. There are those who think that the tribe into which they were born is the main thing about themselves. And nothing can change that. And if they could only like themselves more for it, congratulate themselves more about it, they would be only too happy. And there are people who realize that internationalism is not just a desirable thing. It's actually the only way the world can be organized.[197]

One of the reasons Hitchens admired the Marxist intellectual Rosa Luxemburg was the fact that her internationalism was "so strong that she despised anything to do with lesser or sectarian 'identities.' This led her to oppose any nationalist claims made by her fellow Poles and fellow Jews."[198] He cited a letter Luxemburg sent to her friend Mathilde Wurm, in which she asked: "What do you want with this theme of the 'special suffering of the Jews?' . . . I have no special place in my heart for the ghetto. I feel at home in the entire world, wherever there are clouds and birds and human tears."[199]

Had Luxemburg lived to see what would happen in the decades after she wrote those words (she was assassinated in 1919 by a division of the *Freikorps* in Berlin), she would have seen why a friend of Victor Klemperer's once referred to Jews as a "seismic people."[200] As Hitchens argued: "Because anti-Semitism is the godfather of racism and the gateway to tyranny and fascism and war, it is to be regarded not as the enemy of the Jewish people alone, but as the common enemy of humanity and of civilization."[201] Still, Luxemburg's letter expressed a simple ethical principle that always underpinned Hitchens's work: human suffering doesn't matter more or less depending on the ethnic or national or religious group victims belong to.

Hitchens believed our species has to transcend the racial, religious, and national divisions it has riveted upon itself. This belief became firmer with every anxious frontier he crossed, carved into the map by colonial architects and deepened by decades of senseless violence and hatred. It's why he regarded nationalism with scorn and suspicion—he would have been horrified at its resurgence over the past several years—while advocating the development and expansion of international institutions like the European Union. Religion is yet another source of tribalism that makes the individual subordinate to the group: "The critical and oppositional stance does ultimately rest on a belief in the capacity and pride of the individual," Hitchens writes, "while religion tends to dissolve this into a sickly form of collectivism."[202] He argued that religion arose in the "bawling and fearful infancy of our species"[203]—a reference not only to the fact that it was our first fumbling attempt at science and philosophy, as he often put it, but also one of the clearest manifestations of our basest tribal instincts.

These instincts will always be with us, but they can be resisted. After all, despite centuries of religious warfare and oppression, religion was also one of the forces that made the establishment of large and complex societies possible (by replacing kinship and other narrow forms of tribal identification with a more universal source of solidarity, as Francis Fukuyama observes in *The Origins of Political Order*).[204] Hitchens was right to call sectarianism an addiction—what he described as the "familiar old garbage about tribe and nation and faith" is familiar and old because human beings are natural classifiers and in-group loyalists, distrustful of outsiders, eager to expel deviants, and ready defend the arbitrary borders we've erected around just about everything.

What's especially strange about left-wing identitarianism is the fact that it presents a relentless focus on differences between people as the only way to strengthen the bonds between them. Instead of embracing universal methods of inquiry and discourse, the identitarian left insists that objectivity is an illusion and people with the wrong skin color or genetic makeup should take a step back and shut up. Instead of recognizing that individualism is an appreciation of diversity at the most fundamental level, the identitarian left says we should only care about the superficial diversity of demography. Instead of voting for candidates on the basis of their principles and positions, as some out-of-touch old socialists insist, we should vote for the ones who have the right skin color and reproductive organs.

Recall Crenshaw's observation that there are "potential coalitions waiting to be formed" between members of an endless profusion of intersecting identity groups. Hitchens spent his entire life arguing that there are potential coalitions waiting to be formed between people who couldn't care less about the boxes their political allies check on the census or who they sleep with or which restrooms they use—coalitions based on solidarity around ideas and convictions rather than the divisive and suffocating demands of tribal loyalty.

3 One Cannot Be Just a Little Bit Heretical

Hitchens on Radicalism

In *Koba the Dread: Laughter and the Twenty Million*, Martin Amis starts an argument that had clearly been decades in the making. "Comrade Hitchens!" begins the chapter titled "Letter to a Friend"[1]—a letter that turns out to be a crackling indictment of Hitchens for his many years of avowed (and still not completely disavowed) Trotskyism. Amis attacks Hitchens's "reverence for Lenin" and "unregretted discipleship of Trotsky,"[2] observing that "These two men did not just precede Stalin. They created a fully functioning police state for his later use."[3]

Hitchens responded in an essay titled "Lightness at Midnight" (a reference to Arthur Koestler's anti-Stalinist novel *Darkness at Noon*),[4,5] which accused Amis of overstating the extent to which the horrors and victims of Stalinism have been overlooked—especially on the left. For example, Amis writes, "Everybody knows of Auschwitz and Belsen. Nobody knows of Vorkuta and Solovetsky.... Everybody knows of the 6 million of the Holocaust. Nobody knows of the 6 million of the Terror-Famine."[6] Hitchens replied:

Orwell once remarked that certain terrible things in Spain had really happened, and "they did not happen any the less because the *Daily Telegraph* has suddenly found out about them when it is five years too late." Martin Amis can be excused for coming across some of the above names and numbers rather late in life, but he cannot hope to get away with accusing others of keeping these facts and names from him, or from themselves.[7]

Hitchens argued that Amis ignored members of the anti-Stalinist left—some elements of which were known as the Left Opposition: "The crucial questions about the gulag were being asked by left oppositionists, from Boris Souvarine to Victor Serge to C.L.R. James, in real time and at great peril. Those courageous and prescient heretics have been somewhat written out of history."[8] In a different essay, Hitchens observed that these figures "exposed and opposed Stalin while never ceasing to fight against empire and fascism and exploitation."[9]

These "heretics" were among Hitchens's most important early political influences because they demonstrated how to be an unapologetic Marxist without making excuses for Soviet repression. He shared the view Orwell expressed in 1947: "If one could somewhere present the spectacle of economic security without concentration camps, the pretext for the Russian dictatorship would disappear and Communism would lose much of its appeal."[10] In *Koba the Dread*, Amis acknowledges that "Christopher (like James Fenton, and all other Trotskyists known to me) was, of course, strenuously anti-Stalinist."[11] In a 2012 interview, the novelist Ian McEwan broadened this point, describing Hitchens as a "member of the anti-totalitarian left."[12]

Hitchens joined the Labour Party in 1965, "on the very first day that I was old enough to be eligible," as he later explained, "delightedly clutching a membership card that called for common ownership of the means of production, distribution, and exchange."[13] He was promptly expelled from the party for protesting the Vietnam War, along with many other students in Labour.[14] When he arrived at Oxford in late 1967, he joined the International Socialists—specifically what he described as a post-Trotskyist, "Luxemburgist" sect.[15] Later asked if there was any "-ism" he was associated with at the time, Hitchens said, "Luxemburg . . . the International Socialists were often referred to as Trots, which wasn't completely right. We were Rosa Luxemburgist. Rosa Luxemburg was— still is for me—a great personal and intellectual heroine."[16]

In a 2011 essay, Hitchens explained why he venerated Luxemburg[17]—a Polish-German Marxist intellectual who was one of the most important figures in the German Social Democratic Party until she was assassinated in Berlin in 1919. Luxemburg condemned the Bolsheviks for their suppression of rival political parties and other brutal anti-democratic measures; she was opposed to Prussian militarism and imperialism; she argued that freedom of speech was meaningless unless it extended to "the one who thinks differently"; and she was a staunch internationalist.[18] To Hitchens, Luxemburg represented a tradition of Marxist thought and action which was more humane, rational, and democratic than the version that took hold in the Soviet Union. Although he described himself as a Trotskyist for much of his career, he argued that this was an umbrella term for an international movement of anti-Stalinist Marxists.[19]

Hitchens claimed that he was "never, ever tempted" by communism.[20] As he put it in a 1997 interview: "The communists never appealed to me. And I was to a certain extent inoculated against it. I read *Darkness at Noon* before I read *The Communist Manifesto*."[21] The influence of Koestler and other anti-Stalinist intellectuals was reflected in Hitchens's political commitments in the late 1960s and 1970s—as he later recalled: "Our faction . . . was in close touch with student and worker groups in Poland and Czechoslovakia, where open rebellion against the sclerotic Warsaw pact regimes was breaking out."[22] But this is all the more reason why Amis was right to condemn Hitchens's attraction to communists like Trotsky who often endorsed the repression that dissidents in Eastern Europe fought against. Hitchens could always find venerable Trotskyist dissidents to celebrate, but using the term as a synonym for "anti-Stalinist" was an echo of Trotsky's own mythmaking and propaganda.

Hitchens spent many years calling himself a Trotskyist, and it's difficult to fault Amis for making a few caustic observations about this fact in *Koba the Dread*: "An admiration for Lenin and Trotsky is meaningless without an admiration for terror," he writes.[23] However, Amis goes on to argue that the anti-Soviet revolutions in Eastern Europe were transformative for Hitchens: "A while ago I told you that 1989 was a turning point in your evolution as a writer. Until then your prose had always given me the impression of less than complete disclosure—the sense that certain truths might have to be postponable. Then you lost that inhibition, and your writing voice gained a new quality: freedom."[24] Earlier in *Koba the Dread*, Amis makes the same point:

> Although I always liked Christopher's journalism, there seemed to me to be something wrong with it, something faintly but pervasively self-defeating: the sense that the truth could be postponed. This flaw disappeared in 1989, and his prose made immense gains in burnish and authority. I used to attribute the change to the death of Christopher's father, in late 1988, and to subsequent convulsions in his life. It had little or nothing to do with that, I now see. It had to do with the collapse of Communism. Truth had at last become time-urgent.[25]

In *Letters to a Young Contrarian*, Hitchens draws a connection between the revolutionary era that catalyzed his radical politics and the one which (according to Amis) liberated him as a writer: "I began to feel the weight of every millisecond that marked me as a grizzled soixante-huitard, or survivor of the last intelligible era of revolutionary upheaval, the one that partly ended and partly culminated in les evenements de quatre-vingt neuf" (the events of '89).[26] Hitchens later called these events—the fall of the Berlin Wall and the democratic revolutions that brought the Soviet system to an end—a "huge release of human energy and emancipation. It was a great day, November 9, 1989."[27]

When Hitchens said he was a *soixante-huitard*, he was referring to the revolutionary fervor that swept the world in 1968: the May protests in Paris (why the common term for *'68er* is French) that brought millions of students and workers into the streets, virtually shut down the French economy, and almost brought an end to Charles de Gaulle's presidency; the Civil Rights Movement in the United States; international protests against the Vietnam War, intensified by images of the Tet Offensive in early 1968; and a revolution in Czechoslovakia, the Prague Spring, which was met with Soviet tanks. During this period, a wave of uprisings in Latin America, the United States, and Europe seemed to set a course for what Paul Berman describes in his 1996 book *A Tale of Two Utopias: The Political Journey of the Generation of 1968* as a "new society coming into being."[28] Berman writes:

> It was going to be a society of direct democracy . . . a socialism of the poor countries and of their friends around the world, neither Stalinist nor liberal. A worldwide shift in power from the elites to the masses. A society of individual liberty (as per the revolution in middle-class customs). A society of spiritual grandeur (as per the revolution in the zone of the spirit). Something soulful. A moral advance. And in the glow of that very grand and utopian idea, a thousand disparate events from around the world . . . seemed to merge into a single tide.[29]

As this new global society appeared to take shape, Hitchens writes, "I didn't just think that I was right: I thought that 'we' (our group of International Socialists in particular) were being damn well *proved* right. If you have never yourself had the experience of feeling that you are yoked to the great steam engine of history, then allow me to inform you that the conviction is a very intoxicating one."[30]

At Oxford, Hitchens met with the Polish dissident intellectual Leszek Kołakowski—an important figure in the Polish Spring of 1956 and one of the most influential historians of Marxism in the twentieth century. Kołakowski left Poland during another major uprising in 1968—

after being stripped of his academic post at Warsaw University[31]—which was suppressed by the communist authorities, who launched a simultaneous campaign of anti-Semitic propaganda, abuse, and expulsion.[32] By the time Kołakowski published his three-volume study *Main Currents of Marxism: Its Rise, Growth, and Dissolution* in 1976, he believed totalitarianism was a natural outcome of Marxist thought.[33] As Kołakowski explains in the preface to the 2005 edition of *Main Currents of Marxism*: "Marxist doctrine was a good blueprint for converting human society into a giant concentration camp; to be sure, this was not Marx's intention, but it was an inevitable effect of the glorious and final benevolent utopia he devised."[34]

According to Hitchens, this view was the subject of a disagreement he had with Kołakowski: "I would not concede that Leninism and Stalinism were the same thing, or that the second logically followed from the first," he writes in *Hitch-22*.[35] "Yes, the germ of Stalinism had been in Leninism to begin with. But had there not been other germs as well? And what historical conditions led to the dominance of which germs? I suppose I still hope to show that not everything about this debate was a complete waste of time."[36]

From the conviction that he was yoked to the great steam engine of history to the hope that he hadn't completely wasted his time, Hitchens moved a long way from the convinced radicalism of his youth. In a 2009 article, he acknowledged that "in the longer run, [Kołakowski] was proved right, in the sense that though the system could in fact 'reform' itself, it could do so only by reforming itself out of existence."[37] Hitchens emphasized the historical importance of Trotskyism as a political and intellectual movement until the end of his life—and he continued to argue that the "materialist conception of history hasn't been bettered as an explanation of the way things happen"[38]—but he ultimately considered himself unbound by any formal political party, movement, or ideology. In 2002, he explained why he stopped calling himself a socialist: "If you've concluded that there is no longer an international socialist movement, that it's not going to revive, you're really only being a *poseur* if you say that you're a socialist nonetheless. And that's the position I'm in now. But I miss it. I miss it like an amputated limb."[39]

At that point, Hitchens believed claiming to be a socialist was "more like expressing an attitude than really a politics."[40] But this was an acknowledgment of an unwelcome political reality rather than a rejection of socialism as a concept, and he often split the difference by arguing that the "general socialist critique of capitalism" simply ceased to be politically actionable[41]—which fell short of repudiating the critique itself. This partly explains why he likened his abandonment of socialism to the pain of a phantom limb—he still argued that socialism was the "best political moment humans have ever come up with."[42] In the same interview, he said, "I gave a good deal of my life to [the International Socialists] before realizing that in fact the '68 upheaval was the last flare-up, the last refulgence . . . and not the beginning of a new wave."[43]

Many of the political figures Hitchens most admired were "men and women convinced of the rationality and justice of socialism"[44]—Orwell, Luxemburg, C.L.R. James. But Hitchens always had more fundamental reasons for venerating these figures: their commitment to democratic values, their internationalism, their hatred of totalitarianism. Even when he believed socialism was dead after the Cold War, he recognized that these principles were as important as ever.

When Amis, McEwan, Rushdie, and the poet James Fenton appeared on Charlie Rose to discuss Hitchens several months after his death, Amis made a familiar point: "It was not until the fall of communism in 1989 that he really blossomed as a writer."[45] Later in the conversation, Fenton took issue with this characterization: "1989 was something he would have welcomed at any time—i.e., the fall of Eastern Europe, of communism. But he would have welcomed it from a socialist point of view."[46] They were both right—the end of the Cold War put Hitchens on a new political trajectory, but his essential principles remained the same.

* * *

In the fall of 1992, Hitchens traveled to Bosnia-Herzegovina as Sarajevo was under siege by Slobodan Milošević's forces. After seeing the
blitzed houses of worship, government buildings, and homes; witnessing
a mortar crash into the national library; learning of artillery assaults that
left scores of civilians dead and maimed; and speaking with Bosnian
volunteers who were woefully under-equipped to resist the assault, his
assessment of the situation was grim: "With dismaying speed, and by
a macabre metamorphosis, the World War II Partisan slogan of One
Yugoslavia has mutated into yells for a Greater Serbia, and the army
devised by Tito for defense against foreign intervention has been turned
loose, along with various militias, against civilians and open cities."[47] He
argued that the attack on Bosnia was a threat to the fundamental principles of the European project:

> Bosnia matters, because it has chosen to defend not just its own self-
> determination but the values of multicultural, long-evolved and mu-
> tually fruitful cohabitation. Not since Andalusia has Europe owed
> so much to a synthesis, which also stands as a perfect rebuke to the
> cynical collusion between the apparently "warring" fanatics. If Sarajevo
> goes under, then all who care for such things will have lost something
> precious, and will curse themselves because they never knew its value
> while they still had it.[48]

Hitchens wrote those words at a time when the United States and
other Western countries didn't seem particularly concerned about the
possibility of Sarajevo going under. President-elect Bill Clinton called
for airstrikes and the enforcement of no-fly zones in Bosnia,[49] but once
he occupied the Oval Office, months slipped by before he would even
consider lifting the UN arms embargo.[50] And even then, the Clinton
administration's case for allowing arms into Bosnia was muted. The
"lift and strike" policy—which would have provided Bosnian fighters

with weapons and authorized airstrikes to protect civilians and facilitate arms deliveries—was shelved after the Clinton administration's meager attempt to convince the United States' NATO allies to support it failed.[51, 52] Secretary of State Warren Christopher told the Europeans he was in "listening mode" during a humiliating trip in May 1993, after which the German newspaper *Die Welt* suggested that he should be replaced, while American diplomats told the *New York Times* he should've sent lower-ranking officials instead.[53] Two American Black Hawks were shot down in Mogadishu a few months later, igniting a battle that left 19 American soldiers dead. This made Clinton even more apprehensive about the use of military force in Bosnia and virtually guaranteed his failure to act on the Rwandan genocide in 1994.

In late 1993, Hitchens published an essay in *Boston Review* that demonstrated how uneasy he had become with certain currents on the left—particularly a reflexive anti-interventionism that revealed a strange indifference to aggression and violations of basic human rights:

> Milosevic's war of cleansing in Bosnia-Herzegovina forced a grumbling and self-centered political community to confront the issue of, if not fascism, something uncommonly like it. Perhaps Bosnia was not much of a state (no harm in that, I hope) but it was an identifiable society and culture based on the principle of multi-communal solidarity. And it was appealing for help. Military help at that, since it was threatened with military extinction.[54]

Many accounts of Hitchens's political evolution highlight September 11 as the sole catalytic force that changed his attitude toward U.S. foreign policy—as if he decided on the wholesale exchange of one worldview for another the moment he turned on a TV and saw the World Trade Center ablaze. But Hitchens's campaign for intervention in Bosnia—which was so fervent and persistent that he said he had become a "bore and a fanatic" about the subject in a February 1994 interview[55]—refutes this narrative. The arguments Hitchens would make about the left after September 11 were on his mind years earlier. As he put it, when "thousands of Bosnians lost their lives and the great multi-cultural city of Sarajevo was almost levelled, no serious march or rally expressed any solidarity with the Bosnian cause."[56]

For Hitchens, one of the most vexing aspects of the anti-war left's indifference to Bosnia was the way in which it aligned with what he described as an "outbreak of establishment pacifism." In a March 1994 speech, he said, "It was as if all the arguments I'd ever had with people about how war is really the last thing you want had suddenly all won everybody over. Because they sure didn't think there was anything worth fighting about in Bosnia-Herzegovina, and they did not mind saying so. . . . 'Quagmires,' they said knowingly. 'Wider war.' 'Remember Vietnam?'"[57] In the same speech, Hitchens described Bosnia as a "moral test for the institutions of order and civilization that claim to rule in our name."[58] He accused the United Nations of "persistent, cynical inaction," while the United States, which "disposes of fantastic budgets and treasuries and fleets and armies," decided to "sit the whole crisis out"[59] (this was a year and a half before the Dayton Accords, negotiated under the threat of NATO force, brought the Bosnian War to an end).

In a different speech the same year, Hitchens argued that the left no longer had a "moral core or a decided political position on the matter of internationalism."[60] He pointed out that Bosnia "meets all the conditions under which it can be said that a country should offer military help to another."[61] Bosnia was the victim of "unprovoked aggression"; it was in "no position to threaten any other nation, and has never shown any inclination—let alone ability—to do so"; it was a sovereign state and a multicultural democracy; it had requested assistance through the proper international channels (such as the United Nations); it faced the "third attempt made in this century to physically exterminate a European minority"; and the United States and other Western governments had effectively intervened on Milošević's side by enforcing an arms embargo on the Bosnians.[62] In response to the left's "pathology of quagmire dread," Hitchens pointed out that military intervention, when it was finally undertaken, worked:

> What happened when one white-collar pinky was raised by NATO? Did the skies fall? By no means. Within two days of the credible threat of the use of force, not only had the siege of Sarajevo been lifted, but the Croatian fascist regime had abandoned its attempt to create a separate Croatian-speaking state on Bosnian soil—had come to the conference table and was prepared to discuss autonomy with the Bosnian government. The food aid was sent to Srebrenica . . . cities like Tuzla received their first deliveries just of food aid in two years. I would like to know what was said when those food aid deliveries arrived and the citizens of those towns asked, "Where have you been for the last two years?"[63]

At the beginning of his essay in *Boston Review*, Hitchens wrote, "To state my own prejudices clearly, I should say that as a British socialist I once took, in the heartland of imperialism, a straightforward anti-intervention position."[64] However, he noted that there were several cases that had given him cause to rethink this position over the years. For example, he believed Britain should have defended Cyprus after the Greek coup and Turkish invasion in 1974,[65] which Fenton believes was a decisive moment in his political development.[66] He also said he "didn't take the standard British left line that Thatcher was whipping up chauvinism and imperialist nostalgia" when she sent the British fleet to recapture the Falkland Islands from Leopoldo Galtieri's military dictatorship in Argentina in 1982.[67] He believed Britain had the right to defend its territory under international law.

In *Unhitched: The Trial of Christopher Hitchens*, Richard Seymour argues that Hitchens's position on the Falklands exposed his "faith in empire."[68] McEwan has a different interpretation: "His argument was, and it turned out to be absolutely right, that to wage war against the Argentinians would lead to the fall of the junta and the fall of Galtieri. And that was a consistent theme. That ran all the way through. His Iraq stand was in line with that."[69]

In the introduction to his collection of essays *Arguably*, published a few months before his death and several days before the tenth anniversary of September 11, Hitchens observed that there has always been tension between the anti-imperialist and anti-totalitarian left.[70] After the Cold War, he increasingly found himself on the "anti-totalitarian side," despite his decades as a fierce critic of Western imperialism. He no longer cared when his former comrades attacked him as a servant of empire for arguing that the West should halt an ongoing genocide in Europe, or when he concentrated his rhetorical fire on the "fascism with an Islamic face" that descended on Lower Manhattan, punched a hole in the side of the Pentagon, and flew a plane full of passengers into the ground in Pennsylvania on September 11. He recognized that the gravest threats didn't come from the governments of Western liberal democracies—they came from the totalitarian enemies of those democracies.

While Hitchens no longer considered himself a socialist by the time *Arguably* was published, when he presented his anti-imperialist versus anti-totalitarian political dichotomy, he didn't say he'd moved toward neoconservative or post-ideological anti-totalitarianism. He said he moved toward the anti-totalitarian *left*.[71] He may have severed his connections with the left-wing parties and movements on offer, but he belonged to the left to the very end.

* * *

Patrick Cockburn was no fan of Hitchens's interventionism, but he recognized that "it would be a pity if Christopher's words and writing on Anglo-American military interventions should be ignored.... He was the most intelligent and eloquent defender of these interventions as a means of removing dictators or preventing massacres."[72] Although the tradition of left-wing writers and intellectuals arguing for the removal of dictators and the prevention of massacres is quickly being forgotten, interventionism was once a live issue on the left. Hitchens discussed this historical context in his *Boston Review* essay about Bosnia:

> There is here a noticeable difference between the American and the European left. In England especially, but in other Western European countries also, there were insistent calls for intervention on the Bosnian side, and denunciations of NATO complicity with the Tudjman/ Milosevic partition plan. In my opinion, this was an echo of the great international campaign to defend the Spanish Republic between 1936 and 1939, where the words "non-interventionist" became a term of contempt unloosed against the European realpolitik which used them as an alibi for permitting unfettered Italian and German intrusion into Spanish affairs.[73]

While Hitchens chose to emphasize the left-wing support for the Republican government in the Spanish Civil War (during which Orwell took up arms against Francoism and fascism), he could have mentioned a more recent cadre of interventionist European intellectuals—the French *Nouveaux Philosophes* ("New Philosophers") including André Glucksmann, Bernard-Henri Lévy, Alain Finkielkraut, and Pascal Bruckner, as well as politicians and activists like Joschka Fischer, Daniel Cohn-Bendit, and Bernard Kouchner. Many of these European interventionists (Fischer and Cohn-Bendit are German; Kouchner is French) were disillusioned with Marxism in the 1970s as the brutal nature of the Soviet system and the backwardness and violence in other communist countries became more apparent.[74] This willingness to challenge ideological conformity on the left would persist in the decades to come.

It's no surprise that members of the European left were more committed to defending Bosnia than their American counterparts. In the 1970s and 1980s, the Europeans were developing the ideas that would fuel the emergence of humanitarian intervention as a new principle in Western foreign policy and inform concepts such as "Responsibility to Protect"—which holds that the international community should privilege the protection of human rights over state sovereignty when extreme violations of those rights occur—in the 1990s and early 2000s.[75]

Kouchner, for instance, co-founded Médecins Sans Frontières (Doctors Without Borders) in 1971 and went on to serve as the UN Special Representative for Kosovo and French Minister of Foreign and European Affairs. He was also one of the lead organizers of an international rescue effort for refugees who were fleeing the newly unified communist Vietnam in the late 1970s.[76] The "Boat for Vietnam" likely saved thousands of Vietnamese who would otherwise have drowned in the South China Sea and provided medical care for tens of thousands more.[77]

In a 2014 article, the Vietnamese human rights advocate and poet Vo Van Ai—one of the organizers of the Boat for Vietnam—observed that dissidents in the Soviet Union were the first to support his *samizdat* magazine *Que Me*, which he described as an outlet for "publicizing a movement for democracy and human rights"[78] in Vietnam. But he noted that it was "much harder to convince the Western public, especially people of the left."[79] He recalled a similar reluctance on the Western left to support the Boat for Vietnam:

> During the Vietnam War, thousands of people in Paris, Berlin, Washington, Tokyo, and elsewhere had taken to the streets to denounce US intervention in Vietnam and call for an end to the killings. But these same people remained silent as thousands of Vietnamese died in re-education camps or drowned on the South China seas. The antiwar left could not admit that the "heroic" freedom fighters of yore had turned into tyrants, and the "henchmen of US imperialists" were now the victims. With our campaign for the boat people, the spontaneous and wholehearted engagement of many French intellectuals would not only save thousands of people in distress, but also break these stereotypes and deeply impact the thinking of sectors of the French and European left.[80]

These French intellectuals included New Philosophers like Glucksmann and Lévy, but also major figures such as Foucault, Raymond Aron, and Jean-Paul Sartre.[81] They didn't just raise public awareness and funds for the Boat for Vietnam—they also successfully lobbied the French government to increase the immigration quota for Vietnamese refugees.[82]

In his 2005 book *Power and the Idealists: Or, the Passion of Joschka Fischer and Its Aftermath*, Paul Berman traces the interventionist ideas that gained currency during the Cold War—many of which were catalyzed by humanitarian efforts like the Boat for Vietnam—to policies that were enacted in the 1990s.[83] Berman also explains why the advocates of these ideas and policies viewed them as extensions of their left-wing values. Alongside Kouchner, the other major figures in *Power and the Idealists* are former German Foreign Minister Joschka Fischer and Daniel Cohn-Bendit, who served as the co-president of the Greens-European Free Alliance in the EU Parliament. Cohn-Bendit is also known as "Danny the Red," a nickname he earned while leading the massive student uprising in Paris in 1968.[84] Kouchner, Fischer, and Cohn-Bendit all recognized that Western governments had a responsibility to prevent ethnic cleansing and further disintegration in the Balkans.

Kouchner led the United Nations effort to restore civil administration, rebuild infrastructure, provide humanitarian relief, develop civic institutions, and protect human rights in Kosovo after Milošević launched yet another campaign of ethnic cleansing in the late 1990s.[85] As German Foreign Minister, Fischer played a crucial role in committing his country to the 1999 NATO operation in Kosovo, making the case to his fellow Greens that "with the end of the Cold War there has been a return to ethnic warfare and to nationalistic policies that Europe must not accept."[86] Cohn-Bendit supported military action in Bosnia and Kosovo.[87]

Fischer and Cohn-Bendit took these positions in the face of fierce political opposition—a demonstrator threw a bag of red paint at Fischer during a 1999 Green Party congress and broke his eardrum, while other protesters denounced him as a "warmonger," held up posters of his face graffitied with a Hitler mustache, and paraded naked in front of his podium.[88, 89] Cohn-Bendit was shouted down at the same congress for backing Fischer and arguing in favor of the NATO intervention in

Kosovo.[90] While Fischer initially opposed Western military intervention in Bosnia,[91] Cohn-Bendit said the horrors of that war, particularly the genocidal massacre at Srebrenica, "simply transformed" his colleague's position.[92] As hecklers attempted to disrupt Fischer's speech, he told them: "You can whistle as much as you want, but go and talk to the deportees in the refugee camps in Macedonia."[93]

The intervention in Kosovo was the first time Germany sent its air force into combat since World War II. It's no surprise that Fischer and Cohn-Bendit received intense pushback from the German left (which has a long history of pacifism), but in his speech to the Greens, Fischer questioned this status quo: "I would be interested in hearing how, from a left-wing perspective, we can refer to everything that has gone on in Yugoslavia since 1992, including ethnic warfare and nationalistic policies; what do you call this from a left-wing perspective, from your point of view?"[94] This was the question Hitchens asked his left-wing allies throughout the 1990s, and he didn't receive much of an answer. One German Green Party member said she was afraid the NATO campaign in Kosovo would lead to World War III and argued that her party "has no right to survive because it is not the party of pacifism anymore."[95]

The German Greens certainly aren't the party of pacifism now. After Russia's invasion of Ukraine in early 2022, Vice Chancellor Robert Habeck and Foreign Minister Annalena Baerbock—two of the top Greens in the German Cabinet—were among the leading voices urging German Chancellor Olaf Scholz to send arms to the Ukrainian resistance.[96] The Greens even pushed for the delivery of heavy weaponry (such as tanks and artillery) at a time when Scholz and many other leaders in Europe and the United States believed this move would be a dangerous act of escalation. When protesters screamed "warmonger!" at Habeck during a speech in April 2022, he argued: "In this situation, where people are defending their lives, their democracy and their freedom, Germany and also the Greens must be ready to deal with the reality—and this reality is a reality that must reject an aggressor."[97] A poll conducted around the same time found that Habeck and Baerbock were two of the most popular politicians in Germany.[98]

Other leading Greens, such as Anton Hofreiter, the chair of the Bundestag's European Affairs Committee, are now more likely to argue that *refusing* to confront aggression in Europe will lead to World War III. In an interview on April 20, 2022, Hofreiter warned that the failure to prevent Vladimir Putin from dominating Ukraine could mean "further countries will be invaded and . . . we will end up de facto sliding into a third world war."[99] Major factions of the German left—as well as most of the German political establishment—have finally abandoned the complacent pacifism that had long seemed like an immovable feature of German political culture. Fischer and Cohn-Bendit just recognized the necessity of doing so sooner than most.

After the genocides in the Balkans and Rwanda, new international norms were taking shape around the concept of humanitarian intervention. In an address to the UN General Assembly in 1999, Secretary-General Kofi Annan argued that governments which commit atrocities against their populations or the populations of other states should expect to have their sovereignty challenged.[100] This idea was formalized as the aforementioned "Responsibility to Protect" doctrine, which was accepted by UN member states in 2005.[101] Annan responded to the critics of this doctrine in a 2000 report: "Surely no legal principle—not even sovereignty—can ever shield crimes against humanity. Where such crimes occur and peaceful attempts to halt them have been exhausted, the Security Council has a moral duty to act on behalf of the international community."[102]

In *Letters to a Young Contrarian*, Hitchens observes that, unlike the Armenian and Nazi genocides, which "took place under the cover of a wider war . . . the attempt to destroy the Muslims of Bosnia took place in broad daylight, and was captured on film, and was the cause of the war and not a vile subtext of it."[103] The fact that the slaughter in Bosnia occurred in full view of the rest of the world was one more reason it was a frontal challenge to the very idea of a European (as well as international) community. Hitchens recalls how jarring it was to witness a "full-dress reprise, in Europe, of internment camps, the mass murder of civilians, the reinstitution of torture and rape and deportation as acts of policy."[104] In *Hitch-22*, he emphasizes the historic and cultural significance of the assault on Sarajevo:

> An ancient and civilized town, famous in European history as the site of a tragic drama but also celebrated as a symbiotic meeting place of peoples and cultures and religions (the name itself derives from the antique word *serai*, as in "caravanserai" or place of shelter and hospitality), was being coldly reduced to shards by drunken gunners on the surrounding hills who sniggeringly represented the primeval hatred of the peasant for the city and the illiterate for the educated.[105]

Despite these crimes, Hitchens observed that much of the left wouldn't even offer forms of support that stopped well short of direct military involvement (such as lobbying against the arms embargo or marching in support of the Bosnian resistance): "It was as if the fear that such solidarity might be misconstrued as a demand for bombing or intervention had paralyzed the limited forces of internationalism altogether."[106] He concluded that anti-interventionism had become a reactionary position, as any demand for action would call upon the "U.S. government to act in some sense as a morally confident agent, and thus could not be right."[107] He thought the left was abdicating its responsibility to take an active role in debates about war and human rights by retreating to this position: "It is, in short, going to be very hard to discuss foreign policy in the future if the main thrust of radical and critical argument is purely non-interventionist. In real terms, this will amount to abstention from the debate rather than participation in it."[108]

At the end of the Cold War, some factions on the left saw an opportunity to work toward an international system capable of punishing war criminals, preventing aggression against civilians, and securing human rights as widely as possible. In a footnote near the end of *Hitch-22* (which refers to Susan Sontag's "call for NATO and the White House to abandon an ignoble neutrality and save the name of Europe"),[109] Hitchens mentions the European interventionists whose ranks he and Sontag had joined from the other side of the Atlantic: "In spite of the general nullity of the Left on this question, Susan was only the best known of several, including Bernard-Henri Lévy, Peter Schneider, Daniel Cohn-Bendit, Adam Michnik, and others, who in their way traced a line from 1968 through 1989 to future combats with the totalitarian."[110]

* * *

A few years after the disintegration of the Soviet Union, Hitchens observed that the "1989 European and Russian revolutions" were the "axis, pivot and subtext of all commentary since," and he described those revolutions as "one of the greatest episodes of liberation in the human record."[111] But there was a certain uneasiness in this acknowledgment—he also described the immediate post–Cold War era as a "bogus triumphal period," mocked Francis Fukuyama's "end of history"[112] thesis—that liberal democracy will prove to be the most durable and universal form of government—and argued that the defeat of communism didn't license "Western liberal self-congratulation."[113]

In a 1993 interview, Hitchens took issue with "all those who say that, since the 1989 revolution, that there's really no need for the left critique of society or politics anymore. That we've moved beyond all that. That society is just basically a liberal problem-solving matter and no more."[114] While he described 1989 as a "real emancipating revolution that I'd long hoped for and worked for and supported,"[115] he thought the collapse of communism had led to the emergence of a bloodless, consensus-driven form of politics in the West. Deep ideological divides were being filled in and flattened out by an opportunistic and hubristic political establishment.

One of the reasons Hitchens despised Clinton was the fact that he embodied the centrist and technocratic view of politics that became increasingly common in the 1990s. Clinton was a "New Democrat" who focused on what his political advisors called "triangulation"—blending the ideas of both major parties to create a new position in the center[116] (Hitchens's 1999 book about Clinton is titled *No One Left to Lie To: The Triangulations of William Jefferson Clinton*).[117] Hitchens regarded this electoral strategy as ethically and ideologically vacuous—just eight months into Clinton's presidency, he already believed there was "something completely hollow at the very center of the guy."[118] However, there was one center-left political movement Hitchens decided he *could* support during this period: "I didn't vote Labour in 1979 which is the last time I could have done," he said in a 1997 interview. "But I will vote Labour in May; I would like the Labour Party to win."[119] Hitchens's younger self would have been shocked to discover that he would one day support a Labour leader like Tony Blair, who certainly didn't put the common ownership of the means of production, distribution, and exchange at the top of his agenda.

It would be difficult to come up with a politician who believes more firmly that society should be "basically a liberal problem-solving matter" than Blair. But Hitchens argued that "Blair is an improvement on the hypocrisy of the Labour Party. Old Labour was no fucking bargain, I can tell you that."[120] In other words, British voters knew exactly what they were getting with Blair—he was the face of New Labour, a movement that embraced free markets and abandoned the party's formal commitment to socialism. In 1997, Labour won its largest majority since 1945 (as well as the most total seats of any election in the party's history) on the strength of this platform,[121] which Hitchens later attributed to Blair becoming the "first senior member of the party to feel that it had to undergo a makeover, or rebranding, not for reasons of 'image' alone, but as a matter of integrity. And because he believed it himself, he made it convincing to others."[122]

When an interviewer asked Hitchens if the Labour Party could still consider itself socialist in 2005, he replied: "Not in any sense that would have been recognizable to me when I joined it many years ago, forty years ago, now, no. Because it completely accepts . . . the permanence of the capitalist free enterprise system."[123] In the same interview, he credited Blair's government for its commitment to "something that's very important to me, which is internationalism,"[124] and he described this commitment as a reaffirmation of a vanishing left-wing tradition:

> Prime Minister Blair considers it a matter of principle that we don't coexist—our party doesn't coexist with totalitarian or racist or aggressive or theocratic regimes or movements, and has sent British forces to defend Sierra Leone against the hand loppers and barbarians who were sent in from Liberia . . . to Afghanistan to oppose the Taliban, and to Iraq to assist in the liberation—long overdue—of Mesopotamia. The finest traditions, I think, of the socialist movement have always been internationalist and in solidarity. And on that, I think he scores very high.[125]

While Hitchens originally described his support for Blair as a case of "lesser evilism" and noted that "the word 'new' has no more charms for me"[126] (as in, *New* Labour and *New* Democrat), his willingness to endorse a Labour leader who many on the traditional left loathed was suggestive—especially at a time when his disgust with Blair's American counterpart was reaching its zenith. Hitchens didn't accept the idea that Blair was the British Clinton, despite their political similarities. In the summer of 1999, he argued that "Clinton has had the orphaned Kosovo issue forced on him for adoption. But his heart, his gut, and his nerve are not involved at all. He wishes it could have been avoided."[127] By contrast, Hitchens observed that "Tony Blair has been out there every day saying 'This is a matter of principle and we must stand firm.'"[128] Despite the common smear of Blair as Washington's vassal or "poodle" after the invasion of Iraq, Hitchens observed that he deployed "British force on its own, and to try to persuade the international community that the evil of dictatorship had not ended with the Cold War."[129] He continued:

> The Tories had been all but pro-Milošević during the Balkan horrors—a cause of shame that Blair did much to redeem by pressing a hard line on the attempted Serbian cleansing of Kosovo. The record plainly shows that he was more determined than Washington on this occasion, while expressing the imperative for a badly compromised Europe to face the responsibility for its neglected Adriatic front. Before the fall of Milošević, furthermore, he went to Chicago in April 1999 to deliver a significant speech, in which he stressed that internal affairs were not a disguise under which despots should be allowed to conduct genocide or rearmament.[130]

Hitchens argued that "it was Blair who leaned heavily on [Clinton] to intervene in Kosovo. . . . There was no easy talk of 'poodles' then: Blair was the one pushing Washington and not the other way about."[131] In the 1999 Chicago speech Hitchens cited, Blair argued that the conflict in Kosovo was a "just war, based not on any territorial ambitions but on values."[132] He called for a "new Marshall Plan"[133] for the war-ravaged Balkans, declared that "acts of genocide can never be a purely internal matter,"[134] and outlined the political context of the intervention: "Globalization is not simply economic—it is also a political and a security phenomenon. We live in a world where isolationism has ceased to have a reason to exist. . . . We cannot turn our backs on conflicts and the violation of human rights within other countries if we want still to be secure."[135] The view that state sovereignty had to be redefined in the post–Cold War era had made its way to 10 Downing Street.

This was the principled and unequivocal internationalist position that Hitchens had demanded from Western leaders since he first visited Sarajevo in 1992. A year after Blair made the case for a "new doctrine of international community" in Chicago,[136] he deployed British troops to Sierra Leone in a successful effort to assist the UN mission in the country and bring the civil war between the Sierra Leone Army and the

Revolutionary United Front—a paramilitary group backed by the Liberian dictator and war criminal Charles Taylor—to an end.[137] Hitchens applauded Blair's decision to "send troops to put down the barbaric invasion of the hand-loppers and diamond-dealers,"[138] and argued that "It is not too much to say that another Rwanda had been averted."[139]

Hitchens's admiration for Blair would only increase. "Despite his genius for public relations and political manipulation," Hitchens wrote, "the record still shows a consistent attachment to at least two important precepts: hostility to totalitarianism and a strong belief that Britain has both an Atlantic and a European future."[140] Blair was the most prominent Western leader whose politics appeared to be in alignment with the European liberal interventionists, which is one of the reasons he regarded the United States as a defender of democracy and human rights rather than an exporter of imperial violence—unlike so many on the left.

Blair closed his speech in Chicago with an appeal for American internationalism: "We need America engaged. We need the dialogue with you. Europe, over time, will become stronger and stronger, I believe, but its time is some way off yet. And so I say to you: never fall again for the doctrine of isolationism, because the world truly cannot afford it."[141] After observing that the Anglo-American relationship became stronger "under the British center-Left"—a political movement embodied by Blair more than any other figure—Hitchens speculated about why this might be: "Perhaps," he wrote, it "has something to do with the old devotion of the British Left, from Thomas Paine onward, to the ideals of the American Revolution."[142]

* * *

Though his political transition was well underway in the 1990s, the September 11 attacks pushed Hitchens to formally discard his remaining political loyalties. There was no clearer signal of this shift than his decision to leave the *Nation*—the magazine that brought him across the

Atlantic and printed his "Minority Report" column for almost two decades. In a 2006 article for the *Kenyon Review*, John Rodden argued that leaving the *Nation* was the necessary final stage of Hitchens's political development:

> Hitchens' good-bye to the *Nation* was not just a personal milestone; it can also be seen as a symbolic event. It signified that he no longer needed the magazine, either as a professional platform or an intellectual community. Outside its orbit, he could affirm (or indulge) his iconoclasm and rebel individualism without restraint, firing salvos on whatever targets and from whatever vantage point he deemed most appropriate.[143]

While Rodden was right that Hitchens's departure from the *Nation* was symbolic, he overstated its practical significance. The *Nation* never ordered Hitchens to hold his fire or direct it at different targets. As *Nation* editor Katrina vanden Heuvel put it when Hitchens resigned: "We have enjoyed publishing someone who has always had the freedom to write what they wanted and challenge many of our readers' assumptions."[144] Hitchens later noted that he wasn't under any editorial constraints at the *Nation*, and he demonstrated the point when he accused the magazine of being the "voice and the echo chamber of those who truly believe that John Ashcroft is a greater menace than Osama bin Laden" in his final Minority Report.[145]

Hitchens's resignation from the *Nation* after 20 years as a columnist wasn't necessary to maintain his independence, which had already been established at that point in his career—it was a declaration that he no longer wanted to be associated with what he regarded as the official outlet of the "Chomsky-Zinn-Finkelstein quarter" of the left.[146] In the 1990s, Hitchens parted with this faction over the Balkans, and September 11 turned this gap into a chasm. He supported the United States' interventions in Afghanistan and Iraq because the Taliban and Saddam Hussein had turned their countries into monstrous tyrannies, while major figures on the left like Noam Chomsky, Howard Zinn, and Norman Finkelstein dismissed this argument as an excuse for American imperialism.

It wasn't just witnessing the horrors in the Balkans that led Hitchens to question the left's priorities before September 11—it was his early encounter with theocratic assaults on liberal societies and the uneasy commitment to liberal principles in the face of those assaults. During a 2005 interview about the fall of the Berlin Wall, the conversation shifted to the fatwa against Rushdie, which was issued when the Soviet Union was just months away from extinction:

> I thought [the fatwa] was an unprecedented challenge, not just to what we might call First Amendment values, but to civilization, really. What impressed me then—and depressed me, too—was how many people said, no, no, the problem is not the Ayatollah. The problem is Rushdie. Rushdie asked for this. He brought it on himself by writing a novel critical of Islamic tradition or of the literal interpretation of the Quran.[147]

As Rushdie later put it, the fatwa "changed something in Christopher. It made him understand that a new danger had been unleashed upon the earth, that a new totalizing ideology had stepped into the down-at-the-heels shoes of Soviet Communism."[148] There was clear alignment between what Rushdie described as the "appeasement politics of sections of the Western left"[149] after the fatwa and the attitudes toward Islamism and jihadism after September 11, such as the impulse to shift the conversation from theocratic violence to religious grievances and the habit of redirecting blame from the attackers to the victims. In both cases, this usually took the form of tedious recitations of all the ways Western governments have antagonized the "Muslim world," as if the Ayatollah Khomeini and al-Qaeda spoke for all Muslims.

For many on the left, Hitchens's support for the wars in Afghanistan and Iraq was always difficult to understand. This is why left-wing writers and intellectuals came up with cynical, groundless, and often bizarre explanations for these positions, such as the idea that Hitchens was actually an imperialist in disguise all his life or a bigot who just wanted to kill Muslims. In an article published a few days after Hitchens's death, Glenn Greenwald wrote:

> When it came to the defining issues of the post-9/11 era, [Hitchens] was largely indistinguishable from the small army of neoconservative fanatics eager to unleash ever-greater violence against Muslims: driven by a toxic mix of barbarism, self-loving provincialism, a sense of personal inadequacy, and, most of all, a pity-inducing need to find glory and purpose in cheering on military adventures and vanquishing some foe of historically unprecedented evil even if it meant manufacturing them.[150]

It's difficult to see how Hitchens "manufactured" the threat of theocratic terrorism, the evidence of which isn't exactly difficult to ascertain: the massacre of three thousand civilians in the United States; the incitement and prosecution of a savage civil war in Iraq by thugs like Abu Musab al-Zarqawi; the thousands of corpses jihadists have piled up everywhere from Paris to Mumbai to Nairobi to Peshawar; the millions of dollars on offer to assassinate Rushdie (and all the bloodshed that accompanied the fatwa); the machine gunning of journalists for printing cartoons; and the takeover of large tracts of Iraq and Syria in an attempt to establish a new caliphate, which led to the genocide and sexual enslavement of Yazidis in northern Iraq, as well as the public execution of journalists, aid workers, homosexuals, and members of other ethnic and religious minorities.

Considering Hitchens's close relationships with the targets of jihadist assassins (Rushdie, Hirsi Ali, Kurt Westergaard, and so on), it's no surprise that he was especially attuned to the reality of theocratic violence. Greenwald's contribution to the debate after the *Charlie Hebdo* massacre was to publish a series of anti-Semitic cartoons in the *Inter-*

cept—an attempt to demonstrate that the West is selective about which forms of controversial speech it celebrates.[151] But this tawdry exercise merely demonstrated that you can publish whatever you want about Judaism without heavily armed theocratic firing squads showing up at your magazine's offices.

Greenwald argued that Hitchens was "vindictive and barbaric about his war cheerleading" and that his "glee over violence, bloodshed, and perpetual war dominated the last decade of his life."[152] He cited Hitchens's former colleague and friend Dennis Perrin, who wrote in *Minneapolis City Pages* that Hitchens was "energized by the violence" in Bosnia and, after September 11, joined the ranks of the "Beltway's A List" who "like the view from atop the growing pile of bodies."[153] "Unlike Christopher," Perrin wrote, "I do not revel in blasting apart strangers."[154] In *AlterNet*, Chris Hedges decried Hitchens's "blood lust"; "chauvinism"; support for "violent projects of apocalyptic killing" and "imperialist projects"; use of "language that is racist, crude and intolerant"; and alleged belief that the world should be divided into "superior and inferior races"[155] (consider this particular calumny in the context of Hitchens's actual beliefs on race and racism discussed in chapter 2).

The most generous explanation for this flood of cartoonish vitriol is a near-total lack of familiarity with Hitchens's work and political history. If he was so "eager to unleash ever-greater violence against Muslims," for instance, he wouldn't have been a "fanatical" advocate of Western intervention to defend Bosnian Muslims from a genocidal campaign launched by actual imperialists and war criminals. In fact, Hitchens argued that "anti-Muslim prejudice" was one of the reasons Western politicians couldn't be roused to support Bosnia earlier than they did.[156] To prove his point, he presented a thought experiment:

> If Christian churches, whether Orthodox or Catholic, were being burned, and if Christian civilians were being burned by Muslim irregulars with . . . definite support from a neighboring Muslim power in Europe, who is there here who thinks that Western Europe would

have regarded it as a matter of indifference? Or as a proof that the Balkan people are incorrigible? Or as another proof that the warring factions of the Balkans are at it again? I don't think so. Thus, we have to add to the charge that we bring against our betters and our leaders and the masters of the new world order that they are sick. They're sick with cultural racism and religious prejudice. They have not advanced Europe out of a Medieval mindset that thinks of the Gates of Vienna as the only place where civilization can be said to begin. And what a condemnation that is.[157]

Hitchens also noticed that the Bosnians were "invariably described as 'the Muslims' whereas no broadcast ever reported that 'today, Catholic forces destroyed the bridge at Mostar' or 'Orthodox bombardment set fire to the national library of Bosnia in Sarajevo.'"[158] Contra Greenwald, Perrin, Hedges, et al., the atrocities in New York, Washington, and Pennsylvania didn't suddenly fill Hitchens with violent hatred toward Muslims. A month after September 11, a C-SPAN caller asked him if the attacks were evidence of a "clash of civilizations"[159]—a term used and popularized by political scientist Samuel P. Huntington to describe the future of global conflict after the Cold War[160]—and he responded: "It isn't a clash of civilizations, no, because there's too much civilization on what other people would otherwise call the other side, the Muslim side."[161] Hitchens frequently argued that talk of Muslim and Western "sides" made no sense in the first place, as Muslims are the most important allies against theocracy around the world and integral members of Western societies.[162, 163]

It would be strange if a fulminating anti-Muslim bigot was also the best-known advocate of Kurdish self-determination in the Western media (the Kurds are predominately Sunni Muslims)—the primary motivation behind Hitchens's support for the Iraq War. He wore the flag of the Patriotic Union of Kurdistan on his lapel like American politicians wear Old Glory, and he spent many years chronicling the horrors inflicted on the Kurds by Saddam Hussein (often with the acquiescence or active support of the United States). Hitchens challenged those on the left who were "all frenzied about an American-led 'attack on the Muslim world'" before the Iraq War. He asked: "Are the Kurds not Muslims? Is the new Afghan government not Muslim? Will not the next Iraqi government be Muslim also?"[164]

A clear connection between Hitchens's pre- and post-September 11 positions was his solidarity with the Kurds, whose plight as a besieged stateless minority was a longstanding left-wing cause. In 1993, he described the "betrayal of the Kurds" as one of the most atrocious aspects of the Gulf War[165]—a reference to the Kurdish and Shia uprisings against Baghdad after the war, which President George H.W. Bush encouraged before abandoning the rebels to face Saddam Hussein's forces alone.[166] Tens of thousands of rebels and civilians were massacred as U.S. forces stood by, and this was just a few years after Hussein launched the genocidal Anfal campaign against Iraq's Kurds, which left between 50,000 and 100,000 dead.[167] Washington had reason to believe the genocide was taking place, but U.S. officials didn't interrogate the evidence as actively as they could have because Iraq was then considered an ally against Iran.[168]

In a 2002 article, Hitchens wrote: "I haven't seen an anti-war meeting all this year at which you could even guess at the existence of the Iraqi and Kurdish opposition to Saddam."[169] During a debate with Tariq Ali the same year, Hitchens pointed out that American aircraft were patrolling the airspace over northern and southern Iraq—a policy that protected the Kurds and other vulnerable Iraqis instead of leaving them at the mercy of Saddam Hussein.[170] Had the anti-interventionists "won the argument about Iraq," Hitchens argued, "there would not now be an embryonic Kurdish state in the north of Mesopotamia, growing steadily and beginning to flourish, under an umbrella of international protection."[171] He continued:

> I'm old enough to remember that Kurdistan is a much older cause of
> the left in the Middle East even than Palestine. But a creepy silence

falls when I ask my former comrades about this example. It can't be right, can it? That Kurds benefit from American and European military guarantees? It can't be right. It doesn't compute to some minds who are not yet prepared for it.[172]

When Hitchens died, Iraqi President Barham Salih (then the prime minister of Kurdistan) described him as a "tenacious moral warrior" and said the "Kurds lost [a] good friend."[173] In an article for the *Nation*, Hitchens recalled a conversation with Salih about how the left regarded the prospect of U.S. intervention in Iraq: "'I am very disappointed with the left,' Salih told me. In the past the Kurdish cause was a major concern of the internationalist, human rights and socialist movements, but now a slight shuffling and evasiveness seems to have descended."[174]

In a 1994 discussion about military interventionism—seven years prior to September 11 and almost a decade before the Iraq War—Hitchens reflected on how he "began to develop serious misgivings"[175] about the anti-war movement during the Gulf War, which "to this day has failed to evolve any consistent position on the Kurdish people, whose position in that war was and remains a matter of principle, and whose survival as a people . . . and as an emerging semi-autonomous area of the Middle East does, in fact, depend on a protective nexus of intervention on the Iraqi-Turkish-Syrian border."[176] In the debate with Ali, Hitchens criticized those who only take the side of the victims when it's politically convenient to do so:

> I think if you run into someone who only mentions Serbian and Christian Orthodox grievances when Muslims are being massacred, and who only mentions Muslim grievances when Muslims are the aggressors and the murderers, and who keeps weirdly silent about Kurdistan and Rwanda and Sierra Leone, you may have encountered someone who is suffering . . . not from a principled anti-imperialism, but from something quite different: which is a pathological anti-Americanism.[177]

Despite his decades of writing and speaking about the subject, some of Hitchens's critics describe his solidarity with the Kurds as an affectation. As Richard Seymour put it: "For Hitchens, the Kurds provide a crucial ideological quilting point in relation to Iraq, in which support for imperialism can be suffused with the drama of revolution."[178] He added that the "main function of the Kurds for Hitchens is to cover his guilt, and shame, and embarrassment about allowing himself to be made a conduit for lies in the service of mass murder."[179] However, in *Unhitched,* Seymour quotes the writer and activist Mike Davis, who has a "recollection of Hitchens in the 1990s, as 'a charming and bighearted guy' who 'had a tendency to develop profound emotional attachments to third world groups, particularly the Cypriots and the Kurds, and I think that eventually blinded him to the reality of American wars.'"[180] Condescending as this comment was, it doesn't suggest that Hitchens was using the Kurds to justify buried imperial impulses.

A major theme of *Unhitched* is the idea that Hitchens was a faux leftist who only used the language of solidarity and human rights to mask his imperialism. But again and again, Seymour is forced to concede that Hitchens actually had principled left-wing reasons for the positions he took. Consider Hitchens's support for the Falklands War—according to Seymour, the "left gloss that he put on this position was that the defeat of the Argentinian forces would precipitate the downfall of [Leopoldo] Galtieri, whom he characterised as a fascist."[181] Seymour continues: "In one sense Hitchens was proved right. Galtieri was indeed stripped of his post by the Argentinian military after an inquiry into the strategic and tactical failures of the war."[182] He proceeds to acknowledge that the war "pushed the regime into economic turmoil," points out that Galtieri was "wildly mistaken" about the strategic implications of the invasion, and closes by admitting that the military dictatorship was "undoubtedly further weakened and divided by the defeat. This hastened the subsequent transition to civilian rule."[183]

In other words, Hitchens was right in every sense. But without breaking his stride, Seymour runs back to his narrative: "In reality, however, the fall of Galtieri was a by-product of something that Hitchens wanted more, the reassertion of British power, particularly of its naval power."[184] In *Unhitched*, Seymour never even comes close to proving what he set out to prove—that Hitchens was a closet imperialist and right-winger. What Seymour despises is the fact that, like the European interventionists, Hitchens realized that his left-wing principles didn't put him in permanent opposition to Western governments, alliances, and institutions. This was a logical extension of his belief that radical internationalists should be consistent advocates for the resistance to aggression and the defense of vulnerable populations—whether they were under siege in Sarajevo or fighting for their freedom on the scarred hillsides of northern Iraq.

* * *

When Hitchens resigned from the *Nation*, his colleague Eric Alterman told the *New York Times* that "Christopher had long ago ceased to feel comfortable with his friends on the left."[185] This comment assumes there's a rigid set of doctrines that constitutes an official or authentic left—it doesn't consider the possibility that, like Orwell, Hitchens attacked the left *from* the left.

Hitchens defended the wars in Afghanistan and Iraq, but he was also a plaintiff in an ACLU lawsuit against the Bush administration for its authorization of warrantless surveillance.[186] He believed the "War on Terror" was a just cause, but he condemned the use of torture by American interrogators and even underwent waterboarding to demonstrate the ugly deceptiveness of euphemisms like "enhanced interrogation"—an experience he recounted in an essay titled, "Believe Me, It's Torture."[187] He despised Islamist groups like Hamas, but he was an ardent supporter of Palestinian rights and statehood.[188, 189] Hitchens was derided as a right-winger despite his lifelong opposition to capital punishment (the earliest political position he could remember taking)[190, 191] and support for universal healthcare,[192] reparations for the descendants of slaves,[193] and the decriminalization of drugs in the United States.[194] But for Hitchens, political positions themselves didn't matter as much as a person's reasons for holding them—by the last decade of his life, he said, "I don't have any allegiances. . . . I don't ask what people's politics are. I ask what their principles are."[195]

The main reason left-wing intellectuals and journalists slandered Hitchens so brazenly ("eager to unleash ever-greater violence against Muslims," "bloodlust," "chauvinism," "imperialism," "racism," "genocide," etc.) was their conviction that he had become an apologist for Western imperialism. This view is rooted in a belief that has become axiomatic on many parts of the left—if the United States or any other Western power intervenes in another country, it can't possibly be to protect human rights or resist aggression. Much of the left has been fundamentally opposed to the main currents of Western foreign policy since the Cold War—the expansion of NATO, the promotion of free trade, the emergence of liberal interventionism, and support for a broad range of international political and economic institutions (such as the United Nations, World Trade Organization, and International Monetary Fund).

Hitchens could always draw upon a vast mental encyclopedia of the crimes and failures of American foreign policy, but after September 11, he was contemptuous of the way those on the "anti-imperialist" left were invoking this history. As he explained in his *Nation* column immediately following the attacks (titled "Against Rationalization"):

> I was apprehensive from the first moment about the sort of masochistic e-mail traffic that might start circulating from the Chomsky-Zinn-Finkelstein quarter, and I was not to be disappointed. With all due thanks to these worthy comrades, I know already that the people of Palestine and Iraq are victims of a depraved and callous Western statecraft. . . . But there is no sense in which the events of September 11 can be held to constitute . . . a reprisal, either legally or morally.[196]

During a panel discussion in October 2001, Oliver Stone implicated U.S. foreign policy in the "revolt of September 11th." Hitchens replied: "Excuse me, 'revolt'? . . . It was state-supported mass murder, using civilians as missiles."[197] While intellectual critics of U.S. foreign policy like Chomsky were more sophisticated than Stone, their central argument wasn't much different. When confronted with the incineration of three thousand civilians by theocratic murderers on American soil, Chomsky's first instinct was to list all the ways in which this assault was the predictable reaction to decades of American imperialism (see his book *9-11*, published shortly after the attacks).[198] Hitchens summarized this attitude as the insistence that "we must change the subject" from theocratic terrorism "and change it at once, to Palestine or East Timor or Angola or Iraq. All radical polemic may now proceed as it did before the rude interruption."[199]

Reviewing the argument between Hitchens and Chomsky in *Guernica*, George Scialabba noted that Chomsky merely thought the slaughter of American civilians should prompt "some reflection on the question raised by President Bush in the bombing's immediate aftermath: 'Why do they hate us?'"[200] For a whole lot of good reasons, Scialabba explained, including:

> Our longstanding opposition to independent Arab nationalism and Iranian democracy; our ardent support for the brutal dictatorship of Saddam Hussein in the 1980s, followed abruptly by our horrifying degradation of Iraqi society through bombing and boycott in the 1990s; our indifference to the dispossession of Palestinian Arabs, especially since 1967; and in the background of these, of moral if not immediate historical relevance, the holocaust visited on Indochina in the 1960s and 70s; our collaboration with massacre and repression in Latin America, and particularly Central America, throughout the 20th century; our material and diplomatic support for near-genocidal violence by Indonesia against East Timor and by Turkey against the Kurds, and so on.[201]

Scialabba doesn't tell us how this gallery of American criminality and cruelty explains what motivated al-Qaeda to attack the United States. And not only does he imagine that the "holocaust visited on Indochina" is in some way morally relevant to discussions about September 11 (how?), but he also ignores the grievances Osama bin Laden *actually* had about U.S. policy—American military bases in Saudi Arabia, for instance.[202] It's remarkable that one of Scialabba's explanations for September 11 was the United States' "material and diplomatic support for near-genocidal violence by Indonesia against East Timor." As Hitchens often noted, this argument is exactly backwards—Bin Laden wasn't furious with the West for *supporting* Indonesian imperialism in East Timor. He was outraged when Western forces helped to *liberate* East Timor from Indonesian rule.

An overwhelming majority of East Timorese voted for independence in a 1999 referendum, despite a campaign of intimidation and violence mounted by local militias (which were created and supported by the Indonesian armed forces).[203] After the 2002 Bali bombings that killed more than 200 people, including 88 Australians,[204] the Southeast Asian jihadist group responsible (Jemaah Islamiyah)—along with Bin Laden, who supported the perpetrators—cited Australia's leadership in the UN peacekeeping effort to facilitate East Timor's transition to independence as the reason for the attack.[205]

Imam Samudra, a member of Jemaah Islamiyah who helped plan the bombings, explained why Australian civilians deserved to be massacred: "Australia has taken part in efforts to separate East Timor from Indonesia which was an international conspiracy by followers of the Cross."[206] A year before the bombing, Bin Laden offered his analysis of the international effort to protect the East Timorese as they exercised their right to self-determination: "The crusader Australian forces were on Indonesian shores, and in fact they landed to separate East Timor, which is part of the Islamic world."[207] In a 2005 article, Hitchens pointed out that "East Timor was for many years, and quite rightly, a signature cause of the Noam Chomsky 'left.' The near-genocide of its people is an eternal stain on Indonesia and on the Western states that were complicit or silent. Yet Bin Ladenism wants not *less* of this killing and repression but *more*. Its demand to re-establish the caliphate is a pro-imperialist demand, not an anti-imperialist one."[208] Hitchens made the same point in a 2007 interview:

> You may have noticed that when the al-Qaeda forces, with their Baathist allies, blew up the U.N. office in Baghdad to murder the great Sérgio Vieira de Mello—the wonderful Brazilian human rights envoy who Kofi Annan had sent there—they said they'd done it to revenge themselves for his help in getting East Timor independence from Indonesia. . . . So you see, if you want to make these people happy and address their complaints, you have to say, "Well, we'd be better off not having liberated East Timor"—not a demand that can easily be met. If you really want al-Qaeda to go away, you have to let Pakistan take over Kashmir and tear the heart out of the Indian Federation and start a horrible religious war in the subcontinent. The cause of Islamist terrorism, in other words . . . is the ideology of Islamic terror.[209]

Like Oliver Stone, when Chomsky and Scialabba witnessed the incineration of thousands of civilians in New York, Washington, DC, and Pennsylvania, they saw a revolt. It was the whole world against the United States. "If the subject is 'What should America do about terrorism?'" Scialabba wrote, "then at least part of the answer must be: we should understand why others commit it, against us in particular."[210] Or as former Labour MP George Galloway put it in a 2005 debate with Hitchens in New York: "You may think that those airplanes in this city on 9/11 came out of a clear, blue sky. I believe they emerged out of a swamp of hatred created by us."[211]

* * *

In *The Tyranny of Guilt: An Essay on Western Masochism*, Pascal Bruckner explores a subject that became a major undercurrent of Hitchens's thinking, especially in the last decade of his life: the tendency among Western intellectuals to ceaselessly condemn their own cultures and lament the horrors their societies have inflicted on the world.[212] Bruckner believes this incessant self-criticism has become fanatical and mindless—a view Hitchens shared, and a habit he often described as "masochistic."[213, 214] One of the most prominent themes of left-wing activism and scholarship over the past several decades has been what Bruckner would describe as guilt: for slavery and racism, for other forms of prejudice and exclusion throughout history, for colonialism. Though Bruckner focuses on Europe, this phenomenon isn't confined to the continent—large swaths of the American left insist that the United States is incurably racist at home and relentlessly imperialistic abroad.

There are many examples. After September 11, Susan Sontag demanded to know: "Where is the acknowledgment that this was not a 'cowardly' attack on 'civilization' or 'liberty' or 'humanity' or 'the free world' but an attack on the world's self-proclaimed superpower, undertaken as a consequence of specific American alliances and actions?"[215] Chomsky claimed that the United States was responsible for a "silent genocide" in the early days of the war in Afghanistan.[216, 217] Many on the left blamed NATO when Vladimir Putin invaded Ukraine and launched the largest conflict on European soil since World War II (the Democratic Socialists of America, for instance, called for the United States to withdraw from the alliance and demanded that Washington "end the imperialist expansionism that set the stage for this conflict" two days after Russian tanks rolled across the border).[218] Left-wing apologists for Bashar al-Assad like Max Blumenthal howl about Western involvement in Syria as hundreds of thousands are killed by Russian and regime forces.[219] Blumenthal and his colleague Ben Norton echo Putin and accuse the United States and its allies of supporting neo-Nazis in Ukraine,[220] while slandering pro-democracy demonstrators in Moscow, Minsk, and Hong Kong as violent tools of Western governments.[221, 222, 223]

In Nick Cohen's 2007 book *What's Left? How the Left Lost Its Way*— a book Hitchens described as "exceptional and necessary"—you'll find a chapter titled "Kill Us, We Deserve It."[224] In this chapter, Cohen summarizes the outbreak of left-wing masochism after September 11. He cites a *New Statesman* editorial, for instance, which suggested that the victims in the World Trade Center weren't as "innocent" or "undeserving" as one might think. "If America seems a greedy and overweening power," the editorial explained, "that is partly because its people have willed it. They preferred George Bush to both Al Gore and Ralph Nader. These are harsh judgments but we live in harsh times."[225] Documentary filmmaker Michael Moore was horrified that al-Qaeda targeted cities that tend to vote for Democrats: "If someone did this to get back at Bush," he wrote on his website, "they did so by killing thousands of people who DID NOT vote for him! Boston, New York, DC, and the planes' destination of California—these were places that voted AGAINST BUSH."[226] Mary Beard, a professor of classics at Cambridge with a lot of royal letters next to her name, declared that the "United States had it coming."[227]

In 1969, Chomsky summarized a view that has become a pillar of left-wing thought for many in Europe and the United States: "I restrict myself to discussing American terror," he said. "For one thing, because it's just qualitatively different in scale. And for another thing, because I feel that we have some responsibility for it."[228] According to Chomsky— who expounded on this principle in *On Power and Ideology: The Managua Lectures* (1987)—it's "very easy to denounce the atrocities of someone else. That has about as much ethical value as denouncing atrocities that took place in the 18th century."[229]

For someone who considers *Homage to Catalonia* Orwell's "greatest book,"[230] it's curious that Chomsky expresses so much contempt for writers and intellectuals who denounce atrocities committed abroad. *Homage to Catalonia* is a memoir of Orwell's experience fighting in the Spanish Civil War, but it's also a bitter exposé on the Stalinist subversion of the war effort through the repression and liquidation of factions like the Partido Obrero de Unificación Marxista—the party under whose flag Orwell fought in Spain.[231] Should Orwell have stopped wasting his time on Stalin and penned an attack on the governments of Stanley Baldwin and Neville Chamberlain instead? For that matter, what does Chomsky have to say about *Animal Farm*? That Orwell's devastating critique of the Soviet Union (which some publishers refused to print because it didn't criticize totalitarianism more generically) had no ethical value? Recall that Hitchens described the support for intervention in Bosnia among members of the European left as "an echo of the great international campaign to defend the Spanish Republic between 1936 and 1939."[232] The left hasn't always observed Chomsky's insular maxim.

Hitchens often pointed out that there's no such thing as a neutral policy when massacre and repression are taking place. In 1994, hundreds of thousands of people were killed in Rwanda in just a few months,[233] a number that almost certainly would have been significantly lower had the United States and other Western countries provided even a modest commitment of troops, as Clinton later acknowledged.[234] The same applies to the Darfur genocide where a small number of forces could have prevented many deaths (Hitchens argued that the UN and Western powers should have taken much more robust action than they did).[235] If American activists, intellectuals, and editorial boards had urged the Clinton administration, NATO, and the United Nations to stop the atrocities taking place in Rwanda and Sudan—an outcry which shamefully failed to materialize (with several notable exceptions, such as Nicholas Kristof's *New York Times* columns on Darfur)[236]—would Chomsky have accused them of doing something ethically suspect?

For two years, Western powers allowed the war on Bosnia to continue unabated—a policy that led to thousands of deaths and the displacement and immiseration of many more. Hitchens couldn't even convince many of his fellow left-wingers to join calls to end the arms embargo against Bosnia,[237] which ensured that the Bosnians (who had nowhere near the military resources as Serbian forces, which were outfitted with weapons and equipment left over from the Yugoslav People's Army) would be forced to endure a grinding conflict and blockade with no chance of mounting a significant resistance. Left-wing interventionists like Cohn-Bendit, on the other hand, were signing appeals to the United Nations, the Clinton administration, and Congress to "lift the cruel arms embargo imposed against Bosnia" and abandon the "policy of pseudo-evenhandedness that has in fact strengthened the side of aggressive Serb expansionism."[238]

Chomsky's predictable response to September 11 put Hitchens "in mind of something from the opening of Marx's *The Eighteenth Brumaire of Louis Bonaparte* ... the observation that when people are learning a new language, they habitually translate it back into the one they already know."[239] This is what Chomsky has been doing since the end of the Cold War: habitually insisting that every intervention, no matter how justified on humanitarian grounds, was just the latest example of American hegemony and imperialism. In a 1999 debate with Chomsky about Kosovo in the *Nation*, Hitchens argued against the idea that the NATO campaign was "mere power-projection for the New World Order. We appear to be in a new era, where old reflexes serve us less well. However, this does not relieve us of our responsibility to take the side of the victims, as Chomsky once taught me and many others to do."[240]

In the final chapter of his memoir, Hitchens says he was "being called a traitor and a warmonger by quite a lot of the Left" during the wars in the Balkans, but he was "both appalled and relieved to find that I no longer really cared."[241] In the same chapter, Hitchens again mentions how he felt after relinquishing his left-wing affiliations: "On some days, this is like the phantom pain of a missing limb." But this time he includes an addendum: "On others, it's more like the sensation of having taken off a needlessly heavy overcoat."[242] Throughout the chapter, Hitchens cites several examples of former communists who could point to the exact moment they decided to abandon *The God That Failed* (the title of a collection of anti-communist essays by André Gide, Richard Wright,

Ignazio Silone, Stephen Spender, Arthur Koestler, and Louis Fischer).[243] After the Hitler-Stalin pact, Koestler said, "I no longer cared whether Hitler's allies called me a counter-revolutionary."[244] Hitchens writes about his own disillusionment (not with communism, but with the left), observing that he "wanted the moral arithmetic to add up, while still hoping that it could somehow be made to do this on the 'left' side of the column."[245] He continues:

> In Bosnia, though, I was brought to the abrupt admission that, if the majority of my former friends got their way about non-intervention, there would be another genocide on European soil. A century that had opened with the Muslim Turkish slaughter of the Armenians, and climaxed in the lowest sense of that term with an attempt to erase Jewry, could well close with a Christian destruction of the continent's oldest Muslim population. This was an exceedingly clarifying reflection. It made me care much less about the amour propre of my previous loyalties.[246]

This assertion of independence was overdue, but why was Hitchens willing to cede the "left side of the column" to those former allies who were opposed to taking action in the Balkans? During the 1990s, he still felt it was necessary to "phrase any disagreement with actual or former comrades in terms that were themselves 'Left,'"[247] but this wasn't especially difficult to do in the case of Bosnia. Beyond the fact that left-wing friends like Sontag campaigned alongside him, there was the example set by Europe's *soixante-huitards*, whose support for intervention in the Balkans was consistent with the arguments they had been making for decades about defending human rights and civilian lives wherever they're threatened. Today's left should reclaim this history as its own.

* * *

When the United Kingdom held a referendum on whether the country would remain in the European Union in June 2016, Jeremy Corbyn was the British Labour Leader. Corbyn ostensibly supported the Remain campaign, but it would be difficult to find a worse advocate for that position from the left—as a local councillor in Haringey he voted to leave the European Union's predecessor (the European Economic Community, or EEC) in 1975,[248] he voted against ratifying the Maastricht Treaty—which established the modern European Union—as a Member of Parliament in 1993,[249] and he spent decades attacking the union. Unlike many who are anti-EU for practical reasons, such as concerns about excessive bureaucracy in Brussels or the monetary union, Corbyn's opposition to the European project has always been more fundamental—he believes the European Union and NATO constitute a twenty-first century "European empire."[250]

Corbyn's distrust of the European Union is bound up with his paranoia about NATO. In a 2009 speech condemning the Treaty of Lisbon—a set of amendments to the Maastricht Treaty that updated the European Union's democratic procedures, specified the union's powers, and made other institutional changes[251]—Corbyn said: "Europe will become subservient to the wishes of NATO and the aims of NATO" and described the alliance as "this military machine, this military Frankenstein."[252] He condemned NATO as a "global military force with no democratic control, no accountability whatsoever" and argued that "NATO's influence has been malevolent, to say the least, on every economy of every country that's been part of it."[253]

Corbyn has repeatedly called for NATO to be disbanded. In 2011, he said, "We in the radical end, the left, of the unions and the Labour Party, have got to be realistic that NATO is a major problem and a major difficulty, and we have to campaign against NATO's power, its influence and its global reach, because it is a danger to world peace and a danger to world security."[254] In 2012, he argued that the end of the Cold War was the "obvious time for Nato to have been disbanded."[255] When Putin sent 200,000 troops to the Ukrainian border in late 2021 and early 2022—an obvious reminder of why the world needs the "military Frankenstein" which so terrifies Corbyn—and demanded that NATO formally refuse Kyiv entry to the alliance, Corbyn repeatedly blamed "both sides" and attacked NATO.[256]

The "anti-imperialist" left has a history of blaming "both sides" in the face of one-sided—even genocidal—imperial aggression. In the 1990s, the Committee for Peace in the Balkans (a left-wing group co-founded by Diane Abbott, who would later serve as Corbyn's Shadow Home Secretary) published a letter in opposition to NATO's involvement in Bosnia: "The reality," the letter stated, "is that all sides have committed atrocities," while the "one-sided nature of NATO's intervention is breath-taking."[257, 258] In 2004, Corbyn sponsored a motion signed by 24 other MPs which celebrated an article by John Pilger in the *New Statesman* that described the NATO intervention as an "illegal, unprovoked attack on a European country" (as if Milošević had been quietly minding his own business) and a campaign of "bombing of defenseless people."[259] Pilger closed his piece by arguing that the "show trial of Slobodan Milosevic proceeds as farce." The motion Corbyn signed "congratulates John Pilger on his expose of the fraudulent justifications for intervening in a 'genocide' that never really existed in Kosovo."[260]

In 2014, Corbyn argued that the true motives behind the interventions in the Balkans were purely mercenary: "Noam Chomsky analysed the whole war," he wrote, "and concluded that the real 'winners' were Western arms manufacturers and that 'the US was able to enforce its domination over the strategic Balkans region.'"[261] Corbyn uncritically accepted Chomsky's interpretation, but it's belied by the two years the Clinton administration spent vacillating on Bosnia—the last thing Clinton wanted was to get the United States involved in an expanding war in Europe.

Corbyn represented one faction of the left in the post-Cold War era, but there were others that didn't share his conviction that NATO posed a bigger threat than the return of genocidal nationalism to Eu-

rope. *Power and the Idealists* is a study of how, as Berman puts it, "someone with an extremely radical New Left orientation could have ended
up, in the fullness of time, a friend of NATO."[262] According to Berman,
after the fall of the Soviet Union, the European interventionists "finally
had to put aside matters of mere philosophy or attitude and adopt actual
positions and accept the political consequences."[263] He mentions the fact
that some '68ers supported the Gulf War, for instance, but argues that
the "big moment of left-wing evolution came the next year . . . when the
ethnic massacres got underway in the Balkans."[264]

Berman explains that many factions of the left could be relied upon
to demand *inaction* during this period: "There was an old-fashioned and
even reactionary left," best represented in the United States by the *Nation*, which "published an amazing series of anguished editorials about
the need not to upset the Russians and especially the nationalists among
them, therefore the need to stay out of the Balkans."[265] Then there were
the "realpolitik liberals in the first years of the Clinton administration,"
who were "hardly going to press for forceful interventions in the name
of something as vaporous as human rights."[266] But finally, there were the
"veterans of the student uprisings circa 1968"[267]—the people who, as
Berman puts it,

> had imagined that they were building a new civilization in Europe.
> Those people, in looking at the Balkans in the nineteen-nineties, were
> guaranteed to give at least a few thoughts to matters of genocide, to
> questions of resistance and non-resistance—the issues that, in their
> youth, had brought them to the left-wing barricades. A hatred of
> genocide was these people's oldest and deepest idea, together with the
> worried conviction that Nazism was capable of reappearing under new
> disguises.[268]

Just a few pages later, though, Berman refers to this faction as the
"former left."[269] This echoes Hitchens's observation that opposition to
genocide in the heart of Europe was no longer a position on the "'left'

side of the column." But why did Berman and Hitchens make these concessions? Throughout *Power and the Idealists*, Berman frequently points out that there are and always have been "multiple lefts." Why can't the interventionist left—which, Berman argues, stood for "antitotalitarianism" and "humanitarian action"[270]—be one of them? Beyond arguing that "many good '68ers became very good '89ers,"[271] Hitchens observed that the war in Bosnia mobilized this faction of the left while other factions maintained their indifference and neutrality. At the end of *Letters to a Young Contrarian*, Hitchens discusses the implications of this neutrality:

> Given the uneven way that borders and populations actually intersect, in Europe and the Balkans and the Caucasus, it would be suicidal to allow the forcible triumph of a demagogic and dictatorial regime, which sought to impose the tyrannical notion of congruence between "race" and "state." This would negate the whole idea of Europe, not to say civilisation, and could only lead to more war and further despotism.[272]

Hitchens recognized that those who wanted to prevent this catastrophe from destroying the idea of Europe were, in fact, still fighting for the principles that had brought them to the left-wing barricades decades earlier. He argues that Bosnia "brought together the best of the Sixty-Eighters and the Eighty-Niners, and showed that there had always been a potential symbiosis of the two."[273] This alliance represented a left-wing tradition that's far more progressive and internationalist than Corbynism, which is a grudging, evasive, and anachronistic ideology that gets reheated and repackaged as "anti-imperialism" every time there's a conflict between the liberal democratic world and its enemies. But Hitchens reminds us that there have always been plenty of real anti-imperialists on the left: "In Sarajevo and Mostar and Tuzla and Zagreb and Dubrovnik, I repeatedly met, without any arrangement to do so, just the people I remembered, and I might have hoped to encounter, from earlier battles."[274]

* * *

"A map of the world that does not include Utopia," according to Oscar Wilde, "is not worth even glancing at."[275] While Hitchens "used to adore that phrase," he found himself reflecting "more upon the shipwrecks and prison islands to which the quest has led."[276] What became clearer and clearer to Hitchens after the revolutions of 1989—which were, above all, revolutions for liberal democracy and rejections of the utopian fantasies that had built and populated so many prisons in Europe—was that the principles of internationalism and freedom could be defended without the dead weight of ideology: "I have actually seen more prisons broken open, more people and territory 'liberated,' and more taboos broken and censors flouted," he writes, "since I let go of the idea, or at any rate the plan, of a radiant future."[277]

But Hitchens didn't abandon the idea of a better future. Berman refers to the '68ers as "idealists" because they recognized that the political developments we've grown accustomed to are actually powerful and even revolutionary affirmations of their left-wing principles. Hitchens describes the political transformation of these intellectuals and activists during the "fairly long interval between 1968 and 1989" as a process by which "many of the revolutionaries against consumer capitalism metamorphosed into 'civil society' human-rights activists."[278] This wasn't a departure from their left-wing values. After the Cold War, "the future seemed to belong to liberal democracy," Berman writes.[279] With the establishment of the European Union in 1993, Berman observes that the "stalwarts from the student left of many years before . . . had begun to see in the new institutions of the European Union the realization of some very old left-wing dreams. Nor was this a delusion."[280] He continues:

> Most of the old-fashioned proletarian doctrines of the nineteenth-century revolutionary left may have evaporated during the course of the 1989 revolutions, but this one element in the classic left-wing imagination—the vision of a borderless, federal, peaceful, technocratic

Europe—turned out to be solid and lasting. People with backgrounds in the revolutionary left could recognize some of their own principles in the European project. And the left-wing stalwarts duly threw themselves into the planning and negotiations, in the belief that now, finally, they had stumbled on a way to realize their own most fondly held ideas in a new and improved version, stripped of the grotesque errors of the left-wing past.[281]

Hitchens viewed Bosnia as a microcosm of this enlightened and integrated Europe (although it isn't part of the European Union). During the war, he mentioned a poster he saw in a Bosnian government building: "Executed in yellow and black, it was a combined logo featuring the Star of David, the Islamic star and crescent, the Roman Catholic cross and the more elaborate cruciform of the Orthodox Church. *Gens Una Summus*, read the superscription. 'We Are One People.'"[282] He rescued the poster from an office that was later struck by a mortar and took it back to the United States.[283] Hitchens's arguments for the defense of Bosnia and Kosovo didn't just make a case for liberal interventionism—they made a case for building a radical international politics for the world as it actually exists. "In bloody Bosnia," he writes, "I realised that all the disparate and random struggles in which some of us had participated earlier could be made, by this recognition of a hinge or crux moment, to make more than retrospective sense."[284]

Hitchens's Europeanism wasn't always optimistic. He predicted that the euro wouldn't last,[285] arguing: "How tragic it is that the euro system has already, in effect, become a two-tier one and that the bottom tier is occupied by the very countries—Greece, Portugal, Spain, and Ireland—that benefited most from their accession to the European Union."[286] Despite these concerns, he was a firm supporter of European integration, and he saw the European Union as an affirmation of liberal, democratic, and internationalist principles. When he lived in Europe, he was

one of the few on the left to advocate an enlargement of the community and to identify it with the progressive element in politics. This was mainly because I had seen the positive effect that Europeanism had exerted on the periphery of the continent, especially in Spain, Portugal, and Greece. Until the middle of the 1970s, these countries had been ruled by backward-looking dictatorships, generally religious and military in character and dependent on military aid from the more conservative circles in the United States. Because the European community allowed only parliamentary democracies to join, the exclusion from the continent's heartland gave a huge incentive to the middle class in these countries to support the overthrow of despotism.[287]

Hitchens believed Europeanism also had a galvanizing effect on Eastern Europeans, who "even while the Berlin Wall still stood, measured their aspirations by how swiftly they, too, could meet the criteria for membership and escape the dreary, wasteful Comecon system that was the Soviet Union's own parody of a supranational agreement."[288] He argued that Germany's "decision to give up the deutsche mark in 2002 must rank as one of the most mature and generous decisions ever taken by a modern state, full confirmation of the country's long transition from Nazism and Stalinism and partition, Europe's three great modern enemies."[289]

The European Union still gives European citizens powerful incentives to resist authoritarianism and embrace liberal democracy today. As Hungary and Poland have shifted toward right-wing nationalism and authoritarianism over the past several years, their membership in the European Union has imposed limits on the anti-democratic measures their governments can take. For example, after the European Court of Justice ruled in 2019 that the Polish government's efforts to undermine the independent judiciary were contrary to EU law, the country's Constitutional Court declared that Polish law took precedence.[290, 291] As a fight between Warsaw and Brussels looked imminent, the majority of Polish citizens—who know their country is one of the largest recipients of EU aid—wanted the government to retreat from the confrontation.[292] Other countries that want to join the European Union (such as Ukraine) recognize that they have to build more robust democratic institutions and get corruption under control before doing so.

When a fact-checking website published by the European Commission accused *Christopher* Hitchens of describing the European Arrest Warrant as an "outrageous EU intrusion into our [the British] legal system" in the summer of 2014, Peter Hitchens (Christopher's brother and the actual author of those words) responded in the *Daily Mail*: "My late brother, alas, has not been writing for anyone since December 2011, and never did so for the Mail on Sunday. Had he done so, he would have been supportive, not critical of the EU (many of his admirers do not realise how keen he was on the project)."[293] There's a long tradition of left-wingers keen on the project of European integration, including the one who influenced Hitchens more than any other. In a 1947 essay titled "Toward European Unity," Orwell wrote:

> . . . a Socialist United States of Europe seems to me the only worthwhile political objective today. Such a federation would contain about 250 million people, including perhaps half the skilled industrial workers of the world. I do not need to be told that the difficulties of bringing any such thing into being are enormous and terrifying. . . . But we ought not to feel that it is of its nature impossible, or that countries so different from one another would not voluntarily unite. A western European union is in itself a less improbable concatenation than the Soviet Union or the British Empire.[294]

Orwell went on to say that the establishment of a United States of Europe "seems to me a very unlikely event. . . . But I also can't at present see any other hopeful objective."[295] The alternative to the European Union and the international institutions that have expanded since the end of the Cold War is a reversion to the atomized, nationalistic Europe of the twentieth century. At a time when nationalist governments in Europe are increasingly hostile to the basic liberal democratic principles of the European Union—and after Britain succumbed to a dishonest campaign to cancel its membership in the union—a revival of Europeanism is more important than ever.

In *Hitch-22*, after noting that he was "called a traitor and a warmonger by quite a lot of the Left" for supporting the defense of Bosnia, Hitchens emphasizes a "truth that all riveters of the mind-forged manacles most fear, and that I here repeat: *One cannot be just a little bit heretical.*"[296] Hitchens thought the European project—uninspiring and counterrevolutionary as it may seem to Corbyn, Chomsky, and the rest of the "anti-imperialist" left—was worth fighting for. And when NATO was doing the fighting, he supported NATO. If this heresy was enough to get him barred from the left, he embraced his excommunication.

But it's time to retire the notion that Hitchens was no longer on the left after the Cold War. The record of left-wing support for universal human rights, interventionism, and international integration is just as clear as the history of anti-utopianism among ex-communists and other former hard leftists. Did Bernard Kouchner suddenly become a conservative when he left his communist illusions behind and founded Médecins Sans Frontières? Were the ex-communist dissidents of Eastern Europe mere reactionaries? It's a mistake to regard anti-utopianism as a surrender to the forces of cynicism and reaction. "In rejecting Perfectionism," Hitchens writes, "I don't want you to fall into the opposite error, which is that of taking human nature just as you find it. . . . civilisation can increase, and at times actually has increased, the temptation to behave in a civilised way. It is only those who hope to *transform* humans who end up by burning them, like the waste product of a failed experiment."[297]

While Hitchens often criticized the casual use of the word "experiment" by the "sort of radical who claims to act like a pitiless surgeon or a ruthless engineer,"[298] there was one context in which he could invoke the word without a shudder: when discussing the American experiment. In what he described as the battle between those "who regard the American experiment as essentially complete and those who do not,"[299] he counted himself among the latter. As we saw in the previous chapter, he had an acute awareness of America's brutal historical contradictions, as well as all the ways it fails to affirm its revolutionary ideals today. But he also recognized that America still retains the capacity to uphold and export those ideals: liberal democracy, individual rights, the rule of law, pluralism. These are also the ideals that underpin the European project, and they rapidly spread across the continent after the Cold War.

We live in an era of collapsing institutional trust,[300] which has led to political upheavals like the rise of nationalist authoritarianism and Brexit. One reason for this phenomenon is historical amnesia—Europe collapsed into fascism and war within living memory; the Iron Curtain lifted only 30 years ago; and the level of political and economic integration since then has no precedent in human history. The post-Cold War period has been the most peaceful and democratic era the world has ever experienced—achievements that today's radicals should defend and expand. To many left-wingers, however, there's something suspicious or even odious about working within existing structures and institutions— they believe it's more authentically radical to demand demolition and recreation. They're even willing to work with nationalist and populist demagogues to do the job (you'll read more about this ugly development in chapter 5). But at a time when the post-World War II international order really has proven to be a successful framework for global cooperation and democratic expansion, the left is making a grievous mistake by seeking to discredit and erode that order at every turn.

Instead of imagining that the most powerful liberal democracies and the institutions they've built are irredeemable imperial machines, Hitchens decided that the left should urge those nations and institutions to use their power for liberal ends. But he did so without ignoring or attempting to excuse the history of crimes committed by Western governments. "To exchange one orthodoxy for another is not necessarily an advance," Orwell wrote in 1945. "The enemy is the gramophone mind, whether or not one agrees with the record that is being played at the moment."[301] The gramophone minds on the left who accused Hitchens of being an imperialist didn't regard the defense of Europe from the re-emergence of genocidal violence as a worthwhile campaign because they believe the European project is a reactionary, neo-imperialist enterprise. But Hitchens could see how the world changed after 1989:

> . . . the Communist leaderships of Eastern Europe had almost wholly ceased to believe in anything but their own survival and self-interest, which is one of the reasons their demise was so swift. While the revolution from below was not animated by any great "new" idea, as had been the case in 1789, 1848, or even 1917, the intellectuals and the masses were agreed that they wanted the unexciting objective of "normality"—a life not unlike that of Western Europe, where it was possible to express everyday criticism, register a vote, scrutinize a free press, and become a consumer as well as a producer. These unexciting demands were nonetheless revolutionary in their way, which gives you an idea of the utter failure and bankruptcy of the regimes that could not meet them.[302]

In *Hitch-22*, the chapter titled "The Sixties: Revolution in the Revolution" contains a suggestive footnote: " . . . those who bang their heads against history's wall had better be equipped with some kind of a theoretical crash helmet. It was to take me some time to doff my own."[303] This crash helmet was Hitchens's discovery that the Marxism of his youth wasn't the only way to be a radical. Modern Europe isn't a utopia, but it's nonetheless revolutionary in its way. If today's left-wingers could rediscover this simple fact, they wouldn't just realize that NATO and the European Union aren't in the process of building a new European "empire"—they would see that these institutions have prevented the old European empires from returning.

In his introduction to *Elements of the Philosophy of Right*, Georg Wilhelm Friedrich Hegel wrote that the "owl of Minerva begins its flight only with the onset of dusk."[304] Though Hitchens thought this image had been overused, he admitted that it had "always been attractive to me because it is only at the close of an epoch that you can really say that it

was an epoch at all—you can give it some kind of measure and depth."
He continued: "I don't think the owls of '68 became Minerva-like until
'89."[305]

When Fukuyama published his essay "The End of History?" Hitchens jeered: "At last, self-congratulation raised to the status of philosophy!"[306] He continued to be intensely critical of Fukuyama in the decades that followed. It's strange, though, that a writer who spent many
years as a Marxist—and never stopped thinking like one—would be so
contemptuous of Fukuyama's theory, informed as it was by a Hegelian
sense of historical mechanics and progress (and supported by far more
real-world evidence than any strain of Marxism could ever claim). It's
even stranger because, as we'll see throughout the rest of this book,
Hitchens and Fukuyama appeared to have converged on a belief in the
power and sustainability of liberal democracy after the dissolution of the
Soviet Union.

Despite Hitchens's suspicion of utopianism, he still believed radical
progress was possible: "The next phase or epoch is already discernible,"
he wrote at the beginning of the twenty-first century, "it is the fight to
extend the concept of universal human rights, and to match the 'globalisation' of production by the globalisation of a common standard for
justice and ethics. That may sound mild to the point of herbivorous: I
can assure you it will not be in the least a moderate undertaking. It will
provide more than enough scope for the most ambitious radical."[307]

It's suggestive that Hitchens added the disclaimer about how this
political project—a more sweeping and inspiring project than anything
our species has ever attempted—wouldn't be a "moderate undertaking."
Radicals aren't supposed to call for NATO to enforce international law
and protect human rights, nor are they supposed to defend "neoliberal"
institutions like the European Union or call upon America to use its
power to prevent and punish atrocities. And they certainly aren't supposed to make the case that good old liberal democracy is the most revolutionary force on earth. But that's what Hitchens did, and it's why his

work as a left-wing heretic after 1989 will long outlive his work as a socialist who had no idea how soon dusk would fall.

4 Iraq

Hitchens on Interventionism

Hitchens died on December 15, 2011—the day a ceremony was held in Baghdad to mark the end of the Iraq War.[1] While tributes to Hitchens poured in, a headline in the *Huffington Post* announced: "Christopher Hitchens, Despite Criticism And Casualties, Defended Iraq War To The End."[2] An article in the *Economist* observed that "Hitchens's support for the invasion of Iraq largely ruined his writing for me, for most of the last decade."[3] In a piece published the day after Hitchens's death, *Gawker* reporter John Cook argued that his position on Iraq was the "unforgivable mistake" of his career: ". . . it must not be forgotten in mourning him that he got the single most consequential decision in his life horrifically, petulantly wrong."[4]

These posthumous indictments weren't much of a surprise. In the years following the invasion of Iraq, many pro-war writers and intellectuals retreated from their position when it became clear that the occupation would be bloodier, longer, and more destabilizing than they had anticipated. But Hitchens became all the more immovable in his support. He sometimes admitted what he got wrong, such as underestimating the strength of the insurgency (a word he wouldn't have used) and overestimating the Bush administration's competence—for example, he decried the "near-impeachable irresponsibility in the matter of postwar planning."[5] But on the core issue of whether Saddam Hussein should have been removed by force, he never yielded.

Hitchens was wrong about many of the issues that were central to the administration's case for war. In October 2002, he told readers of the *Nation*: "I don't particularly care, even in a small way, to be a hostage of Saddam Hussein myself. There is not the least doubt that he has acquired some of the means of genocide and hopes to collect some more."[6] A few months later, he argued that Iraq would soon be buying plutonium from North Korea if Hussein wasn't removed from power.[7] This was part of his case that Baghdad was prepared to purchase all the components it needed for a nuclear weapons program "off the shelf"[8]— an argument that drastically overstated Iraq's ability to build such a program. At a time when Bush administration officials were terrifying Americans with apocalyptic imagery—"We don't want the smoking gun to be a mushroom cloud," National Security Advisor Condoleezza Rice said in January 2003[9]—Hitchens contributed to this hysteria. He later argued that "Bush and Blair made a hash of a good case, largely because they preferred to scare people rather than enlighten them or reason with them."[10] But this is exactly what he did with loose talk of retail plutonium, weapons of genocide, and so on.

In April 2004, after the evidence for the existence of Iraqi weapons of mass destruction had fallen apart, Hitchens said "we can now be sure" the weapons posed no threat.[11] This was an argument he made frequently—that it would have been reckless to "accept Saddam Hussein's word for it"[12] on the question of compliance with the relevant UN resolutions. He believed the only way to confirm that Iraq didn't have stockpiles of illegal weapons was to invade the country: ". . . no credible inspection could be conducted on any other terms," he wrote,[13] despite the fact that

UNSCOM had spent almost a decade cataloging and dismantling Iraq's arsenal after the Gulf War.[14] This means he thought the entire debate about weapons and UN inspections was pointless from the outset—the invasion had to take place no matter what.

In February 2003, Hitchens declared that al-Qaeda and Saddam Hussein "operate in an unspoken but increasingly obvious alliance. It's a sort of Hitler-Stalin pact."[15] Hitchens was right to reject the idea that "there's no connection between Saddam Hussein and the world of terror"[16] (Hussein was a notorious sponsor of international terrorism), but Baghdad's support for the Abu Nidal Organization, the Palestine Liberation Front, and other terrorist groups shouldn't be conflated with support for al-Qaeda—much less a role in September 11.

Hitchens also severely misjudged the length and intensity of the war. During a different 2003 debate, he announced: "I haven't used the word war all evening. There will be no war, but there will be a fairly brief and ruthless military intervention to remove the Saddam Hussein regime, long overdue."[17] His opponent, Mark Danner, replied, "Orwell would be proud of that construction."[18] Hitchens had a habit of making confident declarations about how quickly and painlessly conflicts would end. In a November 2001 article, he argued that "The Taliban will soon be history."[19] Two weeks later, he observed that the overthrow of the Taliban had been accomplished with "no serious loss of civilian life."[20] Hitchens's early analysis of the Iraq War didn't age any better. In a December 2003 article, he observed that there had been "no humanitarian meltdown" and "no mass civilian casualties" in the country.[21]

Hitchens's critics have no shortage of material to work with, but no argument should be judged by its weaknesses alone. Yet this is what has happened to Hitchens's case for the removal of Saddam Hussein—it has been disfigured by summary after summary like the one you just read with no attempt to consider his views as a whole. While Hitchens was often wrong about Iraq, he was right that Saddam Hussein's regime was one of the most crushing tyrannies on earth. Grant every argument about his lack of foresight and his insistence on the presence of weapons and terrorist connections that didn't exist, and you're still left with that terrible, unalterable fact.

Patrick Cockburn observed that nobody at Hitchens's memorial—during which many of his friends read excerpts of his work—spoke about the "main feature of Christopher's literary and political career over the past decade. This was his support for the wars fought by the U.S., with Britain as its main ally, in Iraq and Afghanistan."[22] Cockburn noted that Hitchens's editor at *Vanity Fair*, Graydon Carter, mentioned his "'curious pro-war stance before the invasion of Iraq,' as if he was noting a bizarre taste in socks or ties."[23] Hitchens's adversaries recall his support for the Iraq War with relish—as if the words "Hitchens supported the invasion of Iraq" constitute an argument in and of themselves—while many of his admirers reflect on it with incredulity and embarrassment. But Hitchens's position on Iraq wasn't incidental to his political identity in his final decade. In fact, when placed in the context of his evolving views about the United States, interventionism, and universal human rights, it wasn't even all that surprising.

* * *

To many left-wing critics of the Iraq War, it's absurd to claim that Hitchens was doing anything other than shilling for an imperial project launched by a Republican administration and supported by a cabal of sinister neoconservatives. The evidence that Hitchens had crossed over to the right appeared overwhelming: he became friends with Paul Wolfowitz, wrote pro-war articles for the *Weekly Standard*,[24] and spoke about the threat of "Islamofascism" at the David Horowitz Freedom Center[25]—what more did you need to know? But the Iraq War had plenty of supporters on the left, such as Paul Berman, George Packer, and Kanan Makiya. Several of the New Philosophers in France also supported the war, including André Glucksmann and Pascal Bruckner. In a 2007 essay,

Hitchens wrote, "Of the defenders of the liberation of Iraq in the British media and political spheres ... most of the best-known spokesmen—Nick Cohen of the *Observer*, the *Financial Times's* John Lloyd, and parliamentarians Denis MacShane, Peter Hain, and John Reid—belonged to the traditional Left."[26]

Even if there had been no left-wing support for the Iraq War, it wouldn't have mattered to Hitchens, who wasn't particularly concerned about who his political allies happened to be in the last decade of his life. In *Hitch-22*, he dismisses the idea that "by taking up some out-of-line position I would find myself 'in bed with,' as the saying went, unsavory elements. It's good to throw off this sort of moral blackmail and mind-forged manacle as early in life as one can."[27] In *Letters to a Young Contrarian*, he counsels readers not to "worry too much about who your friends are, or what company you may be keeping."[28] He continues:

> Any cause worth fighting for will attract a plethora of people: I have spoken on platforms with Communists about South Africa and with "Cold Warriors" about Czechoslovakia; in the case of Bosnia I spoke with Muslims who disagreed with me about Salman Rushdie and Jews who suspected me because I have always supported statehood for the Palestinians.[29]

Although he wrote that passage years before the invasion of Iraq, he also mentions "making common cause with neoconservatives" on intervention in the Balkans. In a 1997 interview, he criticized the factions on the right that were opposed to taking action in Bosnia, observing that the "only ones who said any differently were the neocons, and for them the alarm-bell word was 'genocide.' Left and liberal people were saying, 'Well, we don't want another quagmire like Vietnam.'"[30] Many neoconservatives were in favor of the interventions in Bosnia and Kosovo, while right-wing realists such as Brent Scowcroft, James Baker (who famously said the United States had "no dog in that fight" as the former Yugoslavia imploded),[31] and Colin Powell were opposed.[32] The future

Bush administration wasn't keen on interventionism—just before the 2000 election, George W. Bush said he would bring the United States' peacekeeping mission in the Balkans to an end. "We don't need to have the 82nd Airborne escorting kids to kindergarten," Condoleezza Rice declared.[33, 34]

In *The Assassins' Gate: America In Iraq*, Packer points out that "several of the most prominent Iraq hawks came from the left. Most prominent of all was Hitchens."[35] But the Iraq War also split the interventionist left, especially in Europe. German Foreign Minister Joschka Fischer rebuffed Secretary of Defense Donald Rumsfeld at a European defense conference in Munich when Rumsfeld attempted to make the case for war: "Excuse me, I am not convinced," Fischer said. "I cannot go to the public and say these are the reasons [to go to war] because I don't believe in them."[36] Daniel Cohn-Bendit was less delicate: ". . . your government has been behaving like the Bolsheviks in the Russian Revolution," he told Bush administration advisor Richard Perle a few weeks before the invasion. "You want to change the whole world!"[37]

According to Hitchens, his brother Peter once described the invasion of Iraq as a "stupid, left-wing war"—a comment he believed was "nearer to the mark" than the claim that he had moved to the right by supporting it.[38] A central theme of Hitchens's pro-war writing was the idea that the left had become conservative—even reactionary—in what he regarded as necessary confrontations with post–Cold War dictatorships. He attacked left-wingers who preferred the "stolid pragmatism of Nixon, Kissinger, and Scowcroft to the Utopian schemes and dreams of the neocons. In such a conservative worldview, what's the need for a left in the first place?"[39] When the left "hears the term 'regime change' and responds with anxious whimpers about 'destabilization,'" he asked, "Who are the radicals here?"[40]

Hitchens always bristled when interlocutors described Saddam Hussein as a "bad guy." As in: *Sure, Saddam was a bad guy, but the Iraq War was still a disaster.* "Anyone who starts a sentence saying that," Hitchens argued, "knows and cares nothing about Iraq."[41] He observed that Hussein was one of a handful of dictators who had "done their considerable best to ruin the promise of the post Cold War years and to impose themselves even more ruthlessly on their own peoples and neighbors."[42] In the face of these persistent threats, Hitchens accused the left of an "affectless, neutralist, smirking isolationism" and asked "since when is the Left supposed to argue for preservation of the status quo?"[43] He continued:

> You might think that the Left could have a regime-change perspective of its own, based on solidarity with its comrades abroad. After all, Saddam's ruling Ba'ath Party consolidated its power by first destroying the Iraqi communist and labor movements, and then turning on the Kurds (whose cause, historically, has been one of the main priorities of the Left in the Middle East). When I first became a socialist, the imperative of international solidarity was the essential if not the defining thing, whether the cause was popular or risky or not.[44]

Hitchens never forgot how brutal and dysfunctional the status quo was in Iraq, nor did he forget the horrors that created it. A year after a bloody purge of Baath Party officials in 1979, which marked Saddam Hussein's formal seizure of power, he launched an eight-year war with Iran—one of the longest conventional interstate wars of the twentieth century, which left 680,000 dead and missing and over 1.5 million wounded.[45] Hussein invaded Iran to annex territory in the southwest of the country,[46] but much of the war was fought in a state of grinding stasis with grisly echoes of World War I:[47, 48] soldiers dug into trenches, human wave assaults, massive battles that left tens of thousands dead and wounded (such as Operation Ramadan,[49] a major Iranian offensive near Basra and one of the largest land battles since World War II), and the systematic use of chemical weapons[50]—the largest deployment of weapons of mass destruction since the atomic bombings of Hiroshima and Nagasaki.

The United States supported Baghdad during the Iran-Iraq War (which began a year after the Iranian Revolution removed the U.S.-backed Shah).[51] In a 1991 essay, Hitchens asked readers to "imagine Washington's response if Saddam Hussein had launched an attack when the Shah ruled Iran. Or, to bring matters up to date, ask yourself why Iraq's 1980 assault was not a violation of international law or an act of naked aggression that 'would not stand'"[52]—a reference to President George H.W. Bush's rhetoric about Iraq's invasion of Kuwait.

Many of the principles that led Hitchens to support the Iraq War were the same ones that drove his opposition to the callous and amoral realpolitik that had long characterized the United States' involvement in the Middle East. "Crimes and blunders" like the United States' support for Saddam Hussein, Hitchens argued, "will necessitate future wars."[53] At the time, this was a mordant observation about what he viewed as an incompetent, war-mongering establishment in Washington. But it was prescient in a way he couldn't have anticipated in 1991, and he would have been shocked to discover that he would one day be among the voices arguing that a war with Saddam Hussein was necessary.

Hitchens was always a strong critic of the realist school of international relations scholarship, the proponents of which often counsel inaction in the face of humanitarian catastrophes that don't sufficiently threaten America's "vital interests." When realists call for action, it's typically to maintain a volatile balance of power like the one between Iran and Iraq in the 1980s. In *The Hell of Good Intentions: America's Foreign Policy Elite and the Decline of U.S. Primacy*, realist scholar Stephen Walt celebrates the virtues of "offshore balancing"—the strategic mechanism through which realists argue that the United States can prevent other powers from becoming dominant in their regions—with reference to America's support for eight years of pointless war prosecuted by Saddam Hussein: "The Reagan administration," Walt writes, "helped thwart an Iranian victory in the Iran-Iraq War (1980–88) by giving Saddam Hussein military intelligence and other forms of assistance."[54] To Walt, this is an example of the "reassuring history" of offshore balancing—part of a broader strategy which "prevented the emergence of dangerous regional hegemons and preserved a global balance of power that maximized U.S. security."[55] But to Hitchens, it was evidence of the way Washington had long used human beings as raw material to secure its short-term interests in the region.

What about its long-term interests? As Hitchens noted, U.S. support for Saddam Hussein as his forces slaughtered hundreds of thousands of Iranians in a pointless land grab wasn't quickly forgotten in Tehran, and the Iran-Iraq War was the training ground for a cadre of hardened Iranian officers like Qasem Soleimani, who would go on to foment chaos and bloodshed across the region for decades.[56] Syrian President Bashar al-Assad has received significant military support from Iran's Quds Force, which Soleimani led, and the malign influence of Iranian proxies in countries like Iraq and Lebanon has fueled sectarianism and violence for decades.[57] These proxies were also responsible for the deaths of many American soldiers during the Iraq War, one of the reasons cited by the Trump administration for assassinating Soleimani with an airstrike in early 2020.[58]

Of course, none of this is to say the Revolutionary Guards wouldn't have exploited the sectarian conflict in Iraq to increase Iranian influence in the country if the United States had adopted a different policy during the Iran-Iraq War. But it's a reminder that Washington's support for Baghdad may have had unforeseen consequences beyond the horror of subsidizing and perpetuating a war that left hundreds of thousands dead. As Hitchens put it in a 2010 interview: "... this playing off of Iran against Iraq is one of the foulest parts of the recent statecraft. What one wants is to end it by putting both countries in the control of their own people."[59]

* * *

Supporting Saddam Hussein's insane war against Iran was bad enough, but continuing to support him as he committed genocide against Iraq's Kurds was the nadir of the United States' ugly relationship with Baghdad in the 1980s. During the Iran-Iraq War, Kurdish *peshmerga* forces took advantage of the conflict to launch a guerrilla campaign against the regime.[60] As the war neared its end, Hussein appointed his cousin Gen. Ali Hassan al-Majid to wage a merciless campaign against the rebels who had taken refuge in villages across northern Iraq, or as al-Majid put it in a haunting echo of Nazi propaganda, to "solve the Kurdish problem and slaughter the saboteurs."[61] The Iraqis called this campaign "Anfal" ("Spoils of War"), and it was by no means limited to the rebels who were waging war on Baghdad.

As a 1993 Human Rights Watch report explained, Anfal led to "mass summary executions and mass disappearance of many tens of thousands of non-combatants, including large numbers of women and children, and sometimes the entire population of villages."[62] It was a scorched earth assault on Iraq's Kurds, targeting homes, schools, mosques, and infrastructure; forcibly displacing hundreds of thousands; and imprisoning victims in "conditions of extreme deprivation" or leaving them to die in the desert with no food, water, or basic necessities.[63]

Al-Majid, who Human Rights Watch described as the "overlord of the Kurdish genocide,"[64] became known to the world as "Chemical Ali."[65] During the Iran-Iraq War, Baghdad repeatedly used chemical weapons against Iranian troops, often with the knowledge of the CIA and other Western intelligence agencies.[66] In *A Poisonous Affair: America, Iraq, and the Gassing of Halabja*, Joost R. Hiltermann argues that Iraq's deployment of chemical weapons was likely the "qualitative factor that led to the Kurdish insurgency's collapse, as well as the Iranian leadership's decision to sue for peace."[67] Hiltermann points out that chemical weapons were instrumental in grinding down a resilient Kurdish resistance: ". . . the Anfal campaign led to the methodical murder of tens of thousands of Kurdish civilians—first flushed out of their villages by poison gas, then hauled to transit centers, sorted by age and sex, and carted off to execution sites in Iraq's western desert, far from Kurdistan."[68]

The single most horrific event of the Anfal campaign was the chemical attack on Halabja in March 1988, which caused the agonizing deaths of several thousand Kurdish civilians.[69] The United States didn't just fail to take action after Halabja—it masked Iraqi culpability. Hiltermann outlines this sordid history in a chapter titled "Fixing the Evidence," which observes that the United States publicly questioned Iraq's role in the Halabja massacre by suggesting that Iran was responsible, despite a mountain of evidence to the contrary.[70] As Hiltermann explains, officials in Washington "worked actively to oppose a strong and unambiguous Security Council condemnation of their Iraqi allies."[71] The motives were no secret: "Powerful factions inside the Reagan administration, the DIA [Defense Intelligence Agency] in particular, were squarely behind the Iraqi war effort."[72] Hiltermann argues that Washington may have emboldened Hussein to continue the Anfal genocide by obscuring the evidence of his crimes and sending "repeated signals to Iraq that the regime could continue, and even escalate, chemical weapons use."[73]

As the Gulf War came to a close in February 1991, the United States offered a different sort of encouragement—this time to Saddam Hussein's enemies. In a speech delivered two weeks before the end of the war, President George H.W. Bush called upon the "Iraqi military and the Iraqi people to take matters into their own hands, to force Saddam Hussein, the dictator, to step aside."[74] Bush made the same appeal in a speech later that day at a Raytheon plant in Massachusetts.[75] During the war, Coalition aircraft dropped leaflets that read, "O you soldier and civilian, young man and old, O you women and men, let's fill the streets and the alleys and bring down Saddam Hussein and his aides."[76]

Rebels in the Kurdish north and Shia south heeded Bush's words and took up arms against the regime with the reasonable expectation of American support.[77] But despite the fact that hundreds of thousands of U.S. troops were still deployed in the Gulf, that support never materialized. Some members of the Bush administration argued that the United

States should aid the rebels with airstrikes and other forms of military assistance,[78] but Bush and Scowcroft preferred to allow the regime to slaughter the rebels with no interference from the colossal military machine that had just pushed that regime's forces out of Kuwait in a matter of months. Scowcroft later described the rebels as "malcontents" and dismissed the significance of Bush's "impulsive ad lib" about overthrowing Hussein, which he claimed amounted to little more than a "routine speech in Washington."[79]

Beyond the routine cruelty and cynicism on display from the Bush administration, the United States directly facilitated the massacre of Iraqi rebels and civilians. When an Iraqi commander asked Gen. Norman Schwarzkopf if the regime could continue using armed helicopter gunships after the war, he replied, "Yeah. I will instruct our Air Force not to shoot at any helicopters that are flying over the territory of Iraq where we are not located."[80] Schwarzkopf later claimed that he was "suckered" into allowing Saddam's air force to cut down Kurdish and Shia rebels along with many Iraqi civilians,[81] but he explicitly granted this permission. He even told the commander how Iraqi helicopters should be marked to avoid being shot at, and said he wanted to "make sure that's recorded, that military helicopters can fly over Iraq."[82] He continued: "If they must fly over the area we are located in, I prefer that they not be gunships, armed helos, and I would prefer that they have an orange tag on the side as an extra safety measure."[83]

Washington could have ordered the airborne assault to stop at any time. On March 30, 1991, the *Washington Post* reported that "U.S. military commanders say pilots flying routine combat air patrols over Iraqi territory could readily shoot down many of the helicopters if Washington so authorized."[84] But Bush could only muster a warning that helicopters "should not be used for combat purposes inside Iraq."[85] When the United States announced that it wouldn't shoot down Iraqi helicopters, thousands of Kurds fled across the Turkish border. In a 2003 article, Hitchens summarized what happened after Schwarzkopf assured the Iraqis that Coalition forces wouldn't fire upon their military helicopters—there was a

> rain of horror from the sky as the Baath Party and its airborne gunships restored order, cleared a space for the special police squads and Republican Guard, slaughtered as many as 60,000 Shia civilians, shelled the holy sites of Najaf and Karbala, and recaptured all of the other places whose names have lately become familiar to a mass readership, or in some cases familiar again.[86]

Chemical Ali was in charge of putting down the Shia revolt in the south, and he did so with indiscriminate massacres of rebels and civilians, medieval methods of execution (such as drawing and quartering between trucks), and the destruction of entire villages.[87] Regime forces killed more than 20,000 Kurds and displaced as many as 2 million, who believed a second Anfal was underway.[88] This humanitarian disaster prompted the United States, Britain, and France to launch Operation Provide Comfort, which assisted Kurdish refugees and established a no-fly zone over northern Iraq. Another no-fly zone was imposed over southern Iraq in August 1992, and both were patrolled by Western aircraft until the Iraq War in 2003. Meanwhile, Saddam Hussein remained in power and Iraqis suffered under 13 years of sanctions.

* * *

In an essay published immediately after the invasion of Iraq, Hitchens referred to the post-Gulf War period—during which Saddam Hussein repeatedly fired on Coalition aircraft, threatened to invade Kuwait a second time in 1994, continued to menace the Kurds and Shia, and held onto power even as his country fell to pieces—as part of a continuous conflict that had "smoldered on for more than a dozen years, like a fire deep in a bad old mine, and was only now being brought to a conclusion."[89] Hitchens said he felt déjà vu when in 2003 he recalled what he saw during an earlier visit to Iraq after the Gulf War:

> When I look at my old notes and photographs I start to quiver. Here it all is. The victims of chemical bombing in the city of Halabja, some of them with injuries that were still burning and festering. Villages voided and scorched by Saddam's ethnic cleansing, in a darkened landscape that seems to stretch to hell and back. White-faced refugees and defectors from the South, telling stories of oppression that harrow the soul.[90]

Hitchens argued that the years between those conflicts were "eaten by the locusts." This is the theme of his 2003 collection of essays *A Long Short War: The Postponed Liberation of Iraq*—that the status quo in Iraq was intolerable, and that the United States had essentially been at war with Hussein since the invasion of Kuwait.[91] While the invasion of Iraq turned into a long long war, Hitchens argued that the country was already on the precipice of implosion before 2003—it was a "ruined and tortured and collapsing" state that would have eventually necessitated an intervention whether the United States invaded or not.[92] Hitchens insisted that Iraq would have "become to the region what the Congo is to Central Africa: a vortex of chaos and misery that would draw in opportunistic interventions from Turkey, Iran, and Saudi Arabia."[93] There's no way of knowing what would have happened had the United States not invaded (Hitchens often presented counterfactual scenarios with too much confidence), and interventions from regional powers took place in Iraq despite the presence of American troops. However, Hitchens's basic point that it's important to "compare the current state of the country with the likely or probable state of it had Saddam and his sons been allowed to go on ruling"[94] deserves to be taken seriously.

Hitchens argued that the post-invasion civil war in Iraq was partly a manifestation of sectarian hatreds that were suppurating beneath the surface of Iraqi society for many years. When he was asked if he should have predicted that a civil war would erupt after the invasion, he responded, "Only to the extent that there was pre-existing unease and mistrust between the different population groups in Iraq. Since it was the policy of Saddam Hussein to govern by divide-and-rule and precisely to exacerbate these differences, it is unlikely that civil peace would have been the result of prolonging his regime."[95] This divide-and-rule policy was intensified after the Gulf War, and it fed the sectarianism that ghoulish outsiders like Abu Musab al-Zarqawi (the leader of Al-Qaeda in Iraq) exploited to foment a civil war after the invasion. As Hitchens often pointed out, Zarqawi fled from Afghanistan to Iraq after the fall of the Taliban, so he was already operating in the country when the invasion took place (he also spent time in Iran and Syria during this period).[96] Iraqi society was completely Balkanized in the years after the Gulf War, as Kanan Makiya explains in his introduction to the 1998 edition of *Republic of Fear: The Politics of Modern Iraq*:

> The regime turned to inculcating sectarianism, confessionalism, and tribalism as its new legitimating instruments of rule. . . . Virtually from the day the cease-fire in the Gulf War came into effect, Saddam Husain switched to a policy of promoting sectarianism between Shi'is and Sunnis in Iraq. (In much the same way, Slobodan Milosevic, a former Communist, fomented Serbian nationalism as a way of holding on to power in a collapsing Yugoslavia.)[97]

Although *Republic of Fear* is an analysis of how the Baath Party managed to dominate Iraq for decades—through a totalitarian system of pervasive brutality and shared complicity, in which as many Iraqis as possible were implicated in the regime's crimes—by the time Makiya wrote his introduction to the updated edition (September 1997), he believed this system was unraveling. As he explains, the "absolutism of the Republic of Fear was breaking down. Rank-and-file soldiers were deserting Saddam Husain's army in record numbers. Iraqis were speaking out and telling their stories like they had not done before."[98] Meanwhile, Makiya observes that middle-class Iraqis were "learning what it meant to be hungry for the first time in their lives"[99] as the economy collapsed under sanctions, the rule of law frayed in Baghdad and across the country, and Hussein's forces continued to torment the Kurds in the north and the Shia in the south as punishment for the uprising. "Under such conditions," Makiya writes, "it was neither effective nor possible to shoot and torture everybody."[100]

Hitchens argued that "Iraq was headed straight for implosion and failure, both as a state *and* a society, well before 2003."[101] He observed that "All the crucial indices, from illiteracy to unemployment to the emigration of talent and skill, were rapidly heading south," going on to contend that "U.S. policy could hardly be indifferent to this distress and misery and demagogy, if only because the whole context was shaped by two largely American decisions. The first was to allow Saddam to remain in power after 1991 and to watch while he massacred the Shiites and Kurds. . . . The second was to impose sanctions, which, unduly prolonged, did far more damage to an already distraught society than they did to the ruthless and corrupt regime."[102]

The dire conditions in Iraq were summarized in an October 1994 article in the *New York Times*: "This country of 20 million people . . . remains financially broken, lurching from one crisis to another. Unable to sell its oil and buy food, medicine and spare parts except under United Nations conditions that it refuses to accept, Iraq faces famine and economic collapse."[103] The article documented surging rates of burglary, theft, and rape; a 9 percent rise in malnutrition among Iraqi infants (reported by UNICEF); and engineers, doctors, and lawyers making between $6 and $10 per month, while retirees tried to survive on $3.[104] An Iraqi dinar was worth about $3 before the Gulf War, but a single dollar was worth between 500 and 600 dinars by 1994.[105] Iraqis weren't exactly flourishing in the late 1980s, either, as Saddam Hussein gassed the Kurds and the nation staggered out of eight years of warfare with Iran (which cost billions of loaned dollars to wage[106]—one of the factors that led to the invasion of Kuwait).

Meanwhile, the regime remained an Orwellian presence in the lives of many Iraqis. Despite the immense suffering and discontent of the Iraqi people, Hussein maintained what Makiya describes as a "coup-proof" grip on the country under the protection of his sprawling and impenetrable security and intelligence apparatus.[107] The above-mentioned *New York Times* article captured the dystopian experience of Iraqi citizens, particularly in areas where the regime was in full control:

> The Iraqi President has rarely appeared in public in the last few years, but his presence remains overwhelming. He appears in taped television programs broadcast daily. His face peers down from thousands of posters and statues throughout the country. He continues to claim victories and inveigh against enemies from the United States to Saudi Arabia, promising almost weekly an imminent lifting of the United Nations sanctions.[108]

Although the Iraqi government had lost considerable influence in the north and south of the country, Iraq's Kurds and Shia still weren't safe from Baghdad during the 1990s, despite the presence of NATO aircraft in their skies. Makiya reminds us that, on August 30, 1996, Hussein "sent his tanks and forty thousand crack Republican Guard troops into Arbil, inside the safe-haven area set up by the allied coalition in 1991. The secret police followed in their wake, penetrating deep into Iraqi Kurdistan, killing hundreds and arresting thousands of oppositionists who had believed in American promises of protection."[109] Hussein was invited to Erbil (sometimes spelled as Arbil) by Massoud Barzani, head of the Kurdistan Democratic Party, amid fighting between this party and the Patriotic Union of Kurdistan. Hitchens emphasized other ways Iraqis remained vulnerable after the Gulf War, writing that the no-fly zones "managed to protect the Kurds and Shiites from a repeat performance of the mass murders of 1991 and earlier but did not prevent, for example, the planned destruction of the largest wetlands in the Middle East, home to the 5,000-year-old civilization of the Marsh Arabs."[110] As

Baghdad continued to torture its own population, Iraq's neighbors could never relax, either—in 1994, Hussein shocked the world by positioning his troops to invade Kuwait again.[111]

U.S. policy toward Iraq in the 1990s maintained a grim and unstable status quo—significant chunks of the country remained outside Hussein's control, the economic crisis was becoming more desperate by the day, and there was no reason to believe the situation would improve. In a 1999 essay, Hitchens argued that the "policy toward Baghdad has been without pulse or direction or principle ever since Mr. Clinton took office. As one who spent some horrible days in Halabja, the Kurdish city that was ethnically cleansed by Saddam's chemical bombs, I have followed Washington's recent maneuvers with great attention."[112] One of these maneuvers was the bombing of Iraq in December 1998, after which the "Saddam Hussein regime survived with contemptuous ease," Hitchens wrote, "while its civilian hostages suffered yet again."[113] Despite the mounting crises in Iraq, there was no indication that the regime would fall—Makiya explains that this condemned Iraqis to a state of permanent immiseration:

> The Iraqi case has a lot to teach us about what happens to an outlaw state that is not overthrown when it consistently breaches international norms but is subjected to a combined regime of sanctions and unbridled tyranny: it corrodes and rots, devastating and impoverishing the vast majority of the population, without necessarily becoming any easier to revolt against or overthrow from the inside.[114]

After Iraq's humiliating defeat in the Gulf War, a column of tanks was rolling through Basra when a commander parked in front of a huge mural of Hussein. As a crowd gathered, he climbed on top of his tank and shouted down the regime before getting back in, swiveling the turret toward the mural, and puncturing the dictator's face with several shells. Makiya describes this as a "classic revolutionary moment"[115]—the sort of image the Western world celebrated as Soviet governments fell across

Eastern Europe less than two years earlier. But instead of taking advantage of this unprecedented revolutionary moment at the end of the Gulf War—when Iraqi dissidents were calling upon the forces that had just bombarded their cities to depose their leaders—the United States allowed Hussein to slaughter the rebels with impunity and launch a years-long campaign of reprisal during which thousands more were killed, tortured, and imprisoned.

Like Hitchens, Makiya argues that this betrayal was to blame for the slow-moving calamity that befell Iraq between 1991 and 2003: "All the important issues since then go back to that war's unfinished business," Makiya writes, "and a veritable American obsession with containing the adversary, as opposed to getting on with the obvious business of helping Iraqis to topple him."[116]

* * *

In April 1991, the United Nations adopted Resolution 688, which called upon Iraq to "allow immediate access by international humanitarian organizations to all those in need of assistance in all parts of Iraq and make available all necessary facilities for their operations."[117] While the resolution affirmed the commitment to "respect the sovereignty, territorial integrity and political independence of Iraq,"[118] Makiya argues that it represented the "first time that the United Nations had asserted a right of interference in the internal affairs of a member state."[119] Bernard Kouchner helped to draft the text.[120] The United States launched Operation Provide Comfort immediately after Resolution 688 was adopted.[121]

According to Hitchens, the "only speech by any statesman that can bear reprinting from that low, dishonest decade [the 1990s] came from Tony Blair when he spoke in Chicago in 1999."[122] But in that speech—which argued for Western military action in Kosovo and the necessity of interventionism more broadly—Blair emphasized the "need to focus in a serious and sustained way on the principles of the doctrine of international community *and on the institutions that deliver them.*"[123] He criticized the "ad hoc" approach to issues of international security and called for a "reconsideration of the role, workings, and decision-making process of the United Nations, and in particular the UN Security Council."[124] This demand is all the more pressing today, as Russia and China become more aggressive and authoritarian—the opposite of what many governments and analysts expected in the optimistic years following the Cold War, and a reality that cripples the Security Council in the face of flagrant violations of international law and human rights.

In Chicago, Blair made the case for establishing and strengthening formal international structures that could protect human rights and punish those who violate them—a project the Iraq War undermined, as it demonstrated that large states would submit to the rule of law only when it suited them. A decade later, Blair delivered another speech in Chicago, which noted that pre-September 11 military interventions had been "undertaken with . . . a humanitarian purpose, had been relatively self-contained, short in duration and plainly successful."[125] Blair cited the British intervention in Sierra Leone: "The gangsters were stopped, the Government saved and in late 2007, the people of Sierra Leone changed [the] ruling party by the ballot box, and without bloodshed."[126] After September 11, Blair acknowledged that circumstances "changed radically"—the long wars in Afghanistan and Iraq had led to "fatigue with an interventionist foreign policy,"[127] and "as time has passed, so has the familiar certainty that our power would always triumph."[128] While Blair still believed in the interventionist principles he outlined in 1999, he recognized the political cost of putting those principles into practice.

Hitchens argued that Iraq in 2003 "met all the conditions under which a country may be deemed to have sacrificed its own legal sovereignty. To recapitulate: It had invaded its neighbors, committed genocide on its own soil, harbored and nurtured international thugs and killers, and flouted every provision of the Non-Proliferation Treaty."[129] Of course Saddam Hussein could have been convicted on all these charges, but it's impossible to argue that the Iraq War was launched in compliance with international law. The United States justified the war with reference to UN Resolutions 678 and 687, which authorized the use of force if Hussein was in material breach of his disarmament obligations.[130, 131] Though the resolutions were adopted during and after the Gulf War, they were affirmed in Resolution 1441, which was adopted in November 2002.[132] This didn't mean the United States could unilaterally decide that Iraq wasn't in compliance and invade the country—military action has to be authorized by the Security Council.

Hitchens often criticized the United Nations for its failures in Rwanda and Sudan.[133, 134, 135] But in a case like Rwanda, where 800,000 people were killed in under one hundred days, relatively modest military action could have prevented an imminent massacre on a vast scale—a situation hardly analogous to Iraq, brutal as conditions were under Saddam Hussein and sanctions. One of the tragedies of the Iraq War is the fact that it slowed the momentum toward the establishment of new laws and norms around sovereignty and intervention. Just a few years after UN Secretary General Kofi Annan declared that "state sovereignty, in its most basic sense, is being redefined" and argued that intervention was necessary in cases of "gross and systematic violations of human rights that offend every precept of our common humanity,"[136] he described the Iraq War as illegal and said, "I hope we do not see another Iraq-type operation for a long time."[137]

The Iraq War didn't just have a corrosive effect on the authority of the United Nations; it was also harmful to the world's most important military alliance. After September 11, NATO immediately invoked Article V—the collective defense provision which affirms that an attack on one member state is an attack on all—and took an active role in the war in Afghanistan. Iraq, on the other hand, led to a major break within the alliance. France and Germany were opposed to the war—recall Fischer's comment to Rumsfeld: "Excuse me, I am not convinced"[138]—and although NATO countries took part, the alliance as an entity did not.

The Iraq War made American voters wary of interventionism as well. Presidents Barack Obama and Donald Trump both campaigned on their opposition to the war (in the latter's case, disingenuously), and its unpopularity[139] in the United States has made interventionism a significant political liability. This is why a catastrophe like the Syrian Civil War—which has left hundreds of thousands dead and created one of the largest refugee crises since World War II—doesn't prompt much self-criticism in the United States or other Western countries. Regardless of how nightmarish the situation becomes in Syria, it can always be argued that intervention would only make matters worse. This is the case Obama made as president. As the death toll exploded in Syria and refugees poured across its borders, he resisted "calls for military action, because we cannot resolve someone else's civil war through force, particularly after a decade of war in Iraq and Afghanistan."[140] While Obama wanted the Assad regime out of power, he argued: "I don't think we should remove another dictator with force—we learned from Iraq that doing so makes us responsible for all that comes next."[141]

However, after Assad allegedly used chemical weapons against Syrian civilians in 2013, Obama couldn't decide what to do. A year before the attacks, he said the deployment of such weapons crossed a "red line," which would mean "enormous consequences" for the Assad regime.[142] When evidence emerged that Assad's forces had indeed massacred hundreds of people (including many children) with chemical weapons in Ghouta in August 2013,[143] the administration appeared to be preparing to launch airstrikes. But the following month, Obama delivered a convoluted speech that attempted to explain why the United States wouldn't retaliate against Assad after all. First, he argued that it was necessary to seek Congressional approval for airstrikes. Then he asked Congress to postpone this decision while the United States worked with Russia to remove Assad's stockpile of chemical weapons.[144]

While the main point of the speech was to announce a diplomatic response to the attack, Obama spent much of it justifying a military strike he didn't intend to launch. In response to the allegation that such a strike would merely be a "pinprick," he retorted: "Let me make something clear: The United States military doesn't do pinpricks. Even a limited strike will send a message to Assad that no other nation can deliver. . . . a targeted strike can make Assad, or any other dictator, think twice before using chemical weapons."[145] Why would Assad think twice before using chemical weapons when Obama declared in advance that a demonstrative strike was all he was willing to consider? The successful effort to remove most of Assad's chemical weapons was an important non-proliferation victory, but Human Rights Watch reported that the regime's use of these weapons remained "widespread and systematic" in the years that followed.[146]

Obama's Syria policy was warped by domestic politics and the incapacitating fear of getting into "another Iraq." He returned to Iraq again and again in his speech about Assad and chemical weapons,[147] but he didn't mention Saddam Hussein's gassing of the Kurds when he discussed the history of chemical warfare, despite the fact that the attack on Halabja was a far more apposite historical parallel than the examples he used: World War I and the gas chambers of the Holocaust.[148] As always, Obama only emphasized Iraq as a warning.

Obama was well aware that military action doesn't invariably draw the United States into costly Iraq-like occupations. In 2011, the United States took part in a NATO-led campaign to protect Libyan civilians from a massacre at the hands of Muammar Gaddafi's forces, which were poised to attack Benghazi after Gaddafi announced that he would clear out the "cockroaches" and "rats" who resisted him "inch by inch, room by room, home by home, alleyway by alleyway, person by person."[149] Around the same time, Gaddafi's son declared that "rivers of blood" would run through Libya.[150] On March 17, 2011, the UN Security Council approved Resolution 1973, which authorized "all necessary measures . . . to protect civilians and civilian populated areas under threat of attack in the Libyan Arab Jamahiriya, including Benghazi."[151] The air campaign lasted seven months—Gaddafi's forces were defeated and the Security Council voted unanimously to end the NATO civilian protection mandate on October 27, 2011, despite the transitional government's request for the operation to be extended.[152, 153] After the intervention, the country remained mired in violent factionalism and another civil war erupted in 2014.

Here's how Obama later recalled his decision to get involved in Libya: ". . . we actually executed this plan as well as I could have expected: We got a UN mandate, we built a coalition, it cost us $1 billion—which, when it comes to military operations, is very cheap. We averted large-scale civilian casualties, we prevented what almost surely would have been a prolonged and bloody civil conflict. And despite all that, Libya is a mess."[154] When Obama was asked to name his greatest mistake as president, he said, "Probably failing to plan for the day after what I think was the right thing to do in intervening in Libya."[155]

Many headlines misrepresented Obama's comment, such as this one in the *Guardian*: "Barack Obama says Libya was 'worst mistake' of his presidency."[156] But he made it clear that *Libya* wasn't his worst mistake—he explicitly argued that the first civil war would have been longer and bloodier without the intervention. However, he also recognized that the United States and other Western countries abandoned Libya when it still desperately needed security and other forms of assistance in the aftermath of the civil war. Derek Chollet, who worked on Libya for the National Security Council, explained what was on Obama's mind when he made this decision: "The president was like, 'We are not looking to do another Iraq.'"[157] When Hitchens argued in favor of Western intervention in the Balkans, he criticized "spurious analogies from Vietnam" as excuses for complacency,[158] and he could have said the same about Iraq in the years after the invasion. Obama's wariness of sustained interventionism—of getting into another Iraq—led to what he admitted was the biggest mistake of his presidency.

In an article published a few days before the Security Council authorized no-fly zones in Libya, Hitchens acknowledged that intervention "might inadvertently ignite a sectarian regionalism culminating in fragmentation or partition."[159] But he made a point that's often ignored in the aftermath of the intervention: Gaddafi had "reached his Ceausescu moment" and there was probably a "very sharp limit to the duration of his regime,"[160] regardless of what action NATO took. The civil war was already well underway when NATO got involved, and there's no reason to assume Libya would have been any more stable or less violent without that involvement. Hitchens continued: "If that regime implodes while [Gaddafi] is still 'in place,' then all the grim consequences . . . will be incurred in any case. Weapons will get into the wrong hands; divide-and-rule tactics (already a stock in trade) will intensify; religious and tribal passions will be deliberately inflamed. The main difference will be that we merely watched this happen."[161]

In April 2011, Hitchens criticized the neurotic Western policy that sought the removal of Gaddafi without making this aim official.[162] An article by Obama, French President Nicolas Sarkozy, and British Prime Minister David Cameron declared that "Our duty and our mandate under UN Security Council Resolution 1973 is to protect civilians, and we are doing that. It is not to remove Qaddafi by force. But it is impossible to imagine a future for Libya with Qaddafi in power."[163] Obama, Sarkozy, and Cameron argued that Gaddafi's involvement in any new Libyan government would be an "unconscionable betrayal" and observed that "so long as Qaddafi is in power, NATO must maintain its operations."[164] They went on to declare their commitment to the reconstruction of post-Gaddafi Libya: "Qaddafi must go and go for good. At that point, the United Nations and its members should help the Libyan people as they rebuild where Qaddafi has destroyed—to repair homes and hospitals, to restore basic utilities, and to assist Libyans as they develop the institutions to underpin a prosperous and open society."[165]

This is exactly what the international community failed to do, and Hitchens could see the flimsiness of the Western commitment to Libya early on. Obama was immediately searching for an exit strategy as soon as NATO warplanes were in the air—he even told a senior White House official he wanted the campaign to take "Days, not weeks."[166] Hitchens contended that "What is utterly lacking in Libya, still, is an *entrance* strategy."[167] He argued that NATO countries should be more heavily involved: "Where is the virtue in pursuing this sporadically, with inadequate firepower, with no serious fighting forces on actual Libyan soil, and in letting the pace of events be dictated by the slowest-moving forces?"[168] And he pointed out that relying on the rebels—a "rabble" who weren't "cemented by any historic tradition of resistance or common experience,"[169] unlike the Kurdish *peshmerga* or the Northern Alliance in Afghanistan—would pointlessly prolong the conflict. Hitchens understood that the rebel militias would cause problems as the interim government sought to consolidate its control over the country. Most importantly, he recognized that the "collapse of the Qaddafi system is necessarily absolute and complete."[170] He continued:

> It is symbolized precisely by the tearing down and tearing up of the statues and posters, all showing The Leader in the various uniforms and regalias he has designed for himself over the years. The sub-Mussolini effect; the combination of Ruritania and the Gulag; a certain style of neo-fascist camp and kitsch will be virtually all that remains to study. For the rest, an unpunctuated record of cultural annihilation and the obliteration of any concept of autonomous or independent institutions.[171]

As with Iraq, it was this obliteration of Libyan civil society—which produced what Hitchens described as a "pitiless 42-year tabula rasa"[172]—that created the conditions for social and political dissolution after the fall of Gaddafi. These conditions would have been present even without the Gaddafi family's "obscene decision to keep their regime-spectacle going until the last possible moment, regardless of any cost in blood or treasure."[173]

The Libya campaign was an affirmation of the interventionist principles and frameworks that were developed at the end of the twentieth century. Not only did NATO aircraft have a UN warrant to bypass
another country's sovereignty in defense of its citizens, but the campaign was also sanctioned by regional governments[174]—a fact Hitchens
emphasized: "The Arab League has . . . broken with decades of torpor,
declared the Gaddafi regime illegitimate, and called for the imposition
of a no-fly zone."[175] But instead of regarding Libya as a successful mul-
tilateral effort to protect civilians who were staring down the turrets of
a dictator's tanks, many critics (especially on the left) now remember it
as a mini Iraq—yet another tragic episode of American overreach and
hubris. This is an injustice to history and a dismissal of the idea that
governments should not be allowed to murder their populations at will
and a reminder to dictators everywhere that powerful political forces are
at work to ensure their security.

On March 18, 2011, Iraqi Foreign Minister Hoshyar Zebari traveled to Paris, where he made the case for intervention in Libya and cited
the no-fly zone over northern Iraq after the Gulf War as a precedent.[176]
Zebari was "helping to tilt the whole axis of local diplomacy against
one-man rule," according to Hitchens, a moment that was "especially
gratifying for those of us who remember Zebari as the dedicated exile
militant that he was 10 years ago, striving to defend his dispossessed
people from the effects of Saddam Hussein's chemical weapons."[177] As
Iraq prepared to host the annual Arab League summit, Deputy Foreign
Minister Labid Abawi explained that his country was "back to play a
major and positive role in the Arab region. We take pride in that Iraq has
already exceeded all these other Arab countries in establishing a democratic regime."[178] Despite the violence and corruption that were still rife
in Iraq, Hitchens observed that the country "already has, albeit in rudi-
mentary and tenuous form, the free press, the written constitution, and
the parliamentary election system that is the minimum demand of Arab
civil society."[179]

Hitchens was writing at a time when the Arab Spring was just a few months old, and he didn't live to see its collapse: military dictatorship in Egypt, devastating violence in Syria, the civil war in Yemen, the rise of the Islamic State, and the European migration crisis (which contributed to resurgent right-wing nationalism on the continent). He died as the demands for democracy and an end to decades of repression in the Arab world still carried the promise of radical political transformation. It seemed possible that 2011 could be the Middle East's 1989, and Hitchens believed other dictators were on the precipice of their own Ceausescu moments. He argued that it was time for the West to abandon these brutal clients and finally take the side of their victims:

> Although there have been some intermittent noises from the International Criminal Court, it ought to be said in very unequivocal tones, by our government and others, that the Qaddafis and Assads and their accomplices are on notice. They should be told that the names of their military and security officers have been taken down, as have the names of their victims, and that prosecutions are even now being readied for a range of serious crimes. The continuing slaughter of those who will be needed in the rebuilding of Libya and Syria will not be countenanced. This is no longer a matter of asset seizures or sanctions, or of statements saying that the Baath Party has lost its legitimacy. It is a matter of raising the cost of war crimes, and of doing so while there is still time.[180]

In the early days of the Syrian Civil War, Hitchens thought Assad would soon go the way of Gaddafi and Saddam Hussein. But thanks to Russian and Iranian support—and perhaps more decisively, Western indifference—he will almost certainly stay in power after waging a decade-long war against his own population.

The Syrian Civil War has caused more than half a million deaths and created a vast refugee crisis—well over half of all Syrians have been forced from their homes, with 6.7 million internally displaced and 6.6 million living abroad.[181] In March 2020, UNICEF reported that 4.8 million children had been born in Syria since the conflict began, along with another million born as refugees in neighboring countries.[182] They've never known anything other than war. Between May 2019 and January 2020 alone, 700,000 civilians were displaced as Syrian and Russian forces launched a major assault on Idlib, western Aleppo, and other areas still under rebel control.[183] A UN commission found that this assault included a wave of indiscriminate attacks on hospitals, schools, markets, and neighborhoods. As commission chair Paulo Sérgio Pinheiro explained: "Children were shelled at school, parents were shelled at the market, patients were shelled at the hospital . . . and entire families were bombarded even while fleeing."[184]

But there were no op-eds by Western leaders in the *New York Times* about the need to protect Syrian civilians as they were pulverized from above. Instead, the outside intervention came from Russia and Iran—on the side of the tyrant. As COVID-19 began to dominate the headlines, it was easy to ignore the massacre taking place in northern Syria—even though the Syrians fleeing that massacre were hit by the pandemic as well. While the world stopped caring about the indiscriminate bombing of Syrian civilians long ago, there was widespread horror and incredulity at Russia's use of similar tactics—which had been honed in places like Aleppo—in Ukraine. As we survey the carnage of the Syrian Civil War, we would do well to recall Hitchens's point that inaction is a policy, too.

* * *

In the summer of 2007, the *New Statesman* republished an article Hitchens wrote about Iraq in 1976, which described Saddam Hussein as "perhaps the first visionary Arab statesman since Nasser."[185] As one of the best-known defenders of the Iraq War—largely on the grounds that Hussein's Iraq was a "concentration camp above ground and a mass grave underneath it"[186]—this was undoubtedly embarrassing. The editors at the *New Statesman* jeeringly noted that, despite being "one of the fiercest and most unrepentant enthusiasts for the U.S.-British over-throw of Saddam Hussein," Hitchens once "took a more admiring view of the Iraqi dictator." Dennis Perrin wrote: "Considering all of the bile he has heaped on those who differed with him over Iraq . . . His upcoming rationale for once publicly hailing Saddam as 'perhaps the first visionary Arab statesman since Nasser' should be amusing."[187] In a review of *Hitch-22*, Richard Seymour said Hitchens neglected to mention the remark in the book.[188]

But Seymour—ever scrupulous and fair to his subject—didn't bother to tell his readers that the chapter on Iraq in *Hitch-22* opens with a lengthy discussion of the *New Statesman* article. Because Iraq was a "British colonial invention," Hitchens explains, "as a British socialist, I had an instinctive sympathy with its nationalists."[189] In the article, Hitchens mentioned a conversation with a man who had been imprisoned and tortured by the Baathist secret police: "And yet he declared that he thought the present government the best Iraqi Administration he had seen. Why? 'Because it has made us strong and respected.' There seems no getting round this point."[190] This is the theme of the article—the Baathists may have been brutal, but they were remaking Iraq into a regional power. In 1976, Hitchens understated—but didn't ignore—the cruelty that was being inflicted on Iraqis in pursuit of this goal:

> Ba'ath party spokesmen, when questioned about the lack of public dissent, will point to efforts made by the party press to stimulate criticism of revolutionary shortcomings. True enough, there are such efforts, but they fall rather short of permitting any organized opposition. The argument then moves to the claim, which is often made in Iraq, that the country is surrounded by enemies and attacked by imperialist intrigue. Somewhere in the collision between Baghdad and Teheran on this point, the Kurdish nationalists met a very painful end.[191]

Despite its lenient rebuttal of Baath Party propaganda, this passage acknowledges many of the elements that made Baathist rule so uniquely

destructive in modern history: its crushing of dissent; its feverish paranoia about foreign plots, which led to frequent purges and explosions
of violence; and its gruesome campaigns against minorities. Though
Hitchens failed to appreciate how vicious the Baathists were in 1976,
his solidarity with the Iraqi opposition was already taking shape. He
condemned the "Nixon-Kissinger strategy of arming and encouraging
a Kurdish revolt, not for the purpose of creating a Kurdish state (which
would have horrified the Shah) but for the purpose of destabilizing
Iraq."[192] The following passage from the *New Statesman* article, in which
Hitchens discussed an investigation chaired by Rep. Otis Pike on the
United States' policy toward the Kurds, could have come straight out of
The Trial of Henry Kissinger:

> They were allowed to take heavy casualties and suffer appalling refugee
> problems; and then were dumped unceremoniously when it became
> clear that the Iraqi government was not going to crumble. "Even in
> the context of covert action," says the report, "ours was a cynical en-
> terprise." As one who had, on previous visits to Baghdad, scorned the
> argument that the Kurds were foreign puppets, I should say that "cyni-
> cal" is the mildest adjective that could be used about this latest triumph
> of the Secretary of State.[193]

Hitchens was 26 years old when he wrote those words, but his attitude
toward American statecraft in 1976 anticipated his support for the war
that would be launched more than a quarter of a century later. By 2003,
Hitchens's view had changed, but so had U.S. policy. While his critics wanted to humiliate him by calling attention to what he had written decades earlier (long before Saddam Hussein committed his most
egregious crimes), the *New Statesman* article didn't just reveal how his
thinking had evolved—it demonstrated how the world changed between
1976 and 2003.

There were clear warnings of the fate that awaited Iraq during
Hitchens's 1976 visit to the country: a prominent figure in the Iraqi

Communist Party informing him that party leaders and activists were being arrested by the Baathist secret police; the fact that "people almost automatically flinched at the mention of the name Saddam Hussein"; Iraqis asking if he could get them out of the country.[194] Hitchens would later discover that Iraqis he knew had been murdered by the regime—including his friend Mazen al-Zahawi, a gay Kurdish interpreter for Saddam Hussein who had shown him around Baghdad in 1976 (and who, Hitchens later wrote, was "denounced as a homosexual" after he was killed).[195] But when the opportunity to remove Hussein arrived in 1991—the moment dissidents like Makiya had long hoped for—Hitchens was too concerned with the machinations of the United States to make the case for regime change.

In the years before the Gulf War, Hitchens knew the Baathists were becoming more "theatrically cruel," but that didn't stop him from arguing that U.S. and Coalition forces had no business expelling Hussein's invading army from Kuwait.[196] He didn't support the Gulf War because he was suspicious of the motives of the George H.W. Bush administration, and he was all too aware of the United States' history in Iraq. He argued that the administration had tacitly authorized a limited invasion of Kuwait—U.S. Ambassador April C. Glaspie infamously told Hussein, "We have no opinion on the Arab-Arab conflicts, like your border disagreement with Kuwait"[197]—and as we've seen, the United States supported the Iraqi government as it waged war on Iran and attempted to exterminate the Kurds during the Anfal campaign. These were the same arguments opponents of the Iraq War would make in 2002 and 2003—how could the United States be trusted to rebuild a country it spent so many years helping to destroy? But this view is an acknowledgment that the Iraq War was a repudiation of the policies that had accommodated and actively supported Saddam Hussein. Hitchens came to believe that "anyone who really cared for the well-being and survival of Iraqis should be arguing for the removal of the insane despotism that had necessitated the sanctions and that was eating the country alive."[198] He didn't care if this effort made the United States look hypocritical, or if his support for it exposed him to the same accusation.

In November 2003, President George W. Bush delivered a speech at the National Endowment for Democracy in which he announced that the United States had "adopted a new policy, a forward strategy of freedom in the Middle East."[199] Bush noted that the number of democracies in the world had surged after the Cold War, and he argued that the "next stage of the world democratic movement" was underway.[200] While comments like these are now dismissed as opportunistic bromides from a president who was trying to sell a war, it's easy to forget that the invasion of Iraq was a radical departure from U.S. foreign policy in the Middle East in the second half of the twentieth century. Bush didn't just call for a new strategy—he also recognized that the old strategy of defending and subsidizing dictatorships in the region had been a failure:

> Sixty years of Western nations excusing and accommodating the lack of freedom in the Middle East did nothing to make us safe—because in the long run, stability cannot be purchased at the expense of liberty. As long as the Middle East remains a place where freedom does not flourish, it will remain a place of stagnation, resentment, and violence ready for export. And with the spread of weapons that can bring catastrophic harm to our country and to our friends, it would be reckless to accept the status quo.[201]

Bush was right to describe the Iraq War as a rejection of this status quo (Obama was accused of inaugurating an "apology tour" when he made the same argument about America's support for dictatorships in the Middle East during a 2009 speech in Cairo).[202, 203] While critics pointed to the hypocrisy of pursuing a "forward strategy of freedom" while continuing to provide billions of dollars of military aid to Egypt, Saudi Arabia, and other dictatorships—support Hitchens constantly criticized—this didn't change the fact that the United States had finally taken the side of the victims and dissidents in Iraq. During a 2003 debate, Hitchens explained why he endorsed this shift: "People say it's risky. Alright then, I'll admit it. That's part of what I like about it. It does take the risk that democracy and self-government is both more desirable—more stable and more defensible—than dictatorship or proxy rule. And I think it can be consistently argued."[204]

Hitchens reminded the audience that democratization often generates fears of instability.[205] Many realists, for instance, considered the democratic revolutions in Eastern Europe destabilizing. In an August 1990 essay titled "Why We Will Soon Miss The Cold War," the University of Chicago's John Mearsheimer (one of the best-known realist scholars in the world) argued that the "prospect of major crises, even wars, in Europe is likely to increase dramatically now that the Cold War is receding into history."[206] While Mearsheimer acknowledged that the "spread of democracy across Europe has great potential benefits for human rights," he believed "it will not guarantee peaceful relations among the states of post–Cold War Europe."[207]

Realists are primarily concerned with the balance of power between states, which is why Mearsheimer believed the West had an "interest in maintaining the Cold War order, and hence has an interest in continuing the Cold War confrontation."[208] Without the common threat of the Soviet Union, he expected Western Europe and the transatlantic alliance to disintegrate—the glue that held NATO together was gone, Germany would attempt to dominate Europe (possibly even invading an Eastern European state to create a buffer against Russia), and the continent would plunge into the multipolar instability that preceded World War I.[209] He was wrong on all fronts—NATO almost doubled its membership, the modern European Union was established, and Europe has seen an unprecedented period of democratic integration.

Mearsheimer's pessimism about post–Cold War Europe is a reminder that realists often think of authoritarian regimes as forces for stability. Many realists (including Walt and Mearsheimer) believe the realpolitik of the Cold War was a better guiding principle than what

Walt describes as the "liberal hegemony" of the past 30 years.[210] In an essay published several months after Mearsheimer's paean to the Cold War, Hitchens attacked the idea that realpolitik had maintained stability in the Middle East.[211] For example, the United States' support for Iraq in the 1980s only prolonged a devastating war, emboldened Saddam Hussein to commit genocide and other atrocities, and created the conditions for the invasion of Kuwait. The "regional status quo has for the past two decades known scarcely a day of peace," Hitchens wrote in 1991. "In the Persian Gulf, it has been a balance of terror for a long time. Realpolitik, as practiced by Washington, has played no small part in this grim situation."[212]

In a 2006 article critical of an essay by Walt and Mearsheimer in the *London Review of Books* about the influence of pro-Israel organizations in the United States[213, 214]—their book *The Israel Lobby and U.S. Foreign Policy* was published a year later[215]—Hitchens criticized the authors for regarding the "death-squad regime of Assad's Syria . . . as a force for stability."[216] Walt and Mearsheimer still held this view five years into the Syrian Civil War—the most devastating and destabilizing conflict on the planet at the time. As they put it in a 2016 essay in *Foreign Affairs*:

> In Syria, the United States should let Russia take the lead. A Syria stabilized under Assad's control, or divided into competing ministates, would pose little danger to U.S. interests. Both Democratic and Republican presidents have a rich history of working with the Assad regime, and a divided and weak Syria would not threaten the regional balance of power. If the civil war continues, it will be largely Moscow's problem, although Washington should be willing to help broker a political settlement.[217]

Hitchens argued that the United States' "rich history" of working with tyrants wasn't just a shameful counterpoint to its professed commitment to democracy and human rights (we've also seen how Moscow deals with its "problems" everywhere from Aleppo to Bucha). He also believed it would eventually lead to massacres, invasions, civil wars, and other calamities because he regarded dictatorships as inherently aggressive and unstable. While this argument has more or less force depending on the regime in question, it was certainly true of the Assad regime—just as it was true of Iraq before 2003.

Saddam Hussein wasn't just a "bad guy." He was a uniquely cruel and erratic tyrant who controlled one of the most extravagantly sadistic totalitarian regimes on the planet and violated the most fundamental international laws and norms for decades. He didn't just launch a pointless and pitiless eight-year attrition war against Iran—he repeatedly deployed chemical weapons on the battlefield and threatened to bombard Iranian cities with chemical warheads. He didn't just abuse the Iraqi population—he waged a campaign of extermination against civilians, gassed and leveled entire villages, and allowed psychopathic killers like Chemical Ali to torture and massacre Iraqis at will during the Anfal genocide and the post–Gulf War uprisings. And this decades-long spree of aggression and repression made Iraq a perennial emergency for the international community. As Hitchens observed: "Iraq was not a sovereign country in 2003. It was under international sanctions already. Large parts of its airspace were patrolled by American and British planes. It didn't really have control over its own borders."[218]

Meanwhile, Iraq's economy imploded while the regime went on committing what UN Special Rapporteur for the Commission on Human Rights Max van der Stoel described as "massive violations of human rights," such as "summary and arbitrary executions"; the "widespread routine practice of systematic torture"; "enforced or involuntary disappearances"; and "routinely practised arbitrary arrests and detention."[219] Van der Stoel argued that this catalog of crimes was "so grave that it has few parallels in the years that have passed since the Second World War."[220]

The compendium of crimes Van der Stoel presented to the United Nations in February 1994 is just over one hundred pages long. Encyclopedias could be filled with the horrors inflicted by the Baath Party—Van der Stoel possessed "18 metric tons of official Iraqi documents, testimonies, analytical reports, forensic and other scientific reports, etc." on abuses against the Kurds alone.[221] The report refers to "an order which permits the secure enjoyment of essentially no human right or freedom. Through the construction of a web of informers including community leaders, friends and family, and the existence of a security apparatus which may intrude into the most private affairs of the individual, it is difficult to speak of the enjoyment of any freedom in Iraq."[222] The section titled "Abuse of Power" observes that "some dehumanizing practices appear to surpass any apparent objective" and explains that "those in power accord little or no value to human life."[223] Van der Stoel's report substantiates the major themes of *The Republic of Fear*, from the ubiquity of state violence in Saddam's Iraq to the caprice with which it was carried out. Hitchens observed that, while terror and cruelty are necessarily systematic in totalitarian regimes, these regimes are also unpredictable and chaotic—a way to keep the population in a constant state of obedient fear and anxiety.[224]

When confronted with a record of crimes as vast and lurid as the one generated by Saddam Hussein, there are several natural tendencies. One is to simply disbelieve the reports. In *A Problem from Hell: America and the Age of Genocide*, Samantha Power discusses the habit of denial that was common among policymakers and the general public when they heard of crimes like the Armenian genocide, the Holocaust, mass exterminations in Cambodia, ethnic massacres in the Balkans, the Rwandan genocide, and the Anfal campaign.[225] Even when people accept that these crimes took place, they're fully capable of downplaying, ignoring, or even excusing them. As Power notes, one Bush administration official referred to Iraq's "legitimate attempts to suppress" the Kurds.[226] Despite the overwhelming evidence of genocide, displacement, and torture in Iraq, other American officials found plenty of excuses for inaction. Power writes:

... those who did not want to punish Hussein told themselves that the crime was not necessarily genocide, that the Kurds had invited repression upon themselves, and that the evidence of gassing was not foolproof. The United States had intelligence that distinguished Iraqi military engagement with armed Kurds from Iraqi destruction of whole communities. And although senior policymakers were right that the information flow was imperfect, U.S. policy is rarely predicated on foolproof evidence. U.S. officials certainly knew enough to know that Saddam Hussein was prepared to use any means available to him to solve his "Kurdish problem."[227]

The *bad guy* view of Saddam Hussein was common within the U.S. government, which made it possible to argue that Iraq's human rights violations weren't serious enough to prevent Washington from providing Baghdad with agricultural credits and maintaining a fruitful economic relationship with Saddam Hussein.[228] After all, the United States often has to work with countries that don't have blemishless human rights records. But while plenty of autocrats are brutal and ruthless—from Abdel Fattah el-Sisi to Recep Tayyip Erdogan to Mohammad bin Salman—it doesn't make sense to classify these thugs and murderers alongside Hussein, who constructed and maintained one of the most suffocating totalitarian regimes on the planet and regularly violated the most fundamental precepts of international law regarding genocide, chemical weapons, and invasion.

In a 2002 article about the junior Bush's often derided use of the word "evil," Hitchens invoked one of the greatest chroniclers of twentieth century totalitarianism: "Faced with the evidence of genocidal politics in 20th-century Europe, Hannah Arendt ... posed the existence of something she termed 'radical evil' and suggested that intellectuals were failing to allow for its existence as a self-determining force."[229] Hitchens attempted to define "evil" as an "irrational delight in flouting every customary norm of civilization."[230] Whether or not you agree with this definition, it captures something essential about Iraq under Baathist rule. Recall Van der Stoel's observation about abuses that "surpass any apparent objective"—Hussein's irrationality had implications for how the international community should or could deal with his regime.

Hitchens often emphasized Hussein's destructive behavior even in the absence of any strategic rationale, such as his decision to set hundreds of Kuwaiti oil wells ablaze as his forces retreated from the country at the end of the Gulf War. The resulting conflagration burned for ten months and belched millions of barrels of oil into the earth, ocean, and atmosphere.[231] Beyond the environmental catastrophe this crime created, it was another reminder that regular mechanisms of deterrence and incentive didn't work with Hussein—he was capable of taking spectacular risks, even when there was no discernible benefit. Hitchens summarized this tendency:

> It's wearisome at this late date to read again the bland assertion that Saddam Hussein did not do things because it would have been unwise or irrational for him to do so. On that very basis, our intelligence establishment concluded that he would not invade Kuwait, would not set fire to the oil fields, and would not perform any number of other insane actions. His megalomania and volatility were consistently underestimated, with real consequences in the real world. No policy based on the assumption of his rational conduct ever worked.[232]

Hussein's megalomania and volatility were his defining characteristics, and they ensured that Baathist Iraq was as capricious in its relationship with the world as it was regimented in the oppression of its people.

* * *

In September 2013, Vladimir Putin published an op-ed in the *New York Times* portentously titled "A Plea for Caution From Russia," which urged the United States not to take military action in Syria.[233] The article was full of high-minded rhetoric about the importance of respecting international law and restraining the use of force—the deployment of which "could throw the entire system of international law and order out of balance."[234] A few months later, Russia invaded and annexed Crimea. Two years after that, Russian aircraft would begin blasting Syrian neighborhoods, hospitals, and schools alongside Assad's air force. And in February 2022, Russia launched the largest conflict in Europe since World War II when it invaded Ukraine.

As Ukrainian cities were blitzed by Russian artillery and cruise missiles in early 2022, leftists like Corbyn (along with many realists) blamed NATO expansion for the war. These academics and commentators have a hard time explaining Russian aggression elsewhere in the world—is NATO responsible for Russia's role in the destruction of Syria as well? Since late 2015, Russian forces have relentlessly bombarded Syrian cities—a campaign thinly disguised as an effort to recapture those cities from terrorists. Russia's sustained assaults on Aleppo, Ghouta (where Assad used chemical weapons against civilians), and Idlib were particularly ferocious, with hundreds of sorties every day, intentional attacks on hospitals and civilian infrastructure, indiscriminate bombings of civilian areas, and other war crimes.[235, 236, 237] These were clear precedents for the crimes Russian forces would later commit in Ukraine.

In his *New York Times* op-ed, Putin celebrated the "profound wisdom" of the "veto by Security Council permanent members . . . enshrined in the United Nations Charter," which he argued has "underpinned the stability of international relations for decades."[238] It makes sense that Putin would be fond of his permanent veto power on the Security Council, but not because it's a mechanism for maintaining international stability. As Russian aircraft continued to blast Syrian civilians on behalf of the dictator who has been slaughtering them since they rose up against his regime in 2011, Moscow repeatedly vetoed Security Council resolutions to authorize the delivery of humanitarian assistance because those resolutions didn't contain legal exemptions for its airstrikes.[239] Of course, Russia's veto also precludes any robust action from the Security

Council on the war in Ukraine, despite the fact that the invasion makes a mockery of the most basic precepts of the UN Charter that Putin once claimed to care so much about.

Near the end of his article, Putin argued: "It is alarming that military intervention in internal conflicts in foreign countries has become commonplace for the United States."[240] He continued: "But force has proved ineffective and pointless. . . . In the United States, many draw an analogy between Iraq and Syria, and ask why their government would want to repeat recent mistakes."[241] Putin was right that many Americans drew an analogy between Iraq and Syria, and he has cited the Iraq War as evidence of the West's hypocrisy in condemning the invasion of Ukraine. These analogies have always served Moscow well. Without a serious American presence in Syria, Putin was free to protect what he saw as Russia's strategic interests, which were contingent on Assad staying in power. To take just one example: in December 2017, Putin signed a deal with the Syrian government that will allow Russia to keep warships at its port in Tartus, enter Syrian territorial and internal waters, and use all its other ports for almost half a century.[242] But Putin has a more pressing concern than the strategic value of Syria—he fears the establishment of any norm that puts dictators on notice by supporting those who would depose them.

This attitude is nothing new for Moscow. In a 2006 article, Hitchens observed that "Putin has been noticeable for his efforts to protect Saddam Hussein, Kim Jong-il, the Iranian mullahs, and the Sudanese racist cleansers from any concerted action by the United Nations."[243] For Putin, it doesn't matter how homicidal a regime is toward its own population or the populations of other states—if it's an enemy of the West, its sovereignty must be upheld. Of course, this standard doesn't apply to any government Putin opposes, and he's especially eager to trample the sovereignty of democratic neighbors like Ukraine, which present a clear ideological challenge to his decaying autocracy. (The idea that Kyiv posed a *military* threat to Russia before the invasion, Moscow's justification for the use of force against Ukraine, is as absurd as the idea that Putin is a stalwart defender of the UN Charter). This blaring hypocrisy is no surprise coming from a revanchist dictator who believes the collapse of the Soviet Union was the greatest geopolitical catastrophe of the twentieth century—and who has a nineteenth-century view of great power politics.

Putin is deeply hostile to the norms that Blair, Annan, Kouchner, Hitchens, et al. were trying to establish in the 1990s and 2000s around interventionism, the Responsibility to Protect, and state sovereignty. He uses the language of international law merely as a cudgel against the United States, and his duplicity has never been clearer than when he followed up his plea for peaceful dialogue and multilateralism in Syria with a ruthless bombing campaign to defend a ruthless dictator. "We are not protecting the Syrian government," Putin wrote, "but international law. We need to use the United Nations Security Council and believe that preserving law and order in today's complex and turbulent world is one of the few ways to keep international relations from sliding into chaos."[244] A few months after writing those words, Putin seized Crimea in flagrant contravention of the most fundamental tenets of international law—a move that began the process of carving up Ukraine, which preceded a long proxy war in the Donbas and culminated in the full invasion several years later. None of this would have surprised Hitchens, who emphasized Moscow's contempt for international law during the Russian invasion of Georgia: "Does anybody remember the speeches in which the Russian ambassador to the United Nations asked the General Assembly or Security Council to endorse his country's plan to send land, air, and sea forces deep into the territory and waters of a former colony that is now a UN member state? I thought not."[245]

Russia is not alone in wanting to maintain a status quo in which autocracies remain undisturbed by any democratic stirrings among their populations. China, for example, also opposed the provision of humanitarian aid to millions of Syrians, blocking the resolutions to authorize this assistance alongside Moscow.[246] In 2019 and 2020, there was a wave of protests in Hong Kong over extradition, draconian national security laws, and other encroachments from the mainland—what the *New York Times* described as the "semiautonomous Chinese city's biggest political crisis and the broadest expression of public anger with Beijing in decades."[247] The Chinese government constantly accuses the United States of fueling unrest in Hong Kong and interfering in other ways.[248] While it's true that the United States supports the protesters, the uprisings are massive and organic expressions of democratic sentiment. But Beijing benefits from the perception that the protesters are American agents out to destabilize the country—a theory which has found champions on the "anti-imperialist" left.

In the spring of 2021, Russia was gripped by protests over the imprisonment of Aleksei Navalny—an opposition leader who survived an assassination attempt (likely perpetrated by Moscow) in August 2020. Protesters took to the streets in cities across Russia, and thousands were arrested and beaten by security forces.[249] Just a month after the invasion of Ukraine, more than 4,300 Russians had already been arrested for protesting the war.[250] Navalny frequently encouraged these protests, and he was sentenced to nine more years in prison on March 22, 2022.[251]

The United States is supportive of these movements for strategic reasons, but also because the defense of democracy is supposed to be a core part of its national identity. While America can boast of remarkable democratic achievements—from the Marshall Plan and the reconstruction of Western Europe and Japan after World War II to its contributions to the dissolution of the Soviet Union—much of U.S. foreign policy during the Cold War exposed its commitment to democracy and freedom as selective and self-serving.

Unlike much of the left, however, Hitchens ultimately thought the end of the Cold War brought the United States into closer alignment with its democratic ideals. Despite the tragic consequences of the Iraq War, Hitchens was unwavering in his conviction that the effort to facilitate the transition from totalitarianism to democracy in the country was worthwhile. And he didn't just believe this was the case for Iraq's sake—he also thought the removal of Saddam Hussein was a significant step toward a world in which dictators and war criminals are finally held accountable. When an interviewer asked Hitchens if there was any "point at which the consequences of the Iraq War would outweigh the benefits," Hitchens replied, "No, certainly not. Because apart from everything else, it's invariably a good thing to see Caligula on trial in front of his own people."[252] Just like Slobodan Milošević, Hitchens argued, Saddam Hussein ended up where he belonged: in the dock (though he believed the decision to execute Hussein was a mistake).[253]

Months before the September 11 attacks, Hitchens was making the case against former U.S. Secretary of State Henry Kissinger in what he described as the "context that's evolved post-Milošević, in other words, the decision by the international community to become seized of the idea of war crimes and crimes against humanity, and to hold people responsible."[254] He thought Kissinger should be held accountable for offenses ranging from the "deliberate mass killing of civilian populations in Indochina"[255] to a CIA-sponsored abduction which led to the assassination of Chilean General René Schneider in 1970.[256] Hitchens's prosecution of Kissinger was a demand for the equal and active enforcement of international law—as he puts it in *The Trial of Henry Kissinger*: ". . . we now enter upon the age when the defense of 'sovereign immunity' for state crimes has been held to be void."[257]

Beyond the precedents established by the International Criminal Tribunals for Rwanda and the former Yugoslavia, Hitchens cites the indictment of former Chilean President Augusto Pinochet by Spanish Judge Baltasar Garzón and Pinochet's subsequent arrest in London: "The Pinochet verdict in London, the splendid activism of the Spanish magistracy, and the verdicts of the International Tribunal at The Hague have destroyed the shield that immunized crimes committed under the justification of *raison d'état*"[258] (reason of state or national interest). He argues that the failure to proceed with similar legal action against Kissinger would

> constitute a double or triple offense to justice. First, it will violate the essential and now uncontested principle that not even the most powerful are above the law. Second, it will suggest that prosecutions for war crimes and crimes against humanity are reserved for losers, or for minor despots in relatively negligible countries. This in turn will lead to the paltry politicization of what could have been a noble process, and to the justifiable suspicion of double standards.[259]

The title of Hitchens's book on Kissinger reflected his belief that human rights law should "apply to the whole of humanity."[260] He asked Americans: "Do we expect to abide by the standards we impose on others?"[261] But even when he was promoting the essays in *Harper's* that became *The Trial of Henry Kissinger*,[262] Hitchens wasn't myopically focused on the United States' crimes. During a January 2001 appearance on C-SPAN to discuss Kissinger, Hitchens acknowledged that the American efforts to enforce laws and norms around human rights were necessary, if inconsistent.[263] When a caller said Milošević was no worse than the other belligerents in the Balkans, Hitchens said, "I think we would disagree about Mr. Milošević . . . the vast orchestration of crimes against humanity in what was Yugoslavia originates in the hysterical plan for a Greater Serbia."[264] When another caller insisted that the sanctions against Iraq made the United States "as bad as Adolf Hitler," Hitchens replied:

> Mr. Saddam Hussein could feed those people if he wanted to, and chooses not to. And Mr. Saddam Hussein is everything that is said about him. I mean, I've been to Iraq several times, I've been since the war, and I've been in Kurdistan. I've been to towns that have been bombed by him with chemical weapons. I've sat on an unexploded chemical bomb in the town of Halabja with Iraqi air force markings on it. I know that this stuff is not propaganda. And I've interviewed people who are still burning from what they were sprayed with.[265]

Hitchens made those comments nine months before September 11. He couldn't have known that he would become one of the best-known advocates for a war on Saddam Hussein within two years. Nor could he have anticipated the fact that this war would be invoked for many years after that to justify inaction in the face of future conflicts and humanitarian catastrophes—whether cynically by dictators like Putin or honestly by world leaders like Obama (as well as millions of war-weary Americans and Europeans). Could the West have been roused to take action in Syria if the United States had never invaded Iraq? Would the Obama administration have deserted Libya so quickly? Would the United States have continued to uphold its commitment to the people of Afghanistan instead of abandoning them to a new era of Taliban rule? What were the consequences of the Iraq War for the project of trying to build a coherent and enforceable system of international law?

When the United Nations asked to deploy 20,000 peacekeepers in Darfur, Sudanese President Omar Hassan al-Bashir refused, declaring that he didn't want his country to become another Iraq.[266] That certainly wasn't going to happen, because as Hitchens put it at the time, the government-backed janjaweed militias had already killed or deported huge numbers of people: "the ethnic cleansers of that province have made good use of the 'negotiation' and 'mediation' period to complete their self-appointed task."[267] In March 2009 and July 2010, the International Criminal Court issued arrest warrants for al-Bashir that included

> five counts of crimes against humanity: murder, extermination, forcible transfer, torture, and rape; two counts of war crimes: intentionally directing attacks against a civilian population as such or against individual civilians not taking part in hostilities, and pillaging; three counts of genocide: by killing, by causing serious bodily or mental harm, and by deliberately inflicting on each target group conditions of life calculated to bring about the group's physical destruction, allegedly committed at least between 2003 and 2008 in Darfur, Sudan.[268]

The words "another Iraq" will, of course, continue to be used by dictators and ethnic cleansers who wish to kill and torture with impunity. But they will also be used by well-meaning citizens, diplomats, scholars, journalists, and heads of state who sincerely believe any intervention—no matter how justified, urgent, or proportionate—can only end in disaster. This is a legacy of the Iraq War Hitchens didn't take seriously enough.

* * *

Was the Hitchens who supported the Iraq War the same Hitchens who called for the arrest of Henry Kissinger? While there was certainly a shift—his opposition to the Gulf War can't be reconciled with his support for the invasion of Iraq in 2003—there's far more overlap than his critics are willing to acknowledge. His attitude toward Kissinger was a proxy for his hostility toward Cold War U.S. foreign policy more generally, and Iraq featured prominently in that analysis. As he explains in *The Trial of Henry Kissinger* (echoing what he wrote in the *New Statesman* a quarter of a century earlier):

> . . . in my capacity as a political opponent I might have mentioned Kissinger's recruitment and betrayal of the Iraqi Kurds, who were falsely encouraged by him to take up arms against Saddam Hussein in 1974–75, and who were then abandoned to extermination on their hillsides when Saddam Hussein made a diplomatic deal with the Shah of Iran, and who were deliberately lied to as well as abandoned. The conclusions of the report by Congressman Otis Pike still make shocking reading, and reveal on Kissinger's part a callous indifference to human life and human rights. But they fall into the category of depraved realpolitik, and do not seem to have violated any known law.[269]

This episode wasn't part of the bill of indictment in *The Trial of Henry Kissinger*—which was an effort to outline what an actionable legal challenge might look like—but that made it especially noxious from Hitchens's point of view. He despised the United States' "depraved realpolitik" and the idea that, as he put it, "great states have no permanent friends or permanent principles, but only permanent interests."[270] He questioned the conceit of statesmen who believed they could be the architects of stability in the Middle East by maintaining what he described as a "balance of terror"[271] while befriending dictators and ignoring the people who actually had to suffer the consequences of their policies. But he believed something changed after the Cold War. Policymakers stopped viewing the world through the distorting prism of the conflict with the Soviet Union, which led to so many grotesque calculations—from the subversion of democracy in Central and South America to the expansion of the Vietnam War. Human rights certainly didn't become a major priority for Washington, but it was difficult to see how interventions like the ones in the Balkans were examples of American imperialism.

The Iraq War wasn't another example of realpolitik in action. It wasn't an opportunistic alliance or compromise with dictatorship. It didn't treat the Kurds as expendable. It wasn't an attempt to tilt the regional balance of terror in the United States' favor (if anything, the invasion strengthened Iran's position in the region). This isn't to say Bush's "forward strategy of freedom" should be taken at face value—of course the administration had motivations beyond securing democracy and human rights in Iraq. Nor is it a defense of the conduct of the war or even a comment on the wisdom of launching that war in the first place. It's an acknowledgment of reality—a policy that actively supports a genocidal totalitarian regime is not interchangeable with a policy which removes that regime by force. In a 2010 interview, Hitchens argued that his position on Iraq meant he had "taken the side of Jalal Talabani and Barham Salih and Kanan Makiya and the other Iraqi left and secular revolutionary intellectuals that the Saddam Hussein regime had to go, that no policy was conceivable that allowed it to retain private ownership of Iraq."[272] He summarized the general principle that informed this view: "There is a radical incompatibility between the civilized world order, which aspires at any rate to democracy and free exchange, and totalitarian, expansionist, fanatical regimes."[273]

For Hitchens, Iraq was always a war of liberation. While he didn't share Fukuyama's view that the end of the Cold War put the world on a trajectory toward liberal democracy, he recognized that totalitarianism and one-party rule had been discredited in Europe, and the totalitarian idea was being confronted elsewhere in the world.

Hitchens didn't support efforts to resist and depose Milošević, the Taliban, Hussein, Gaddafi, and Assad because he suddenly discovered that he had a taste for war and imperialism in his advancing years. He supported these efforts because he believed the United States should stop siding with dictators over their people. At the end of the Cold War, Hitchens understood that the true revolutionaries in the world were the people who took to the streets in Prague, Bucharest, Warsaw, and the other European cities that had been trapped behind the Iron Curtain for decades. He observed that these people "asked for so little in Eastern Europe up to 1989. It was revolutionary to demand something like a bill of rights modeled on the American constitution. That was a revolutionary demand."[274] As the United States has learned painfully and slowly in Afghanistan and Iraq, those who demand liberal democratic institutions and rights aren't asking for "so little"—they're asking for a system of government and social organization that has taken the West centuries to build.

More than three decades after the fall of the Berlin Wall, millions of people across the Middle East remain shackled to theocracies, military dictatorships, and other tyrannies—a status quo that was shaken but not dislodged during the Arab Spring. Hitchens believed the revolutionaries in the twenty-first century are the dissidents and liberals in these societies—particularly in Iraq, which was subjected to decade after decade of totalitarianism. Hitchens was no longer a socialist campaigning against the American empire in the last decade of his life, but he felt "no less radical"[275] because he supported resistance movements in states where basic democratic ideas are just as revolutionary as they were in 1776,

1789, or 1989. When Washington treated Saddam Hussein as a client and a partner, Hitchens condemned the policy as yet another example of undisguised contempt for human rights from American policymakers who believed they could engineer a self-serving balance of power in the Middle East. When the United States reversed this policy in 2003, he decided that the removal of Hussein and the reconstruction of Iraq were causes worth defending—causes that finally put America on the right side in the region.

Many of Hitchens's colleagues lamented this position as if it wasn't just a defection, but a form of intellectual death. This led to articles with titles like "Farewell, Hitch" and lugubrious observations like this one from journalist David Corn, with whom he once shared an office at the *Nation*: "It pains me to engage in this sort of tussle with Hitchens," who had "become a full-fledged ally of the reality-defying advocates of the Iraq invasion. I sadly count that as another casualty of the war."[276, 277] Hitchens responded: "I begin to tire of this sickly idea that I used to be a great guy until I became fed up with excuses for dictators and psychopathic murderers." Those who believed "I was a complete shit and traitor all along," he argued, were "surely nearer the mark."[278]

5 The Enemy

Hitchens on Authoritarianism

After World War II, Orwell was more pessimistic than ever about the future of democracy and freedom in the world. In his 1947 essay "Toward European Unity," he said he would "give the odds against the survival of civilization within the next few hundred years,"[1] but suggested that survival might not be such a good thing, anyway:

> The fear inspired by the atomic bomb and other weapons yet to come will be so great that everyone will refrain from using them. This seems to me the worst possibility of all. It would mean the division of the world among two or three vast super-states, unable to conquer one another and unable to be overthrown by any internal rebellion. In all probability their structure would be hierarchic, with a semi-divine caste at the top and outright slavery at the bottom, and the crushing out of liberty would exceed anything that the world has yet seen.[2]

Orwell published those words when he was writing *1984* (and made a similar case in "You and the Atom Bomb" two years earlier),[3] which demonstrates that he believed the totalitarian nightmare of the novel wasn't just possible, but likely. It doesn't matter how right or wrong Orwell turned out to be—while China and North Korea seem fixated on making *1984* a reality, the most powerful liberal democracies didn't become unbreakable tyrannies. We don't continue to read *1984* almost three-quarters of a century after it was published because it offered an accurate vision of the future. We read it because the impulses Orwell identified—to dominate other human beings, to warp language in the service of some political end, to worship and obey—remain as real today as they have ever been.

"The totalitarian," Hitchens observed a few months before his death, "is the enemy—the one that's absolute, the one that wants control over the inside of your head, not just your actions and your taxes."[4] Hitchens's critics found plenty of ways to dismiss this principle: they accused him of attempting to appropriate some of Orwell's prestige[5] and argued that anti-totalitarianism in the twenty-first century is anachronistic and platitudinous: "Isn't that about the easiest target for anyone (and especially a writer) to pick?" asked Stephen Walt after Hitchens's death.[6] Considering the fact that anti-totalitarianism as Hitchens understood it led to several of his most controversial positions—on Iraq and terrorism, for instance—which lost him many friends and made him a pariah on the left, the answer to Walt's question is no. Hitchens often described monotheistic religion as fundamentally totalitarian (like living in a "celestial North Korea"),[7] and while this position didn't lead to as much turmoil in his personal and political life as his attitude toward terrestrial totalitarianism, it isn't quite the consensus view in America, either.

In the mid-1970s, the Polish dissident Adam Michnik made a comment which, according to Hitchens, "over time was to change my life. The crucial distinction between systems, he said, was no longer ideological. The main political difference was between those who did, and those who did not, think that the citizen could—or should—be 'the property of the state.'"[8] In his memoir, Hitchens explains that the implications of this observation "for all political positions were enormous . . . in order to stay true to the principle—once again, the principle of consistent anti-totalitarianism—one might have to expose oneself to steadily mounting contradictions."[9] Hitchens's career looked like one big contradiction to many of his ex-allies on the left because he ended up supporting policies he would have once decried, such as the wars in Afghanistan and Iraq. But Hitchens observes that other left-wingers followed a similar political trajectory:

> I was a member of a rather idiosyncratic minority of the left that based itself on the original Left Opposition to Stalin's version of communism. So there was always a war within the left going on, and going on within myself as well. And there is a common thread, I think, that binds or can be traced through the experience of 1968, the great *annus mirabilis* of youth revolution, 1989, the final collapse of state socialism in Eastern Europe and Russia, and 2001, the rallying of democratic society against a third form of totalitarianism: the Islamic jihadist one.[10]

"Who's going to rise to totalitarianism's defense in this day and age?" Walt wanted to know.[11] Benito Mussolini used the term *totalitario* in the early 1920s to describe his core philosophy—"Everything in the State, nothing outside the State, no one against the State"[12]—and of course the concept now makes us think of fascism and Stalinism. But Hitchens emphasized how the totalitarian impulse mutates and persists over time. Contrast China's industrial-scale, high-tech censorship with the primitive and violent zealotry of jihadist organizations and Islamist regimes that believe in a theocratic variant of Mussolini's formulation: *Everything in the faith, nothing outside the faith, no one against the faith.* Ian McEwan says Hitchens was a member of the anti-totalitarian left,[13] and this designation is more controversial and relevant than critics like Walt assume.

While it would be an overstatement to describe the rise of populist nationalism in the United States and Europe over the past several years as a totalitarian phenomenon, it's certainly *authoritarian*. This distinction may be helpful to those who regard totalitarianism as an outmoded concept in the twenty-first century. The possibility that outright totalitarianism of the sort Orwell envisioned will take hold in liberal democracies is remote, but the authoritarian moment in Western countries has been a jarring reminder that they aren't immune from the anti-democratic forces that predominate elsewhere in the world. Democracy is a recent innovation, after all, and it's a deviation from the emperors, feudal lords, religious authorities, and Big Men who have ruled throughout history. In a 2010 interview, Hitchens was asked if there's a single principle that "underpins everything you've attached yourself to through your life." He replied: "It would be that no one is good enough to be another person's master. If they're going to be giving orders, they have to earn the right to do it. They can't inherit it. It can't be assumed of them."[14]

While this is a more modest position than anti-totalitarianism, it's also more broadly applicable. Even if every totalitarian regime and movement disappeared overnight, the importance of democratic accountability, the free exchange of information, individual rights, and all the other principles and institutions that authoritarian rulers seek to undermine would remain unchanged. Orwell recognized that the defense of these principles requires a constant struggle against the totalitarian impulse, and even if that impulse doesn't lead to the creation of a modern Airstrip One, it will always be capable of causing incalculable damage to liberal democracy.

* * *

When Donald Trump was elected President of the United States in 2016, many Americans already understood that he was fundamentally hostile to the liberal democratic norms that guided and restrained his predecessors. Trump wasn't just an opportunistic demagogue who recognized that he could exploit voters' prejudices and fears. He was also an inveterately anti-democratic leader who regarded any constraints on his power as obstacles to overcome instead of rules to observe. There are many terms that describe Trump's political movement, from right-wing populism to nationalism—but authoritarianism may be the most apt.

While Trump's ascension to the White House was in many ways unprecedented, he represents a strain of American politics that has been around for a long time—the nationalist, populist right embodied by figures like political advisor, commentator, and politician Pat Buchanan (who Hitchens described as a "fascist windbag")[15] and aviator Charles Lindbergh (a "crackpot and a racist").[16] Like Trump, Buchanan touted his "America First" foreign policy when he ran for president in 1992, 1996, and 2000, which was in turn a homage to Lindbergh's America First Committee.[17]

This political history isn't edifying. When Lindbergh argued that the United States should stay out of World War II, he did so with shameless anti-Semitic appeals to Americans' crudest nationalist instincts. In a September 11, 1941 speech, Lindbergh said the three main lobbies pushing for war were "the British, the Jewish and the Roosevelt administration,"[18] observing that "leaders of both the British and the Jewish races, for reasons which are as understandable from their viewpoint as they are inadvisable from ours, for reasons which are not American, wish to involve us in the war."[19] Buchanan celebrated Trump's place in the American political tradition of nationalism and isolationism, and he described the America First Committee as an "honorable group of American patriots" looking out for the country's best interests.[20]

Hitchens wrote about Buchanan often, and in many ways, he may as well have been writing about Trump. After Trump won in 2016, Buchanan told *Politico*: "The ideas made it, but I didn't."[21] Buchananism prefigured Trumpism almost perfectly: the insular zero-sum worldview that regards trade agreements as stealth mechanisms to cripple the American economy; the belief that NATO is a foreign plot to overextend and weaken the United States; the hatred for international institutions such as the United Nations and the European Union; the fetishization of national sovereignty; the instrumentalization of nativist anxieties and hatreds; the insistence that immigration will destroy the country; the paranoia about "globalism" and a "new world order" allegedly embodied by (often Jewish) figures like George Soros; and the nostalgia for a homogeneous and harmonious American past that never existed.

Nationalists often celebrate authoritarianism abroad—perhaps because so many authoritarians have nationalistic tendencies—and Trump is no exception. He described Egyptian President Abdel Fattah el-Sisi as his "favorite dictator"—a "fantastic guy" with whom he had "great chemistry."[22] As Egyptian defense minister, Sisi oversaw the massacre of more than a thousand protesters in August 2013.[23] Trump described Turkish President Recep Tayyip Erdogan—who has a long record of subverting democracy and the judicial system in his country, violently repressing Kurdish populations in Turkey and its neighbors, and arresting journalists and activists—as a "hell of a leader" and a "tough man."[24] According to John Bolton, Trump's former national security advisor, the president told Chinese President Xi Jinping that imprisoning over a million Uighurs in "reeducation" camps in Xinjiang was "exactly the right thing to do."[25]

Trump's affinity for dictators makes sense: he's contemptuous of the free press, the American judicial system, and the very idea of the separation of powers in the U.S. government. He assailed the press as the "enemy of the people."[26] He repeatedly insisted that a U.S. District Judge was incapable of issuing impartial decisions because he has Mexican heritage.[27, 28] When a caravan of migrants was traveling from Central America to the United States, Trump declared (with no evidence) that "unknown Middle Easterners" were "mixed in" with the crowds.[29] He deployed National Guard troops to the border and said U.S. forces should "consider it a rifle" if migrants threw rocks.[30] He later suggested to aides that American soldiers should shoot migrants in the legs.[31]

Trump had no interest in securing and facilitating the democratic transition of power in the United States if this process didn't benefit him. Before the 2016 election, he refused to say whether he would respect the results: "I will keep you in suspense," he said during the final presidential debate.[32] Despite his victory in the Electoral College, he refused to accept that he lost the popular vote by more than 2.8 million votes, so he declared (without a scrap of evidence) that between 3 and 5 million votes had been cast illegally—none of which could conceivably have been cast for him, of course.[33] He established a Presidential Advisory Commission on Election Integrity to uncover the massive fraud he alleged, but it found nothing and disbanded in early 2018.[34] As the 2020 election approached, Trump declared that there would be "fraud like you've never seen"[35] and repeatedly described the electoral system as "rigged."[36] This claim, which was a transparent effort to preempt a defeat that was starting to look inevitable by undermining faith in the entire democratic process, became a central element of his campaign.

Trump's efforts to sabotage the election became even more relentless after he lost, this time in the Electoral College and by more than 7 million popular votes.[37] He announced that the result was a "fraud on the American public" and declared victory.[38] His legal team filed over 60 lawsuits to challenge the results.[39] He asked state legislators across the country to overturn their constituents' votes and appoint pro-Trump electors to the Electoral College.[40] He told Georgia Secretary of State Brad Raffensperger "I just want to find 11,780 votes, which is one more than we have" and threatened legal consequences if Raffensperger failed to do so.[41] And he told supporters to show up in Washington, DC, for a "Stop the Steal" rally on January 6, 2021—a day that culminated in a violent mob assaulting the U.S. Capitol.[42] Protesters chanted "Hang Mike Pence" because Pence refused to support Trump's attempt to steal the election,[43] while others built a gallows,[44] flaunted white nationalist and neo-Nazi insignia,[45] marched through the Capitol holding a large Confederate flag,[46] and broke into offices. The Congressional certification of the election was interrupted—representatives and senators were rushed out of their chambers while Capitol police tried to hold back rioters who were smashing through windows and barricades, assaulting officers, and hunting down public officials.[47]

Trump acted like a dictator at home and praised dictators abroad. His authoritarianism isn't just central to his worldview—it's an ineradicable part of his character. As we saw in chapter 2, Hitchens was prescient about the political and cultural forces that would lead to Trump's rise. He urged Americans to be wary of the prejudices and resentments that Trump was uniquely capable of summoning, and he represents a form of politics that's anathema to Trumpism—from his internationalism to his disdain for populism and authoritarianism.

Far from earning the right to give other people orders, Trump constantly proved himself unfit for even the most modest positions of authority while arrogating to himself as much personal power as he possibly could. The robust institutional constraints in the United States prevented him from doing far more damage than he otherwise would have done, but his presidency was a stark reminder that the authoritarian impulse can only be contained—it can never be completely suppressed, and it can threaten even the most powerful liberal democracy on earth.

* * *

Immediately after the San Bernardino terror attack in 2015—in which a couple inspired by jihadist propaganda killed 14 people—Trump declared that he wanted to ban all Muslims from the country, create a registry of American Muslims, and place mosques under surveillance.[48,49,50] After Omar Mateen—who declared his allegiance to the Islamic State[51]— massacred 49 people at a nightclub in Orlando, Trump boasted about "being right on radical Islamic terrorism," warned that the attack was "just the beginning," and reiterated his call for a ban on all Muslim immigration to the United States.[52] He also said the United States should institutionalize torture and promised to "bring back a hell of a lot worse than waterboarding."[53]

Journalist Matt Yglesias argued in 2018 that Hitchens would have been "loudly pro-Trump," adding that he somtimes pondered "how annoying Christopher Hitchens' 'contrarian' pro-Trump columns would be if he were still alive."[54] Yglesias believes Hitchens's attitude toward Islam would have convinced him to support Trump,[55] who cynically scapegoated Muslims when the aforementioned attacks tilled fertile ground for an endless harvest of insular, fear-mongering rhetoric. But this is exactly the sort of nativist propaganda that Hitchens spent his entire career resisting. Trump regarded Muslims as a single uniform bloc—a nefarious and unwelcome one at that—but Hitchens always emphasized the diversity of Muslim communities around the world. As he observed in a 2007 essay:

> Islam is as fissile as any other religion. . . . Little binds a Somali to a Turk or an Iranian or an Algerian, and considerable friction exists among immigrant Muslim groups in many European countries. Moreover, many Muslims actually have come to Europe for the advertised purposes—seeking asylum and to build a better life. A young Afghan man, murdered in the assault on the London subway system in July 2005, had fled to England from the Taliban, which had murdered most of his family. Muslim women often demand the protection of the authorities against forced marriage and other cruelties.[56]

Hitchens loathed Islamism—the fusion of Islam and politics—because it's hostile to pluralism, corrosive to free expression, and above all, compulsively authoritarian. He didn't believe a state should be governed by the dictates of a holy book, which will necessarily elevate the rights of some citizens over others. He viewed the Taliban's domination of Afghanistan, to take the clearest example, as a negation of the liberal democratic idea: contempt for non-Islamic art and culture; the trampling of the rights of women, homosexuals, and minority religious groups; and revulsion at the very idea of modernity. The Taliban's vicious and backward ideology, he wrote, motivated it to use "heavy artillery to destroy the Buddha statues at Bamiyan," while the "co-thinkers of bin Laden in Egypt have been heard to express the view that the Pyramids and the Sphinx should be turned into shards as punishment for their profanely un–Islamic character."[57] Hitchens didn't just support the war in Afghanistan as a response to the September 11 attacks—he recognized that Afghanistan "belongs on that list of countries where we have a responsibility whether we like it or not,"[58] and not just a responsibility to protect Americans from terrorism, but also to help the Afghans rebuild their civil society. This conviction would be unintelligible to Trump, whose animus toward Islam has nothing to do with secularism or liberalism, but is merely an expression of his bigotry and opportunism.

The main victims of Islamic theocracy and violence are Muslims. After September 11, Hitchens observed that al-Qaeda's "main military triumphs have been against such targets as Afghan schoolgirls, Shiite Muslim civilians, and defenseless synagogues in Tunisia and Turkey."[59] During the Iraq War, he was especially disgusted with reptilian theocratic murderers and thugs like Abu Musab al-Zarqawi who did everything in their power to foment a savage religious civil war in the country—a tactic even Bin Laden found a little too cold-blooded. A 2005 letter to Zarqawi from Bin Laden's deputy (and the future leader of al-Qaeda) Ayman al-Zawahiri expressed particular concern about attacks on mosques: "My opinion is this matter won't be acceptable to the Muslim populace, however much you try to explain it, and aversion to this will continue."[60] Hitchens was revolted by the destruction of the Golden Dome (al-Askari Shrine) in Samarra less than a year later by the same fanatics who made "Iraqi life very nearly unlivable" and tried to "wreck the prospects of a federal democracy there."[61] And he observed that the United States, far from waging war on the "Muslim world," was on the side of Muslims who wanted to peacefully coexist with members of other faiths and sects.[62]

When commentators like Yglesias imagine that Hitchens's hostility toward Islam would have led him to support Trump, they may be thinking of passages like this:

> All over the non-Muslim world, we hear incessant demands that those who believe in the literal truth of the Quran be granted "respect." We are supposed to watch what we say about Islam, lest by any chance we be considered "offensive." A fair number of authors and academics in the West now have to live under police protection or endure prosecution in the courts for not observing this taboo with sufficient care. A stupid term—Islamophobia—has been put into circulation to try and suggest that a foul prejudice lurks behind any misgivings about Islam's infallible "message."[63]

The conflation of legitimate criticism of the doctrines of Islam with bigotry was a major subject for Hitchens. For one thing, he didn't believe a liberal society could function without the right to criticize religion, especially when the self-appointed representatives of one faith in particular try to silence that criticism with violence. But he also understood that the taboo against criticizing and satirizing Islam is an insult to the millions of Muslims who wouldn't dream of threatening their fellow citizens for exercising their right to free expression in a secular society. It allows the most extreme factions to speak for much wider communities that they don't, in fact, represent: "Europe's multicultural authorities, many of its welfare agencies, and many of its churches," Hitchens wrote, "treat the most militant Muslims as the minority's 'real' spokesmen. As Kenan Malik and others have pointed out in the case of Britain, this mind-set cuts the ground from under the feet of secular Muslims."[64] This tendency also energizes demagogues like Trump and his nationalist allies in Europe who present the entire faith as fundamentally illiberal and violent.

Hitchens argued that liberal democratic governments and citizens should forge alliances with Muslims who "want to practise their religion but otherwise neither to impose it or to be stifled by it." In 2002, he reminded readers that "There is a civil war raging within the Muslim world, where many believers do not wish to live under sharia any more than I do."[65] He observed that "Muslims want to travel, to engage with others, and to have access to information and enlightenment (to which they have already made quite majestic contributions)."[66] While it may seem like an affront to Muslims to make these needless-to-say observations, consider how often Western liberals treat the extremes as the norms within Islam—from Jimmy Carter writing an incensed op-ed about *The Satanic Verses* as if Ayatollah Khomeini spoke for all Muslims to the presumption that Muslims are so inclined toward violence that it's necessary to censor Western media outlets, academic presses, and artists to avoid their ire.

"In a broadcast just after September 11," Hitchens wrote in 2002, "bin Laden deputy Suleiman Abu Gheith warned Muslims living in the West not to reside in tall buildings or fly on airplanes, because the rain of death was not going to stop. There are many, many Muslims, and not just in the West, who do not care to be spoken to in that tone of voice."[67] In the same article, Hitchens celebrated the fact that

> The Iranian people, with no interference from outside, have in the past few years developed their own civil-society riposte to the archaic and bankrupt rule of the mullahs. With its dress and its music and its thirst for contact with the outside world, a generation has begun to repudiate theocracy and to insist that election results be respected. A free press is exploding from under the carapace, and electronic communications are eroding superstition.[68]

Just as Hitchens recognized that Muslims are indispensable allies in the fight against theocracy, he could see that many who shared his hostility toward the authoritarian elements within Islamic communities were, in fact, enemies. He refused to align himself with the xenophobic and nationalist parties and movements in Europe that used the threat of Islamic extremism as an argument against pluralism and other liberal values. While he worried that shifting demographics in Europe could make religious illiberalism more common, he also pointed out that those who make arguments of this kind should be wary: "... paranoia about population did mutate into Serbian xenophobia and fascism, and a similar consciousness does animate movements like the British National Party and [Jean-Marie] Le Pen's *Front Nationale*."[69, 70] Hitchens described Front Nationale, a French party that now calls itself National Rally under the leadership of Marine Le Pen (Jean-Marie's daughter), as "neofascist" in 2006.[71]

Anyone who believes Hitchens was motivated by anti-Muslim prejudice should consult his recommendations for resisting Islamism and jihadism while empowering secular forces around the world. He argued in favor of a "declaration at the UN of our solidarity with the right of the Kurdish people of Iraq and elsewhere to self-determination as well as a further declaration by Congress that in no circumstance will Muslim forces who have fought on our side, from the Kurds to the Northern Alliance in Afghanistan, find themselves friendless, unarmed, or abandoned."[72] This point is particularly salient today, after Trump abandoned the United States' Kurdish allies in northeastern Syria and Biden abandoned Afghanistan. Hitchens also made the case for "energetic support for all the opposition forces in Iran," which would put the United States "on the side of an internal reform movement within Iran and its large and talented diaspora."[73] And he argued for "unconditional solidarity, backed with force and the relevant UN resolutions, with an independent and multi-confessional Lebanon."[74]

We can be fairly certain that these aren't projects Donald Trump has spent much time thinking about. The notion that Hitchens would have become an overnight propagandist for nativist authoritarianism in the United States because he was critical of Islam is just as absurd as the idea that he supported the invasion of Iraq because he wanted to wage war on Muslims. The most powerful illiberal forces in Western democracies have repeatedly used anti-Muslim bigotry to build and maintain support. From Trump's demand for a "total and complete shutdown of Muslims entering the United States" after the San Bernardino attack to the burst of right-wing populism in Europe after the migrant crisis peaked in 2015, anxiety about Islam has proven to be a potent political force in the West. But this doesn't mean we should accept the fiction that there's a "clash of civilizations" between an amorphous "Muslim world" and the West. Nor does it mean we should lie to ourselves about the very real forms of Islamist repression and jihadist violence that afflict millions of people around the world.

* * *

While Hitchens became increasingly suspicious of left-wing utopianism in his later years, he argued that the "worst crimes are still committed in the name of the old traditional rubbish: of loyalty to nation or 'order' or leadership or tribe or faith."[75] Though this is to some extent a false dichotomy (many of the most brutal utopians throughout history dutifully invoked nation, tribe, and faith), it indicates that Hitchens would have been well-equipped to diagnose and resist a threat like Trumpism. Authoritarian populism is nothing new in America—it's a very traditional piece of rubbish. From the popularity of Father Charles Coughlin's putrid anti-Semitic and pro-fascist broadcasts in the 1930s to the original America First movement led by Lindbergh to the internment of Japanese Americans during World War II to McCarthyism, the United States has had plenty of powerful demagogues and authoritarian moments.

Hitchens recognized that nationalism and authoritarianism are often symbiotic, a fact that's particularly relevant in the context of the liberal democratic world's drift toward both over the past decade. After Trump's election, a cadre of intellectuals—such as the political theorist Yoram Hazony and the editor of *National Review*, Rich Lowry[76]—emerged to offer a positive vision of nationalism. In his 2018 book *The Virtue of Na-*

tionalism, Hazony argues that "universal political ideals—of the kind that are so prominent, for example, in the European Union—seem invariably to generate hatred and bigotry to at least the same degree as nationalist movements."[77] Considering the fact that the unprecedented period of European integration since World War II coincided with a 75-year respite from large-scale interstate warfare on the continent—the Russian invasion of Ukraine was resisted by a reenergized European Union, an exception which proves the rule—it's difficult to see how Hazony arrived at this conclusion.

Despite the best efforts of nationalist intellectuals to present a deodorized version of their movement, the resurrection of nationalism in Europe predictably led to surging authoritarianism and xenophobia. Beyond the devastating consequences of resurgent Russian nationalism, European democracies have faced an extended period of democratic decay driven by the return of nationalist politics across the continent. In Hungary, for instance, Prime Minister Viktor Orbán's efforts to transform the country into what he affectionately describes as an "illiberal democracy" have included packing the Constitutional Court and flagrant encroachments on judicial independence; the politicization of regulations for media organizations, NGOs, and educational institutions; and government intrusions on the democratic process through politicized audits, controlled access to the media, and the appropriation of public resources for political purposes.[78]

In March 2019, Orbán's party (Fidesz) was suspended from the European People's Party in the European Parliament, which stated, "We cannot compromise on democracy, rule of law, freedom of press, academic freedom or minorities rights. And anti-EU rhetoric is unacceptable."[79] Orbán celebrated Britain's decision to leave the European Union, and Hungary's membership in the union is in question over its antidemocratic behavior. Orbán has also made xenophobia a central element of his political platform and rhetoric. In 2018, he told the German newspaper *Bild* that he regards refugees as "Muslim invaders," going on to argue that "Christian and Muslim societies will never unite" and that "multiculturalism is just an illusion."[80] Orbán's bigotry is particularly demagogic and opportunistic considering the fact that Muslims comprise just 0.4 percent of Hungary's population.[81] Regardless, 72 percent of Hungarians held unfavorable views of Muslims in 2016, while the median in the rest of the European Union was 43 percent.[82] Orbán has also said "migration is not a solution but a problem . . . not medicine but a poison, we don't need it and won't swallow it."[83] In 2015, he declared, "all the terrorists are basically migrants."[84]

In Poland, the ruling Law and Justice party has brazenly manipulated the judiciary by preventing the appointment of Constitutional Tribunal judges (who are responsible for deciding whether laws comply with the Constitution) and selecting its own through Parliament.[85] Law and Justice has also taken control of the public prosecutor's office, increased the government's authority over lower courts, and established mechanisms for disciplining judges, which prompted the European Commission to take action against the government in 2020.[86]

According to the democracy monitor Freedom House, Law and Justice has enacted "measures that increase political influence over state institutions and threaten to reverse Poland's democratic progress. Recent years have seen an increase in nationalist and homophobic rhetoric."[87] The public broadcaster TVP has been pumping out pro-government propaganda since Law and Justice took power, even campaigning for the party during elections in 2019 and 2020 and attacking the opposition— what Freedom House describes as a "flagrant breach of statutory obligations to present news in a 'reliable and pluralistic manner.'"[88] The leader of Law and Justice, Jarosław Kaczyński, relied on xenophobic rhetoric before elections in 2015, warning voters that Muslim migrants would try to impose sharia and bring "very dangerous diseases long absent from Europe."[89] He also accused Muslims of using Catholic churches as "toilets."[90]

Despite the chaos of Brexit, the European Union faces the prospect of further dissolution. Along with Hungary, Poland's departure from the union is a possible (if remote) consequence of tensions between the government and Brussels over issues like judicial independence and human rights. But the popularity of the European Union among Poles has put pressure on Law and Justice to improve relations with Brussels—after Poland's Constitutional Tribunal declared that domestic law supersedes European law in October 2021, almost three-quarters of Poles said their government should back down from a direct confrontation with the European Union over the issue.[91, 92] Poland's membership in the union is restraining an authoritarian government's efforts to undermine the rule of law—a development that wouldn't have surprised Hitchens.

After the Russian invasion of Ukraine, Poland welcomed millions of refugees and immediately became a staging area for deliveries of weapons and supplies to its eastern neighbor. As a March 2022 *New York Times* report put it: Warsaw was the "capital through which all diplomatic, military and humanitarian roads to Ukraine now pass."[93] Even right-wing populists in Poland who have been voluble in their opposition to Brussels (and often sympathetic to Moscow) have embraced Poland's new role as Europe's most important shield against Russian aggression. Law and Justice remains a deeply illiberal party, and it's likely that Brussels will exert less political pressure on Warsaw at a time when Poland is so integral to relief efforts for Ukraine and the wider defense of Europe. This could empower politicians who have historically been illiberal, anti-democratic, and anti-European. But the war has also inspired a surge of Europeanism across the political continuum in Poland.[94] Even if the Polish government exploits the good will it has earned with its response to the invasion of Ukraine, the war has shown nationalists on the continent how important European unity and solidarity can be.

Poland and Hungary are the largest net recipients of aid from Brussels,[95] and the European Union remains popular in both countries—facts that make the prospect of an exit in either case unlikely. Both governments know they're taking a significant political risk by defying the union on issues such as minority rights, election manipulation, press freedom, judicial interference, and so on. Given the benefits of EU membership, direct confrontations with Brussels are unpopular. Contra Hazony, the European Union has served as a brake on the anti-democratic ambitions of the nationalist governments in Warsaw and Budapest. This is particularly important at a time when these governments will likely remain in power for years to come—Orbán won a sweeping victory in Hungary's 2022 parliamentary elections, while Law and Justice is by far the most popular party in Poland.[96]

While nationalist authoritarians hold power in Poland and Hungary, the populist right has also made inroads in other European countries. The European debt and migrant crises led to an increase in support for the anti-immigrant and Eurosceptic Alternative for Germany, though this support subsequently fell from its peak in the summer of 2018.[97] In the Netherlands, Geert Wilders leads the Party for Freedom—the third-largest party in parliament (it was the second-largest in 2017), and the second-most-popular as of June 2022.[98] Wilders has argued that Islam is a "Trojan horse in Europe," compared the Quran to *Mein Kampf*, and called for it to be banned in the Netherlands (meanwhile, he loudly declares his commitment to free speech when it comes to criticizing Islam).[99, 100] In France, National Rally is a powerful political force—Marine Le Pen made it to the runoffs against President Emmanuel Macron in the past two elections, and her share of the vote jumped from 33.9 percent in 2017 to 41.5 percent in 2022.[101] In June 2022, National Rally won a record 89 seats in the French Parliament.[102]

Hitchens would have been especially appalled at the recrudescence of nationalism in Bosnia. Milorad Dodik, a Serbian nationalist who controls roughly half the country as of this writing in 2022, has declared that he wants the "peaceful dissolution" of Bosnia—including the creation of an exclusively Serbian army.[103] Orbán traveled to Banja Luka in support of Dodik and promised to veto any potential EU sanctions against him.[104] Putin is a supporter of Dodik as well.[105] In a 2003 essay,

Hitchens observed that the "Serbian Orthodox fanatics who had proclaimed an artificial 'Republica Srpska' on stolen and cleansed Bosnian soil" cited other partitioned states (such as Cyprus) as precedents: "Even xenophobes," he wrote, "can practice their own perverse form of internationalism."[106] The cooperation between xenophobic nationalists across Europe is one of the gravest political threats on the continent today.

Hitchens recognized the threat posed by resurgent right-wing authoritarianism in Europe decades ago. In a 1996 article, he discussed the electoral victories of the Freedom Party of Austria (FPÖ) under Jorg Haider—a notorious right-wing politician who was killed in a car accident in 2008.[107] Haider's father Robert was a leading member of the Austrian Nazi Party, and his son praised the Nazis on multiple occasions—at one point celebrating Hitler's employment policies.[108] Like today's FPÖ, Haider was hostile to immigration and European integration. Hitchens believed Haider had "every chance of becoming Chancellor of Austria in the not-too-distant future,"[109] and he was right to be concerned about Haider's influence: three years after Hitchens published his piece, the FPÖ won 27 percent of the vote in Austria's parliamentary elections and formed a coalition with the mainstream Austrian People's Party.[110] Hitchens's explanation for the rise of right-wing populism in the mid-1990s would have been just as accurate two decades later: "In Austria," he wrote, "as in much of the rest of Europe, right-wing populists are 'playing on the piano of social anxiety'—over immigration, unemployment, and resentment against an over-centralized bureaucracy in Brussels."[111]

When Hitchens interviewed Haider, he was "reminded more of British Labor leader Tony Blair than of some lederhosen-clad nostalgic. . . . His answers to all my questions were deft and polished. No, he was not against Europe, only against the bureaucratic aspects of the Maastricht Treaty. He was not against immigrants, only against uncontrolled immigration."[112] Hitchens worried about the possibility that oleaginous politicians like Haider could convince European publics to accept dangerous and reactionary policies under the guise of innocuous-sounding rhetoric about reform: "This modern, yuppified and somewhat ecumenical version of the Euro-Right is no aberration.... Populist and nationalist forces have been able to re-emerge in respectable colors and either take power or come close to doing so."[113] A decade and a half later, Hitchens recognized that a populist shift toward xenophobia and authoritarianism was happening in Europe and the United States simultaneously. As he observed in 2010,

> almost every European country has seen the emergence of populist parties that call upon nativism and give vent to the idea that the majority population now feels itself unwelcome in its own country. The ugliness of Islamic fundamentalism in particular has given energy and direction to such movements. It will be astonishing if the United States is not faced, in the very near future, with a similar phenomenon. Quite a lot will depend on what kind of politicians emerge to put themselves at the head of it.[114]

The politicians who emerged—Trump, Orbán, Le Pen, etc.—took a volatile situation in many Western democracies and made it combustible. Le Pen vowed to end all immigration to France. "This is our home," she told a crowd in the final days of the 2017 French election. "French people feel strangers in their own country . . . because they have fewer rights than immigrants, even than illegal ones."[115] In 2017, Le Pen promised to hold a referendum on French membership in the European Union.[116] While she backed away from talk of a potential "Frexit" in 2022 (part of an effort to make her sound less extreme to French voters—an effort that largely worked), she was still relentlessly hostile to the union. For example, she believes French law should override EU law—the central issue fueling tension between Brussels and Warsaw.[117]

Hazony is the chairman of National Conservatism, an organization that aspires to present nationalism as an "intellectually serious alternative to the excesses of purist libertarianism, and in stark opposition to political theories grounded in race."[118] While there aren't many well-subscribed political theories grounded in race in the United States and Europe today (and it's slightly unsettling that the advocates of a gentle new nationalism feel the need to point out that their ideology isn't explicitly racist), it's no coincidence that *actual* nationalists have built their political movements around chauvinism and xenophobia.

Hazony believes nationalism should be inclusive, but this ambition never seems to make the jump from theory to practice. Nationalists often have a narrow conception of what constitutes a nation—they're more inclined to believe that specific aspects of a country's culture, traditions, and demographic makeup are integral to its identity, and that people who don't observe those traditions or fit into the right demographic categories are suspect. Hitchens had a more capacious and pluralistic definition of national identity, centered on the universal political ideals that Hazony dismisses. He believed, for instance, that internationalism should come naturally to Americans and described nationalists like Buchanan as "chronically un-American."[119]

Hitchens's universalism didn't just make him wary of politicians who appeal to voters' tribal impulses—it also helped him understand how various forms of tribalism (including national identity), populism, and authoritarianism are inextricably linked. In *Letters to a Young Contrarian*, he urges readers to be suspicious of

> all those who employ the term "we" or "us" without your permission. This is another form of surreptitious conscription, designed to suggest that "we" are all agreed on "our" interests and identity. Populist authoritarians try to slip it past you. . . . Always ask who this "we" is; as often as not it's an attempt to smuggle tribalism through the customs.[120]

During his inauguration speech, Trump announced that "we are transferring power from Washington, D.C., and giving it back to you, the people."[121] Over and over again, Trump referred to "the people" and presented himself as their authentic representative: "For too long, a small group in our nation's capital has reaped the rewards of government, while the people have borne the cost"; "Washington flourished, but the people did not share in its wealth"; "What truly matters is not which party controls our government, but whether our government is controlled by the people"; "January 20th, 2017 will be remembered as the day the people became the rulers of this nation again."[122] When Hitchens observed that populist authoritarians often conscript their audiences into their own essentialized, self-glorifying versions of the collective, he anticipated the mechanics of Trumpism.

Hitchens was aware of the threat posed by right-wing populism in the United States. Consider his view of Sarah Palin, who George Packer aptly described as "John the Baptist to the coming of Trump."[123] When Hitchens was asked who he supported in the 2008 presidential election, he acknowledged that Sen. John McCain's position on the Iraq War was closer to his own, but he argued that a serious vote couldn't be cast for the Republican ticket because Palin was on it.[124] In his *Slate* column, Hitchens made the case that Palin was an "absurd choice of running mate" and a "deceiving and unscrupulous woman utterly unversed in any of the needful political discourses but easily trained to utter preposterous lies and to appeal to the basest element of her audience."[125] He explained that Palin was a "deputy who does the innuendoes and slanders" for the McCain campaign, and who had the "nasty and lowly task of stirring up the whack-job fringe of the party's right wing."[126]

Hitchens observed that "Some condescending right-wing intellectuals are calling her [Palin's] style 'populist' and comparing it with Andrew Jackson and William Jennings Bryan. The true name for it is *demagogy*, descending from Joseph McCarthy, Robert Welch, and the nastier elements of the old Nixon gang—people to whom slander and defamation was second nature."[127] He was referring to Palin's declaration that those who demanded proof of the president's citizenship were asking a "fair question," only to immediately retreat from that position: "At no point," Palin announced, "have I asked the president to produce his birth certificate, or suggested that he was not born in the United States."[128] Hitchens's response: "Could anything be more cowardly and contemptible?"[129] And could anything be more indicative of the state of today's GOP than the fact that the man who trumpeted birtherism louder than anyone—and boasted of having done so long after the birth certificate was produced—was propelled to the Oval Office by many of the same voters Palin was courting? Trump didn't need a deputy to stir up the whack-job fringe of the GOP—he was happy to do the work on his own.

Hitchens recognized that Palin is, in fact, a populist. And in a 2009 article, he observed that the "difficulty with populism is that it exploits the very 'people' to whose grievances it claims to give vent."[130] During the 2008 campaign, when talk show host Chris Matthews asked Pat Buchanan if Palin was "one of the people wielding the pitchforks in your brigade back in '92," Buchanan said she was a "brigader in 1996, as was her husband, Chris. They were at a fundraiser for me. She's a terrific gal. She's a rebel reformer."[131] (Buchanan often referred to his supporters as the "Buchanan brigade.") While Palin didn't formally support Buchanan for president, she's firmly rooted in his political tradition, which is why he supported her. Hitchens could see how Palin functioned as a conduit for the most radical ideas on the populist right, noting that she was "close enough (and also far enough away to be 'deniable') to the paranoid fringe elements who darkly suspect that our president is a Kenyan communist."[132] By the time Trump took office, this sort of political chicanery was no longer necessary: Republican voters had already been primed to accept populist politics in its brashest and nastiest form.

In a 1998 essay, Hitchens drew a direct connection between authoritarianism and populism, emphasizing the use of "anti-elitism as a weapon with which to stir the masses against the competing elites that the regime may not like."[133] This is what Trump, Palin, and European populists like Orbán and Le Pen instinctively understand how to do. In *Letters to a Young Contrarian*, Hitchens offers a few historical examples of what he describes as the "manipulation of populism by elitism" (is it possible to think of a better way to describe Trumpism?):

> The "Church and King" mobs unleashed by the authorities in Georgian England were—I don't believe I exaggerate—outlets for energy that might otherwise be directed *at* Church and King. Instead, those who could not read were given cakes and ale for making a pyre of copies of *The Rights of Man*. If you read Dickens's depiction of the Gordon Riots in *Barnaby Rudge* you will strike much the same idea. For the party of order, disorder has always had its uses. It is not only reformers and revolutionaries who claim to speak in the name of the "general will."[134]

The political forces that conceived and nourished Trumpism were at work long before he took office. Hitchens was particularly critical of the mainstream conservatives who made excuses for those forces: "Looking back on the domestic political 'surge' which the populist right has been celebrating since last month," he wrote in December 2010, "I found myself most dispirited by the manner in which the more sophisticated conservatives attempted to conjure the nasty bits away"[135] (recall Ross Douthat's belief that the Tea Party would be folded into mainstream conservatism). These nasty bits included Glenn Beck's fevered conspiracy theories about the machinations of a secret government within the government; the racist "birther" theory; hostility to science and expertise; the exploitation of cultural, economic, and racial anxiety; and the weaponization of disinformation. "A whole new audience has been created," Hitchens wrote, "including many impressionable young people, for ideas that are viciously anti-democratic and ahistorical. The full effect of this will be felt farther down the road, where we will need it even less."[136] The populist right in 2010 was a nascent form of the populist movement that would send Trump to the White House a few years down the road.

As Hitchens explained, populist politicians often deceive and exploit the people they claim to represent. It was clear early on that Brexit would be a disaster for the British economy, but leaders of the Leave movement like Nigel Farage cared more about capitalizing on the nationalist momentum in Britain and pushing the referendum through than honestly weighing the costs and benefits of exiting the European Union. This isn't to say every advocate of Brexit supported it for cynical reasons, but the campaign as a whole misled British voters about the economic consequences, as well as the regulatory and political morass that awaited them. Populists in Europe and the United States have a dismal record of governance—from the Brexit fiasco to the corruption and anti-democratic rot of Trumpism.

The most unsettling political development of the past several decades has been the emergence of authoritarian populism. As Hitchens could see, this phenomenon was menacing when Glenn Beck was spewing hateful and paranoid propaganda on TV every night—but it became one of the gravest threats to liberal democracy when it found its way into the Oval Office and parliaments throughout Europe.

* * *

When Vladimir Putin invaded and annexed Crimea in early 2014, Noam Chomsky wrote a piece about what he regarded as the historical and geopolitical context of the crisis. He observed that Russia's decision to absorb Crimea was trivial compared to the "era's most extreme international crime, the United States–United Kingdom invasion of Iraq."[137] He also reminded readers about the Vietnam War. Despite America's insistence that it maintains international security and stability, Chomsky wrote, the "world thinks differently and regards the United States as a 'pariah state' and 'the greatest threat to world peace,' with no competitor even close in the polls."[138]

Even when Chomsky acknowledged that the annexation of Crimea was illegal, he hastened to add: "the Iraq invasion is a vastly greater crime." A more comparable crime, according to Chomsky, is the United

States' control of Guantanamo Bay in Cuba. Still, he wrote, "Russia has a far stronger case" in this comparison as well. "Even apart from strong internal support for the annexation, Crimea is historically Russian; it has Russia's only warm-water port, the home of Russia's fleet; and has enormous strategic significance. The United States has no claim at all to Guantanamo, other than its monopoly of force."[139] In other words, what business did the United States have condemning Putin? Chomsky also reminded readers of how the United States treated Russia after the Cold War: "When President Gorbachev accepted the unification of Germany as part of NATO—an astonishing concession in the light of history—there was a quid pro quo. Washington agreed that NATO would not move 'one inch eastward,' referring to East Germany. The promise was immediately broken, and when Gorbachev complained, he was instructed that it was only a verbal promise, so without force."[140] Chomsky believes this explains Russian aggression a quarter of a century later.

Many of the most prominent members of the "anti-imperialist" left made similar arguments in 2014. For example, Tariq Ali echoed Chomsky and explained that Russian imperialism in Ukraine should be viewed as a reaction to American perfidy at the end of the Cold War. Ali woefully observed that "One reason Gorbachev has publicly supported Putin on the Crimea is that his trust in the west was so cruelly betrayed."[141] This "cruel betrayal" was allegedly the expansion of NATO after Secretary of State James Baker promised that the alliance would not move eastward.[142] This is bad history—there was no official policy guaranteeing that NATO wouldn't extend to the east (Chomsky was right—the promise *was* verbal and didn't carry anything like the force of a formal treaty). And what kind of left believes a handshake deal between Russia and the United States several decades ago—which was far less serious or binding than Chomsky and Ali imply—should permanently determine the geopolitical makeup of Eastern Europe? Isn't the left supposed to be opposed to imperial carve-ups and hegemonic powers that believe they own their neighbors? Don't the Eastern Europeans get a say?

When the Euromaidan protests erupted in 2013, it was clear that the Ukrainian people were tired of being shackled to the backward, autocratic petro-state next door. The first protest was held in November 2013 when the Ukrainian government suspended the Ukraine-EU Association Agreement that would have established closer political and economic relations between Ukraine and Europe. Despite the passage of an anti-demonstration bill in December, the protests continued to intensify and confrontations with police often turned violent.[143, 144] On February 20, 2014, security forces opened fire on demonstrators and killed dozens.[145] This culminated in a period of intense fighting between protesters and security forces in Maidan Nezalezhnosti (Independence Square), which took the lives of over one hundred people—the climax of what became known as the Revolution of Dignity. After a political settlement was reached in February 2014, Russian-backed President Viktor Yanukovych fled the country and the Ukrainian Parliament voted overwhelmingly to remove him from office.[146]

It isn't difficult to imagine what Hitchens would have said as Soviet statues were stripped down and smashed with a sledgehammer in Kyiv. Or when other statues were torn down across the country, prompting Russia's Foreign Ministry to complain: "Russia is outraged at the ongoing monument demolition campaign in Ukraine. . . . We demand that new Ukraine authorities put an end to this mayhem."[147] At the sight of these images of defiance and self-determination—which were strikingly reminiscent of the 1989 revolutions—many on the left weakly complained that James Baker promised Gorbachev sole ownership of Eastern Europe.

In early 2022, Russia moved 200,000 troops—along with large concentrations of tanks, artillery units, and other heavy weaponry—into strategic positions along the Ukrainian border.[148] Putin then demanded that NATO offer formal assurances that Ukraine would never become a member of the alliance,[149] which was intolerable to Washington, Kyiv, and NATO. Putin's massive build-up of force around his neighbor's borders—following the invasion and annexation of Crimea in 2014 and the long proxy war Russia waged in the Donbas after that—was already the most audacious example of imperial coercion in the twenty-first century. And on February 23, 2022, Russia invaded Ukraine, launching the largest conflict in Europe since World War II.

Before the invasion, Moscow insisted on making the ludicrous claim that its belligerence was a form of self-defense, but Ukraine's relationship with the West posed no military threat to Russia—the threat was always political. Putin was terrified that an autonomous, pro-Western liberal democracy next door would be a standing rebuke to his stagnant oligarchy, and he spent years broadcasting his imperialist vision for Russia. In July 2021, he published a 7,000-word essay on the "historical unity of Russians and Ukrainians," which argued that Ukraine was a Soviet confection that shouldn't be considered a sovereign state.[150] In a paranoid, historically illiterate address days before the invasion, Putin insisted that the "disease of nationalism" (i.e., Ukraine's right to self-determination) had gutted Russian unity.[151]

Despite the overwhelming evidence that the invasion of Ukraine was the centerpiece in Putin's effort to restore as much of the Russian Empire as possible, the "anti-imperialist" left still found a way to blame NATO. The Democratic Socialists of America (DSA) issued a statement which "reaffirms our call for the US to withdraw from NATO and to end the imperialist expansionism that set the stage for this conflict."[152] Left-wing pundits brought up Iraq over and over again.[153, 154] Much of the left's response to Russia's invasion in 2022 was exactly the same as 2014. The only difference was that the obscurantism and moral confusion were all the more conspicuous with Russian missiles and artillery crashing down on Ukrainian cities.

Russia's invasion of Ukraine was the destination of a course Putin set many years earlier. In a 2010 interview, Hitchens worried about the "dangerous alliance between Russian nationalism and chauvinism revived under various pretexts of humiliation that I think are very dubious."[155] He described this move toward embittered nationalism and revanchism as a "terrible outcome for the Russian people and for the people who live within Russian borders who are non-Russian. But also for Russian neighbors, because this expresses a clear nostalgia for days of Russian glory and domination and empire."[156] Just a few years later, Putin justified the annexation of Crimea with the toxic language of nationalism and humiliation that Hitchens was concerned about—language that anticipated his justifications for starting the largest war in Europe in 75 years.

In an address on March 18, 2014, Putin argued that Russia was entitled to absorb Crimea on the grounds that its transfer to Ukraine in 1954 took place "within the boundaries of a single state. . . . Unfortunately, what seemed impossible became a reality. The USSR fell apart."[157] Putin has long regarded the collapse of the Soviet Union as the "greatest geopolitical catastrophe" of the twentieth century,[158] and he longs to restore some semblance of transnational political and economic authority over former Soviet states. According to Putin, after the Cold War, "Russia realised that it was not simply robbed, it was plundered."[159]

Hitchens understood that Putin's irredentism isn't just a reaction to Western policy—he had a sense of historical perspective and proportion that many on the left lack. In 2005, he discussed the "great Russian chauvinist resentment ever since the events of 1989—the feeling that they are on the losing side and that they're becoming a victim country. This is incalculably dangerous."[160] A few years later, Hitchens described Putin's invasion of Georgia as part of an "undisguised plan for the forcible restoration of Russian hegemony all around his empire's periphery."[161] And in 2010, he argued that the "menace of a recrudescent, nationalist, expansionist, reactionary Russia" made the reinforcement of vulnerable NATO allies (particularly the Baltic states) necessary.[162] In a review of Bernard-Henri Lévy's *Left In Dark Times: A Stand Against the New Barbarism*, Hitchens mocked those on the left who are "prone to sympathize with Vladimir Putin concerning the 'encircling' of his country by aggressive titans like Estonia and Kosovo and Georgia."[163] After the invasion of Georgia in August 2008, he pointed out that Russian imperialism shouldn't be confused with self-defense:

> The fans of moral equivalence may or may not have noticed this, but the obviously long-meditated and coordinated Russian military intervention in Georgia comes in the same month as explicit threats to the sovereignty of Poland and Ukraine, and hard on the heels of a Russian obstruction of any U.N. action in the case of Zimbabwe [a reference to the Security Council's failure to impose sanctions on Zimbabwean President Robert Mugabe for a violent campaign against opposition figures in the country]. Those who like to describe Prime Minister Vladimir Putin and President Dmitry Medvedev as reacting to an 'encirclement' of Russia may wish to spill some geopolitical ink on explaining how Kosovo forms part of this menacing ring of steel—or how the repression of the people of Zimbabwe can assist in Moscow's breakout strategy from it.[164]

Hitchens often emphasized Russia's support for Slobodan Milošević during and after the NATO intervention in Kosovo, which Moscow viewed as an affront to its regional hegemony. NATO's effort to halt yet another campaign of ethnic cleansing in the Balkans is the sort of thing many on the left now cite as the source of Putin's aggression, as if his rabid imperial ambitions would magically disappear without all these Western provocations. Given the scope of these ambitions and Putin's willingness to act on them, isn't it possible that he would have exploited NATO's *absence* from the region if the alliance had never expanded?

While Putin has made threatening noises about NATO allies like the Baltic states and Poland, President Biden and European leaders have made it clear to him that Russian forces on NATO territory would immediately be met with a swift and overwhelming military response. This is why Finland and Sweden are, as of July 2022, preparing to join the alliance—the invasion of Ukraine ensured that NATO would continue to expand instead of the other way around. The top concern in Helsinki and Stockholm is that they will be vulnerable to Russian attack before they formally join NATO and receive Article V protection.[165] If NATO had done what so many on the left wanted and refrained from moving one inch to the East (or disbanded altogether), would Putin have kept to himself and respected his neighbors' borders? Or is NATO expansion just one of the many pretexts for Putin's plan to remake Russia as a great imperial power through intimidation and war? Hitchens wasn't naive enough to believe the former.

After the invasion of Ukraine, it should be clear that Putin isn't going to stop making revanchist claims backed by the threat of force. Unlike much of today's left, Hitchens didn't believe appeasing Putin would lead to a new era of tranquil relations with Russia. He understood that the synthesis of bitter historical grievances, pan-nationalist ambitions, and naked militarism didn't bode well for Russia's neighbors.

And unlike the realist scholars who argue that state behavior is determined by the distribution of power in the international system—which leads to the view that any country would behave like Russia given similar geopolitical conditions—Hitchens recognized that the unique internal characteristics of regimes matter. History matters. Ideology matters. The personality of a leader like Putin—especially when there aren't many institutional constraints on his power—matters. Moscow wouldn't be obsessed with reestablishing its regional power if it wasn't for Putin's conviction that Russia was robbed and plundered at the end of the Cold War (or his fanatical admiration for the Russian Empire), just as the Ayatollah Khomeini wouldn't have issued the fatwa against Rushdie if he wasn't the spiritual leader of a theocratic state.

After Russia's invasion of Georgia, Hitchens made an eerily prescient observation about the future of Russian imperialism in Europe: "Russia had never expressed any interest in Ossetian or Abkhazian micronationalisms, while Georgia was an integral part of the Soviet Union. It is thus impossible to avoid the suspicion that these small peoples are being used as 'strategic minorities' to negate the independence of the

larger Georgian republic and to warn all those with pro-Russian populations on their soil of what may, in turn, befall them."[166] Putin justified the
annexation of Crimea, the proxy war in eastern Ukraine, and the subsequent invasion with the exact argument Hitchens anticipated: that Russian-speaking segments of the population were under threat and wanted
to be citizens of Russia. Putin even declared that the invasion was a
"peacekeeping" mission necessary to protect Russian-speaking Ukrainians from "genocide" and ultimately "de-Nazify" the country[167,168,169]—a
country with a Jewish president, Volodymyr Zelensky, who was elected
with 73 percent of the vote.[170]

In countries where Moscow exerts less direct influence, it's still relentlessly hostile to the interests and values of the liberal democratic
world. Hitchens cited Russia's attempt to fracture and undermine Europe by supporting Milošević in Kosovo and counterposed this policy
with the Western effort to help the Balkans escape an era of genocide
and war:

> Heartbreakingly difficult though the task has been, and remains, the
> whole emphasis of Western policy in the Balkans has been on de-
> emphasizing ethnic divisions; subsidizing cities and communities that
> practice reconciliation; and encouraging, for example, Serbs and Alba-
> nians to cooperate in Kosovo. One need not romanticize this policy,
> but it would nonetheless stand up to any comparison with Russian
> behavior in the Caucasus (and indeed the Balkans), which is explicitly
> based on an outright appeal to sectarianism, nationalism, and—even
> worse—confessionalism.[171]

Russia continues to support nationalists and ethnic chauvinists with
secessionist ambitions in the Balkans, such as Dodik in Bosnia.[172] This
is because Putin's ambitions aren't just territorial—he argues that the
"liberal idea has become obsolete,"[173] and he wants liberal democracies
to become less liberal and democratic. As we've seen, populist autocrats
(and would-be autocrats) across Europe and the United States share this

ambition, and they haven't been shy about working together. Orbán has long sought closer relations with Moscow, arguing in 2020 that the European Union shouldn't maintain sanctions on Russia over the annexation of Crimea and the proxy war in eastern Ukraine.[174] Even after the invasion, he refused to allow arms shipments to Ukraine on Hungarian territory while attempting to delay and limit the EU oil embargo on Moscow.[175,176] Le Pen is notoriously sympathetic to Moscow—her party accepted an $11.7 million loan from a Russian bank in 2014—while Trump has repeatedly expressed his admiration for Putin.[177,178]

This authoritarian solidarity is particularly dangerous at a time when the commitment to the liberal idea in the United States and many other Western democracies isn't as strong as it once was. Unlike the left-wingers who think activism and criticism should be confined to their own countries, Hitchens believed the left had a responsibility to confront illiberalism everywhere—a political orientation that's only becoming more important.

When Russia invaded Crimea, the Stop the War Coalition in the United Kingdom released a list of "Ten things to remember about the crisis in Ukraine and Crimea,"[179] but it may as well have asked readers to remember just *one* thing: as always, the West is to blame. "Who is the aggressor?" the article asked. "The obvious answer seems to be that it is Russia, but that is far from the whole picture." After opening with the standard line about the evils of NATO expansion, the article condemned the wars in Afghanistan and Iraq, the intervention in Libya, and drone strikes in Yemen, Somalia, and Pakistan.[180] It even pointed out that the United States helped to "bring down a pro-Russian regime" by supporting the *mujahideen* in Afghanistan in the 1980s, as if this somehow justified Putin's imperialism in Eastern Europe 30 years later. Stop the War implored readers to look at the "background to what is going on," but it actually wanted them to divert their eyes from any crime—no matter how terrible or undeniable—that didn't implicate the West.

The rest of the article is indistinguishable from Russian propaganda.

Putin declared that "Nationalists, neo-Nazis, Russophobes and anti-Semites executed this coup"[181]—his description of the Revolution of Dignity in Ukraine—while Stop the War emphasized the "role of fascists and far right parties in Kiev and elsewhere in the country."[182] Putin argued that the West has strategically encircled Russia with "controlled 'colour' revolutions,"[183] while Stop the War complained of "puppet regimes sympathetic to the West, often installed by 'colour revolutions.'"[184] Like Stop the War, Chomsky, Ali, et al., Putin condemned "NATO's expansion to the East, as well as the deployment of military infrastructure at our borders," along with Western interventions in the Middle East and North Africa.[185] And like Putin, Stop the War urged readers to remember that "many Russian speakers, there [in Ukraine] and in the Crimea, do not oppose Russia."[186]

After the invasion of Ukraine in 2022, Stop the War issued a statement which declared that the war was not the "responsibility of the Russian or Ukrainian governments alone" (as if both of those governments deserved blame) and argued that the "conflict is the product of thirty years of failed policies, including the expansion of NATO and US hegemony at the expense of other countries as well as major wars of aggression by the USA, Britain and other NATO powers which have undermined international law and the United Nations."[187] Left-wing organizations like Stop the War and the DSA are incapable of condemning any act of aggression—no matter how horrific and pointless—without simultaneously arguing that Western behavior is even worse.

There's considerable overlap between the "anti-imperialist" left and America Firsters like Pat Buchanan. After Putin annexed Crimea, Buchanan made all the familiar arguments about the perils of NATO expansion, American hypocrisy, Russia's legitimate security concerns and geopolitical interests, and so on. He decried the United States' support for pro-EU protesters in Kyiv as "direct U.S. intervention in the internal affairs of Ukraine."[188] Buchanan pointed out that George H.W. Bush had "implored Ukraine not to set out on a course of 'suicidal nationalism' by declaring independence from the Russian Federation."[189] Buchanan often declares his support for the principle of state sovereignty, but he doesn't believe this principle should extend to states on Russia's periphery—regardless of their aspirations for independence and democracy. In a review of Buchanan's 1999 book *A Republic, Not an Empire: Reclaiming America's Destiny*, Hitchens observed that, while isolationists often purport to be anti-war, the "blunt fact is that the tradition of Lindbergh and Buchanan would not have kept America out of war, or innocent of overseas adventures." Rather, the representatives of this tradition often "pledged a not-so-surreptitious neutrality to the other side."[190, 191]

While many Western intellectuals—on the left and right—are quick to assume the lowest possible motives for the actions of their own governments, they're willing to accept the most transparent rationalizations for the crimes committed by the West's enemies. An open letter in *Compact* signed by several prominent right- and left-wing intellectuals (including Greenwald, Murtaza Hussain, Sohrab Ahmari, Samuel Moyn, and Christopher Rufo) after the invasion of Ukraine called upon the Biden administration to work toward a "permanent peace that takes into account Ukraine's right to self-determination and Russia's legitimate security needs."[192] It's unclear how the Biden administration was supposed to find this balance at a time when Moscow believed its most essential security need was the denial of Ukrainian self-determination.

For all their lectures about the prudence and honor of isolationism, nationalists tend to admire and apologize for authoritarian aggression. Hitchens emphasized how "highly compatible the concepts of expansionism and racism are with the ideas of the parochial and the nativist."[193] In 2019, Buchanan's acolyte Tucker Carlson dropped the pretense of isolationist neutrality and openly declared his support for Putin: "Why do I care what is going on in the conflict between Ukraine and Russia? And I'm serious. Why do I care? And why shouldn't I root for Russia? Which I am."[194] During the 2016 campaign, Trump bizarrely refused to acknowledge that the annexation of Crimea had even occurred, arguing that Putin was "not going into Ukraine, OK, just so you understand. He's not going to go into Ukraine, all right? You can mark it down. You can put it down. You can take it anywhere you want."[195] This was two years after Russia invaded and annexed Crimea.

The nationalist right has nothing but sympathy for Putin, but it has inexhaustible contempt for the institutions and alliances forged in the liberal democratic world over the past 75 years: ". . . why should my son go to Montenegro to defend it from attack?" Carlson asked Trump in July 2018 (Montenegro became a member of NATO in 2017).[196] The president responded: "I understand what you're saying. I've asked the same question"[197] Trump wanted to withdraw from the alliance[198]—a decision that would have been catastrophic for the United States' allies in Europe, particularly those closest to Russia. Imagine if Trump had pulled the United States out of NATO before the invasion of Ukraine— or if Corbyn had been prime minister when the war started.

Many realists share Buchanan's view that Western encroachment is the proximate cause of Putin's aggression. After Russia absorbed Crimea, Mearsheimer argued that the "taproot of the trouble is NATO enlargement, the central element of a larger strategy to move Ukraine out of Russia's orbit and integrate it into the West."[199] Walt agreed, adding that Russia's invasion of Georgia in 2008 was a response to NATO expansion as well.[200] As Russia prepared to invade Ukraine almost a decade and a half later, Walt wrote: "Had the United States and its European allies not succumbed to hubris, wishful thinking, and liberal idealism and relied instead on realism's core insights, the present crisis would not have occurred."[201]

For realists and nationalists, helping an independent Ukraine move toward liberal democracy was never worth the risk of upsetting the autocrat next door. But what about the left? Aren't left-wingers supposed to be in favor of anti-imperialist and democratic independence movements? According to Pew, two years before the invasion of Ukraine, 78 percent of Ukrainians already expressed no confidence that Putin would "do the right thing regarding world affairs," while just 11 percent expressed confidence—the lowest proportion in Europe.[202] Despite the fact that the Euromaidan protests were a reflection of the genuine hostility toward Moscow's efforts to keep Ukraine trapped in its sphere of influence, many of the loudest voices on the left insisted on parroting Putin's propaganda about how the West, fascists, etc. were ultimately to blame for the unrest.

Hitchens was under no illusions about Russia's efforts to interfere in the affairs of its neighbor. After the main Ukrainian opposition candidate, Viktor Yushchenko, was poisoned with dioxin in 2004 (which left his face gravely disfigured),[203, 204] Hitchens observed that "Putin intervened outrageously in the attempt of the people of Ukraine to make a self-determined government of their own. . . . I do not believe anyone in the Ukrainian KGB would have dared to try to poison the opposition leader if they thought the Russians didn't know or might disapprove."[205] Hitchens was referring to Volodymyr Satsyuk, the former head of Ukrainian intelligence and likely perpetrator of the Yushchenko poisoning, who fled to Moscow where he's shielded from extradition because he has Russian citizenship.[206]

In August 2020, Russian dissident Alexei Navalny was poisoned by Novichok (a nerve agent that Russia has used to assassinate its opponents) during a flight from Tomsk to Moscow.[207] Several months later, after Navalny was imprisoned upon his return to Russia, tens of thousands took to the streets from Moscow to Yakutsk (in eastern Siberia), where protesters couldn't even be deterred by sub-60 degree Fahrenheit temperatures—the largest protests in years.[208, 209] Thousands were arrested as Russian state media condemned the "wave of aggression" and reminded protesters that "hundreds of videos were shot. All the faces are on them."[210]

Rather than expressing solidarity with these protests, many "anti-imperialist" left-wingers—like Max Blumenthal, who runs the *Grayzone* (which describes itself as an "independent news website dedicated to original investigative journalism and analysis on politics and empire")—made the case that Navalny is a Western stooge.[211] In January 2021, the cohost of Blumenthal's podcast *Moderate Rebels*, Ben Norton, posted a video of protesters beating someone up in Moscow and observed: "These are the Western media's and NATO's favorite angelic 'peaceful protesters' in Russia: fanatical supporters of far-right fringe opposition figure Navalny who brutally beat up counter-protesters who dare to hold up signs. This is NATO's hope for Russia's future."[212] During the Euromaidan movement, Blumenthal emphasized the fact that neo-Nazis and other far-right elements were among the protesters.[213] This is one of Putin's favorite tactics: ignore the huge mobilization of Ukrainians who oppose Moscow and smear the entire movement as a bunch of fascists and Western puppets. Since the invasion, Blumenthal has been busily denouncing the Western support for Kyiv as support for neo-Nazis in the Ukrainian military.[214]

This basic script is copied and reprinted over and over again on the "anti-imperialist" left. When tens of thousands of Belarusians turned out in an unprecedented protest against the 26-year reign of Aleksandr Lukashenko and faced the threat of imprisonment and state-sponsored violence, Norton declared that the "US/NATO are attempting a 'color revolution' to overthrow the government in Belarus, the only remaining ex-Soviet state that still has socialistic policies and state control over the economy."[215, 216] Lukashenko later allowed Moscow to use Belarus as a base of operations during the war on Ukraine. Meanwhile, Blumenthal denounces the democracy movement in Hong Kong as a violent right-wing sham funded by the United States government to perpetuate a "new Cold War" narrative, and he dismisses reports about the "so-called concentration camps" in Xinjiang as imperialist propaganda.[217, 218, 219, 220] In a 2021 interview, Blumenthal urged a realignment of priorities: "I just want to extend my invitation to the Chinese government right now to investigate our concentration camps on the U.S.-Mexico border."[221]

Blumenthal and Norton assume that American support for protesters in Eastern Europe and Hong Kong is automatically some kind of scandal. But the fact that the United States seeks to empower democratic forces in anti-Western dictatorships isn't exactly a revelation—of course Washington will seize opportunities to put political pressure on its foes while positioning itself as a defender of democratic values. Two things can be true at once: the democratic movements in Eastern Europe and Hong Kong can be organic and legitimate, even if they have Western support. The presence of violent and anti-democratic forces within the ranks of these movements doesn't change the fact that the vast majority of protesters are peaceful and democratic. The presence of far-right forces in the Ukrainian military shouldn't prevent Western governments from supporting the much larger number of heroic Ukrainians who are defending their country against imperialist aggression and subjugation.

Blumenthal and Norton propagandistically use slivers of truth—yes, there were far-right agitators among the Euromaidan protesters, and yes, some of the anti-Putin and anti-Beijing protests have been violent—to discredit entire democratic movements that challenge their worldview. It doesn't matter how legitimate the grievances of Ukrainian, Russian, Belarusian, or Chinese dissidents are, nor does it matter how autocratic (or imperial, for that matter) their governments happen to be. When the United States declares its support for a movement or government, the "anti-imperialist" left immediately starts searching for ways to discredit and malign it.

* * *

Pat Buchanan believes "Democracy lacks content. As a political system, it does not engage the heart."[222] He describes tribalism and nationalism as the "most powerful currents running in this new century" and deplores the "democracy worshippers of the West" who fail to appreciate this fact. His attitude toward liberal democracy has become more and more spiteful over the years: "America has become the most secularized and decadent society on earth," he argues, "and the title the ayatollah bestowed upon us, 'The Great Satan,' is not altogether undeserved."[223]

In a 1998 essay about populism, Hitchens lamented what he saw as the lack of self-confidence in liberal democratic cultures and institutions: "What of those," he asked, "who affect to believe that an open society, based on an association of equals with no divine warrant and no crowned head, is worth defending?"[224] Those who ostensibly believe in an open democratic society, he argued, offer "little but hesitation, apology, confusion and cowardice." While Buchanan thinks Ayatollah Khomeini was right to describe the United States as The Great Satan, Hitchens learned a different lesson from the pronouncements issued by Iranian theocrats—not that America had become too secular and liberal, but that it refused to defend its secularism and liberalism. This faltering commitment to the West's foundational principles has opened the gates for the nationalist authoritarianism Buchanan embraces.

Hitchens cited two examples of how the liberal democratic world had been "bleating and crying before it can be hurt, and capitulating before a shot can be fired."[225] The first was the response to the Rushdie fatwa. He mentioned a few of the white flags hoisted after Khomeini issued his death sentence: George H.W. Bush observing that no American interests were involved, the Cardinal Archbishop of New York and the Archbishop of Canterbury condemning Rushdie's alleged blasphemy, the refusal of major bookstores to stock *The Satanic Verses*, Viking's cancellation of the paperback edition, and the intellectuals on the right and left who cared more about Rushdie's politics and indulging the pious than defending free expression.[226]

While the Rushdie fatwa demonstrated how quickly many in the West would exchange their most basic rights and freedoms for a bit of security in their own societies, Hitchens's second example of liberal surrender had to do with the protection of those rights and freedoms abroad. When Bosnia was under siege by "ethnicised and clerical fascism," Hitchens observed, "It appealed for help in the clear and intel-

ligible terms that democracy and pluralism were values worth fighting
for, both for their own sake and for the sake of the common peace."[227]
Hitchens's case for the intervention in Bosnia went beyond arguments
about geopolitical necessity, stability, or even human rights. He believed
the conflict was a proving ground for the European idea—if the West
couldn't be mobilized to intervene on behalf of a defenseless multiethnic democracy when it was under sustained assault by irredentist ethnic
cleansers, it had lost its civilizational moorings. His support for interventionism wasn't just a modification of his views on foreign policy—it
was an affirmation of his commitment to liberalism, internationalism,
and democracy.

The nationalist right has become increasingly hostile to those values,
and the descent into something like Trumpism was always the logical
outcome of this process. The United States is the most powerful democracy on earth, but Trump subverted democratic institutions at every
turn. The United States presides over the world's most powerful military alliance, but Trump spurned relationships with NATO countries,
introduced doubt about the American commitment to Article V of the
NATO Charter, and wanted to pull out of the alliance altogether.[228] The
United States helped to build the post–World War II international order, but Trump believed America should turn its gaze inward and let that
order decay.

One of Trump's longest-held convictions (of which there aren't
many) is the idea that the United States is just one power among many
with no special responsibility to protect human rights, promote liberal
institutions, or maintain international security. He thought about relationships between states in strictly transactional and zero-sum terms—
he believed other countries (including allies and trading partners) were
constantly trying to swindle and sabotage the United States. In his inauguration speech, he complained that "we've enriched foreign industry at the expense of American industry" and "subsidized the armies of
other countries."[229] He continued: "We've defended other nations' bor-

ders while refusing to defend our own and spent trillions and trillions of dollars overseas, while America's infrastructure has fallen into disrepair and decay. . . . The wealth of our middle class has been ripped from their homes and then redistributed all across the world." He declared: "We must protect our borders from the ravages of other countries making our products, stealing our companies, and destroying our jobs." And he concluded: "From this day forward, it's going to be only America First."[230]

Unlike Hitchens and the liberal interventionists who argue that sovereignty shouldn't be considered inviolable when states commit atrocities against their populations or neighbors, Trump doesn't believe the international community has a responsibility to get involved: "We will seek friendship and goodwill with the nations of the world," he said, "but we do so with the understanding that it is the right of all nations to put their own interests first."[231] If putting China first means putting a million Uighurs in "reeducation" camps, it's Beijing's right to do so. Trump said he looked forward to Japan, South Korea, and even Saudi Arabia putting their interests first by developing nuclear weapons,[232] despite the fact that this would be in contravention of the Nuclear Non-Proliferation Treaty. When Trump moved U.S. forces out of northeastern Syria, Ankara believed invading and killing America's Kurdish allies—who suffered heavy losses in the fight against the Islamic State—was in Turkey's best interests.

Hitchens was always hostile to the "hard-nosed merchants of realpolitik"[233] who spoke in terms of interests rather than values. These were the people who counseled inaction in Bosnia as the death toll climbed and the process of carving a multiethnic democracy into racialized ministates continued apace. They claimed that the United States didn't have any "vital interests" in the Balkans. They rejected what they saw as a call for the world's lone superpower to use its military might for softhearted humanitarianism. They refused to acknowledge the fact that defending democracy and pluralism from ethno-nationalist imperialism *was* in the United States' interests. They believed the United States' democratic values could be divorced from its interests, just like a long line of "America First" nationalists—from Lindbergh to Buchanan to Trump. And though their reasons weren't always the same, the right and left found plenty to agree about when it came to the Rushdie fatwa and the wars in the Balkans.

The Trump presidency was a distillation of the post–Cold War anxiety about globalization, immigration, cultural change, the projection of American power, and international institutions that were designed to promote the interests of liberal democracies around the world. Trump and his fellow authoritarians in Europe represent a turn away from liberal democracy itself—a temptation that has always been latent in Western societies, but which exploded into full view the moment a demagogue arose to give voice to the fear, anger, and nativism that can so easily be transmuted into political power. But at a time when the left should have offered a counterpoint to Trumpism, many left-wingers decided that America Firstism wasn't so bad after all.

* * *

For many on the left, the predominant concern is always the crimes and depredations of their own governments, which is why they view democratic movements in authoritarian states like China and Russia as secondary to their concerns about Western support for those movements. Recall Chomsky's maxim: "I restrict myself to discussing American terror."[234] This is a defensible principle in some cases, but it has become the *only* principle for much of the left—an attitude that invariably leads to the exaggeration of Western (particularly American) misdeeds and the whitewashing of crimes committed by anti-Western governments and movements.

This is one of the main reasons Hitchens diverged so sharply from several of the major currents of Western left-wing thought after the Cold War. With the international socialist movement in decline and market-based neoliberal systems seemingly triumphant around the world, many on the left made resistance to American hegemony their central cause. They didn't regard solidarity against oppression and violence as a good in and of itself—it had to be filtered through the prism of opposition to the United States (and to a lesser extent, other Western countries). This hasn't just led to an attenuated and impotent form of internationalism on the left—it has warped left-wing thought and discourse, which is why today's "anti-imperialist" left is often indistinguishable from the isolationist right.

At the time of this writing in summer 2022, Trump remained the gravitational center of populist right-wing politics in the United States. But the second-best-known champion of his brand of grievance mongering and xenophobic nationalism was Tucker Carlson, who hosts one of the most popular cable news shows in history.[235] Carlson is a direct descendant of the America First tradition: hostile toward international institutions and interventionism (particularly in defense of human rights); wary of free trade, cultural exchange, and immigration; aggressively nationalistic; contemptuous of ethnic and religious diversity; and willing to exploit populist sentiments around all the above. It's no surprise that, in 2016, Carlson said: "No one is smarter than Pat Buchanan. That guy is a genius."[236]

You aren't going to find many left-wingers who agree with Carlson's reactionary attitudes on social issues, immigration, etc., but when it comes to foreign policy, the different worldviews of the "anti-imperialist" left and the nationalist right suddenly converge. In a June 2020 article, Glenn Greenwald pointed out that there's "ample agreement on specific, consequential issues between the factions that identify as the 'populist left' and 'populist right.'"[237] For example, according to Greenwald, Trump "viciously scorned the Bush family's imperialism and regime change wars." Here's what Trump's vicious scorn for imperialism looked like in practice: he repeatedly argued that the United States should have "kept the oil" in Iraq.[238] He endorsed the use of torture (vowing to use torture methods that were "a hell of a lot worse than waterboarding") and promised to massacre the families of terrorists.[239, 240] While he constantly reiterated his opposition to "endless wars," he also vetoed a bipartisan resolution which would have ended the United States' involvement in the civil war in Yemen.[241, 242]

Whenever Trump proved to be an unreliable anti-imperialist, the left could turn to plenty of other allies on the populist right. Before Trump launched airstrikes against Syria in retaliation for the Assad regime's use of chemical weapons, Greenwald went on Carlson's show to denounce the "neocons" who were in favor of punishing Assad for gassing civilians.[243, 244] Greenwald mocked supporters of the airstrikes who, according to him, believe presidents should "just drop bombs on other countries with no declaration of war, no reason why U.S. interests or the U.S. borders are at stake when it happens."[245]

After the Russian invasion of Ukraine, Greenwald went on Carlson's show to condemn the "incredibly provocative" expansion of NATO and complain about the "extreme hostility created in Washington due to Russiagate."[246] Greenwald later speculated about the possibility that Washington wanted to turn Ukraine "into Syria or Afghanistan where war rages for years and destroys the country, bogging down Russia," while Carlson described Ukrainian President Volodymyr Zelensky as a dictator and argued that "Ukraine isn't a democracy. It's a State Department client state."[247, 248, 249]

Greenwald is excited about the prospect of forging stronger relationships between populists on the left and right. While he claims that the populist right is an admirable aberration which challenges Republican orthodoxies and taboos, he ignores the fact that it's also a manifestation of provincial and reactionary attitudes that have a long and sordid history on the American right. Imagine what Hitchens would have said about a left which, upon learning of a chemical attack against civilians in Syria, urged inaction because American "interests" and "borders" didn't appear to be at stake. Or a left that has repeatedly proven to be incapable of calling Russian imperialism by its right name. Greenwald says people on different ends of the political continuum should cooperate when they share certain principles, but he may want to take a closer look at how progressive those principles actually are.

* * *

The left should reconsider the political wisdom of bringing its "anti-imperialist" contingent into the mainstream. Jeremy Corbyn led the Labour Party from 2015 to 2020, a period when he was the most influential left-wing politician in Britain. This was also one of the most controversial periods in the modern history of the party, during which Corbyn's scandal-plagued leadership inflicted incalculable damage on the populist left in his country and around the world.

When Corbyn became Labour leader, the party saw a dramatic surge in membership—from 193,000 at the end of Ed Miliband's tenure to well over half a million in December 2016.[250] Corbyn's leadership was especially exciting to young Labour voters, who were attracted to his undiluted populist left-wing message and his unconventional style of politics. But Corbyn ended up leading his party to its most devastating Parliamentary defeat in almost a century: Conservatives won 365 seats, while Labour only managed to secure 203.[251] One of the clearest explanations for this defeat was Corbyn himself—64 percent of Britons said he was doing "very badly" as leader of the Labour Party in December 2019, while just 4 percent thought he was doing "very well."[252]

Corbyn's unpopularity was partly due to an anti-Semitism scandal that became one of the biggest stories in British politics in the mid to late 2010s—even amid the Brexit debacle. Beyond the findings of an independent investigation which found that there was a culture of anti-Semitism in the Labour Party,[253] Corbyn's own record and behavior fueled the crisis from beginning to end. For example, in 2012 he trumpeted support for an anti-Semitic mural in London, arguing that it shouldn't be taken down and pointing out that the artist was in "good company. Rockerfeller [sic] destroyed Diego Viera's [sic] mural because it includes a picture of Lenin."[254] Corbyn was referring to Diego Rivera's 1932 mural at Rockefeller Center, which was chiseled off the wall in 1934.[255] The mural in London depicted several conspicuously Jewish businessmen playing Monopoly on the backs of naked, brown-skinned figures with smokestacks belching in the background, a man holding a sign condemning the "new world order," and the "Eye of Providence" watching over the scene.

In 2019, Labour member Jackie Walker was expelled from the party for claiming that Jews were the "chief financiers of the sugar and slave trade" and complaining that Holocaust Memorial Day places too much emphasis on Jews.[256, 257] The first investigation of Walker ended with her reinstatement as a member of the party, and Corbyn said he was content with this outcome, arguing that "Jackie Walker is a woman of black Jamaican heritage and European Jewish heritage. I think she is somebody that does have a deep understanding of issues of racism that have affected her and her family in her life."[258] Walker framed the criticism she received for her blatant anti-Semitism as racism, even putting on a one-woman play about the controversy titled "The Lynching."[259] Recall Hitchens's point about how identity politics can be cynically instrumentalized for many political purposes.

In 2010, Hitchens said he was shocked at the amount of anti-Semitism that had emerged on the left: "I didn't expect to see in my home country leading leftists, members of Parliament, and activists making common cause with the Muslim Brotherhood, with Islamic jihad, with the people who publish the Protocols [of the Elders of Zion]."[260] He continued:

> I would've thought it was unthinkable. But it's not. And given the immense contribution that the Jewish people have made to the liberal left in every society, this seems to me almost the most painful of the insults that this prejudice is currently holding against us. I take it, shall

I say, a bit more personally than some of the others. I'm used to it from Mosley, I don't care. I don't care about it from Jean-Marie Le Pen, I expect it from him. I hate its spread on campus and on the left. And it really needs to be fought without pity wherever it shows itself there.[261]

From 2011 to 2015, Corbyn was chairman of the Stop the War Coalition (the organization that regurgitated Russian propaganda when Putin invaded Ukraine). When he resigned, he said the group "represents the very best in British political campaigning" and emphasized his ongoing support: "I hardly need to say. In stepping down as Chair, I want to make absolutely clear my continuing solidarity with the Coalition and its work against wars of intervention."[262] Corbyn kept his promise to continue supporting his old "anti-war" comrades as Labour leader. After the 2015 terror attacks in Paris, Stop the War received a torrent of criticism for posting an article under the headline: "Paris reaps whirlwind of western support for extremist violence in Middle East."[263] Under pressure to distance himself from the organization, Corbyn instead reaffirmed his support, describing Stop the War (through a spokesperson) as a "vital democratic campaign" that had "repeatedly called it right over 14 years of disastrous wars in the wider Middle East."[264]

John Rees is one of Stop the War's most active officers, and during a meeting in March 2009, he explained that the Western left "must rely on the resistance of people who are at the sharp end of imperialism"[265]—those who attacked Israel and Western forces in Iraq and Afghanistan. At the same meeting, Corbyn told the crowd (to a stupid crackle of applause): "Tomorrow evening, it will be my pleasure and my honor to host an event in Parliament where our friends from Hezbollah will be speaking. I also invited friends from Hamas to come and speak as well. Unfortunately, the Israelis would not allow them to travel here, so it's going to be only friends from Hezbollah."[266] Corbyn then described Hamas as an organization "dedicated towards the good of the Palestinian people and bringing about long-term peace and social justice and political justice in the whole region."[267]

Rees and Corbyn dismissed the idea that their criticisms of Israel and Zionism were tantamount to anti-Semitism. As Rees put it: "Zionism is a political project to which we are opposed, and the Jewish people are something entirely different to that."[268] Corbyn described the idea that "somehow or other, because we're pro-Palestinian, we're anti-Semitic" as "nonsense."[269] It would be easier to take these complaints seriously if Corbyn and Rees hadn't just expressed their fervent support and admiration for an organization that explicitly references the Protocols of the Elders of Zion in its charter and blames Jews for both World Wars, the French and Russian Revolutions, and the formation of the League of Nations—which was actually a plot "through which they [Jews] could rule the world."[270] The charter also claims that Jews have amassed "great and substantive material wealth," taken "control of the world media, news agencies, the press, publishing houses, broadcasting stations, and others," and used "Zionist organizations" like the Freemasons and Rotary Clubs as "cells of subversion and saboteurs."[271]

If Hamas was dedicated to "long-term peace and social justice and political justice in the whole region," its charter wouldn't be filled with lines like this: "Israel will exist and will continue to exist until Islam will obliterate it, just as it obliterated others before it."[272] Or this: "In [the] face of the Jews' usurpation of Palestine, it is compulsory that the banner of Jihad be raised."[273] Recall Rees's support for the "people who are at the sharp end of imperialism." He may want to note that many of those people have a different sharp end in mind: Hamas describes itself as the "spearhead of the circle of struggle with world Zionism" and a galvanizing force in the "fight with the warmongering Jews."[274] In *God Is Not Great*, Hitchens observes that Hamas claims the "whole of Palestine as an Islamic *waqf* or holy dispensation sacred to Islam"[275]—a position that's not exactly conducive to peace—and notes that the organization's methods of governance don't seem particularly focused on securing social and political justice:

In Gaza, a young woman named Yusra al-Azami was shot dead in April 2005, for the crime of sitting unchaperoned in a car with her fiancé. The young man escaped with only a vicious beating. The leaders of the Hamas "vice and virtue" squad justified this casual murder and torture by saying that there had been "suspicion of immoral behavior." In once secular Palestine, mobs of sexually repressed young men are conscripted to snoop around parked cars, and given permission to do what they like.[276]

Corbyn didn't explain how Hamas's indiscriminate rocket attacks on civilian areas secure peace and political justice in the region. Nor did he explain how these attacks contribute to the good of the Palestinian people, who are the victims of retaliatory airstrikes and raids launched by Israel. According to Corbyn, dialogue with his "friends" from Hezbollah (who, he argues, should immediately be taken off Britain's list of designated terrorist organizations) is the "only way forward to bringing back peace."[277] Hitchens was less enamored with the organization "modestly named 'Party of God,' which mobilized the Shia underclass [in Lebanon] and gradually placed it under the leadership of the theocratic dictatorship in Iran. . . . It was in lovely Lebanon, too, having learned to share the kidnapping business with the ranks of organized crime, that the faithful moved on to introduce us to the beauties of suicide bombing."[278]

In a 2009 essay, Hitchens recalled a conversation with Walid Jumblatt, leader of the Progressive Socialist Party in Lebanon, who explained that "Hezbollah is not just a party. It is a state within our state."[279] Hitchens added that it's "also the projection of another state"—foreign subversion facilitated by proxies like Hezbollah is just one example of what he described as the "parties of god" fomenting religious hatred and crushing civil society in the region. When Iranian President Mahmoud Ahmadinejad visited Lebanon in October 2010, Hitchens emphasized the ugly form of solidarity that drives Iran's support for Hezbollah:

A man who has managed to escape serious inconvenience for his illegal pursuit of nuclear weapons and who has pitilessly repressed and cheated his own people can appear on neutral soil as the patron of the Party of God because his regime shares that party's pitiless attitude toward the state of Israel and its biting contempt for all the Arab and Muslim "moderates" who would even consider a compromise with it.[280]

Hitchens summarized the malign influence of Hezbollah (and by extension, Iran and Syria) in Lebanon—from campaigns of intimidation and violence directed at politicians and journalists to the exacerbation of sectarian tensions in the country.[281] He observed that Hezbollah masquerades as the "party of the downtrodden" when it's actually a "puppet of two of the area's most retrograde dictatorships."[282] Hitchens made the same point about Hamas. When Hamas won a majority in the 2006 Palestinian legislative election, Hitchens said it was "agonizing to watch the Palestinians choose a leadership that is openly aligned with the moribund and vicious dictatorships in Iran and Syria."[283] While Corbyn was loudly declaring his solidarity with Hamas (and being paid to appear on Iranian state TV),[284] Hitchens was denouncing its anti-Semitism and imperialism: "Hamas says that it wants an Islamic state all the way from the Jordan to the Mediterranean. It publishes and promulgates the Protocols of the Elders of Zion. Why not assume that it is at least partly serious about all this?"[285]

Recall that Hitchens was critical of the realists and left-wingers who refuse to acknowledge that the internal characteristics of regimes and movements matter. Realists will tell you Putin's Russia is behaving like any other great power. The "anti-imperialist" left will tell you Hamas and Hezbollah fire rockets into civilian areas, assassinate secular politicians, and strangle civil society in countries like Lebanon because they see no other way to resist Western imperialism. This type of analysis leaves sparse room for the role of politically inconvenient ideological or religious motivations, which Hitchens recognized as some of the most powerful drivers of human behavior. Putin *really is* a radical nationalist and imperialist who believes he has a duty to reconstitute the Russian Empire. The leaders of Hezbollah *really are* anti-Semitic theocrats whose organization is a proxy for the anti-Semitic theocrats in Tehran.

Because he failed to confront basic facts about the ideology of Islamism and jihadism, Corbyn uncritically accepted Hamas's propaganda, while Hitchens pointed out that the group is less interested in improving conditions for Palestinians than waging holy war on Jews: "For years, the PLO [Palestine Liberation Organization] leadership has been at least officially committed to a two-state solution and has at least officially made a distinction between Judaism and Zionism. It has also renounced the disgusting tactic of suicide murder. The emergence of a party that considers all of these evolutions as betrayals may have to do with something more than the provision of welfare."[286] Hitchens was a lifelong critic of Zionism, and he was often withering in his condemnations of Israel. In a 1988 essay about his discovery late in life that he was of Jewish descent, he noted that he "sympathized instinctively with the Jewish state" in his youth, but explained that he later felt "misery at the rise of the Israeli Right and enhanced appreciation of the plight of the Palestinians, whether in exile or under occupation."[287] In *Hitch-22*, he writes: "I regard anti-Semitism as ineradicable and as one element of the toxin with which religion has infected us. Perhaps partly for this reason, I have never been able to see Zionism as a cure for it."[288]

But Hitchens understood that Israel faces a sleepless threat from one of the most violent totalitarian ideologies on the planet: jihadism, cloaked as it sometimes is in the garb of revolution and anti-imperialism. He offered no excuses for the theocrats Corbyn celebrated and called his "friends": "Do I wish that the Israeli air force could find and destroy all the arsenals of Hezbollah and Hamas and Islamic Jihad? Yes. . . . Do I feel horror and disgust at the thought that a whole new generation of Arab Palestinians is being born into the dispossession and/or occupation already suffered by their grandparents and even great-grandparents? Absolutely, I do."[289] Hitchens demonstrated that it's possible to hold an uncompromising left-wing position on Israel-Palestine without ratio-nalizing the bigotry and cruelty of Hamas, Hezbollah, and other theo-crats who cynically pretend that the plight of the Palestinians is their central cause.

Hitchens argued in 2008 that the "most depressing and wretched spectacle of the past decade, for all those who care about democracy and secularism, has been the degeneration of Palestinian Arab nation-alism into the theocratic and thanatocratic hell of Hamas and Islamic Jihad."[290] Instead of being depressed by this spectacle, Corbyn and many of his comrades are exhilarated by it—they see Hamas and Hezbollah as radical allies standing up to the imperial bullying of Israel and the Unit-ed States. Again and again, from Russia to Palestine, this is the political calculation made by the "anti-imperialist" left: support for illiberal—even totalitarian—movements and governments is justified as long as they oppose the West. In *Christopher Hitchens: What He Got Right, How He Went Wrong, and Why He Still Matters*, Ben Burgis laments the fact that "It's particularly hard to imagine him [Hitchens] having anything kind to say about one of the most important figures in the global revival of the socialist Left—peacenik British Labour leader Jeremy Corbyn."[291] To Hitchens's lasting credit, Burgis is right.

* * *

In a 1944 letter to Noel Willmett, Orwell worried about the rise of what he described as "petty fuhrers" after the defeat of Hitler.[292] He decried the "horrors of emotional nationalism and a tendency to disbelieve in the existence of objective truth because all the facts have to fit in with the words and prophecies" of these leaders.[293] But he expressed optimism in response to Willmett's observation that the United States and Britain hadn't succumbed to totalitarianism: "As to the comparative immunity of Britain and the USA," Orwell wrote, "Whatever the pacifists etc. may say, we have *not* gone totalitarian yet and this is a very hopeful symptom."[294]

Despite Orwell's suspicion that something like the world he created in *1984* was actually in formation—and his concern over what he described as the "decay of democracy"[295]—he wouldn't have written the book if he believed that outcome was inevitable. Although he was an unyielding critic of British imperialism and American cultural and political influence, he also acknowledged that Western democracy should be defended and improved: "I think, and have thought ever since the war began, in 1936 or thereabouts, that our cause is the better, but we have to keep on making it the better, which involves constant criticism."[296]

At the end of the Cold War, Hitchens recalled a "common feeling that the values of pluralism and democracy were worth having for their own sake."[297] The totalitarian idea, it seemed, had collapsed along with the Berlin Wall. In a 1994 essay about his departure from the Socialist Workers Party in the mid-1970s, Hitchens recalled a conversation he had with the Polish dissident Jacek Kuroń when the Iron Curtain was still drawn over Eastern Europe: "He told me that he'd ceased to bother with Trotskyist disputation, and now felt that the real confrontation was between pluralism and state absolutism. However simplistically phrased, this became the slogan of the most thorough-going revolution we ever did live to see."[298]

It wouldn't be long before Hitchens stopped using words like "simplistic" to describe the confrontation between pluralism and absolutism—the central confrontation of his political life after the Cold War. When he saw his old left-wing comrades busily hatching excuses for neutrality as fascism swept through the Balkans, he realized that much of the left was either indifferent about this confrontation or on the wrong side. And he recognized that the dissidents like Kuroń who made the "simple" demand for democracy in defiance of Soviet totalitarianism—rather than wasting time with "Trotskyist disputation" and other endless internecine squabbles—were vindicated in 1989.

Orwell's terror at the idea of centuries of static and oppressive tension between a few totalitarian superstates was misplaced, and while his predictions about a Cold War between the United States and the Soviet Union were prescient, he probably would have been surprised to discover that communism would collapse all on its own. Although a socialist United States of Europe failed to materialize, consider how shocking it would be for a man who fought in the Spanish Civil War and whose London apartment was destroyed by a German rocket to learn that Berlin would become the anchor of a 27-state European Union—a role made all the more significant by Britain's departure from that union.

Hitchens often observed that petty fuhrers like Slobodan Milošević and Saddam Hussein were direct descendants of the great totalitarians of the twentieth century. He described Milošević's revanchist campaign of ethnic cleansing as the return of fascism to Europe.[299] He observed that the "founders and inspirers of the Baath Party . . . modeled themselves basically on European fascism."[300] (For an incisive analysis of this historical phenomenon, see Paul Berman's *Terror and Liberalism*.[301] For an examination of the influence of Nazi propaganda elsewhere in the Middle East, see his book *The Flight of the Intellectuals*.[302]) Of course these petty fuhrers didn't pose the same civilizational threat as Hitler or Stalin, but they still immiserated or destroyed the lives of millions of people.

Hitchens regarded a status quo in which a European country could be subjected to genocidal violence for years with no significant opposition from Western powers as intolerable. He didn't just view the removal of the Taliban as justice for the September 11 attacks—he welcomed the end of the most retrograde and cruel theocracy on earth, and he would be appalled at the Taliban's triumphant return to power after the United States abandoned Afghanistan in the fall of 2021. He believed a reckoning with Saddam Hussein was inevitable and he wanted to see Iraq liberated from a "psychopathic crime family."[303] He argued that the international community had a responsibility to stop the genocide in Darfur and thought the United States and its allies should do everything possible to bring the dictatorships in Libya and Syria to an end.

Hitchens opposed nationalism and authoritarianism in the United States and Europe for the same reason he supported these interventions around the world—he believed in democracy and universal human rights. Like Orwell, he believed our cause—the liberal democratic cause—is the better. In his 2007 biography of Thomas Paine, Hitchens observes that his subject regarded the United States as an "actual and concrete achievement; not an imaginary Utopia but a home for liberty and the conscious first stage of a world revolution."[304] Once Hitchens dropped the idea of utopia, he realized that the true revolutionary forces in the world are the millions of people—from Eastern Europe to Tehran, Kabul, Hong Kong, Moscow, and Yangon—who demand the basic rights that are granted at birth in liberal democracies. Hitchens frequently observed that there are many countries which would benefit from the adoption of a set of rights and rules resembling the U.S. Constitution—he still believed in America's revolutionary purpose 230 years after Paine made the case for independence and representative government.

While these ideas were radical for their time, the endurance of the American Revolution is a testament to its practicality and universality. Even the title of Paine's revolutionary pamphlet, *Common Sense*, captures this essential element of his work: he was naturally and intentionally egalitarian, and his argument was meant to be understood as widely as possible. The intelligibility of Paine's case rested on the obvious fact that what he described as the "two ancient tyrannies" of monarchy and aristocracy were just that: tyrannies. Even in Paine's time, most people could see that democracy was the only real bulwark against authoritarianism—a fact that's no less true today.

6 The Highest Form of Patriotism

Hitchens on Internationalism

"Patriotic and tribal feelings," Hitchens wrote in 1991, "belong to the squalling childhood of the human race, and become no more charming in their senescence. They are particularly unattractive when evinced by a superpower."[1] This was a few months after the Gulf War, when Hitchens was primarily concerned about what he regarded as America's imperial overreach.

Over the next decade and a half, Hitchens's attitude toward patriotism changed: "In America," he wrote in 2005, "your internationalism can and should be your patriotism."[2] In one of Thomas Jefferson's final letters on June 24, 1826, he reflected on the global significance of the American experiment: "May it be to the world what I believe it will be (to some parts sooner, to others later, but finally to all), the signal of arousing men to burst the chains under which monkish ignorance and superstition had persuaded them to bind themselves, and to assume the blessings and security of self-government."[3] Hitchens cited these lines to demonstrate Jefferson's belief in the universality of the principles enshrined in the Declaration of Independence and the Constitution.[4]

Hitchens thought American internationalism should be motivated by a basic set of ideas: first, Enlightenment values such as free expression, pluralism, democracy, and individual rights are, in fact, universal—they can be understood by anyone, and once understood, they will generally be chosen over the alternatives. Second, the United States should simultaneously embody and defend those values in the world. And third, nationalism, religion, and other forms of tribalism should be resisted, as they often lead to the negation of those values.

In *Enlightenment Now: The Case for Reason, Science, Humanism, and Progress* (2018), Steven Pinker emphasizes the universality of the Enlightenment project: reason is the nonnegotiable starting point for any civil society; science nudges us closer to the objective nature of reality, and its hypotheses are universally testable and intelligible; humanism is the belief that human flourishing is more important than the glorification of the nation, god, or some other tribal deity; and progress has taken place on a vast scale everywhere from Europe to East Asia to the United States to sub-Saharan Africa—thanks in no small part to the Enlightenment principles outlined above. To put these principles into practice, Pinker argues for the development of "norms and institutions that channel parochial interests into universal benefits."[5]

George Packer observed that Hitchens, "for all his radicalism . . . was old-fashioned. He once said to me, 'I'm a Paine-ite,' meaning Thomas Paine. That sounded right. Christopher was born a couple of centuries too late."[6] Hitchens became more old-fashioned in his later years, but this isn't to say he moved to the right or became reactionary—he simply moved from socialism toward a more elemental set of principles and political commitments. Consider what Hitchens meant when he described himself as "Paine-ite," for instance. He always appreciated the United States' radical origins, as well as the value of living and working in a country with a secular Constitution that offered robust protections such as the "great roof of the First Amendment."[7] He had long argued that the country of his birth should adopt something like the U.S. Constitution.[8] However, in other ways his attitude toward America underwent a complete transformation—as a socialist he regarded the United States as a marauding imperial power, but he was forced to revisit this view after the Cold War.

When the Soviet Union collapsed, Hitchens understood that most Eastern Europeans were demanding something simultaneously radical and modest; revolutionary and familiar: the blessings and security of self-government. "In Eastern Europe by the end of the 1980s," he wrote in 2011, "one knew not only what the people wanted but also how they would get it. Not to diminish the grandeur of those revolutions, the citizens essentially desired to live in Western European conditions, of greater prosperity and greater liberty."[9] Hitchens also noted that the post-Soviet democracies in Eastern Europe were immediately ready to be integrated into an existing international system of commerce and defense—what Pinker might describe as norms and institutions that channel parochial interests into universal benefits: "The arms of the European Community and NATO," Hitchens wrote, "were already more or less open."[10] There's no clearer example of Eastern Europe's effort to escape its Soviet past and join the Western democratic world than Ukraine's bid for membership in the European Union and NATO in courageous defiance of Putin's massive military machine.

The demand for what Hitchens described as "Western European conditions" was a radical one, even by recent historical standards. There were far more autocracies than democracies in the world at the close of the Cold War, but this distribution has been inverted.[11] Nonviolent resistance was central to the revolutions in Eastern Europe—as Hitchens put it, dissidents like Václav Havel were "ironic, understated, nonfanatical, nonviolent."[12] There has never been a more sweeping political change on the back of largely peaceful civic action: the revolutions in Poland, Hungary, Czechoslovakia, East Germany, and Bulgaria (it should be noted that the transition was sometimes violent, as in Romania) took place under the shadow of overwhelming Soviet military force. But as Hitchens put it, the revolutionaries facilitated the move to liberal democracy "by putting on plays, by writing poems, by publishing essays, by making jokes, by demonstrating the value of the written word and a life lived in truth and by nothing else; no car bombs, no bullying, no fanaticism."[13]

While it's true that political and structural changes within the Soviet Union—particularly the process of decentralization and the empowerment of national governments overseen by Mikhail Gorbachev after Perestroika and Glasnost[14]—had a significant role in its collapse, the discontent within soon-to-be-former Soviet states was a major driver of the 1989 revolutions. The revolutions also sustained and built upon one another, with transitional governments establishing parliamentary procedures and paths to liberalization on the basis of what other European parties and movements had done. The demand for unrestricted freedom of movement throughout Europe led to the most arresting images of the revolution, from the hundreds of East Germans fleeing across the border between Austria and Hungary when it was briefly opened in the summer of 1989 (which preceded the official opening that September) to the hundreds of thousands of people who descended on the Berlin Wall on November 9, 1989. These images didn't just demonstrate how widespread the contempt for communist rule had become—they were a glimpse of what the future of Europe would look like. Recall Paul Berman's observation that "one element in the classic left-wing imagination—the vision of a borderless, federal, peaceful, technocratic Europe—turned out to be solid and lasting."[15]

The existence of a borderless, federal, peaceful, technocratic Europe is taken for granted today, but it's hard to overstate what a historic aberration this is. As Robert Wright observes in *Nonzero: The Logic of Human Destiny*: "If ninety, even sixty, years ago, you had predicted that someday France and Germany would have the same currency, the reply would have been: 'Oh, really? Which nation will have conquered which?'"[16] The post–World War II era has been an unprecedented period of international integration and democratic development, and the two are often entwined: the NATO Charter calls upon states to observe and defend democratic norms and institutions, the rule of law, individual liberty, and economic cooperation. The UN Universal Declaration of Human Rights states that the "will of the people shall be the basis of the authority of government" and affirms basic democratic rights such as freedom of expression and assembly. The Maastricht Treaty declares that the European Union respects the principles of democracy and fundamental human rights. These institutions partially comprise what's referred to—often derisively, especially on the left—as the postwar international order. Through the maintenance of organizations like the United Nations, international economic institutions, alliances like NATO, and mutual defense treaties with South Korea, Japan, and other regional powers, the United States has been the anchor of the international system for the past three-quarters of a century.

During this period, America and its allies have presided over what historians and political scientists refer to as the Long Peace: an era of relative stability during which interstate warfare (particularly between great powers) has seen a precipitous decline. Here's how Pinker describes this period:

> For 450 years, wars involving a great power became shorter and less frequent. But as their armies became better manned, trained, and armed, the wars that did take place became more lethal, culminating in the brief but stunningly destructive world wars. It was only after the second of these that all three measures of war—frequency, duration, and lethality—declined in tandem, and the world entered the period that has been called the Long Peace.[17]

Pinker identifies several causes of the Long Peace: the growth in international commerce, the spread of democracy, and the establishment of international laws and norms that have made war and conquest illegal. He acknowledges that the international prohibition on aggression has been inconsistently enforced—while the United States led a coalition to expel Saddam Hussein from Kuwait in 1990, Putin was able to invade and annex Crimea with relative impunity in 2014—but Pinker rightly observes that "an imperfectly enforced law is better than no rule of law at all."[18] Though Pinker doesn't mention it, the most effective enforcement mechanism when it comes to the Husseins and Putins of the world is American (and increasingly European) power.

Just months after the Berlin Wall was torn down, Hitchens penned a caustic deconstruction of Cold War neoconservatism[19]—an ideology which he believed was adrift after the dissolution of the Soviet Union. He argued that neoconservatives were thinly disguised imperialists whose *raison d'être* vanished with the end of the Warsaw Pact. They needed the Soviet empire to justify the maintenance of the American empire, swollen military budgets, and so on. For many years, Hitchens characterized the Cold War as an "inter-imperial rivalry" because he saw the United States as the inheritor of European imperialism after World War II.[20] In 1990, he ridiculed neoconservatives for believing they had been involved in a "long twilight struggle against the 'totalitarian' foe" during the Cold War.[21]

But there was dissonance in this critique—not because Hitchens had a secret sympathy for the self-aggrandizing Cold Warriors, but because he had nothing but sympathy and admiration for the dissidents of Eastern Europe. Despite the decades of subjugation and stagnation they had endured, they remained "Cheerful, orderly, well-informed, happily familiar with all the values and procedures of democracy, anti-militarist, conscious of history."[22] At the end of the Cold War, Hitchens found it difficult to believe that such principles and temperaments could emerge "under a 'totalitarian' system, where obedience and thought control were the norms,"[23] but he would later admit that this is exactly what happened in the former Soviet Union.

In an article published many years later, after noting that Washington's behavior during the Cold War "involved some episodes of unforgettable arrogance and cruelty," Hitchens pointed out that American "imperialism" is still a historical anomaly: "Unlike the Romans or the British, Americans are simultaneously the supposed guarantors of a system of international law and doctrine." He continued: "The plain fact remains that when the rest of the world wants anything done in a hurry, it applies to American power."[24] As for his comment about the interimperial rivalry during the Cold War, he later challenged the "spurious 'moral equivalence' between the Soviet and American sides."[25] The grandiose claims of the neocons notwithstanding, Hitchens ultimately acknowledged that a long twilight struggle against a totalitarian foe really had taken place in the Soviet Union. And despite the disastrous consequences of many American policies during the Cold War, the United States was on the right side of this global struggle.

The United States has an outsize role in the international system, which is one of the reasons the left has made opposition to the ugly side of American power (B-52s over Cambodia, anti-democratic meddling in Central and South America, decades of support for dictatorships like Saudi Arabia and Egypt, etc.) one of its central causes. But Hitchens's left-wing critics are wrong to insist that his liberal interventionism—a term sure to raise the blood pressure of some readers—is a right-wing position counterbalanced by the left-wing demand to see Kissinger on trial. They were expressions of the same internationalist convictions.

Hitchens's most essential political shift was his reassessment of the United States—especially its role in the post–Cold War world. The carpet bombing of Cambodia was in no way comparable to the NATO intervention to rescue Bosnia from a genocidal siege carried out by petty fuhrers and war criminals like Milošević and Ratko Mladić. The decision to arm and fund the *mujahideen* can't be likened to the effort to remove the Taliban from power. The United States' repeated betrayals of the Kurds can't be compared to the no-fly zone that was established over northern Iraq to protect them. The Iraq War was a reversal of Washington's support for Saddam Hussein as he waged a devastating war against

Iran and committed genocide against the Kurds. You may regard Hitchens's arguments about promoting democracy or defending human rights as smokescreens for other geopolitical aims, but even the most cynical interpretation of the past three decades of U.S. foreign policy has to contend with the fact that these were stark divergences from the policies that were adopted during the Cold War.

Now that the United States and its European allies are trying to help a desperate Ukrainian resistance expel Russian forces from their country after the most brutal and brazen act of imperialism in Europe since World War II, these divergences are even clearer. The "anti-imperialist" left no longer has a cause—at least until it recognizes that the real imperialists in the world today aren't the leaders of Western countries.

Just as Hitchens believed Americans should be natural internationalists, his own internationalism was unthinkable without the United States. And this internationalism was the practical extension of his commitment to the universal values of the Enlightenment, which he believed America should represent and protect. "Internationalism," Hitchens observed in 1991, "is the highest form of patriotism"[26]—an observation that has taken on even greater significance with the return of great power competition and the renewed authoritarian threat to democracy around the world.

* * *

Like Berman, Hitchens saw the connection between the revolutionary movements of 1968 and the collapse of communism in 1989. "Of the dissident heroes of that later revolution," he wrote, "I can think of several who I first met on or around the barricades of 1968."[27] Despite the pervasive left-wing belief that the European Union, NATO, and other international institutions are instruments of neoliberal imperialism, they're actually manifestations of old ideas about European solidarity and political integration.

After the revolutions in 1989, former Soviet states were lining up to be part of the Western system of trade, travel, defense, and political organization—the greatest movement away from totalitarianism in history. This movement continues to this day with Ukraine's effort to decouple from Russia and join the European Union and NATO. When Russia went to war over Ukraine's democratic and internationalist ambitions, many left-wingers, nationalists, and realists argued that it was never worth risking World War III for a Westernized Ukraine. Meanwhile, as Russian missiles and artillery leveled Ukrainian cities and forced millions from their homes, it's no wonder that countries like Kosovo requested membership in NATO and the deployment of U.S. forces on their soil.[28] While many on the left are squeamish about assisting small countries in spite of Moscow's demands, Hitchens always had a bias toward doing so.

The populist right and left have converged on a reactionary view of European integration. Just as Corbyn sees the creation of a new European empire in greater economic, political, and military cooperation across the continent, British Prime Minister Boris Johnson once observed that "Napoleon, Hitler, various people tried this out, and it ends tragically."[29] Johnson also described the European Union as an attempt to "recreate the dream of the Roman Empire." Other Leave campaigners like Jacob Rees-Mogg agreed, arguing that Johnson's comments were "absolutely true." Perhaps the best-known campaigner for Brexit, Nigel Farage, made the same observation in 2019: "They're building an empire, why deny it?"[30]

While the Labour Party under Corbyn officially supported remaining in the European Union, its efforts were muted. As Nick Cohen explained: "The dominant factions of the British far left have shown you since the 1970s that they are anti-European."[31] As we saw in chapter 3, Corbyn was expressing fervent anti-Europeanism right up to the moment he was charged with championing the European cause in the face of powerful forces marshaled in favor of Brexit, and he would soon be echoed by Johnson, Farage, and many of the most prominent Leave campaigners. Corbyn is part of a long tradition of Euroscepticism on the British left. Former Labour MP Tony Benn was notoriously hostile to the European Union, describing it as a corporatized, undemocratic attack on British sovereignty and using the exact same language as the nativist right: "I think they're building an empire there," he said in a discussion at the Oxford Union in 2013, "and they want us to be a part of that empire, and I don't want that."[32]

Critics of the European Union often argue that the union is undemocratic, but a far more urgent threat to democracy in Europe today is the emergence of nationalist authoritarianism—a movement defined by its Euroscepticism and the paranoid insistence that the nations of Europe are subservient to a dictatorship headquartered in Brussels. The European Union has served as a safeguard against the anti-democratic tendencies of Fidesz, Law and Justice, and other populist parties that are moving their countries toward authoritarianism. After the invasion of Ukraine, Europe channeled its political power into military power when it mobilized to resist the other major threat to democracy on the continent: Russian aggression. Benn believed the European Union was an anti-democratic empire that would succumb to partition and war, but it has instead united around the democratic aspirations of a prospective member threatened with extinction by a tyrant who openly wants to restore the Russian Empire.

In a profile of Benn published in 1981, Hitchens took issue with his "nationalistic and populist" rhetoric and attacked his position on European integration:

> Benn's approach to the larger problem of economic revival is misguided. He favors withdrawal from the European Common Market and a policy of protection and import restriction to save British industry. . . . he speaks here for some of the Left, much of the Right, and large sections of business. The major defect of that position is that it assumes an outdated, 'Britain alone' stance and has no perspective for cooperation with the growing European Left (which, though highly critical of the

Common Market, favors increased European integration). There is a point at which patriotism, especially British patriotism, becomes petty chauvinism. Tony Benn is perilously near this point. He also ignores the fact that protectionism has historically and invariably been a conservative cause in Britain—the cry of the inefficient capitalist in the face of competition and the cry of the subsidized worker who wants to export unemployment to poorer countries.[33]

Even when Hitchens was a socialist who was naturally sympathetic to elements of Benn's radical domestic agenda, he was alarmed by the insular tendencies of left-wing populism—tendencies that have always found sympathy and support on the right.

As if the connection between the far left and the nationalist right on the European Union wasn't clear enough, George Galloway decided to start campaigning alongside Nigel Farage in the run up to Brexit. At a rally organized by Grassroots Out (a pro-Brexit organization) in February 2016, Galloway took the stage, warmly thanked Farage, and observed that they agree on the "most important thing not only now but in the lifetime of everyone in this hall and everyone in this country. It is the demand that Britain should be an independent, sovereign, and democratic country, and that means leaving the European Union."[34] Galloway said Britons' power to make decisions about their future had been "given away to a lavishly funded Eurocratic state," and he announced that he wanted to expose the "lie that to be on this side of the argument is to be on the political right. I fought the 1975 referendum behind my then-leader, the late and great Right Honorable Tony Benn, and it's in memory of him that I'm standing here this evening." A few seconds later, Galloway conceded that he wouldn't, in fact, be standing there without the nationalist right: "But for Nigel Farage, we would not be having a referendum on this question."[35]

To many on the left, the story of Trump and Brexit is simple: the failures of a nefarious ruling class in Western countries led to the eruption of a long-smoldering populist uprising. Public confidence in the "elites" or the "establishment" (conveniently vague terms that are palatable to populist demagogues on the left and right) was sapped by the Iraq War, the Great Recession, etc. This explanation is useful because it happens to validate a long list of left-wing grievances. On this view, the rise of populist authoritarianism in Europe and the United States was a direct consequence of neoliberal economics, military interventionism, and so on.

Unlike Corbyn, Benn, and Galloway, Hitchens represented a left-wing tradition in favor of European unity. In a 2003 essay, he celebrated the "straight capitalist and socialist rationality of the EU—where 'Union' means what it says and where frontiers are bad for business as well as a reproach to the old left-internationalist ideal."[36] In *Hitch-22*, he writes: ". . . when I swore out an affidavit to testify to Congress during the impeachment trial of the loathsome Bill Clinton, I was asked to state my citizenship and found myself saying that I was a citizen of the European Union."[37] During a 1999 debate with his brother Peter, Hitchens argued in favor of greater integration across the British Isles and throughout Europe, and said he believed these processes were inseparable.[38] For example, he observed that European mediation was important for handling disputes over the status of Ireland:

> It's . . . seemed to me for a long time to be self-evident that the form—the political context in which [mediation] could take place—must be European. Because where is the solvent, where was the real solvent of the border question between Britain and Ireland, if it was not the fact that both Britain and the Republic of Ireland became members of the same customs union? At once the border began to look absurd and has come to look more absurd ever since.[39]

Hitchens argued that the European Union exerted a moderating influence on conflicts in Europe and prevented them from being expressions of "mere nationalism": "It is the European context," he said, "that has prevented the Catalan and Basque questions in Spain from becoming tribal, and stopped them from being as tribal as they were. Because there is a context in which there's another court—as there is even for us humble subjects—if denied justice, we can go to a court in Europe."[40] He even believed there was a "possibility that the filthy consequences of British policy in Cyprus can be undone by careful European handling of Greek-Turkish relations."[41] He made the case that the European Union pressured autocratic states to become more democratic, explaining that the union

> allowed Greece, Portugal, and Spain—in my lifetime—to with confidence get rid of their dictatorships knowing, as all intelligent citizens in those countries did, they would never be allowed into the European family . . . if they retained their dictatorial or despotic mode of government. The rules of the community forbid the admission of dictatorships or any but parliamentary democracies. It is also this that prevents Hungary and Romania from contesting Transylvania now. Both of them want to be members of the European Union—they will not be allowed to import a tribal quarrel into the European Union. They're on good behavior for that reason.[42]

Four years after Hitchens made that argument, 83 percent of Hungarians voted to join the union.[43] At the end of 2021, Orbán's Hungary faced possible expulsion from the union for his hostility to the independent press, manipulation of the judiciary, and politicization of the democratic process. However, after the disaster of Brexit, European populations aren't eager to abandon their place in it. This pro-European public sentiment restrains states like Hungary and Poland that are moving in an authoritarian direction, as they have to conform to the union's democratic standards to placate their own voters. EU membership also forces pro-Russian leaders in Europe to occasionally join the rest of the bloc in challenging Moscow—even Orbán condemned the invasion of Ukraine and agreed to sweeping sanctions imposed by the European Union.[44]

Hitchens was unsparing in his criticism of those (on the left and the right) who reflexively distrust European integration despite the evidence that it facilitates the spread of democracy and mitigates conflict. After listing the practical benefits of membership in the European Union—as well as the catalytic effect these benefits can have on the broader move toward liberal democracy—he condemned the nativist attitudes of anti-European British conservatives:

> And what does the right wing say? We don't want to do business with foreigners. We don't want them interfering in our internal affairs. We reserve the right to say to the extraordinarily sober and disciplined and decent and conscientious political class in Germany—we don't know how lucky we are to be dealing with such people—we reserve the right to daily visit upon them the crudest and most vulgar and hateful insults. . . . And to say that only English-speaking countries have played a civilized role in Europe in this century. Where does this arrogance come from? How is this demagogy permitted? This is the British version of fascism.[45]

The histrionics of Hitchens's speech, particularly at the end, undermined his point—while there's a contingent of Eurosceptics of the blood-and-soil variety, they make up a small proportion of the anti-EU right. Still, this is the sort of vehement rhetoric Peter Hitchens was probably thinking of when he described his brother as more pro–European Union than his supporters may realize. He (Christopher) was often disappointed by the progress of the European project, but he was an impassioned defender of that project when it came under attack. Peter, who routinely describes the European Union as a modern German empire,[46] is well-acquainted with the perspective his brother denounced in the speech above. Christopher, on the other hand, always celebrated Germany's commitment to Europe:

> In European discussions the most punctilious internationalists are the Germans, whose government even surrendered the special symbol of its deutschmark to the idea of a Europeanized Germany. The large majority of refugees from the recent Balkan wars found hospitality on

German soil. Nobody except the left-Green Joschka Fischer has really ever been able to commit or persuade Germans to send their troops overseas.[47]

Berlin's decision to admit over a million refugees during the European migration crisis in 2015 could be added to this summary of German internationalism, along with its willingness to scrap a major pipeline deal (Nord Stream 2), risk an energy crisis, and drop its neutrality on behalf of Ukrainian sovereignty after the Russian invasion. Though Hitchens focused on the right in the debate with his brother, he knew elements of the left were more interested in decrying an imaginary European empire than doing the hard work of making the European Union a more viable project. And for Hitchens, left-wing parochialism was always more grating than right-wing parochialism. Why would the left, with its stated commitments to openness and internationalism, so clearly echo right-wing xenophobia and nationalism? In *Hitch-22*, he explains why he decided to stop supporting the Labour Party in the late 1970s, and its anti-Europeanism featured prominently: "Labour had become a status quo party, hostile to the union with Europe, suspicious of technological innovation, inward-looking, and envious."[48]

While Hitchens applauded the Germans for the "remarkable sacrifice of the deutsche mark, their greatest postwar achievement," he confessed that he thought the eurozone would be a failure.[49] But he said he took "absolutely no pleasure in saying this. I did not at all care for the alliance of parties, from xenophobic to post-Stalinist, that combined to defeat the [European] constitution and that now yearn for the euro to be undone."[50] His revulsion at this alliance between the far left and far right suggests what he may have thought about the reconstitution of that alliance during the Brexit campaign. He was sometimes pessimistic about the European Union, but at a time when George Galloway and Nigel Farage were fulminating from the same stage about the depredations of a new European empire, it's difficult to imagine Hitchens joining them.

Despite his criticisms of the union, Hitchens understood the significance of Europeanism for Britain: ". . . viewed historically, it is surely neither surprising nor alarming that the British decided to reverse Winston Churchill's greatest mistake—abstaining from original membership in the European common market—and to associate more closely with the neighboring landmass."[51] If Hitchens was this critical of Britain's early failure to join the European Union's predecessor, he almost certainly would have seen Britain's decision to withdraw from the union in an era of far greater economic and political interdependence as an even greater mistake.

The left-wing antipathy toward the union is part of a larger trend— hostility toward globalization more broadly. When Hitchens was asked in 2001 what he thought about the "anti-globalization movement"— which regards institutions like the European Union as puppets of international private interests and believes globalization is a byword for sinister neoliberal economic policies—he argued that it appeared to be a "protest against modernity, and to have a very conservative twinge, in the sense of being reactionary." He continued: "I hear the word *globalization* and it sounds to me like a very good idea. I like the sound of it. It sounds innovative and internationalist. To many people it's a word of almost diabolic significance."[52] Hitchens compared the anti-globalization movement to the "hysterical aversion to world government and internationalism" on the nativist right[53]—a form of paranoia that often takes the form of dark insinuations about the Trilateral Commission, what Trumpist political tactician Steve Bannon described as the "Party of Davos," wealthy philanthropists and activists like George Soros and Bill Gates, and the machinations of a secret world government.

Hitchens argued that economic globalization should coincide with the universalization of protections for human rights and democratic principles—recall his argument that the international community should "match the 'globalization' of production by the globalization of a common standard for justice and ethics."[54] He expanded on this position in a 2002 interview, arguing that the benefits of globalization, whether political or economic, "should be properly shared and administered":

> ...whether you call it globalization or not, the world has increasingly become one economy. We all live in the same economy. . . . Does that mean we all live in the same society? Shouldn't it mean that? No, oddly enough, it doesn't quite mean that. Some of us have different kinds of societies within this, which are better off than the others—and have more claim on human rights and justice. . . . We're always being told of the benefits of [globalization] one way—we should be allowed to claim on our own behalf and that of others the counterpart. That's, therefore, what politics is to me.[55]

The "anti-imperialist" and anti-globalization left are largely one in the same—a connection Hitchens made increasingly often after September 11. This convergence is no surprise, as the motivating force behind "anti-imperialism" isn't genuine opposition to imperialism, but reflexive opposition to the West. Because the world's most powerful military alliance and many of the institutions that have underpinned globalization since World War II are Western, there's a natural connection between what's viewed as Western military and economic hegemony.

There are legitimate criticisms of the European Union and international economic institutions like the World Trade Organization and the International Monetary Fund, such as their lack of democratic accountability and the economic displacement that can result from the free flow of capital, goods, people, and ideas. Economic displacement can result from the free flow of capital, goods, people, and ideas. Hitchens was critical of the IMF in his essay about Benn, and it's clear that he believed the European Union (particularly the eurozone) was in need of significant reform. But much of the left is hostile to the basic elements of globalization and international political integration. Left-wing politicians and activists like Corbyn and Galloway aren't interested in reforming the institutions that represent the most successful effort at international integration in the history of the species—instead, they want to see the postwar global economic and political order overthrown. As Hitchens understood, this project is anything but progressive.

* * *

During a 2017 talk, the historian Stephen Kotkin made an obvious point that has somehow become controversial: "Europe is a profound success," he said. After acknowledging a few of the European Union's perennial issues (he cited the currency union in particular), Kotkin put them into perspective: "But, my God, these are fixable problems . . . how about the Nazi problem? Was that a harder problem to fix than the common currency?"[56] The remarkable unity among EU states after the Russian invasion of Ukraine suggests that Europe is capable of recognizing and mobilizing around real problems when they arise. Putin revitalized the European project in ways that were unthinkable just months before the war.

On a continent that almost succumbed to Nazism in living memory, it's strange that those who consider themselves members of the "anti-imperialist" left would be so blinkered and ahistorical as to describe profoundly successful postwar international institutions as the redoubts of a new empire. Yet this pervasive view is one of the reasons left-wing attacks on the European Union frequently make the awkward leap from economics to foreign policy. At the Grassroots Out rally, Galloway congratulated himself on his role in a debate over whether Britain should have taken military action in Syria. He argued that Prime Minister David Cameron "tried to persuade us to become the air force for ISIS and al-Qaeda and start bombing Syria" before bizarrely suggesting that there's a contradiction between the ability to freely protest a war and EU membership:

> The American Air Force was warming up on the tarmac, just waiting for a rubber stamp from the British Parliament of David Cameron's point of view. But in an epic debate in which speeches changed the outcome . . . we defeated Cameron and the engines had to be switched

off at the Andrews Air Base. And we narrowly, by 13 votes, avoided becoming embroiled in a disaster. That's the kind of Parliamentary sovereignty I believe in, and that's the kind that we can have if we leave this European Union.[57]

This was the biggest applause line in the speech, but Galloway's point was incoherent. The "epic debate" over British involvement in Syria took place when the United Kingdom was still in the European Union and resulted in a decision to avoid direct armed intervention. Of course Parliament was free to vote against the use of force—Galloway didn't even try to make a connection between Brexit and his triumphant speech about halting the American war machine (he didn't explain how the United States was constrained by what the British Parliament decided to do, either). Nor did he recall that Obama wasn't exactly eager to launch a military operation in Syria.

Left-wing antagonism toward the union makes a certain kind of political sense. If you believe the West—drunk with power after winning the Cold War—has spent the past three decades attempting to impose its hegemonic influence on the rest of the world, the image of an oppressive and expansionist European superstate is politically attractive. For one thing, the existence of a democratic Europe after World War II is difficult to imagine without the security provided by NATO and the United States—the other great targets of the "anti-imperialist" left. In *The Tyranny of Guilt*, Pascal Bruckner highlights the connection between democratic self-determination in Europe and the American security umbrella:

It is because NATO represents a serious military threat in Europe that democratic revolutions in Ukraine and Georgia became possible, despite Moscow's hostility to them. Without this strike force, the European Union's virtuous power to propagate democracy by bringing its neighbors into the circle of prosperity and justice would have little chance of succeeding. The perpetual peace to which Europe aspires has its source not in Europe but in the United States.[58]

Now that Europe is becoming more assertive about its right to collective self-defense, expect the "anti-imperialist" left to shift some of its rhetoric about the American empire toward the emerging European empire. Despite the fact that the military threats Europe faces today are clearer than at any point in the past several decades, the Corbynite left will continue to insist that these threats don't warrant a strong defense. Rather, they'll make the case that Europe should disarm, NATO should disband, and the United States should fold up its security umbrella and withdraw from the continent. The populist right will fervently agree, while pro-Russian politicians like Orbán will work to undermine the European unity on display after the invasion of Ukraine (as of May 2022, Hungary wasn't allowing arms shipments to travel through the country and delaying the European Union's effort to impose an oil embargo on Russia).

Once Hitchens cleared away the ideological debris of socialism and "anti-imperialism," several practical realities came into view. The NATO intervention in the Balkans marked the "first and only time in the twentieth century that ethno-fascism was stopped, and reversed, while it was still in progress."[59] Putin may feel encircled or provoked by the expansion of NATO—and the consequences of his paranoia have been catastrophic for the people of Ukraine—but the withdrawal of the alliance would likely have had far worse implications for the continent. The rest of Eastern Europe, for instance, would be trapped in Moscow's sphere of influence indefinitely. Would Putin have invaded Ukraine if the country was already a member of NATO? Could the stationing of NATO troops in Ukraine as Russia massed its forces on the border in late 2021 and early 2022 have prevented a full invasion?

The predictions many realists made about a post-NATO Europe after the Cold War turned out to be exactly wrong because Western governments have no incentive to abandon the most successful military alliance in history—even less so now that great power competition has returned. But NATO isn't just a way for great powers to protect their interests—it's also the only way for less powerful countries to protect their very existence as independent states. When Hitchens was asked whether NATO should guarantee the security of its smallest members, he didn't take the position shared by America Firsters, realists, and the isolationist left—that the Baltics and other states on Europe's eastern flank aren't worth defending. Instead, he urged NATO countries to uphold their commitment to all their allies, no matter how small:

> If I'm asked what responsibility this gives us, the menace of a recrudescent, nationalist, expansionist, reactionary Russia . . . certainly in the case of the Baltic republics that were annexed by the Soviet Union as part of the Hitler-Stalin pact and finally pried loose from that only in the last days of Gorbachev and confirmed as independent states very recently . . . that's a clear responsibility on our part to prevent any bullying.[60]

Considering the risk of a potentially devastating conflict if NATO confronted Russia over the territorial integrity of, say, Estonia or Latvia—something the United States and its allies have unequivocally promised to do in the event of a Russian attack—it's clear that Western powers define their interests more broadly than they used to. They're willing to go to war with a nuclear-armed adversary to defend the principle of state sovereignty. Hitchens argued that NATO could only justify its existence by enforcing international laws and norms against aggression: "If a point of principle like genocide in Bosnia is too difficult to uphold . . . then clearly we could be getting by with a very much smaller armed forces budget, and could probably dispense with NATO altogether."[61] This is a radical reconception of how states should operate. Hitchens believed governments should expand their definition of national interests to encompass the development and defense of a functioning international community, and he thought this community should extend far beyond Europe.

* * *

After the Gulf War, Hitchens observed that the Kurds have "powerful, impatient enemies and a few rather easily bored friends."[62] Many of these friends could once have been found on the left, but their numbers were dwindling by the turn of the twenty-first century. When Barham Salih, a veteran Kurdish politician who now serves as the president of Iraq, told Hitchens he was "very disappointed with the left" for its position on the Iraq War,[63] he was expressing a sentiment that's unintelligible on the left today. It's conventional wisdom that the only sound position to take on the war is one of total condemnation, regardless of the positive effects it had for the fledgling semi-autonomous state in northern Iraq. But Hitchens knew what Salih meant and shared his disappointment—when an interviewer asked him in 2010 to identify the true revolutionaries in the world, he cited the "people who've striven with increasing success to create an independent Kurdistan in northern Iraq."[64] This effort almost certainly would have been extinguished if it wasn't for continuous Western military involvement in the 1990s and 2000s.

During the Iraq War, Hitchens pointed out that the "toughest and most authentic guerrilla army in Iraq—the Kurdish peshmerga—is fighting very effectively on the coalition side."[65] He was friends with Kurdish leaders like Salih and former President Jalal Talabani. He said his support for the war "always was (and still is) a matter of solidarity with the democratic forces in Iraq and Iraqi Kurdistan and of the need for the United States to change its policy and be on their side."[66] The invasion of Iraq was, in fact, a complete and historic policy reversal when it came to the Kurds. In a 1997 article, Hitchens wrote, "Ever since the presidency of Woodrow Wilson, an American signature, for better or worse, has been on various international promises for Kurdish autonomy."[67] And it was always for worse—all those promises were broken. When Salih was deputy prime minister of Iraq in 2007, he told Hitchens: "We are willing to fight and sacrifice for a democratic Iraq. And we were the ones to suffer the most from the opposite case. If Iraq fails, it will not be our fault."[68]

When Iraq's Kurds overwhelmingly voted for independence in September 2017, Qubad Talabani (the deputy prime minister of Kurdistan and Jalal Talabani's son) thought of Hitchens: "If only Christopher could have been with us today, wearing his Kurdistan flag lapel pin, cheering us on."[69, 70] But the celebration was over before it started. Despite the fact that 93 percent of Kurds voted in favor of independence,[71] the Iraqi government had no intention of granting the Kurds their autonomy—in fact, they would soon have even less control over their resources and territory. Not only were Turkey and Iran hostile to the vote (out of fear that it would inspire their Kurdish populations to move toward independence)—the United States was opposed as well. Though the Kurds fought to expel the Islamic State from Kirkuk and other parts of northern Iraq after the Iraqi military fled in 2014, that same military (accompanied by Iranian-backed militias) forced them to relinquish control of the territory in 2017.[72] The Kurdish flags flying over outposts that *peshmerga* fighters had bravely defended against the Islamic State were taken down. Although there were several firefights, the heavily armed *peshmerga* generally withdrew peacefully.

In a failed attempt to convince the Kurds to delay the referendum, the *Washington Post* reported, the Trump administration offered to "support the Kurds' negotiations with Baghdad. The United States offer said that if negotiations with Baghdad had not progressed after two years, the United States would recognize the need for a referendum."[73] A member of the Kurdistan Democratic Party (KDP) dismissed this familiar ploy: "They were promising things that they couldn't implement because there would be opposition in Baghdad. What's the point? We've seen this play out so many times before."[74]

Hitchens always admired the Kurds' commitment to democracy despite these endless disappointments. He recalled meeting with Azzam Alwash, a director at the American University of Iraq in Sulaimaniya, who explained that students would be learning about the "ideas of Locke, the ideas and writings of Paine and Madison." Hitchens continued: "Everybody knows how to snigger when you mention Jeffersonian democracy and Iraq in the same breath; try sniggering when you meet someone who is trying to express these ideas in an atmosphere that only a few years ago was heavy with miasmic decay and the reek of poison gas."[75] When Hitchens's opponents would sneer at the idea that Iraq would somehow become a Jeffersonian democracy, he sometimes corrected them by pointing out that Iraqi democracy wouldn't be strictly speaking Jeffersonian, as the Iraqis aren't slaveholders. Hitchens dedicated his book on Thomas Paine to Jalal Talabani, the "first elected president of the Republic of Iraq; sworn foe of fascism and theocracy; leader of a national revolution and a people's army. In the hope that his long struggle will be successful, and will inspire emulation."[76]

Hitchens regarded the Kurds' fight for independence as one of the most venerable causes of the internationalist left: "The Kurds are the largest nationality in the world without a state of their own," he explained. "The King of Bahrain has, in effect, his own seat at the United Nations, but the 25 million or so Kurds do not. This is partly because they are cursed by geography, with their ancestral lands located at the point where the frontiers of Iraq, Iran, Turkey, and Syria converge. It would be hard to imagine a less promising neighborhood for a political experiment."[77] These onerous conditions make it all the more striking that the Kurdish experiment has been impressively liberal and democratic. In 1994, Hitchens wrote an introduction to *When the Borders Bleed: The Struggle of the Kurds*—a compendium of photos by Ed Kashi. He emphasized the long history of deception and abuse at the hands of neighboring countries and great powers:

> An experienced Kurd can tell his grandchildren of betrayal by colonial Britain and France, of promises made by Iran, Iraq, Syria, and Turkey to support the Kurds for as long as they were fighting only on the rival's territory, of interventions in Kurdistan by Israel to weaken Arab nationalist regimes, and of promises made by both cold war superpowers that turned out to be false.[78]

Hitchens was focused on the promises made by one Cold War superpower in particular: ". . . the Kurds have traditionally looked to the United States," he wrote, "as their deliverer from old injustices. George Bush appeared to sympathize with their cause during Desert Storm, yet his subsequent lack of support has left them baffled. Western politicians seem unable to appreciate the depth of the Kurdish yearning for a homeland."[79] Nor do Americans understand their country's long and fraught relationship with the Kurds, as Hitchens explained in a 1997 article:

> How many Americans know that Henry Kissinger used the Kurds as surrogates and mercenaries and then abandoned them in their hour of trial? How many Americans know that the Bush administration, which later yelled about the fact that the Kurds had been gassed by Saddam Hussein, had kept suspiciously quiet about that very gassing at the time when it occurred?[80]

The Kurds are people who, as Hitchens put it, don't "live on some exotic planet but in the same international community as the Council on Foreign Relations and the Department of State."[81] In other words, he thought it was long past time for Washington to stop treating them as bargaining chips or expendable tools in regional power politics. Hitchens didn't just believe the United States owed the Kurds a debt after decades of duplicity—he regarded the Kurds' fight for self-determination as a harbinger for democracy throughout the region: "Kurdish forces and spokesmen have always been to the fore in democratic and reform movements in all four of their compulsory 'homelands,' and the future of civilized discourse in Iran, Iraq, Turkey and Syria is inextricably bound up with their fate."[82]

Take Syria, for instance, where Kurds managed to carve a democratic enclave (Rojava) out of the most violent and unstable country on earth. During a September 2018 conversation with Noam Chomsky on Jeremy Scahill's *Intercepted* podcast, listeners may have been surprised to hear the world's foremost opponent of American military interventionism call for the United States to keep a contingent of forces in north-eastern Syria: "In my opinion," Chomsky said, "it makes sense for the United States to maintain a presence which would deter an attack on the Kurdish areas. They have the one part of Syria which has succeeded in sustaining a functioning society."[83] He continued: "The idea that they should be subjected to an attack by their bitter enemies the Turks, or by the murderous Assad regime . . . anything should be done to try to prevent that." Scahill was shocked at this decidedly un-Chomskian as-sessment of the situation—which acknowledged that the U.S. military could prevent aggressors from behaving aggressively—and he immedi-ately launched into a more comfortable reinterpretation:

> You are one of the leading people in the world that is consistently re-minding the world that the United States has always adopted a posture of "certain Kurds are good Kurds, certain Kurds are bad Kurds." And the United States has poured money and weapons into the coffers of, for instance, the Turkish military, explicitly to be used for an ongoing attempt at genocide against the Kurds. So I'm curious how you recon-cile that with a position that the United States would, in essence, be the protector of the Kurds in the context of the Syrian war.[84]

Chomsky countered that this history "does not change the fact that now the United States could, with a relatively small presence, deter at-tacks against the Kurds in Syria."[85] Scahill's attempt to change the sub-ject from the policy in question to a well-worn recitation of American crimes should be familiar to Chomsky. In discussions about the Iraq War, for instance, he invariably pointed out that the United States supported Hussein as he waged war on Iran and committed genocide against the Kurds. Would he make the same argument about American hypocrisy to discredit Operation Provide Comfort, which established a no-fly zone over northern Iraq to protect the Kurds after the glut of violence fol-lowing the Gulf War? In Scahill's obstinate refusal to see how American force could be used to protect its friends by deterring their enemies—

and preventing a potential humanitarian crisis in the process—Chomsky should have been able to see the logical outcome of his own approach to analyzing U.S. foreign policy.

In October 2019, President Trump decided to withdraw one thousand troops who were protecting the United States' Kurdish allies in northeastern Syria.[86] Turkey seized this opportunity to invade Kurdish-held territory, which immediately turned one of the most stable parts of Syria into a chaotic and bloody battlefield, displacing hundreds of thousands of civilians and leaving the Kurds at the mercy of their most implacable enemies. Tactically, Trump's decision was unintelligible: it gave Assad an opportunity to recapture lost territory, strengthened the Russian and Iranian positions in Syria, alienated European allies, reduced the United States' leverage in any future political settlement, and made the possibility of a resurgent Islamic State more likely. There was no pretense of Kissingerian realpolitik or strategic rationale at play—Trump abandoned the Kurds because he could.

The consequences of Trump's withdrawal were easily predictable—Chomsky understood exactly what would happen, and argued that the United States had a responsibility to prevent it. Scahill didn't dispute Chomsky's assumption that Turkey would immediately exploit the vacuum left by the removal of U.S. forces—he just didn't appear to care. The idea that the United States could be the "protector of the Kurds" in any context was intolerable to him—even though the Kurds in question desperately needed assistance, and despite the fact that they were conducting a radical political experiment in Rojava that emphasized direct democracy, secularism, and women's rights. As with much of today's left, Scahill allowed his antagonism toward the United States to override all other considerations, including even the most basic solidarity with the Kurds—a group whose interests he only champions when it's politically convenient to do so. Which is what the Kissingers of the world have always done.

* * *

Although Hitchens was a strong advocate of Kurdish sovereignty, there was tension between this position and some of his internationalist inclinations. While he understood the practical value of the Kurds' autonomy, given the decades of harrowing abuse they suffered at Baghdad's hands—as well as the legitimacy of their demand for self-determination as the world's largest stateless minority—these positions clashed with his support for political integration.

As a general principle, from India to Cyprus to Ireland, Hitchens deplored partition as a dangerous and superficial solution to political conflict. As he put it in a 2003 essay: ". . . all partitions except that of Germany have led to war or another partition or both." He observed that the "'fault lines' and 'flash points' of journalistic shorthand are astonishingly often the consequence of frontiers created ad hoc by British imperialism." He argued that the partition of India, "with its enormous military wastage and potentially catastrophic nuclear potential, must count as one of the great moral and political failures in recent human history."[87]

Hitchens wasn't just hostile to partition because it was often overseen by incompetent colonial officials—it also reliably activates blind tribal instincts. Even in countries and regions that had been partitioned many decades earlier, he noticed that "people discuss their injuries as if they had been inflicted yesterday."[88] Although tribalism often fuels provincial quarrels and prejudices that seem only to harm the people who hold them, it can take hold on a much larger scale—and even pose an existential threat to millions of people, as the conflict between India and Pakistan demonstrates. Hitchens recognized the tragic absurdity of this situation:

> One of the great advantages possessed by Homo sapiens is the amazing lack of variation between its different "branches." Since we left Africa, we have diverged as a species hardly at all. If we were dogs, we would all be the same breed. We do not suffer from the enormous

differences that separate other primates, let alone other mammals. As if to spite this huge natural gift, and to disfigure what could be our overwhelming solidarity, we manage to find excuses for chauvinism and racism on the most minor of occasions and then to make the most of them. This is why condemnation of bigotry and superstition is not just a moral question but a matter of survival.[89]

Note the word "superstition." Hitchens often emphasized the instigative role of religion in conflicts caused by partition. The idea that terrestrial claims could be justified with appeals to divine authority was anathema to him, which is why he argued that faith is a force multiplier as well as an "enormous multiplier of tribal suspicion and hatred"[90]—in the Israel-Palestine conflict, the Iraq War, and many other conflicts around the world. He also argued that religion could be exploited by those who favored partition: "The availability of a religious 'wedge,' added to the innate or latent appeal of chauvinism and tribalism, was always a godsend to the masters of divide and rule. Among other things, it allowed the authorities to pose as overworked mediators between irreconcilable passions."[91]

This conviction that conflicts are the consequence of irrational and incompatible passions has long been an excuse for Western powers to ignore massacres and other crimes that they're in a position to mitigate or prevent. President Clinton spent two years stalling while the death toll surged in Bosnia, and one of the reasons was his conviction that violence and tribalism were endemic to the region. As George Packer writes in *Our Man: Richard Holbrooke and the End of the American Century*:

> Clinton was reading a book that his wife had given him—*Balkan Ghosts*, by a journalist named Robert Kaplan. It portrayed the region as soaked in the blood of ancient tribal hatreds—they'd been fighting one another forever. Kaplan, in turn, had traveled around the Balkans avidly reading Rebecca West's enormous classic *Black Lamb and Grey Falcon*, about her journey through Yugoslavia just before World War II, a book with a strong pro-Serb and anti-Muslim bias. Where Eu-

ropeans saw a war of civilizations, Americans threw up their hands at incomprehensible Old World trouble.[92]

Hitchens recognized this attitude—which he encountered constantly when advocating for NATO involvement in the Balkans—for what it was: an instrumental prejudice that presents inaction and indifference as prudence.

The insistence that conflicts are ancient and intractable is a political tactic often used by the isolationist right. When Sen. Rand Paul argued that abandoning America's Kurdish allies in Syria was the right thing to do—asserting falsely that Turkey was going to invade regardless of what Washington did—he observed that the United States should stay out of a "hundred-year-old war between the Turks and the Kurds."[93] Paul has a habit of presenting the entire Middle East as a pit of primitive violence and tribalism: "Anybody read about the Middle East?" he asked during a campaign event in 2015. "They've been killing each other for a thousand years and they'll probably be killing each other for another thousand years. That doesn't mean we just retreat, and do nothing. That means we need to acknowledge what the Middle East is like before we get involved."[94] This position ignores the United States' history of exacerbating tensions and fueling violence in the region, as well as the fact that there are millions of people who don't fit Paul's caricature of bloodthirsty permanent combatants—they're just human beings unfortunate enough to be born and caught in war zones, failed states, and autocracies.

While Western leaders have been all too willing to redraw the map—often with disastrous repercussions—they're reluctant to halt violent partitions in progress. But as Hitchens explained, Western powers can also mitigate the worst consequences of those partitions, such as the genocide in the Balkans: "The largely secular Muslims of Bosnia and Kosovo were . . . the main victims of the cave-in to partition in the former Yugoslavia, and are now the chief beneficiaries of that policy's reversal."[95]

While some religious and ethnic groups have benefited from partition to the detriment of others, Hitchens argued that the people who suffered most were "those of all creeds and of none who believed in modernity and had transcended tribalism."[96] He made this point in a passage about how partition has affected various Muslim communities—as well as secularists and members of minority sects and faiths in those communities—but it reflects his attitude toward partition in many other contexts. Recall the poster he saw in Sarajevo, which featured Muslim, Jewish, and Christian iconography with the superscription "We Are One People." He observed that this display was "all that was left of internationalism" in the country[97]—a declaration of solidarity which was eclipsed by an outbreak of the most vicious and determined nationalism the region had seen since World War II.

As Hitchens understood, the Kurds have more reasons to fiercely value their independence than just about any group. He instantly would have seen through the Trump administration's promise to recognize the need for a referendum on Kurdish sovereignty—yet another insulting lie dressed up as generous mediation. He knew the United States and other countries had long used similar assurances to placate the Kurds or manipulate them into acting as proxies against adversaries. But he still argued that the idea of partitioning Iraq along religious and ethnic lines would likely end in disaster, and he lauded the Kurds' willingness to play a role in the development of a democratic and federal political system in the country.[98] As he explained in a 2005 debate:

> the Kurds have begun to build and help other Iraqis build when they could have been chauvinistic. They could have been xenophobic. They could have said, "Enough with Iraq. We're through with it. We're leaving." Instead, [they] accepted their internationalist responsibilities. President Talabani, it seems to me, is a president of whom any country in the region could be proud, and not just by the sort of comparisons one could make. This is an extraordinary, unarguable, unambiguous gain.[99]

The Kurds' ethnic and religious solidarity helped them build a relatively stable democracy and civil society in northern Iraq. But it isn't their loyalty to their tribal identity that Hitchens admired—it's their commitment to the universal ideal of self-government. None of this is to say the Kurds are above infighting—a civil war erupted between the Patriotic Union of Kurdistan (PUK) and the Kurdistan Democratic Party (KDP) in the mid-1990s, which left thousands dead (this was when Saddam Hussein's forces pushed into Kurdistan in defiance of the Western forces protecting the area). Nor is it to say their democracy is perfect—widespread voting irregularities have been reported in recent elections, while plunging voter turnout has been driven by allegations of fraud, the duopoly of the KDP and PUK, and discontent about the thwarted independence referendum.[100] But democracy is young in Iraqi Kurdistan, as it is in the rest of the country, and it still represents an unarguable and unambiguous gain over the alternatives, especially in a country coming off decades of war and totalitarianism.

Hitchens believed it was possible to reconcile his internationalism with his support for Kurdish self-determination: "Partition in Iraq would be defeat under another name (and as with past partitions, would lead to yet further partitions and micro-wars over these very subdivisions). But if it has to come, we cannot even consider abandoning the one part of the country that did seize the opportunity of modernization, development, and democracy."[101]

Hitchens acknowledged that the Kurds could be as tribal and fratricidal as any group—he noted that, during Operation Provide Comfort, they "reduced their foreign friends to despair by first holding an election and then settling remaining issues at gunpoint" (Makiya has discussed this conflict at length).[102, 103] But he celebrated any move toward democracy in the region, no matter how uneven. In a 2006 article, he recalled the "moment we all now yawn about, with millions of people waiting patiently and getting purple fingers, which has since been repeated twice, to the point where elections in Iraq—Iraq!—have come to seem routine, even banal."[104] Despite the ever-present corruption and violence in the country (especially due to the influence of armed Iranian proxies) and the political popularity of religious thugs like Muqtada al-Sadr, Iraqi democracy remains far more robust than most of the alternatives in the region.[105]

* * *

When some commentators argued in 2005 that elections in Iraq should be postponed for security reasons, Hitchens asked if those making this case "relished the job of telling Iraqis and Kurds, after more than three decades of war and fascism, that it was too soon to hear from them at the polls?"[106] To those who expected instability as a result of the elections, Hitchens replied: "It does not seem very probable to me that the new Iraq will again invade either Iran or Kuwait. . . . So, the risks of democracy seem somewhat slighter than those posed by absolutism."[107] A central theme in Hitchens's work is the idea that dictatorship is inherently volatile and democracy—despite the threat of factionalism, subversion, and manipulation by outside forces, as well as the arduous process of institution-building—is better for long-term stability.

Hitchens died in the early, hopeful days of the Arab Spring, and despite his energetic support for democracy in the Middle East, he had deep concerns about the prospects for a fundamental political transformation in a region roiled by decades of war and dictatorship. In an essay published several months before his death, Hitchens compared the Arab Spring to several revolutions that took place in the second half of the twentieth century: democratic uprisings in Spain and Portugal, "people power" movements in Asia in the 1980s, and the collapse of the Soviet Union.[108] "I was a small-time eyewitness to those 'bliss was it in that dawn' episodes," Hitchens wrote, "having been in Lisbon in 1974, South Korea in 1985, Czechoslovakia in 1988, Hungary and Romania in 1989, and Chile and Poland and Spain at various points along the transition.

I also watched some of the early stages of the historic eruption in South Africa." However, in Egypt—where one of the most significant revolutions of the Arab Spring took place in 2011—he said he couldn't "find any parallels, models, or precedents at all."[109]

Recall Hitchens's observation that the post-Soviet republics in Eastern Europe were primed to be admitted to existing Western institutions. He also emphasized the fact that "everybody from East Berlin to Warsaw was already relatively literate and qualified," while politicians "such as Vaclav Havel and Lech Walesa . . . had already proved that they were ready to assume the responsibility of government."[110] In Portugal, a profusion of competing political parties and a robust civil society immediately swept into the vacuum left by the dictatorship. In Greece, Hitchens explained, the "torturers and despots of the military junta went to jail and the veteran civilian politicians came home from exile, or emerged from prison, and by the end of the year had held an election, in which the supporters of the former system of dark glasses and steel helmets were allowed to run and got about 1 percent."[111] In South Africa, Nelson Mandela's African National Congress was ready to take control when the apartheid regime fell.

In Egypt, Hitchens believed the prospects for the emergence of a functioning civil society after the fall of Hosni Mubarak—who had ruled the country for three decades—were dim: "With the partial exception of the obsessively cited Muslim Brotherhood, the vestigial political parties are emaciated hulks. The strongest single force in the state and the society—the army—is a bloated institution heavily invested in the status quo. As was once said of Prussia, Egypt is not a country that has an army, but an army that has a country."[112] This observation would prove prescient in 2013, when Gen. Abdel Fattah el-Sisi led a coup which removed the Muslim Brotherhood's Mohamed Morsi from power and suspended the recently approved Egyptian Constitution. In August 2013, pro-Morsi protesters in Cairo were massacred by Egyptian security forces—Human Rights Watch puts the likely death toll at more than a thousand.[113] Hitchens closed his article with a warning about the prospects for democratic revolution across the region:

> The same day on which I write was to have been a "Day of Rage" in Damascus, but that was an abject fizzle which left the hereditary Assad government where it was, while having regained much of what it had lost in Lebanon after the wretchedly brief "Cedar Revolution" of 2005. In Yemen there are perhaps five separate and distinct causes of grievance, from a north-south split to a Shiite tribal rebellion to the increasingly sophisticated tactics of al-Qaeda's local surrogate. This doesn't mean that the Arab world is doomed indefinitely to remain immune from the sort of democratic wave that has washed other regions clean of despotism. Germinal seeds have surely been sown. But the shudder of conception is some considerable way off from the drama of birth, and this wouldn't be the first revolution in history to be partially aborted.[114]

Hitchens mentioned Syria and Yemen in his bleak assessment of the Arab Spring in early 2011, but he couldn't have anticipated that both countries would soon be in the throes of devastating civil wars, which would cause hundreds of thousands of deaths, destabilize much of the region, create the conditions for jihadist groups (most notoriously the Islamic State) to flourish, and propel a wave of nationalist authoritarianism in Europe. While the Assad regime's continued existence was horrific enough before it started slaughtering Syrian civilians on an industrial scale, its ruthless prosecution of the civil war (with decisive assistance from Iran and Russia) was yet another reminder that the "stability" offered by dictatorship is often illusory. Beyond the fact that dictators wantonly invade their neighbors, they also create internal conditions that lead to mass disgust and discontent—an engine of permanent civil strife.

Hitchens had plenty of doubts about the Arab Spring, but he recognized the tenacious strength of the democratic impulse among courageous protesters who were demanding the same rights that citizens of liberal democracies take for granted. While he understood the ways in which democratic uprisings in the Middle East and North Africa diverged from their counterparts in other regions, he emphasized the fact that the "common factor of human spontaneity and irrepressible dignity, what Saul Bellow called the 'universal eligibility to be noble,'"[115] was just as visible on the streets of Cairo, Tunis, and Damascus as it was in Prague, Bucharest, and Budapest two decades earlier. He applauded the "exemplary courage and initiative of the citizens of Tahrir Square," but he also knew how ambitious and hazardous their political project was: "This really is a new language: the language of civil society, in which the Arab world is almost completely unlettered and unversed."[116]

Of course, this doesn't imply that the Arab world and the citizens of other countries in the region are incapable of democracy. Hitchens revered the activists and scholars in the Middle East who fought for democratic rights and values in the most difficult possible circumstances. During a 2009 lecture at the American University in Beirut, he celebrated pro-democracy activists in Iran, the Egyptian dissident and professor Saad-Eddin Ibrahim (who he later described as "one of the intellectual fathers of the Tahrir movement"), the Cedar Revolution in Lebanon, the Palestinian reformer Salam Fayyad, and the Kurds who were attempting to sustain and defend their democracy in northern Iraq.[117] In Hitchens's introduction to *Arguably*—the last collection of essays published while he was still alive—he condemned those who think (like Jeremy Corbyn) that "revolutionary authenticity belonged to groups like Hamas or Hezbollah, resolute opponents of the global colossus and tireless fighters against Zionism." He continued:

> For me, this was yet another round in a long historic dispute. Briefly stated, this ongoing polemic takes place between the anti-imperialist Left, and the anti-totalitarian Left. In one shape or another, I have been involved—on both sides of it—all my life. And, in the case of any conflict, I have increasingly resolved it on the anti-totalitarian side. (This may not seem much of a claim, but some things need to be found out by experience and not merely derived from principle.) . . . the forces

who regard pluralism as a virtue, "moderate" though that may make them sound, are far more profoundly revolutionary (and quite likely, over the longer term, to make better anti-imperialists as well).[118]

Hitchens's evolution from the anti-imperialist left to the anti-totalitarian left was a fundamental political shift, and his observation that he was "increasingly resolved" to be on the anti-totalitarian side was an acknowledgment of this transition. His internationalism was interwoven with his contempt for authoritarianism. He opened the above essay with reference to Mohamed Bouazizi, Abu-Abdel Monaam Hamedeh, and Mehdi Mohammed Zeyo—three casualties of the dictatorships in Tunisia, Egypt, and Libya. Bouazizi set himself on fire after the Tunisian authorities harassed him for selling produce in Sidi Bouzid and confiscated his scales—an act that may have single-handedly launched the Arab Spring. Hamedeh was an Egyptian restaurant owner who emulated Bouazizi when he set himself alight in front of the country's Parliament, sparking revolutionary fervor in his country as well. Zeyo loaded his car with propane tanks and rammed through the front gates of a military compound in Benghazi from which Gaddafi's forces were gunning down protesters. These "martyrs," Hitchens argued, "were not trying to take life. They desired, rather, that it be lived on a higher level than that of a serf, treated as an inconvenience by a moribund oligarchy."[119]

Hitchens argued that dismal economic conditions and oppression on their own couldn't account for the mass protests across the Middle East—he believed a pervasive sense of indignity and shame were powerful engines of revolution as well. "One of Francis Fukuyama's better observations," he wrote, "drawing on his study of Hegel and Nietzsche, was that history shows people just as prepared to fight for honor and recognition as they are for less abstract concepts like food or territory."[120] Hitchens often emphasized humiliation and debasement in his analysis of the resistance to authoritarian systems—feelings that animate revolutions regardless of where they take place. In a 2011 essay about Iran, he wrote: "The Islamic republic actually counts all of its subjects as infants, and all of its bosses as their parents. It is based, in theory and in practice, on a Muslim concept known as *velayat-e faqih*, or 'guardianship of the jurist.' In its original phrasing, this can mean that the clergy assumes responsibility for orphans, for the insane, and for (aha!) abandoned or untenanted property."[121]

Hitchens argued that the West should support the democratic movement in Iran, which faces constant repression and "elections" he aptly described as a "crudely stage-managed insult to those who took part in them and those who observed them." He pointed to the choking influence of the religious authorities on Iranian "democracy": ". . . any voting exercise is, by definition, over before it has begun, because the all-powerful Islamic Guardian Council determines well in advance who may or may not 'run.'"[122] The scam was so obvious in 2021 that President Ebrahim Raisi, a loyal acolyte of Ayatollah Khamenei and the anointed victor, urged the Guardian Council to approve a few more candidates[123]—a move that would at least present the illusion of democratic competitiveness. The limited form of democracy that used to exist in Iran (the outcomes of some elections were occasionally unpredictable) has all but disappeared since a flagrantly fraudulent election in 2009, in which popular reformist politician Mir Hussein Moussavi was crushed by Mahmoud Ahmadinejad. When it became apparent that there were widespread irregularities in the vote, millions of Iranians took to the streets in what became known as the Green Movement—the largest protests since the Iranian Revolution in 1979.

Hitchens's revulsion at the infantilization of entire societies wasn't limited to Iran. Of the Egyptian Revolution, he wrote, "In the long term, this sense of being relegated to infancy and immaturity has had a salutary effect, which one hopes will outlast the temptations—of the immature culture of self-pity and victimhood, plus the equally false reassurances of theocracy—that are certain to arise now that the period of enforced adolescence is over."[124] Hitchens wrote those words less than two weeks before Mubarak's 40-year reign came to an end, and he was right to be concerned that many Egyptian voters would prefer the "false reassuranc-es of theocracy" when the time came for their first election. The Muslim Brotherhood won almost half the seats in Egypt's parliament in 2012, and Mohamed Morsi became president.[125, 126] Considering Hitchens's hostility to Islamism, it's difficult to know how he would have inter-preted Egypt's first election—he may have celebrated the process while lamenting the result. But in any case, he recognized that the transition to democracy in the Middle East would inevitably run up against illiberal forces that use democratic mechanisms to secure power.

"Tides will ebb, waves will recede, the landscape will turn brown and dusty again, but nothing can expel from the Arab mind the example and *esprit* of Tahrir," Hitchens wrote.[127] Despite all the ways dictatorships menace their neighbors and create crises for the international communi-ty, this simple reality—along with the universal eligibility to be noble—may turn out to be the most powerful driver of revolutionary instabil-ity. Hitchens often underlined the fact that instability isn't always a bad thing—it can be a necessary intermediate stage between autocracy and democracy. No matter how fitful the move to democracy turns out to be, he believed it's vastly preferable to the alternatives: ". . . the supposed at-tractions of authoritarian 'stability,'" he wrote, "are in fact illusory, since nothing is more volatile and unsafe than dictatorship, which lacks any self-critical method for learning from its mistakes."[128]

Just as this fact is true about dictatorship wherever it's imposed, Hitchens argued that liberal democracy could take root anywhere. After September 11, he called for a "resolute declaration in favor of a fight to the end for secular and humanist values: a fight which would make friends of the democratic and secular forces in the Muslim world."[129] Hitchens believed he was witnessing a historic struggle for human rights and democracy in the Middle East, and he wanted America to be on the right side.

* * *

In articles and discussions about Afghanistan, Hitchens often cited the Welsh Labour politician Aneurin Bevan who, during the Cypriot War of Independence in the 1950s, observed that it was "very hard to discover whether the [British] Government are anxious to have Cyprus as a base, or a base on Cyprus."[130, 131, 132] With this distinction in mind, Hitchens asked: "Extending the analogy, might we not be able to shape events in Afghanistan nearer to our heart's desire without making ourselves responsible for the running of the whole nation and society?"[133] In the decade after Hitchens's death, this is what the United States tried to do—troop levels fell precipitously between 2011 and 2015 (and stayed low in the years that followed),[134] and Washington focused on helping the Afghans keep the Taliban under control and out of the major cities.

But after two decades of war, the United States ultimately decided that it didn't even want a base in Afghanistan. When the Biden administration removed all U.S. forces from the country—which led to a mass exodus of NATO personnel, contractors, NGOs, and everyone else who was trying to build a functioning state there—the Afghan security forces quickly fell apart in the face of the Taliban onslaught. The Taliban captured more than a dozen provincial capitals in a single week, including Kandahar and Herat, before sweeping into Kabul and taking full control of the country.[135]

"If the Taliban are allowed to declare victory in Afghanistan, it means what?" Hitchens asked in 2010. "It means they beat the North Atlantic Treaty Organization and the United States and the United Nations in open warfare, and can boast about it. Well, that's an outcome that's not thinkable."[136] The Biden administration made this unthinkable outcome inevitable, and there's no telling how it will embolden jihadist groups around the world—or what effect it had on the strategic thinking of aggressive dictators like Xi Jinping and Vladimir Putin. The more essential issue for Hitchens, though, was the fact that Afghanistan "belongs on that list of countries where we have a responsibility whether we like it or not"[137]—a responsibility the United States has now recklessly cast aside.

As I wrote this chapter, I couldn't keep pace with events—each paragraph was displaced every day by another horrifying development. Afghanistan's economy was collapsing. Mass starvation appeared imminent. Sanctions were making life unbearable for the Afghan people while posing no threat to the continued rule of the Taliban. In October 2021, the *New York Times* reported that "Female judges and lawyers have left the courts under Taliban pressure," while women who sentenced men to prison for domestic violence, kidnapping and raping women and girls, and other abuses were receiving death threats from those they convicted after the Taliban released hundreds of prisoners.[138, 139] "The women have not only lost their jobs," the *Times* reported, "but also live in a state of perpetual fear that they or their loved ones could be tracked down and killed."[140] Once the Taliban regained power, women were immediately purged from the government, schools, the media, and other institutions and businesses across Afghanistan. Within months, head-to-toe coverings were once again mandatory for all women.[141]

It was impossible to keep up with this stream of horrors as the book went to print, so I'll just ask: as you read these words, what's the current state of Afghanistan? Do the prospects for democracy and human flourishing in the country look better or worse now that the United States has left it in the hands of the most retrograde theocratic force on the planet? While Biden made perfunctory noises about "humanitarian assistance" and "speaking out for the rights of women and girls,"[142] it's clear that his concern for human rights in Afghanistan is next to nonexistent. He claimed that the United States was only in the country to "get the terrorists who attacked us on 9/11 and to deliver justice to Osama Bin Laden."[143] But as chairman of the Senate Foreign Relations Committee in the early days of the war, he argued that "History will judge us harshly if we allow the hope of a liberated Afghanistan to evaporate because we failed to stay the course."[144] By the time he was vice president, Biden believed the United States should have a much smaller presence in the country. As president, he just wanted out at all costs.

The Trump administration's record on Afghanistan is dismal as well. Trump set the withdrawal in motion with a farcical series of negotiations with the Taliban and a declaration that the United States would be out of the country by May 2021, even earlier than the actual exit.[145] This deprived Washington of any meaningful leverage and guaranteed that the negotiations would accomplish nothing—after twenty years of constant warfare, the Taliban could easily wait a few more months. Biden cynically pretended to be stuck with this agreement, despite the fact that he had no problem shredding a long list of Trump's other initiatives.[146]

You won't find much concern for the plight of a re-Talibanized Afghanistan on the left. In May 2021, Jeremy Scahill praised Biden in the *New York Times* for his "bold" decision to withdraw the remaining U.S. forces from the country (just several thousand at that point). "Once the United States pulls out its conventional military forces," Scahill wrote, "hawkish figures in the American security and foreign policy establishment will use every subsequent incident of Taliban violence to argue that withdrawal was a mistake."[147] Scahill made it sound as if the withdrawal would lead to a few pockets of violence here and there instead of a sweeping reassertion of the Taliban's power across the country. He didn't find the space to mention the future of human rights or democracy in Afghanistan anywhere in his piece. Hitchens, on the other hand, argued that Afghanistan was one of the most important battlegrounds in a global struggle between theocracy and civil society, which is why he urged the United States and its allies to support their Afghan friends:

> In one form or another, the people who leveled the World Trade Center are the same people who threw acid in the faces of unveiled women in Kabul and Karachi, who maimed and eviscerated two of the translators of *The Satanic Verses* and who machine-gunned architectural tourists at Luxor. Even as we worry what they may intend for our society, we can see very plainly what they have in mind for their own: a bleak and sterile theocracy enforced by advanced techniques.[148]

The United States' 20-year effort to prevent the return of theocracy in Afghanistan has come to an end, and this is a tragedy for the Afghans who believed they had escaped Taliban rule—especially women. In the decade and a half after the Taliban were removed from power, primary school enrollment among Afghan girls surged from effectively zero to over 80 percent.[149] Girls could expect more years of schooling in 2019 than any Afghan, male or female, two decades earlier.[150] Over a quarter of the seats in the Afghan Parliament were occupied by women.[151] Under the Taliban, women were forced to wear the burqa and beaten in the streets for showing their faces, put to death for adultery, barred from working or studying, required to have a male guardian when outside the home, and banned from public gatherings. Here's how a *New York Times* report summarized the situation for Afghan women in May 2022: "Since the Taliban seized control of Afghanistan in August, Afghan women have been subjected to a cascade of announcements restricting their employment, education, travel, deportment and other aspects of public life."[152]

"I am not sending my boy back there to risk his life on behalf of women's rights!" Biden boomed to Richard Holbrooke in 2010.[153] Nobody who supports the end of the U.S. mission in Afghanistan actually thinks its termination will be good for Afghan women or civil society, but improving the lives of Afghans has never been the primary focus of the "anti-imperialist" left. For these opponents of the war, getting the United States out of Afghanistan was all that mattered, regardless of the fact that millions of Afghans are now condemned to live under Taliban rule—probably for many decades to come. Hitchens, on the other hand, believed supporting the courageous struggle of Afghan women to take part in the social and political life of their country was a central aim of the war. In a 2007 essay, he recounted the sight of women learning about the democratic process at a National Democratic Institute program in Kabul:

. . . three years ago, you could not look an Afghan woman or girl in the eye. Half the population was chattel or other property: invisible, enveloped, and voiceless. The male members of their families could literally give them away as bargaining chips, or prizes. Arbitrary and lascivious punishments, usually totted up in lashes but sometimes in lethal stones, were the enforcement of this slavery.[154]

Once the Taliban retook power in the fall of 2021, Afghanistan immediately became one of just a dozen countries with no women serving in high-ranking government positions.[155] Taliban spokesman Sayed Zekrullah Hashimi explained his government's position on the matter: "There is no need for women to be in the cabinet. . . . You are burdening her with something that she is unable to carry out, she is not capable. What useful thing can come out of that?"[156] Before the Taliban takeover, women held seats in 27 percent of the Afghan Parliament—a proportion comparable to the U.S. Congress.

Despite the systematic destruction of Afghan civil society in the aftermath of the American withdrawal, many on the left believe the real crime was removing the Taliban in the first place. In his book about Hitchens, Ben Burgis condemns his subject's position on the war in Afghanistan and summarizes what he describes as "*twenty years* of sustained imperial violence" in the country:

> . . . twenty years of American soldiers kicking in doors and terrorizing civilians, of Afghan drivers being killed at roadside checkpoints set up around their country by occupying forces, of Afghan children growing up without parents and Afghan parents burying their children because the military occupying a deeply hostile population was too oblivious to local customs and too hair-trigger in its use of deadly force to tell the difference between a gun being fired by an insurgent and one being fired as part of a wedding celebration.[157]

To Burgis, there's only one story to be told about Afghanistan: the story of pitiless American imperialists holding the population down by force.

He doesn't mention the gains made by Afghan women and girls over the past two decades. Or the fact that millions of Afghans *returned* to their country after the invasion, while tens of thousands of desperate Afghans tried to flee when the United States departed (in one especially horrifying episode, an Afghan teenager clung to the landing gear of an American transport plane before falling to his death).[158] Hitchens witnessed how disgusted many Afghans were with the Taliban:

> On my own ventures into the Afghan hinterland, I found that the Taliban . . . labored under one giant disadvantage from which the earlier mujahidin had not suffered: They had already been the government of Afghanistan and had not been loved for it. Countless people, especially women and city dwellers, had ugly memories of their cruel and stupid rule. Many Afghans fled the country to get away from it and only came back when the Taliban were thrown out.[159]

Burgis doesn't say a word about the massive international effort to build a functioning civil society in Afghanistan or the opportunities for women or the collapse in the maternal mortality rate after the removal of the Taliban.[160] He doesn't want to discuss the female judges who now fear for their lives or the female journalists who can no longer report the news or the women who've been thrown out of government and every other important position in Afghan society. Instead, Burgis argues that Hitchens was so blindingly wrong about Afghanistan that anyone who disagrees can be "safely dismissed as the neoconservative equivalent of the kind of leftist who could never quite bring himself to admit that Comrade Stalin could have actually done all the things revealed in Khrushchev's speech." He continues: "The interesting question is not, *Was Hitch right about Afghanistan and Iraq?* Even those on the Left—and I count myself as one of them—who continue to admire the man's overall body of work need to acknowledge that the answer to *that* question is a giant NO written in fire."[161]

As Afghan civil society is extinguished by the return of the Taliban, this level of complacency on much of the left is remarkable. It's also a predictable manifestation of the left's default position on foreign policy. In *A Foreign Policy for the Left*, Michael Walzer observes that the "denial of agency to other countries suggests a fairly radical version of leftist inwardness; the lack of interest in what would happen if the United States actually disengaged suggests an even more radical version."[162] Both versions of leftist inwardness have long been on full display in debates over Afghanistan. Hitchens referred to the left's tendency to deny agency to non-Western states and movements during a 2002 debate with Tariq Ali. He recalled that Ali organized an anti-war demonstration in London after September 11 under the "pathetic slogan 'Stop the war before it starts'"—a slogan that exposed a strange sense of causality and culpability. He continued:

> That's in October and November [2002]. Not only is that the most lame, abject slogan I think any peace movement has ever come up with, but it also makes very clear the view of its organizers, which was and obviously is this: that the war hadn't started yet. Which, in turn, means the war did not start on September the eleventh. It would only be a war if there was a counterattack. I swear to you, Tariq. I look at you and tell you this. I never thought I would live to see the left sink that fucking low.[163]

Those who agreed that a counterattack was necessary—including then-Senator Biden, who said he couldn't "think of any war since World War II more justified" than the one in Afghanistan[164]—were immediately faced with the central dilemma of the conflict. Leaving the country would mean allowing it to succumb yet again to Taliban rule—or letting it collapse altogether. Hitchens didn't just view this possibility as a potential strategic disaster—he believed Washington would be discarding its most pressing moral and political obligations if it left Afghanistan. He emphasized how the United States had contributed to the country's immiseration:

We involved ourselves in the Afghan war against the Soviet Union very deeply. We picked some not-very-desirable allies at that point . . . then we walked away from the country and let it collapse in civil war and factionalism and, worse, the worst possible promulgation of both chaos and tyranny. An Islamic republic manages to get the worst of both worlds: Hobbesian state with iron rules. . . . We've got more reasons than the Taliban to have to undo this and repay some of what we owe to the Afghan people. And that would be true, I think, even if it was not in our interests.[165]

This was the same argument Hitchens made about the Iraq War— that the United States' ugly record was a reason to get involved, not the other way around. But the more salient point was the one Hitchens made about the conditions in Afghanistan: a Hobbesian state with iron rules. This is a good way to summarize the instability and lack of basic necessities combined with the asphyxiating cruelty of a theocratic system. Hitchens's observation that the United States had good reasons to intervene in Afghanistan "even if it was not in our interests" mirrored the point he made about Bosnia—if America refused to defend a secular European republic as it was shelled and ethnically cleansed by a neighbor, it might as well slash the defense budget and stop pretending to be a superpower. Hitchens wanted to live in a world that took the concept of an international community seriously, which meant powerful countries like the United States should be obligated to use their resources to deter aggression and prevent suffering. In *God Is Not Great*, Hitchens outlines several of the reasons why this obligation is particularly strong in Afghanistan—to protect human life and to salvage what's left of a great culture:

So ghastly had been the regime of the Taliban in Afghanistan, which slaughtered the Shiite Hazara population, that Iran . . . had considered invading the country in 1999. And so great was the Taliban's addiction to profanity that it had methodically shelled and destroyed one of the world's greatest cultural artifacts—the twin Buddha statues at

Bamiyan, which in their magnificence showed the fusion of Hellenic and other styles in the Afghan past. But, pre-Islamic as they undoubtedly were, the statues were a standing insult to the Taliban and their al-Qaeda guests, and the reduction of Bamiyan to shards and rubble foreshadowed the incineration of two other twin structures, as well as almost three thousand human beings, in downtown Manhattan in the fall of 2001.[166]

Like many on the left, Burgis believes the war in Afghanistan is nothing more than two decades of "sustained imperial violence." Hitchens, on the other hand, argued that the left should stop viewing the world through the antique lens of Cold War "anti-imperialism" and instead direct its energy toward solidarity with the victims of totalitarian movements and ideologies:

> . . . the years after the implosion of the Soviet Union in 1989 are marked by the recrudescence of danger from different forms of absolutism in Serbia, Iraq, Afghanistan, Iran, Darfur, and North Korea, and, once again, a huge number of "intellectuals" will not agree that the totalitarian principle, whether secular or religious, is the main enemy. There is, apparently, always some reason why this is either not true or is a distraction from some more pressing business or is perhaps a mere excuse for "empire."[167]

These left-wing omissions and diversions are all the more conspicuous at a time when Russian imperial aggression and Chinese totalitarianism have displaced absolutist threats from smaller countries and movements as the gravest geopolitical dangers in the world.

In 2002, Hitchens argued that the "era of the client state is gone and . . . the aim is to enable local populations to govern themselves. This promise is sincere. A new standard is being proposed, and one to which our rulers can and must be held."[168] This "new standard" was an explicit rejection of empire, as well as the Cold War realpolitik that sought friendly relations with authoritarian states as long as they served some immediate (and often shortsighted) material interests. The dictatorships that the United States supported in the second half of the twentieth century certainly didn't enable local populations to govern themselves. Nor did other imperial systems throughout history. Those systems didn't make a habit out of establishing timetables for withdrawal, either. Washington wanted nothing more than to leave Afghanistan in the hands of a capable Afghan government and military. And despite the fact that Kabul was still far from being able to secure and govern the country on its own, the Biden administration withdrew anyway—with disastrous consequences for the Afghans.

You could interpret Hitchens's support for regime change policies as an expression of imperialism and militarism, or you could view it as impatience with a status quo that left tens of millions of people at the mercy of brutal dictatorships for decades. Saddam Hussein controlled Iraq for almost 25 years. Gaddafi's flamboyantly cruel reign in Libya lasted for more than four decades. Bashar al-Assad has been in power since 2000, while his father Hafez al-Assad ruled the country for almost 30 years before that. The clerical dictatorship in Iran has existed for over 40 years. Hitchens often asked audiences to consider what Iraq would look like if Hussein had remained in power for another decade or two, only to be succeeded by one of his ghoulish sons. Or what the Balkans would look like if Slobodan Milošević had built a Greater Serbia atop many more mass graves like the one in Srebrenica. In Afghanistan, we're now witnessing the consequences of American retreat, and they're every bit as ugly as Hitchens feared.

It's easy to deride the international effort to rebuild Afghanistan now that it has failed, but this attitude ignores the sheer scale and ambition of the undertaking—an attempt to build a centralized democratic state in one of the least developed and most fragmented countries in the world. The "anti-imperialist" left insists that Afghanistan will be better off without the United States' presence, but many Afghans don't agree. In the decade and a half after the invasion, the United Nations

High Commissioner for Refugees (UNHCR) reported that more than 5 million Afghan refugees returned to their country.[169] When the United States left, tens of thousands of Afghans fled every week. "I'm not scared of leaving belongings behind, I'm not scared of starting everything from scratch," an Afghan man named Haji Sakhi told the *New York Times* in the summer of 2021. "What I'm scared of is the Taliban."[170]

* * *

For the past couple of decades, nationalism has been ascendant around the world: Trump's America Firstism, Brexit, nationalist dictatorships in China and Russia, and the rise of nationalist parties and leaders throughout Europe. "One cannot see the modern world as it is," Orwell wrote in 1941, "unless one recognizes the overwhelming strength of patriotism, national loyalty. In certain circumstances it can break down, at certain levels of civilization it does not exist, but as a *positive* force there is nothing to set beside it."[171] Meanwhile, globalization can be a powerfully destabilizing force. When people believe their jobs are being shipped overseas and find it increasingly difficult to compete in the international economy—or when immigration drives anxiety about shifting demographics in their country—it's easy for a nationalist demagogue to exploit this fear and resentment. Trump realized this fact early on and made the most of it.

But the power of internationalism shouldn't be underestimated, either. As Peter Singer argues in *The Expanding Circle*, all the seemingly insuperable forms of tribalism that have existed throughout human history have eroded: "The circle of altruism has broadened from the family and tribe to the nation and race, and we are beginning to recognize that our obligations extend to all human beings."[172] We feel a natural connection with hundreds of millions of fellow citizens, and it's difficult to see why the evolutionary forces that have created a sense of national solidarity—such as reciprocal altruism and the ability to recognize that our interests shouldn't take precedence just because of where we live or who we are—would suddenly stop exerting influence beyond a country's borders. But as the revival of nationalism demonstrates, it remains one of the most potent political forces in the world—a force that can easily be instrumentalized by autocrats to scapegoat foreigners, "globalists," and the international system itself. The entrenched resistance to internationalism is a testament to how radical a genuine commitment to universal rights and responsibilities really is.

Although Hitchens no longer consulted a map of the world that included Utopia, the political project he urged the left to support in the last two decades of his life was no less radical than his international socialism. He called for the establishment of an international community in which democratic reformers and dissidents everywhere could expect solidarity and support from the liberal democratic world, dictators could no longer massacre and oppress their citizens with impunity, and powerful states would proactively enforce international laws and norms. He believed it was time for the era of the client dictatorship to end, replaced by a system of alliances and institutions that treats human rights and political development as the most reliable long-term contributors to security and stability. And he argued that the United States' role in this system is indispensable—not only because of its political, economic, and military influence, but also because of its fundamental values. As he put it in the introduction to *Arguably*:

> There is currently much easy talk about the "decline" of my adopted country, both in confidence and in resources. I don't choose to join this denigration. The secular republic with the separation of powers is still the approximate model, whether acknowledged or not, of several democratic revolutions that are in progress or impending. Sometimes the United States is worthy of the respect to which this emulation entitles it; sometimes not. Where not—as in the question of waterboarding . . . I endeavor to say so. I also believe that the literature and letters of the country since the founding show forth a certain allegiance to the revolutionary and emancipating idea.[173]

These principles led Hitchens to support efforts that may have been quixotic and were certainly fraught with risk. His internationalism was destabilizing by definition, as it called for the end of a status quo in which the West accepts and supports violent and oppressive regimes— regimes that don't typically react with measured calm to existential threats. The transition to democracy will be more chaotic in the Middle East than it was in Eastern Europe (the war in Ukraine may seem like a counterpoint, but it isn't—Putin was terrified that his neighbor was de- mocratizing, modernizing, and integrating too quickly). There are many entrenched illiberal forces in the Middle East that have no intention of ceding their power, while democratic institutions and practices remain in their infancy. Still, Hitchens understood that liberal democracy, once established, would ultimately be a greater source of stability than one- party rule.

For all its imperfections, the post–World War II global order has been the most ambitious internationalist project in human history. But on the left, even that term—postwar global order—has become an object of scorn and ridicule. For much of the left, the European Union isn't an effort to integrate the economies and peoples of Europe to make the continent more prosperous and peaceful—it's a new empire run by rapa- cious, anti-democratic elites. NATO isn't a check on Russian and Chi- nese authoritarianism, nationalism, and expansionism—it's an instru- ment of imperial aggression that forced Putin to invade his neighbor by expanding right up to his "doorstep" (or "back yard," both of which imply that Russia owns the states on its periphery). And the United States isn't a defender of democracy and guarantor of European security—it's a global hegemon that simply wants to dominate as many corners of the earth as possible. These attitudes have placed much of the left in per- manent opposition to the forces and structures that have connected the species like never before.

Less than a month before his death, Hitchens recalled a point once made by Bernard-Henri Lévy: that "America had been *essentially* in the right about combating fascism and Nazism, and *essentially* right about opposing and outlasting the various forms of Communism, and that all else was pretty much commentary or, as one might say, *merde de taureau* [bullshit]."[174] Hitchens argued that "Something of the sort seems to apply in the present case," a reference to democratic movements around the world. "The crowds have a tendency to be glad that there is an American superpower, if only to balance the cynical powers of Moscow and Beijing."[175] This essential truth is becoming more obvious by the day.

In *Hitch-22*, Hitchens observes that the "usual duty of the 'intellectual' is to argue for complexity and to insist that phenomena in the world of ideas should not be sloganized or reduced to easily repeated formulae."[176] However, he argues that "there is another responsibility, to say that some things are simple and ought not to be obfuscated."[177] It's easy to imagine the response of many left-wing intellectuals to Hitchens and Lévy's essentialism about the United States: hoarse recitations of American crimes; the insistence that America is the world's "leading terrorist state" (a common Chomskian refrain); that America is institutionally, foundationally racist; that America is aggressive, imperial, ignorant, bigoted, and hypocritical; that America squandered its historically unprecedented power after World War II and the Cold War on the endless pursuit of military and economic hegemony, undergirded by an international order which exists only to facilitate American domination.

I was born in 1989. Fukuyama's original essay about the "end of history" had just been published in the *National Interest*[178] and the Berlin Wall would fall a few months later. The threat of nuclear annihilation was less ominous than it had been in decades. President George H.W. Bush took the United States' nuclear-armed B-52s off 24-hour alert in September 1991,[179] while the arms control treaties START I and II (which heralded the most precipitous reduction in global inventories of nuclear warheads the world has ever seen) were negotiated in July 1991 and January 1993, respectively.[180] The Maastricht Treaty was signed in 1992 and took effect the following year, establishing the modern European Union. Membership in NATO almost doubled over the next few decades (as I write, Sweden and Finland are preparing to join the alliance in the aftermath of Russia's invasion of Ukraine).[181] Between 1990 and 2018, GDP per capita surged in every major region, particularly Asia and the Middle East.[182] Over the same period, the proportion of the global population living in extreme poverty fell from 36 percent to less than 9 percent.[183] There were no wars between great powers. While there were 111 autocracies and 57 democracies in 1990, there were 99 democracies and 80 autocracies in 2018.[184] To echo Lévy, conditions have essentially improved for our species since the end of the Cold War.

Why is it, then, that these achievements are so often presented as footnotes in a larger story about racism, imperialism, and the ravages of marauding neoliberal capitalism? As Pinker notes in *Enlightenment Now*, "Intellectuals hate progress. Intellectuals who call themselves 'progressives' *really* hate progress."[185] Of course the United States and its allies can't take credit for all the achievements outlined above, but as any "anti-imperialist" left-winger will tell you, there's little doubt about which countries have had disproportionate influence on the formation and maintenance of global structures since the end of the Cold War. With the Russian invasion of Ukraine, waning American power, etc., it has become fashionable to declare that the postwar global order has failed. But threats and shocks have a tendency to galvanize the liberal democratic world around a common set of principles and goals—a phenomenon at work in the European and transatlantic solidarity with Ukraine during the war.

The most prominent left-wing intellectuals and publications today will tell you that the economic and security architecture designed by the Western powers after World War II has actually made the world poorer, less safe, and less stable. After Britain decided to abandon the European Union—a calamitous decision that the majority of British voters regretted as the transition process actually took place[186]—Glenn Greenwald was delighted at what he saw as a repudiation of the "profound failures of Western establishment factions" and global institutions that have "spawned pervasive misery and inequality." He expressed his bitter contempt for those who "regard with affection and respect the internationalist institutions that safeguard the West's prevailing order: the World Bank and IMF, NATO and the West's military forces, the Federal Reserve, Wall Street, the EU."[187] As we've seen throughout this book, the "anti-imperialist" left wants to destroy these institutions and replace them with—well, nobody knows.

After observing in *Letters to a Young Contrarian* that many once-dangerous border crossings (such as Checkpoint Charlie in Berlin) have "collapsed or partly evaporated and are just marks in my passport," Hitchens concludes: "The other ones will all collapse or dissolve one day, too."[188] This wasn't a reference to national borders in general—it was a reference to especially absurd and sinister lines on the map like the 38th parallel which separates North and South Korea (a "demilitarized zone" that happens to be the most militarized zone on earth, as Hitchens often observed). To Hitchens, these are the "frontiers that freeze stupidity and hatred in place and time,"[189] and he believed they would eventually be opened. In a 2010 introduction to *Animal Farm*, Hitchens observed that the book "has not been legally published in China, Burma, or the moral wilderness of North Korea, but one day will see its appearance in all three societies, where it is sure to be greeted with the shock of recognition that it is still capable of inspiring."[190] The expectation that these physical and intellectual frontiers would eventually be crossed isn't a form of utopianism, but a radical form of idealism.

Despite the fact that Hitchens dismissed the "end of history" as a concept, he seemed to accept Fukuyama's central premise: that liberal democracy would prove to be more sustainable than any authoritarian alternative. This conviction led him to argue that the United States should do everything in its power to hasten the collapse of ossified dictatorships that menaced their neighbors and populations. As he put it in 2003, there is nothing stable, as well as nothing decent, in a policy that relies on proxy rule, on client states, and on fascistic regimes. It's a great moment, in fact, and one that everyone should be proud of: that the United States has begun to discard the policy of the proxy state and the client regime, and has begun to say that, whatever the risks, democracy is more stable, as well as more justifiable, as an experiment.[191]

There's plenty to criticize in the past 30 years of U.S. foreign policy, but the left is mistaken when it presents this period as an era of Western imperialist tyranny. The decades following the Cold War have seen a democratic renaissance around the world, and Western powers have often been on the side of those in the streets protesting, taking up arms against their brutal and unelected rulers, and defending themselves from the dictator next door. Galling as it is to the "anti-imperialist" left, it remains essentially true that the United States has been a force for the expansion and integration of liberal democracy since the collapse of the Soviet Union. With the increasingly audible demands for democracy in Kyiv, Hong Kong, Moscow, Minsk, Tehran, and Yangon—as well as the persistent, if battered, support for democracy in the Middle East and North Africa a decade after the Arab Spring—the left should stop wasting its time attacking the fictional transatlantic empire and turn its attention toward the anti-democratic regimes that deny their populations even the most basic freedoms that we accept as no more than our due in the West.

As Hitchens understood, American history is replete with examples of breathtaking cruelty and hypocrisy. But he also recognized what many on the left have forgotten: that America does have a certain allegiance to the revolutionary and emancipating idea. And exporting that idea is still the highest form of patriotism.

7 America

Hitchens on Liberalism

What does it mean to be a liberal? The entry for *liberalism* in the *Stanford Encyclopedia of Philosophy* emphasizes the looseness of the term: "Given that liberalism fractures on so many issues—the nature of liberty, the place of property and democracy in a just society, the comprehensiveness and the reach of the liberal ideal—one might wonder whether there is any point in talking of 'liberalism' at all." But the entry concludes: "It is not, though, an unimportant or trivial thing that all these theories take liberty to be the grounding political value."[1]

One key element of liberalism is the idea that no authority has the natural right to rule other human beings: John Locke, Jean-Jacques Rousseau, and Immanuel Kant argued that any limitation on individual freedom must be justified. Other theories of freedom, such as positive liberty, offer a more capacious understanding of the concept—when people are constrained by any impediment (such as poverty or a lack of education), they are unfree. Classical liberals focus on property rights and economic freedom, while liberal egalitarians believe the government should take a more active role in ensuring economic fairness and equality. Kantian contractualism focuses on the collective, while Hobbesian contractualism highlights the importance of individual self-interest. The tension between collectivism and individualism has long been a central conflict within liberalism.[2]

Liberalism has always been a contested concept. As the *Stanford Encyclopedia* puts it: "Liberal theories form a broad continuum," from complete philosophical systems to specific political doctrines.[3] Liberal values can contradict one another: economic freedom, for instance, can lead to inequalities and concentrations of power that restrict the freedom of others. Ideas about what constitutes liberalism change over time, from the classical liberalism of the nineteenth century to the egalitarian liberalism of the twentieth and twenty-first. With so many divergences and inconsistencies, the claim that any figure or set of ideas is "liberal" is difficult to justify. There will always be competing interpretations and values—manifestations of what John Rawls described as the "reasonable pluralism" of liberal democratic societies.[4]

With these contradictions and debates in mind, I'd like to close by arguing that Christopher Hitchens was a liberal. In an essay about Charles Dickens, Orwell described his subject as "a man who is always fighting against something, but who fights in the open and is not frightened ... a man who is generously angry—in other words, of a nineteenth-century liberal, a free intelligence, a type hated with equal hatred by all the smelly little orthodoxies which are now contending for our souls."[5] That's how I would describe Hitchens—even the nineteenth-century part. George Packer is right to observe that Hitchens was an old-fashioned radical and a "figure of the Enlightenment, a coffee-house pamphleteer, a ready duelist, an unreasonable fighter for reason, an émigré from England come to the New World to tell us what the universal words of our Declaration meant, and hold us to them."[6]

Hitchens was always fighting against something—recall Amis's observation: "He likes the battle, the argument, the smell of cordite."[7] He embraced the battle as an end in itself, not only to refine his own arguments but also because (as John Stuart Mill understood) the open exchange of ideas is the foundation of civil society. He fought in the open because debate and discussion are the only tools civilization has to solve its problems short of violence and other forms of coercion. He was an advocate for free expression in opposition to restrictions of any kind: implicit speech codes enforced by one's colleagues and fellow citizens and explicit speech codes enforced by the state or an authoritarian ideology. His nonnegotiable attitude toward free expression derived from the fact that he was a free intelligence—a heterodox thinker in an age of smelly little orthodoxies. "Don't allow your thinking," he wrote, "to be done for you by any party or faction, however high-minded."[8] His critics present him as a typical left-wing apostate, but they can only do so by ignoring all the ways he violates that pattern.

Even Hitchens's more forgiving critics and admirers have a tendency to appreciate him for all the wrong reasons. Burgis's book presents him as a talented polemicist who was at his best as an orthodox Marxist and who made a few decent points about Henry Kissinger, Bill Clinton, and religion (but was still generally sophomoric about the subject). Then came his support for the wars in Afghanistan and Iraq. Along with so many other left-wing critics, Burgis describes this as a tragic coda which forever blackened Hitchens's legacy. "What the hell happened?" he asks. Burgis concludes that Hitchens was "always worth reading and watching and he was always worth thinking about and arguing with in your head. That's very far from being a nothing."[9] *Very far from being a nothing* is praise of a kind, and Burgis doesn't fall into the trap of assuming Hitchens's post–September 11 positions were evidence of his latent sadism, racism, and imperialism—or motivated by pure opportunism. But it's difficult to see why he wrote the book.

After Hitchens's death, most of the tributes and recollections emphasized his terrifying presence on the debate stage or his prodigious memory and eloquence or the fact that he could drink all night and produce a thousand polished words before bed. There are dozens of published stories about Hitchens that seem to follow the same script: after drinking and talking with him into the small hours, his companion would wake up with a jackhammer of a hangover only to discover that Hitchens had pounded out a gleaming, erudite essay about Wilde or Waugh or Wodehouse. It's no surprise that an author known for slugging Johnny Walker Black and making his way through two packs of Rothmans every day—while still somehow managing to maintain a packed book tour and debate schedule, make it to the TV studios on time, and keep up his foreign reporting—is now enveloped in a certain mystique.

Hitchens is a vintage figure, if not straight out of the nineteenth-century coffeehouses, then out of a time when the haze of cigarette smoke still filled American newsrooms and daily papers had large overseas bureaus. He said he could barely use his cell phone and claimed that he refused to stop using his typewriter until the last store that sold ink ribbons closed in Washington, DC. His literary "set" was sometimes compared to the Bloomsbury Group—a homage to the Bohemian atmosphere of public intellectual life in England in the early twentieth century. Hitchens was also a generalist and a polymath, which has become a rarity in an era of rigid academic specialization and bland hackwork for increasingly partisan publications.

After Hitchens's death, journalist Jane Mayer described him as a "supernova in Washington" who stood out among the tedious procession of "dreary, self-editing power-seekers" in the nation's capital.[10] When journalist and social critic Malcolm Muggeridge read through the obituaries for Orwell, he believed he was witnessing "how the legend of a human being is created."[11] I sometimes got the same feeling (to a lesser extent, I'm sure) when I read about Hitchens, but it was a peculiar type of legend that was in formation. He was always annoyed at the "profusion of condescending terms we . . . have for dissent."[12] *Bad boy, maverick, gadfly, contrarian, rabble rouser*. And when he invoked E.P. Thompson's phrase "the enormous condescension of posterity" in anticipation of how his life and work may later be regarded,[13] he didn't realize how right he would prove.

A sort of Hunter S. Thompson effect started to take hold in the public perception of Hitchens in his last decade and the years following his death. The coverage is about Hitchens the celebrity, the pugnacious provocateur, the booze-fueled, chain smoking, Oxford-educated English export who can reel off a few lines of Auden before eviscerating an opponent with his rapier wit. Terms like "rapier wit" make frequent appearances in articles about Hitchens. His presence on YouTube is so extensive that he once referred to the site as "MeTube,"[14] and you get the sense that many of his fans discovered him on the site. There's nothing wrong with that, of course, but when you review the expanding library of "Hitch slaps" with thundering titles about how Hitchens "destroys" or "humiliates" one hapless opponent after another, you get the uneasy feeling that some of these fans never migrated from the videos to the books.

The pyrotechnics of Hitchens's speech and writing make it easy to miss—and misstate—his arguments. Martin Amis argued that he "didn't deal in common sense. That was not his beat. There are plenty of people who can do common sense, and that wasn't Christopher's thing. It was saying something that went against the grain and then having to justify it. So that the Hitch was really debating with Christopher half the time."[15] Amis's implication is that Hitchens really *was* a contrarian—someone who goes around picking fights and spouting unorthodox opinions merely because he loves fighting for its own sake. While there was certainly an element of that attitude in his personality—he acknowledged that many arguments are, in fact, intrinsically worth having—the image of Hitchens as the impulsive combatant and gadfly distracts from the coherent set of principles that informed his work.

Salman Rushdie believed Hitchens's outspoken atheism was a return to form after a series of depressing aberrations: "The *God is Not Great* moment is sort of the moment at which Christopher came back from . . . the Iraq mistake, you know, and kind of regained his genuine intellectual ground."[16] That was the "real Christopher," he said. In an essay published a few weeks after Hitchens's death, Rushdie observed that *God Is Not Great* "carried Hitch away from the American right and back toward his natural, liberal, ungodly constituency. He became an extraordinarily beloved figure in his last years, and it was his magnificent war upon God, and then his equally magnificent argument with his last enemy, Death [a reference to his writing about confronting his own mortality after being stricken with cancer], that brought him 'home' at last from the misconceived war in Iraq."[17] But Hitchens never backed away from his position on Iraq and always regarded his opposition to Saddam Hussein and religion as expressions of the same anti-totalitarian principle. As to whether the post-September 11 Hitchens continued to occupy his genuine intellectual ground, at this point in the book I hope you'll agree that his positions on Afghanistan, Iraq, the Arab Spring, and Islamism weren't such substantial deviations—if they were deviations at all.

The most significant deviation was Hitchens's shift from Marxism to the advocacy of a more fundamental set of liberal democratic principles. Like Paine, he was a radical pragmatist. When he broke from the International Socialists in the mid-1970s, he recalls in *Hitch-22* his sudden realization that "democracy and pluralism were good things in themselves, and ends in themselves at that, rather than means to another end."[18] He says a passage from Conor Cruise O'Brien's *Writers and Politics* "phrased it better than I could then hope to do":

> "Are you a socialist?" asked the African leader.
>
> I said, yes.
>
> He looked me in the eye. "People have been telling me," he said lightly, "that you are a liberal . . ."
>
> The statement in its context invited a denial. I said nothing.
>
> And yet, as I drove home from my interview with the leader, I had to realize that a liberal, incurably, was what I was. Whatever I might argue, I was more profoundly attached to liberal concepts of freedom—freedom of speech and of the press, academic freedom, independent judgment and independent judges—than I was to the idea

of a disciplined party mobilizing all the forces of society for the creation of a social order guaranteeing more real freedom for all instead of just for a few. The revolutionary idea struck me as more *immediately* relevant for most of humanity than were the liberal concepts. But it was the liberal concepts and their long-term importance—though not the name of liberal—that held my allegiance.[19]

According to Hitchens, this passage "brilliantly summarized the contradictions with which I had been living, and with which in many ways I was condemned to go on coexisting for some time to come."[20] Like O'Brien, Hitchens realized that he was incurably liberal. This is why his discovery that the "socialist critique" of capitalism had become static and obsolete[21] didn't fill him with dread or contempt as it once would have. For one thing, he argued that Marx had failed to "grasp quite how revolutionary capitalist innovation really was."[22] But Hitchens's more fundamental political shift had less to do with socialism versus capitalism and more to do with what O'Brien described as the long-term importance of a consistent allegiance to liberalism.

When *Forbes* named Hitchens one of the "25 most influential liberals in America," the article noted that he would "likely be aghast to find himself on this list," as he "styles himself a 'radical'" rather than a mere liberal.[23] You can't blame the *Forbes* author for this impression—in a 1993 interview, Hitchens said, "I don't think liberals make very good writers. I think liberals are always trying to have it both ways. They want to share in the idea that capitalism is basically the best humanity can do, but they want to be able to be compassionate about it. I think that leads to a lot of sickly writing."[24] When Hitchens was still a socialist, he often used words like "sickly" or "invertebrate" to describe liberalism. However, he began to realize that this was merely a form of political posturing: "Alteration of mind can creep up on you," he writes in his memoir. "For a good many years I maintained that I was a socialist if only to distinguish myself from the weak American term 'liberal,' which I considered evasive."[25] O'Brien captures this tension between liberalism and radicalism, and it's no surprise that Hitchens says he underwent "experiences that recall one to the original text [O'Brien's *Writers and Politics*] as if in confirmation."[26]

It's not that Hitchens believed socialism and liberalism are in some way incompatible—he recognized that many of the greatest liberals of the twentieth century (Orwell, Rustin, James, Debs) were socialists, and he revered their radical achievements: "The socialist movement," he explains in *Letters to a Young Contrarian*, "enabled universal suffrage, the imposition of limits upon exploitation, and the independence of colonial and subject populations. Where it succeeded, one can be proud of it."[27] But when Hitchens was "compelled to recognise that its day is quite possibly done," he ignored the sneers of his ex-comrades—*People have been telling me that you are a liberal*—who believe a commitment to liberal democracy as an end in itself is some kind of bourgeois compromise.

At the same time, Hitchens formed alliances with those who shared this commitment—whether on the left or the right. Several of the most influential and incisive liberals in the world today are generally considered to be on the center-right, such as Hitchens's friends David Frum and Anne Applebaum. From the Russian invasion of Ukraine to the rise of Trumpism and nationalist authoritarianism in Europe, certain conservative intellectuals have demonstrated a far more consistent commitment to liberal democratic values than the nativists and isolationists on the right or the pseudo anti-imperialists and identitarians on the left. In the process, they have demonstrated that simple left-right binaries have become less useful in an age of surging authoritarianism and other forms of illiberalism on both ends of the political continuum.

"Many is the honorable radical and revolutionary," Hitchens writes, "who may be found in the camp of the apparent counterrevolution. And the radical conservative is not a contradiction in terms."[28] Hitchens cites the example of Edmund Burke, who was a "very potent advocate for the rights of the American colonies, for the Bengalis robbed and bullied by the East India Company, and for his fellow Irishmen." Meanwhile,

Hitchens argues that the "noblest verdict on Paine is that he wanted the French Revolution to be more temperate and humane, and the American Revolution (by abolishing slavery and being decent to the Indians) to be more thoroughgoing and profound. But in some ways—obscured by his combat with Burke—this makes him more of a conservative figure."[29] Hitchens also emphasized Orwell's conservative (even reactionary) impulses, and he cited Lionel Trilling's observation that these impulses could be put to use in radical politics. Trilling wrote:

> Orwell clung with a kind of wry, grim pride to the old ways of the last class that had ruled the old order. He must sometimes have wondered how it came about that he should be praising sportsmanship and gentlemanliness and dutifulness and physical courage. He seems to have thought, and very likely he was right, that they might come in handy as revolutionary virtues.[30]

Orwell was always a man of the left, but he often reserved his sternest criticism for his fellow socialists. From his vehement anti-communism to his contempt for the pacifist left-wing intellectuals who could only bring themselves to denounce war if it was waged by the West, he was a heterodox radical who consciously avoided intellectual and moral co-option and coercion on the left. Yet when the Duchess of Atholl asked Orwell in early 1945 if he would speak at an event hosted by an anti-communist group called the League for European Freedom, he responded that he couldn't take the stage on behalf of an organization that purported to champion freedom while remaining silent about British imperialism in India: "I belong to the Left and must work inside it," he wrote back to the Duchess, "much as I hate Russian totalitarianism and its poisonous influence in this country."[31]

Recall Hitchens's final words in *Why Orwell Matters*: ". . . what he [Orwell] illustrates, by his commitment to language as the partner of truth, is that 'views' do not really count; that it matters not what you think, but *how* you think; and that politics are relatively unimportant, while principles have a way of enduring, as do the few irreducible individuals who maintain allegiance to them."[32] One of these individuals was Jacek Kuroń (the Polish dissident and major figure in the Solidarity movement), who, according to Hitchens's account of their meeting, "punctured one of my illusions right away, by saying that he no longer had any illusions about Trotskyism. The real terrain of struggle was for democratic liberties and the rule of law."[33] Then there was Adam Michnik's observation that the "real struggle for us is for the citizen to cease to be the property of the state."[34] What Hitchens described as the "principle of consistent anti-totalitarianism"—upheld by dissidents like Kuroń and Michnik—has a way of enduring.

As Hitchens became more explicit and consistent in his opposition to totalitarianism, he became increasingly suspicious of the left-wing fantasies that had once made him feel he was "yoked to the great steam engine of history." By the end of his life, he regarded Utopia as a "fantastically potent illusion": "I suspect," he writes in *Hitch-22*, "that the hardest thing for the idealist to surrender is the teleological, or the sense that there is some feasible, lovelier future that can be brought nearer by exertions in the present, and for which 'sacrifices' are justified."[35] But he also recognized that it was possible to dispense with this illusion and remain an idealist—even a revolutionary: "Those 'simple' ordinary propositions, of the open society, especially when contrasted with the lethal simplifications of that society's sworn enemies, were all I required."[36]

When an interviewer asked Hitchens what socialists could learn from the twentieth century, he said, "They should learn that things such as the Enlightenment, secularism, rationality, [and the] commitment to reason can't be taken for granted."[37] Hitchens argued that there would always be "powerful enemies" of the Enlightenment, and he decided that defeating those enemies and defending the open society was a more worthwhile political project than the effort to resurrect a moribund international socialist movement. And he recognized that this ideological shift "necessitated constant argument about the idea of America."[38]

* * *

Americans, like the citizens of liberal democracies across Europe, shouldn't be complacent about the enemies of the Enlightenment. Trump and his authoritarian allies in Europe view democracy in the same way as Turkish President Recep Tayyip Erdogan—as a train you ride until the time comes to get off.[39] There hasn't been a more overt threat to the basic institutions and practices of liberal democracy in decades. When Trump entered the Oval Office and authoritarian populism seemed ascendant around the world, references to Fukuyama's "end of history" thesis were ubiquitous. The most wised-up thing you could say in a column or speech was something about how we're still living through history after all, Fukuyama's declaration was premature, etc. (these were also familiar refrains after the September 11 attacks). The echoes of the twentieth century, these commentators insisted, reverberated in the twenty-first: nationalism and fascism were on the march and democracy was in peril everywhere.

As with any genuine threat, there were those who dismissed it completely and those who inflated it to apocalyptic proportions. Hitchens may have taken the opportunity to attack Fukuyama yet again during the West's authoritarian moment, but I doubt he would have heralded the end of the liberal democratic experiment, either. It's difficult to imagine him expressing performative horror at "concentration camps" in Texas, as Rep. Alexandria Ocasio-Cortez did in reference to the detention of migrants and the separation of their families on the southern border.[40] But it's impossible to imagine him defending an America First demagogue who declared the press the "enemy of the people;" thought the United States should steal Iraq's oil, reinstitute torture, and murder the families of terrorists; didn't know the difference between the Kurds and the Quds Force, and coldly abandoned the former like so many presidents before him; wanted to ban Muslims from the country; built his presidency around cultural grievances, white Christian identity politics, and many other forms of mindless tribal division; expressed bottomless scorn for the independent judiciary, the First Amendment, and the democratic process itself; shredded arms control treaties and climate change accords; hated the core institutions of the postwar international order; and tried to overturn an American election.

Many on the left will tell you that Trumpism is an indictment of the global liberal order since the end of the Cold War—or even liberal democracy as it has been practiced since the creation of the United States of America. These are several of the left's great projects today: deconstruct the political and economic institutions of the postwar world, shrink or disband the transatlantic and transpacific military alliances that have existed for 75 years, and expose the fact that the liberal democratic pretensions of the United States have been hollowed out by its warmongering, racism, and tireless pursuit of hegemony. Just as so many left-wing critics of Hitchens believed his true motives had to be the lowest ones—racism, greed, imperialism, sadism—they believe the same about their own societies.

While it's easy to blame the neoliberal establishment, Washington elites, and bureaucrats in Brussels for Trump, Brexit, and all the other populist upheavals that have afflicted Western democracies over the past several years, the left refuses to consider its role in this process of democratic decay. Many on the left describe the founding of the United States as a sinister ploy to ratify and expand slavery instead of an establishment of universal democratic principles. This contributes to the cynical and demoralizing idea that liberal democracy has always been a big sham. When the "anti-imperialist" left agrees with the nationalist right that a dictatorship in Brussels is building a European empire and argues that NATO only exists to defend Western imperialism, it erodes confidence in the postwar international order. Whereas Hitchens saw a tremendous release of human energy and liberation in 1989, much of the left now sees the inauguration of an oppressive era of American domination. Instead of directing their moral and political energy toward supporting the dissidents in actual closed societies and totalitarian systems, these factions of the left have wasted decades striking blow after blow against the imperial colossus of the United States.

The idea that the United States was founded on racism and oppression is about as mainstream as ideas get on the left today, and this has led to distrust and hostility toward the principles, institutions, and figures that Americans have always venerated. On this view, Thomas Jefferson wasn't the statesman who authored the most influential declaration of universal human rights in history and erected the wall between religion and the state that made America's secular democracy possible—he was a slaver and a hypocrite. The U.S. Constitution isn't a document that codified, for the first time, a set of individual rights that provided the scaffolding for the most revolutionary experiment in self-government in human history—it's an instrument of oppression designed to maintain the most wretched and anti-democratic institution the species has ever devised. The United States didn't build and maintain a set of international institutions that coincided with an unprecedented period of global integration, collapsing poverty, declining warfare, and increasing democracy after World War II—it torched Vietnam, undermined democracy, and established tyrannical control over as much of the world as possible.

Of course, Jefferson *was* a slaveholder and a hypocrite, the Constitution *did* codify slavery, and the United States *has* subverted democracy and propped up dictators around the world. But it's possible to acknowledge these blights and failures, as Hitchens did, while recognizing the essential radicalism of the American experiment. For an author so wedded to irony—and for a man who was powerfully repelled by America's crimes and excesses, yet caught in the "strong gravitational pull of the great American planet"[41]—Hitchens's final embrace of the United States as a revolutionary force in the world was a fitting epilogue.

Hitchens considered himself a "Paine-ite." His old-fashioned Enlightenment liberalism was more concerned with democratic first principles than the most common forms of liberalism today. It was a form of liberalism unencumbered by any postmodern obscurantism or relativism. It embraced the universalism of the Declaration of Independence without the monumental hypocrisy of its authors. It incorporated the egalitarianism of the twentieth and twenty-first centuries and rejected the forms of tribalism that have hijacked that egalitarianism. Like the great Enlightenment liberal philosophers, Hitchens took liberty to be the grounding political value: the liberty to speak and write openly, to be free of authoritarian domination, and to escape the arbitrary constraints of tribe, faith, and nation.

Immediately after the Soviet Union dissolved, Hitchens said patriotism belonged to the "squalling childhood of the human race."[42] A decade and a half later, he became an American. He did so out of solidarity with a country that was his home for decades—a country that had just been attacked by a group of theocratic murderers who did, in fact, hate its freedoms, its tolerance, its openness, its embodiment of universal democratic values that the literal, one-book mind will never be able to comprehend. "I had lived in the nation's capital for many years," Hitchens wrote, "and never particularly liked it. But when it was exposed to attack, and looked and felt so goddamn vulnerable, I fused myself with it. I know now that no solvent can ever unglue that bond. And yes, before you ask, I could easily name Arabs, Iranians, Greeks, Mexicans, and others who felt precisely as I did, and who communicated it almost wordlessly."[43]

The bond Hitchens felt with America was more fundamental than the bond between fellow citizens. When writing his book about Jefferson, Hitchens found himself "referring in the closing passages to 'our' republic and 'our' Constitution. I didn't even notice that I had done this until I came to review the pages in final proof. What does it take for an immigrant to shift from 'you' to 'we'?"[44] On September 11, 2001, millions of people who had never set foot in the United States shifted from "you" to "we." The world mourned when America was attacked because America isn't just a place—it's an idea, and it belongs to everyone. This was Hitchens's final argument, and whether or not history has a discernible purpose or direction, it's an argument that the left—and anyone else who cares about the survival of liberal democracy—should fight to vindicate.

Notes

Introduction

1.   Christopher Hitchens, *For the Sake of Argument* (London: Atlantic Books, 2021), xii. First published in 1993 by Verso (New York, London). Hitchens was specifically referring to the "left opposition" to Stalinism.

2.   Christopher Hitchens, "Iraq War Debate," C-SPAN 2 Book TV recording, 22:35, September 14, 2005, www.c-span.org/video/?188768-1/iraq-war-debate.

3.   Richard Seymour, "Christopher Hitchens: from socialist to neocon," *Guardian*, January 18, 2013, www.theguardian.com/books/2013/jan/18/christopher-hitchens-socialist-neocon.

4.   Julian Barnes, *Nothing to Be Frightened Of* (Toronto: Vintage Canada, 2009), 79. First published in 2008 by Knopf.

5.   Richard Seymour, *Unhitched: The Trial of Christopher Hitchens* (London: Verso, 2012), xiii.

6.   Barry Gewen, "Irving Kristol, Godfather of Modern Conservatism, Dies at 89," *New York Times*, September 18, 2009, www.nytimes.com/2009/09/19/us/politics/19kristol.html.

7.   Dennis Perrin, "Obituary for a Former Contrarian," *Minneapolis City Pages*, July 9, 2003. Article reprint: Simon Cottee and Thomas Cushman, *Christopher Hitchens and His Critics: Terror, Iraq, and the Left* (New York: New York University Press, 2008), 263.

8. "Hannity & Colmes." Fox News, May 16, 2007.

9. Christopher Hitchens, "Believe Me, It's Torture," *Vanity Fair*, July 2, 2008, www.vanityfair.com/news/2008/08/hitchens200808.

10. Christopher Hitchens, ACLU lawsuit statement, 2006, www.aclu.org/other/statement-christopher-hitchens-nsa-lawsuit-client.

11. George Orwell, *The Road to Wigan Pier* (London: Victor Gollancz, 1937).

12. George Orwell, "Notes on Nationalism," *Polemic*, October 1945.

13. Christopher Hitchens, "Stranger in a Strange Land," *Atlantic*, December 2001, www.theatlantic.com/magazine/archive/2001/12/stranger-in-a-strange-land/302349/.

14. Michael Walzer, *A Foreign Policy for the Left*, (New Haven, CT: Yale University Press, 2018), 3.

15. Christopher Hitchens, *Why Orwell Matters* (New York: Basic Books, 2002), 211.

1 First Amendment Absolutism

1. George Orwell, "The Freedom of the press," initially unpublished introduction to *Animal Farm* (London: Secker and Warburg, 1945), first published by the *Times Literary Supplement*, September 15, 1972.

2. Christopher Hitchens, "Assassins of the Mind," *Vanity Fair*, January 5, 2009, www.vanityfair.com/news/2009/02/hitchens200902.

3. George Orwell, "As I Please," *Tribune*, July 7, 1944.

4. George Packer, "The Enemies of Writing," *Atlantic*, January 23, 2020, www.theatlantic.com/ideas/archive/2020/01/packer-hitchens/605365/. This essay was adapted from a speech Packer delivered on January 21, 2020 after receiving the 2019 Hitchens Prize from the Dennis & Victoria Ross Foundation.

5. Orwell, "The Freedom of the press."

6. George Orwell, "The Prevention of Literature," *Polemic*, January 1946.

7. Christopher Hitchens, "A Dissenting Voice: Conversation with Christopher Hitchens," interview by Harry Kreisler, *Conversations with History*, Institute of International Studies, UC Berkeley, 16:03, www.youtube.com/watch?v=93vTib-WWvs.

8. Christopher Hitchens, *Letters to a Young Contrarian* (New York: Basic Books, 2001), 105.

9. George Orwell, "Why I Write," *Gangrel*, Summer 1946.

10. Christopher Hitchens, *God Is Not Great: How Religion Poisons Everything*, (New York: Twelve, 2007), 153.

11. Martin Amis, "The Boy Can't Help It," interview by Meryl Gordon, *New York Magazine*, April 26, 1999, nymag.com/nymetro/news/media/features/868/.

12. George Orwell, "Politics and the English Language," *Horizon*, April 1946.

13. Christopher Hitchens, "Minority Report," *Nation*, March 13, 1989.

14. Christopher Hitchens, "Siding with Rushdie," *London Review of Books*, October 26, 1989, www.lrb.co.uk/the-paper/v11/n20/christopher-hitchens/siding-with-rushdie

15. Terence Smith, "Iran: Five Years of Fanaticism," *New York Times Magazine*, February 12, 1984, www.nytimes.com/1984/02/12/magazine/iran-five-years-of-fanaticism.html. Smith cited a journalist who "witnessed one of these human-wave assaults, in which tens of thousands of young Iranians have gone willingly to their deaths." He explained that the journalist "could hardly believe what he was seeing, as first one boy, and then another, detonated a mine and was hurled into the air by the explosion. 'We have so few tanks,' an Iranian officer explained to the journalist, without apology."

16. "Child Soldiers Global Report 2001—Iran," *Child Soldiers International*, 2001, accessed May 25, 2022, www.refworld.org/docid/498805f02d.html.

17. Hitchens, "Siding with Rushdie."

18. Ibid.

19. Ibid.

20. Ibid.

21. Christopher Hitchens, "Burned Out," *Slate*, March 7, 2005, slate.com/news-and-politics/2005/03/nuke-this-journalistic-cliche.html.

22. Jimmy Carter, "Rushdie's Book Is an Insult," *New York Times*, March 5, 1989, www.nytimes.com/1989/03/05/opinion/rushdie-s-book-is-an-insult.html.

23. Ibid.

24. Edwin McDowell, "Furor Over 'Satanic Verses' Rises As 2 More Book Chains Halt Sales," *New York Times*, February 18, 1989, archive.nytimes.com/www.nytimes.com/books/99/04/18/specials/rushdie-furor.html.

25. Ibid.

26. "Salman Rushdie and *The Satanic Verses*," interview by Bruce Collins, C-SPAN recording, 00:39, February 21, 1989, www.c-span.org/video/?6308-1/salman-rushdie-the-satanic-verses.

27. Kenan Malik, *From Fatwa to Jihad: The Rushdie Affair and Its Aftermath* (New York: Melville House, 2009), 1.

28. Salman Rushdie, "India Bans a Book For Its Own Good," *New York Times*, October 19, 1988, www.nytimes.com/1988/10/19/opinion/india-bans-a-book-for-its-own-good.html.

29. Sanjoy Hazarika, "12 Die in Bombay in Anti-Rushdie Riot," *New York Times*, February 25, 1989, archive.nytimes.com/www.nytimes.com/books/99/04/18/specials/rushdie-riot.html.

30. Ibid.

31. Ibid.

32. Ibid.

33. Steven R. Weisman, "Japanese Translator of Rushdie Book Found Slain," *New York Times*, July 13, 1991, archive.nytimes.com/www.nytimes.com/books/99/04/18/specials/rushdie-translator.html?mcubz=0.

34. Ibid.

35. Henrik Pryser Libell and Richard Martyn-Hemphill, "25 Years Later, Norway Files Charges in Shooting of 'Satanic Verses' Publisher," *New York Times*, October 10, 2018, www.nytimes.com/2018/10/10/world/europe/norway-satanic-verses.html.

36. Christopher Hitchens, *Hitch-22: A Memoir* (New York: Twelve, 2010), 268.

37. Ibid.

38. Ibid., 269.

39. Ibid.

40. Ibid., 270.

41. Letter from representatives of Turkey, Saudi Arabia, Iran, Pakistan, Egypt, Indonesia, Algeria, Bosnia and Herzegovina, Libya, Morocco, and Palestine to Danish Prime Minister Anders Fogh Rasmussen, October 12, 2005, www.rogerbuch.dk/jpabrev.pdf.

42. Ibid.

43. Ibid.

44. Letter from Danish Prime Minister Anders Fogh Rasmussen to the above-mentioned representatives, October 21, 2005, web.archive.org/web/20060219083657/http://gfx-master.tv2.dk/images/Nyhederne/Pdf/side3.pdf.

45. Hitchens, *Hitch-22*, 272.

46. Letter to Rasmussen.

47. Jeffrey Fleishman, "Protesters Burn Two Embassies in Syria Over Cartoons of Prophet," *The Los Angeles Times*, February 5, 2006, www.latimes.com/archives/la-xpm-2006-feb-05-fg-muhammad5-story.html.

48. Katherine Zoepf and Hassan M. Fattah, "Protesters in Beirut Set Danish Consulate on Fire," *New York Times*, February 5, 2006, www.nytimes.com/2006/02/05/international/middleeast/protesters-in-beirut-set-danish-consulate-on-fire.html.

49. Lydia Polgreen, "Nigeria Counts 100 Deaths Over Danish Caricatures," *New York Times*, February 24, 2006, www.nytimes.com/2006/02/24/international/africa/24nigeria.html.

50. John F. Burns, "Cartoonist in Denmark Calls Attack 'Really Close,'" *New York Times*, January 2, 2010, www.nytimes.com/2010/01/03/world/europe/03denmark.html.

51. Simon Cottee, "Flemming Rose: The Reluctant Fundamentalist," *Atlantic*, March 15, 2016, www.theatlantic.com/international/archive/2016/03/flemming-rose-danish-cartoons/473670/.

52. Christopher Hitchens, "Stand up for Denmark!" *Slate*, February 21, 2006, slate.com/news-and-politics/2006/02/stand-up-for-denmark.html.

53. Joel Brinkley and Ian Fisher, "U.S. Says It Also Finds Cartoons of Muhammad Offensive," *New York Times*, February 4, 2006, www.nytimes.com/2006/02/04/politics/us-says-it-also-finds-cartoons-of-muhammad-offensive.html.

54. Ibid.

55. Christopher Hitchens, "ALOUD at Central Library," Library Foundation of Los Angeles, interview by Tim Rutton, *Los Angeles Times* columnist, June 4, 2007, lapl.org/books-emedia/podcasts/aloud/god-not-great-how-religion-poisons-everything.

56. Christopher Hitchens and Ahmed Younis, interview by Colleen McEdwards, *CNN International*, February 4, 2006.

57. Thierry Leveque, "French court clears weekly in Mohammad cartoon row," *Reuters*, March 22, 2007, www.reuters.com/article/industry-france-cartoons-trial-dc/french-court-clears-weekly-in-mohammad-cartoon-row-idUSL2212067120070322.

58. Ibid.

59. "Charlie Hebdo attack: Three days of terror," *BBC News*, January 14, 2015, www.bbc.com/news/world-europe-30708237.

60. Ibid.

61. Maria Abi-Habib, Margaret Coker, Hakim Almasmari, "Al Qaeda in Yemen Claims Responsibility for Charlie Hebdo Attack," *Wall Street Journal*, January 14, 2015, www.wsj.com/articles/yemens-al-qaeda-branch-claims-responsibility-for-charlie-hebdo-attack-1421231389.

62. Lucy Cormack, "Charlie Hebdo editor Stephane Charbonnier crossed off chilling al-Qaeda hitlist," *Sydney Morning Herald*, January 8, 2015, www.smh.com.au/world/charlie-hebdo-editor-stephane-charbonnier-crossed-off-chilling-alqaeda-hitlist-20150108-12k97z.html.

63. Ibid.

64. Dan Bilefsky, "Kosher Supermarket Attacked in Paris to Reopen," *New York Times*, March 13, 2015, www.nytimes.com/2015/03/14/world/europe/kosher-supermarket-attacked-in-paris-to-reopen.html.

65. "Paris attacks: What happened on the night," *BBC News*, December 9, 2015, www.bbc.com/news/world-europe-34818994.

66. "Paris attacks: Millions rally for unity in France," *BBC News*, January 11, 2015, www.bbc.com/news/world-europe-30765824.

67. "Charlie Hebdo magazine to receive PEN award," *Associated Press*, March 25, 2015, apnews.com/article/afa3801a4f574ab7a62e3ba794818dd7.

68. Letter from PEN members about the decision to honor *Charlie Hebdo* with the Toni and James C. Goodale Freedom of Expression Courage Award, April 26, 2015, pen.org/pen-receives-letter-from-members-about-charlie-hebdo-award/.

69. Ibid.

70. Ibid.

71. "French court OKs cartoons," News24, February 7, 2006, www.news24.com/

news24/french-court-oks-cartoons-20060207.

72. Gérard Biard's remarks at PEN Literary Gala, May 5, 2015, pen.org/2015-pen-literary-gala-alain-mabanckou-dominique-sopo-gerard-biard-and-jean-baptiste-thoret2/.

73. Salman Rushdie, "The Fifth Annual Arthur Miller Freedom to Write Lecture," in conversation with Christopher Hitchens, PEN America, May 2, 2010, pen.org/event/christopher-hitchens-the-fifth-annual-arthur-miller-freedom-to-write-lecture/.

74. Hitchens, *Hitch-22*, 278-279.

75. Ayaan Hirsi Ali, *Infidel* (New York: Simon & Schuster, 2007).

76. Christopher Hitchens, "She's No Fundamentalist," *Slate*, March 5, 2007, slate.com/news-and-politics/2007/03/ayaan-hirsi-ali-is-no-fundamentalist.html.

77. Eve Conant, "A Bombthrower's Life," *Newsweek*, February 25, 2007, www.newsweek.com/bombthrowers-life-105047.

78. Hitchens, "She's No Fundamentalist."

79. Hitchens, *God Is Not Great*, 28.

80. Malik, *From Fatwa to Jihad*, 145.

81. Letter from PEN members.

82. Packer, "The Enemies of Writing."

83. Jennifer Schuessler, "Six PEN Members Decline Gala After Award for Charlie Hebdo," *New York Times*, April 26, 2015, www.nytimes.com/2015/04/27/nyregion/six-pen-members-decline-gala-after-award-for-charlie-hebdo.html.

84. Letter from PEN members.

85. Packer, "The Enemies of Writing."

86. Aurelien Breeden and Constant Méheut, "Trial Over January 2015 Attacks Opens in Paris," *New York Times*, September 2, 2020, www.nytimes.com/2020/09/02/world/europe/charlie-hebdo-trial-france.html.

87. "The cover you won't escape," *Charlie Hebdo*, September 1, 2020, charliehebdo.fr/2020/09/societe/la-couverture-a-laquelle-vous-nechapperez-pas/.

88. Ibid. Translated from the French.

89. Aurelien Breeden, "Paris Attack Suspect Wanted to Target Charlie Hebdo With Arson," *New York Times*, September 29, 2020, www.nytimes.com/2020/09/29/world/europe/france-attack-suspect-terrorism.html.

90. Ibid.

91. "Charlie Hebdo: French magazine's head of HR 'forced out of home,'" *BBC News*, September 22, 2020, www.bbc.com/news/world-europe-54251389.

92. Aurelien Breeden and Constant Méheut, "2 Wounded in Paris Knife Attack Near Charlie Hebdo's Former Office," *New York Times*, Sept. 25, 2020, www.nytimes.com/2020/09/25/world/europe/paris-knife-attack.html.

93. Ibid.

94. Adam Nossiter, "Man Beheads Teacher on the Street in France and Is Killed by Police," *New York Times*, October 16, 2020, www.nytimes.com/2020/10/16/world/europe/france-decapitate-beheading.html.

95. "France teacher attack: Seven charged over Samuel Paty's killing," *BBC News*, October 22, 2020, www.bbc.com/news/world-europe-54632353.

96. Hitchens, *God Is Not Great*, 12.

97. Michael Lipka, "Muslims and Islam: Key findings in the U.S. and around the world," Pew Research Center, August 9, 2017, www.pewresearch.org/fact-tank/2017/08/09/muslims-and-islam-key-findings-in-the-u-s-and-around-the-world/.

98. Christopher Hitchens, "Don't Say a Word," *Slate*, March 2, 2009, slate.com/news-and-politics/2009/03/a-u-n-resolution-seeks-to-criminalize-opinions-that-differ-with-the-islamic-faith.html.

99. "A Bill for Establishing Religious Freedom," June 18, 1779, available here: www.monticello.org/site/research-and-collections/virginia-statute-religious-freedom#footnote1_p8hojko.

100. Hitchens, *God Is Not Great*, 125.

101. Ibid.

102. Ibid.

103. Ibid.

104. Ibid., 124.

105. Christopher Hitchens, "Gods of Our Fathers," *Washington Examiner*, December 11, 2006, www.washingtonexaminer.com/weekly-standard/gods-of-our-fathers.

106. Ibid.

107. Flemming Rose, "Why I Published Those Cartoons," *Washington Post*, February 19, 2006, www.washingtonpost.com/wp-dyn/content/article/2006/02/17/AR2006021702499.html.

108. Hitchens, "Assassins of the Mind."

109. Ibid.

110. Anouar Abdallah, *For Rushdie: Essays by Arab and Muslim Writers in Defense of Free Speech* (New York: George Braziller, 1994), 41.

111. Hitchens, "Assassins of the Mind."

112. Christopher Hitchens and Shashi Tharoor, "Freedoms of Speech," Hay Festival, May 27, 2006, www.hayfestival.com/p-1643-christopher-hitchens-and-shashi-tharoor.aspx.

113. Ibid.

114. Derrick Bryson Taylor, "George Floyd Protests: A Timeline," *New York Times*, November 5, 2021, www.nytimes.com/article/george-floyd-protests-timeline.html?name=styln-floyd-trial&region=TOP_BANNER&block=storyline_menu_recirc&action=click&pgtype=Article&variant=show&is_new=false.

115. Tom Cotton, "Send In the Troops," *New York Times*, June 3, 2020, www.nytimes.com/2020/06/03/opinion/tom-cotton-protests-military.html.

116. Laura Rozen (@lrozen), "Mattis wipes the floor with Tom Cotton. @nytopinion should be embarrassed for running his fascist propaganda," Twitter, June 3, 2020, twitter.com/lrozen/status/1268316355612336129.

117. Joyce Carol Oates (@JoyceCarolOates), "it's one thing to air diverse opinions. but when people are actually being killed, maimed & terrorized by lawless law enforcement, such 'bothsiderism' begins to seem obscene. surely the NYTimes wouldn't present both sides of the Holocaust?" Twitter, June 3, 2020, twitter.com/JoyceCarolOates/status/1268319884573892609.

118. Ben Smith, "Inside the Revolts Erupting in America's Big Newsrooms," *New York Times*, June 7, 2020, www.nytimes.com/2020/06/07/business/media/new-york-times-washington-post-protests.html.

119. Letter from *New York Times* staffers about the decision to publish Sen. Tom Cotton's op-ed, June 4, 2020, int.nyt.com/data/documenthelper/7004-times-letter/efc475797987966bdaab/optimized/full.pdf#page=1.

120. Ursula Perano, "NYT employees say running Tom Cotton op-ed put black staff in danger," *Axios*, Jun 3, 2020, www.axios.com/2020/06/04/new-york-times-cotton-staff.

121. James Bennet, "Why We Published the Tom Cotton Op-Ed," *New York Times*, June 4, 2020, www.nytimes.com/2020/06/04/opinion/tom-cotton-op-ed.html.

122. Ibid.

123. Marc Tracy, Rachel Abrams, and Edmund Lee, "New York Times Says Senator's Op-Ed Did Not Meet Standards," *New York Times*, June 4, 2020, www.nytimes.com/2020/06/04/business/new-york-times-op-ed-cotton.html.

124. Bennet, "Why We Published the Tom Cotton Op-Ed."

125. Cotton, "Send In the Troops."

126. Marc Tracy, "James Bennet Resigns as New York Times Opinion Editor," *New York Times*, June 7, 2020, www.nytimes.com/2020/06/07/business/media/james-bennet-resigns-nytimes-op-ed.html.

127. Ibid.

128. Craig R. McCoy, "Stan Wischnowski resigns as The Philadelphia Inquirer's top editor," *The Philadelphia Inquirer*, June 6, 2020, www.inquirer.com/news/stan-wischnowski-resigns-philadelphia-inquirer-20200606.html.

129. Jenice Armstrong, "Inquirer staffers who called out 'sick and tired' voiced what a lot of us have been thinking," *The Philadelphia Inquirer*, June 6, 2020, www.inquirer.com/opinion/black-lives-matter-george-floyd-inquirer-philly-jenice-armstrong-20200606.html.

130. Sarah Ellison and Jeremy Barr, "A star reporter's resignation, a racial slur and a newsroom divided: Inside the fallout at the New York Times," *Washington Post*, February 12, 2021, www.washingtonpost.com/lifestyle/2021/02/12/donald-mcneil-new-york-times-fallout/.

131. "A Letter on Justice and Open Debate," *Harper's Magazine*, July 7, 2020, harpers.org/a-letter-on-justice-and-open-debate/.

132. Jesse Singal, "The Reaction to the Harper's Letter on Cancel Culture Proves Why It Was Necessary," *Reason*, July 8, 2020, reason.com/2020/07/08/the-reaction-to-the-harpers-letter-on-cancel-culture-proves-why-it-was-necessary/.

133. Hannah Giorgis, "A Deeply Provincial View of Free Speech," *Atlantic*, July 13, 2020, www.theatlantic.com/culture/archive/2020/07/harpers-letter-free-speech/614080/.

134. Jeff Yang, "The problem with 'the letter,'" *CNN Opinion*, July 10, 2020, www.cnn.com/2020/07/10/opinions/the-letter-harpers-cancel-culture-open-debate-yang/index.html.

135. "A More Specific Letter on Justice and Open Debate," *The Objective*, July 10, 2020, objectivejournalism.org/2020/07/a-more-specific-letter-on-justice-and-open-debate/.

136. "America Has a Free Speech Problem," Editorial Board, *New York Times*, March 18, 2022, www.nytimes.com/2022/03/18/opinion/cancel-culture-free-speech-poll.html.

137. Survey of United States residents aged 18 or older, *New York Times* and Siena College Research Institute, February 9-22, 2022, int.nyt.com/data/documenttools/free-speech-poll-nyt-and-siena-college/ef971d5e78e1d2f9/full.pdf.

138. Hitchens, *Hitch-22*, 124–125.

139. Ibid., 125.

140. Ibid.

141. Ibid.

142. Scott Jaschik, "Speech, Interrupted," *Inside Higher Ed*, March 6, 2018, www.insidehighered.com/news/2018/03/06/students-interrupt-several-portions-speech-christina-hoff-sommers.

143. Hitchens, *Hitch-22*, 223.

144. Ibid.

145. Mark Landler, "Austria Frees Holocaust Denier From Jail," *New York Times*, December 21, 2006, www.nytimes.com/2006/12/21/world/europe/21holocaust.html.

146. Christopher Hitchens, "Free Speech Über Alles (Even for David Irving)," *Wall Street Journal*, February 23, 2006, www.wsj.com/articles/SB114066518886080999.

147. Christopher Hitchens, "Hitler's Ghost," Vanity Fair, June 11, 1996, www.vanityfair.com/news/1996/06/hitlers-ghost-christopher-hitchens.

148. Raul Hilberg, *The Destruction of the European Jews* (Chicago: Quadrangle, 1961).

149. Christopher Hitchens, "Hitler's Ghost."

150. Landler, "Austria Frees Holocaust Denier From Jail."

151. Deborah E. Lipstadt, *Denying the Holocaust: The Growing Assault on Truth and Memory* (London: Penguin, 1993).

152. Hitchens, "Free Speech Über Alles (Even for David Irving)."

153. Christopher Hitchens, "Be it resolved: Freedom of speech includes the freedom to hate," TVO, January 7, 2007, www.tvo.org/video/archive/christopher-hitchens.

154. Ibid.

155. John Stuart Mill, *On Liberty* (London: Longman, Roberts, & Green Co., 1859).

156. Rose, "Why I Published Those Cartoons."

157. Hitchens, *Letters to a Young Contrarian*, 29.

158. Packer, "The Enemies of Writing."

159. Hitchens, *Letters to a Young Contrarian*, 31.

160. Christopher Hitchens, interview by Sasha Abramsky, *The Progressive Magazine*, December 16, 1997, progressive.org/magazine/christopher-hitchens-interview/.

161. David Erdos, "Charter 88 and the Constitutional Reform Movement: a Retrospective," *Parliamentary Affairs*, October 2009, academic.oup.com/pa/article/62/4/537/1538934.

162. Hitchens, *Letters to a Young Contrarian*, 123.

163. Christopher Hitchens, "Why Even Hate Speech Needs to Be Protected," *Reader's Digest*, November 2011, www.rd.com/article/freedom-speech-most-important-first-amendment-right/.

164. Mark Twain, *Following the Equator* (Hartford: American Publishing Company, 1897).

165. George Orwell, "As I Please," *Tribune*, July 7, 1944.

166. Humbert Wolfe, "Over the Fire," *The Uncelestial City* (London: Victor Gollancz, 1930).

167. Hitchens, *Hitch-22*, 277–278.

168. Christopher Hitchens, "The Swastika and the Cedar," *Vanity Fair*, March 30, 2009, www.vanityfair.com/news/2009/05/christopher-hitchens200905.

169. Hitchens and Tharoor, "Freedoms of Speech."

170. Ibid.

171. Hitchens, *Letters to a Young Contrarian*, 73.

172. Mill, *On Liberty*.

173. Hitchens, *Letters to a Young Contrarian*, 76–77.

174. Christopher Hitchens, "The Company She Keeps," *Washington Post*, October 29, 1995, www.washingtonpost.com/archive/opinions/1995/10/29/the-company-she-keeps/247eced4-f77b-413a-8615-b887b0127429/.

175. James S. Granelli, "Letter Writers Hope to Sway Keating Judge: S&L scan-

dal. More than 120 people, including Mother Teresa, have written to the court pleading for a sentence of probation, not prison," April 5, 1992, *The Los Angeles Times*, www.latimes.com/archives/la-xpm-1992-04-05-fi-1035-story.html#:~:text=%E2%80%9CI%20only%20know%20that%20he,whenever%20she%20visited%20the%20region.

176. Mother Teresa, Nobel Prize acceptance speech, Aula of the University of Oslo, Norway, December 10, 1979, www.nobelprize.org/prizes/peace/1979/teresa/acceptance-speech/.

177. Michael T. Kaufman, "The World of Mother Teresa," *New York Times*, December 9, 1979, www.nytimes.com/1979/12/09/archives/the-world-of-mother-teresa-mother-teresa.html.

178. Christopher Hitchens, *The Missionary Position: Mother Teresa in Theory and Practice* (New York: Verso, 1995).

179. Hitchens, *Letters to a Young Contrarian*, 99.

180. Pascal Bruckner, *The Tyranny of Guilt: An Essay on Western Masochism* (Princeton: Princeton University Press, 2010), 85. First published by Grasset et Fasquelle (Paris) in 2006.

181. Hitchens, *Letters to a Young Contrarian*, 41.

182. George Orwell, "Through a Glass, Rosily," *Tribune*, November 23, 1945.

183. "College Free Speech Rankings: What's the Climate for Free Speech on America's College Campuses?" The Foundation for Individual Rights in Education, College Pulse, *RealClearEducation*, September 24, 2021, www.thefire.org/presentation/wp-content/uploads/2021/09/24110044/2021-CFSR-Report-v2.pdf.

184. Lisa Feldman Barrett, "When Is Speech Violence?" *New York Times*, July 14, 2017, www.nytimes.com/2017/07/14/opinion/sunday/when-is-speech-violence.html.

185. "Student Attitudes Free Speech Survey," The Foundation for Individual Rights in Education and YouGov, 2017, www.thefire.org/research/publications/student-surveys/student-attitudes-free-speech-survey/student-attitudes-free-speech-survey-full-text/.

186. Don Gonyea, "Trump's Flag-Burning Tweet Brings Back 1980s-Era Controversy," NPR, November 29, 2016, www.npr.org/2016/11/29/503719125/trumps-flag-burning-tweet-brings-back-1980s-era-controversy.

187. Charlie Savage, "Trump Calls for Revoking Flag Burners' Citizenship. Court Rulings Forbid It," *New York Times*, November 29, 2016, www.nytimes.com/2016/11/29/us/politics/trump-flag-burners-citizenship-first-amendment.html.

188. Dan Cancian, "Everything Trump Has Said About NFL Kneeling So Far," *Newsweek*, June 8, 2020, www.newsweek.com/everything-donald-trump-said-nfl-anthem-protests-1509333.

189. Brian Naylor, "Trump Again Blasts Libel Laws, Calling Them 'A Sham'" NPR, January 10, 2018, www.npr.org/2018/01/10/577100238/trump-again-blasts-libel-laws-calling-them-as-a-sham.

190. "Improving Free Inquiry, Transparency, and Accountability at Colleges and Universities," Federal Register, Vol. 84, No. 58, Executive Order 13864, March 21, 2019,

www.govinfo.gov/content/pkg/FR-2019-03-26/pdf/2019-05934.pdf.

191. Susan Svrluga, "Trump signs executive order on free speech on college campuses," *Washington Post*, March 21, 2019, www.washingtonpost.com/education/2019/03/21/trump-expected-sign-executive-order-free-speech/.

192. Letter from PEN members.

193. Packer, "The Enemies of Writing."

194. Hitchens, *Hitch-22*, 271.

195. Hitchens, *Hitch-22*, 272.

196. Jytte Klausen, *The Cartoons That Shook The World*, (New Haven: Yale University Press, 2009).

197. "The Controversy Regarding 'The Cartoons that Shook the World,'" *Yale-News*, December 2, 2009, news.yale.edu/2009/12/02/controversy-regarding-cartoons-shook-world.

198. Hitchens, *Hitch-22*, 117.

199. Ibid.

200. Ibid.

201. Packer, "The Enemies of Writing."

202. Hitchens, "Be it resolved: Freedom of speech includes the freedom to hate," TVO.

203. Christopher Hitchens, "Freedom of Expression Must Include the License to Offend," Intelligence Squared debate, October 17, 2006, www.intelligencesquaredus.org/debate/freedom-expression-must-include-license-offend/#/.

204. Hitchens, "Why Even Hate Speech Needs to Be Protected."

205. "A Bill for Establishing Religious Freedom," June 18, 1779.

206. Hitchens, *Letters to a Young Contrarian*, 140.

2 Sinister Bullshit

1. "The 1619 Project," *New York Times Magazine*, August 2019, www.nytimes.com/interactive/2019/08/14/magazine/1619-america-slavery.html.

2. Hitchens, *Letters to a Young Contrarian*, 112.

3. Hitchens, *Hitch-22*, 121.

4. Ibid.

5. Christopher Hitchens, "Reparations for Slavery" debate, C-SPAN 2 recording, www.c-span.org/video/?167191-1/reparations-slavery.

6. Hitchens, *Letters to a Young Contrarian*, 127-128. After his arrest for incitement, Hitchens says he felt "disappointed as well as relieved when that charge was

dropped; there had been something flattering in this tribute to my rhetorical skill."

7.   "Feminist Epistemology and Philosophy of Science," *Stanford Encyclopedia of Philosophy*, published August 9, 2000, substantive revision February 13, 2020. plato.stanford.edu/entries/feminism-epistemology/#FemiStanTheo.

8.   Christopher Hitchens, "Blood for No Oil!" *Atlantic*, May 2006, www.theatlantic.com/magazine/archive/2006/05/blood-for-no-oil/304798/.

9.   Norman Hill and Leon Lynch, "Rustin Fought Quotas, Not Affirmative Action," *New York Times*, October 3, 1987, www.nytimes.com/1987/10/03/opinion/l-rustin-fought-quotas-not-affirmative-action-769887.html.

10.   Michael G. Long, *I Must Resist: Bayard Rustin's Life in Letters* (San Francisco: City Lights Books, 2012), 358–359.

11.   The King Encyclopedia, "Powell, Adam Clayton, Jr.," Stanford University Martin Luther King, Jr. Research and Education Institute, kinginstitute.stanford.edu/encyclopedia/powell-adam-clayton-jr.

12.   Bayard Rustin, "From Protest to Politics: The Future of the Civil Rights Movement," *Commentary*, February 1965, www.commentary.org/articles/bayard-rustin-2/from-protest-to-politics-the-future-of-the-civil-rights-movement/.

13.   Ibid.

14.   Ibid.

15.   Ibid.

16.   Ibid.

17.   Robin DiAngelo, *White Fragility: Why It's So Hard for White People to Talk About Racism* (Boston: Beacon Press, 2018).

18.   Ibram X Kendi, *How to Be an Antiracist* (New York: One World, 2019).

19.   DiAngelo, *White Fragility*, 9.

20.   Christopher Hitchens, "The Perils of Identity Politics," *Wall Street Journal*, January 18, 2008, www.wsj.com/articles/SB120062413171299477.

21.   Thomas Chatterton Williams, *Self-Portrait in Black and White: Unlearning Race* (New York: W.W. Norton & Company, 2019).

22.   Hitchens, "Reparations for Slavery" debate, C-SPAN 2 recording, 54:22.

23.   "Reparations Move Deplored by Rustin," *New York Times*, May 9, 1969, timesmachine.nytimes.com/timesmachine/1969/05/09/88992857.pdf.

24.   Abraham Lincoln, First Inaugural Address, March 4, 1861, avalon.law.yale.edu/19th_century/lincoln1.asp.

25.   Hitchens, *Letters to a Young Contrarian*, 112.

26.   Hitchens, *Hitch-22*, 121.

27.   Helen Pluckrose and James Lindsay, *Cynical Theories: How Activist Scholarship Made Everything About Race, Gender, and Identity—and Why This Harms Everybody* (Durham, NC: Pitchstone Publishing, 2020), 21.

28. Christopher Hitchens, "Transgressing the Boundaries," *New York Times*, May 22, 2005, www.nytimes.com/2005/05/22/books/review/transgressing-the-boundaries.html.

29. Edward Said, *Orientalism* (New York: Pantheon, 1978).

30. Christopher Hitchens, "Where the Twain Should Have Met," *Atlantic*, September 2003, www.theatlantic.com/magazine/archive/2003/09/where-the-twain-should-have-met/302779/.

31. Pluckrose and Lindsay, *Cynical Theories*, 70.

32. Said, *Orientalism*, 3.

33. Hitchens, "Where the Twain Should Have Met."

34. Ibid.

35. Ibid.

36. Ibid.

37. George Orwell, *The Road to Wigan Pier* (Oxford: Oxford University Press, 2021), 99, Oxford World's Classics, edited by Selina Todd, first published by Victor Gollancz (London) in 1937.

38. Hitchens, *Hitch-22*, 390.

39. Christopher Hitchens, "East is East," *Atlantic*, March 2007, www.theatlantic.com/magazine/archive/2007/03/east-is-east/305607/.

40. Rachelle Hampton, "Why Everyone's Talking About *American Dirt*," *Slate*, January 21, 2020, slate.com/culture/2020/01/american-dirt-book-controversy-explained.html.

41. Chris Bell, "Prom dress prompts 'cultural appropriation' row," *BBC News*, May 1, 2018, www.bbc.com/news/blogs-trending-43947959.

42. Gianluca Mezzofiore, "Gordon Ramsay's new 'authentic Asian' restaurant kicks off cultural appropriation dispute," *CNN Travel*, April 15, 2019, www.cnn.com/travel/article/gordon-ramsey-asian-restaurant-cultural-appropriation-intl-scli/index.html.

43. Hitchens, "Where the Twain Should Have Met."

44. Ibid.

45. Rachel Poser, "He Wants to Save Classics From Whiteness. Can the Field Survive?" *New York Times*, February 2, 2021, www.nytimes.com/2021/02/02/magazine/classics-greece-rome-whiteness.html.

46. Ibid.

47. Letter from Princeton faculty on "antiracism," July 4, 2020, docs.google.com/forms/d/e/1FAIpQLSfPmfeDKBi25_7rUTKkhZ3cyMICQicp05ReVaeBpEdYUCky1A/viewform.

48. Ibid.

49. Joshua T. Katz, "A Declaration of Independence by a Princeton Professor,"

Quillette, July 8, 2020, quillette.com/2020/07/08/a-declaration-of-independence-by-a-princeton-professor/.

50. Poser, "He Wants to Save Classics From Whiteness. Can the Field Survive?"

51. Hitchens, "East is East."

52. Hitchens, *Hitch-22*, 91.

53. C.L.R. James, "The Making of the Caribbean People," lecture at the Second Montreal Conference on West Indian Affairs, summer 1966, reprinted in *Spheres of Existence* (London: Allison & Busby, 1980), 179, files.libcom.org/files/CLR%20James%20-%20Spheres%20of%20Existence.pdf.

54. Hitchens, *Hitch-22*, 280.

55. Deborah Solomon, "The Contrarian," *New York Times*, June 2, 2010, www.nytimes.com/2010/06/06/magazine/06fob-q4-t.html.

56. Pluckrose and Lindsay, *Cynical Theories*, 97.

57. Ibid., 117.

58. "Critical Philosophy of Race, 1.2, Critical Race Theory," *Stanford Encyclopedia of Philosophy*, published September 15, 2021, plato.stanford.edu/entries/critical-phil-race/#CritRaceTheo.

59. "Discrimination, 7, Intersectionality," *Stanford Encyclopedia of Philosophy*, published February 1, 2011, substantive revision April 20, 2020, plato.stanford.edu/entries/discrimination/#Int.

60. Kimberle Crenshaw, "Mapping the Margins: Intersectionality, Identity Politics, and Violence against Women of Color," *Stanford Law Review*, July 1991, www.jstor.org/stable/1229039.

61. Pluckrose and Lindsay, *Cynical Theories*, 124–125.

62. Pluckrose and Lindsay, *Cynical Theories*, 124.

63. Crenshaw, "Mapping the Margins," 1297.

64. "Feminist Epistemology and Philosophy of Science," *Stanford Encyclopedia of Philosophy*.

65. Crenshaw, "Mapping the Margins," 1298.

66. Ibid.

67. Ibid., 1299.

68. Ibid.

69. Anita Hill, *Speaking Truth to Power* (New York: Doubleday, 1997).

70. Christopher Hitchens, "The Wrong Questions," *Washington Post*, November 9, 1997, www.washingtonpost.com/archive/entertainment/books/1997/11/09/the-wrong-questions/4347c53d-2358-43a5-8e41-73ba5d63a807/.

71. Ibid.

72. Hitchens, *Letters to a Young Contrarian*, 113.

73. Ibid., 112–113.

74. Ibid., 113.

75. "Kimberlé Crenshaw on Intersectionality, More than Two Decades Later," Columbia Law School Interview, June 8, 2017, www.law.columbia.edu/news/archive/kimberle-crenshaw-intersectionality-more-two-decades-later.

76. Hitchens, "The Perils of Identity Politics."

77. Rich Lowry, "Can Bernie Sanders Survive the Modern Left?" *Politico Magazine*, February 20, 2019, www.politico.com/magazine/story/2019/02/20/bernie-sanders-left-2020-225190/.

78. Neera Tanden (@neeratanden), "At a time where folks feel under attack because of who they are, saying race or gender or sexual orientation or identity doesn't matter is not off, it's simply wrong.," Twitter, February 19, 2019, twitter.com/neeratanden/status/1097835900468424704.

79. John Bowden, "Sanders on reparations: There are better ways than 'just writing a check,'" *The Hill*, March 1, 2019, thehill.com/homenews/campaign/432254-sanders-on-reparations-there-are-better-ways-than-just-writing-a-check/.

80. "Bernie Sanders: Senator from Vermont," Editorial Board, *New York Times*, January 13, 2020, www.nytimes.com/interactive/2020/01/13/opinion/bernie-sanders-nytimes-interview.html.

81. Pete Buttigieg, keynote address at the 2019 Human Rights Campaign dinner in Las Vegas, May 11, 2019, www.youtube.com/watch?v=CuCKSFtNhRQ&t=3s, www.nytimes.com/2019/05/12/us/politics/pete-buttigieg-speech-2020.html.

82. Ibid.

83. Ibid.

84. Jonathan Easley, "Pete Buttigieg gambles with criticism of identity politics," *The Hill*, May 14, 2019, thehill.com/homenews/campaign/443498-pete-buttigieg-gambles-with-criticism-of-identity-politics/.

85. Ibid.

86. Ibid.

87. Josh Lederman, "Buttigieg calls out Democrats for playing 'identity politics,'" *NBC News*, May 12, 2019, www.nbcnews.com/politics/politics-news/buttigieg-calls-out-democrats-playing-identity-politics-n1004706.

88. Christopher Hitchens, "White Fright," *Slate*, August 30, 2010, slate.com/news-and-politics/2010/08/glenn-beck-s-rally-was-large-vague-moist-and-undirected-the-waterworld-of-white-self-pity.html.

89. Ibid.

90. Ibid.

91. Ibid.

92. Ibid.

93. Ibid.

94. Ibid.

95. Presidential Approval Ratings—Donald Trump, Gallup, news.gallup.com/poll/203198/presidential-approval-ratings-donald-trump.aspx.

96. Donald J. Trump, "Remarks by President Trump at the White House Conference on American History," September 17, 2020, trumpwhitehouse.archives.gov/briefings-statements/remarks-president-trump-white-house-conference-american-history/.

97. Jeanne Kuang, Marina Affo, Patricia Talorico, Ira Porter, "Wilmington removes Caesar Rodney, Christopher Columbus statues Friday amid calls for change," *Delaware News Journal*, June 12, 2020, www.delawareonline.com/story/news/2020/06/12/wilmington-remove-christopher-columbus-caesar-rodney-statues/3175003001/.

98. Erin McPike, "Trump reframes claim that Muslims cheered 9/11," *Reuters*, November 28, 2015, www.reuters.com/article/us-usa-election-trump/trump-reframes-claim-that-muslims-cheered-9-11-idUSKBN0TH0OS20151128.

99. Abby Phillip and Abigail Hauslohner, "Trump on the future of proposed Muslim ban, registry: 'You know my plans,'" *Washington Post*, December 22, 2016, www.washingtonpost.com/news/post-politics/wp/2016/12/21/trump-on-the-future-of-proposed-muslim-ban-registry-you-know-my-plans/.

100. Patrick Healy and Michael Barbaro, "Donald Trump Calls for Barring Muslims From Entering U.S.," *New York Times*, December 7, 2015, www.nytimes.com/politics/first-draft/2015/12/07/donald-trump-calls-for-banning-muslims-from-entering-u-s/.

101. Emily Stephenson and Amanda Becker, "Trump backs surveillance of mosques despite criticism of rhetoric," *Reuters*, November 28, 2015, www.reuters.com/article/us-usa-election/trump-backs-surveillance-of-mosques-despite-criticism-of-rhetoric-idUSKCN0Z12AS.

102. Christopher Hitchens, "Contempt for the Little Colony," *Harper's Magazine*, October 1989, reprinted in *For the Sake of Argument* (London: Atlantic Books, 2021), 32.

103. Alan Fram and Jonathan Lemire, "Trump: Why allow immigrants from 'shithole countries'?" *Associated Press*, January 11, 2018, apnews.com/article/immigration-north-america-donald-trump-ap-top-news-international-news-fdda2ff0b877416c8ae-1c1a77a3cc425.

104. Bianca Quilantan and David Cohen, "Trump tells Dem congresswomen: Go back where you came from," *Politico*, July 14, 2019, www.politico.com/story/2019/07/14/trump-congress-go-back-where-they-came-from-1415692.

105. Christopher Hitchens, "Tea'd Off," *Vanity Fair*, December 9, 2010, www.vanityfair.com/news/2011/01/hitchens-201101.

106. Ross Douthat, "The Seduction of the Tea Partiers," *New York Times*, September 26, 2010, www.nytimes.com/2010/09/27/opinion/27douthat.html.

107. Ibid.

108. Hitchens, "Tea'd Off."

109. Ibid.

110. Kevin Roose, "What Is QAnon, the Viral Pro-Trump Conspiracy Theory?" *New York Times*, September 3, 2021, www.nytimes.com/article/what-is-qanon.html.

111. Matthew Haag and Maya Salam, "Gunman in 'Pizzagate' Shooting Is Sentenced to 4 Years in Prison," *New York Times*, June 22, 2017, www.nytimes.com/2017/06/22/us/pizzagate-attack-sentence.html.

112. "Political Polarization in the American Public," Pew Research Center, June 12, 2014, www.pewresearch.org/politics/2014/06/12/political-polarization-in-the-american-public/.

113. Hitchens, "Tea'd Off."

114. Ibid.

115. Ibid.

116. Hitchens, "White Fright."

117. DiAngelo, *White Fragility*, 9.

118. Christopher Hitchens, "America, Afghanistan, and the Contrarian," Commonwealth Club of California records, published by the Stanford University Hoover Institution Library & Archives, 46:46, December 17, 2001, digitalcollections.hoover.org/objects/3093/america-afghanistan-and-the-contrarian.

119. DiAngelo, *White Fragility*, 10.

120. Hitchens, "Reparations for Slavery" debate.

121. Hitchens, "Siding with Rushdie."

122. Christopher Hitchens, *Unacknowledged Legislation: Writers in the Public Sphere* (London: Verso, 2000), xiii.

123. Ibid.

124. Christopher Hitchens, "Eschew the Taboo," *Slate*, December 4, 2006, slate.com/news-and-politics/2006/12/hatred-will-always-outpace-linguistic-correctness.html.

125. DiAngelo, *White Fragility*, 11.

126. Ibid., 9.

127. Marc Caputo, "Culture wars fuel Trump's blue-collar Latino gains," *Politico*, November 21, 2020, www.politico.com/news/2020/11/21/culture-wars-latinos-trump-438932.

128. Astead W. Herndon, "Alexandria Ocasio-Cortez on Biden's Win, House Losses, and What's Next for the Left," *New York Times*, November 7, 2020, www.nytimes.com/2020/11/07/us/politics/aoc-biden-progressives.html.

129. Joe Biden, State of the Union Address, March 1, 2022, www.whitehouse.gov/state-of-the-union-2022/.

130. Stephen Kearse, "GOP Lawmakers Intensify Effort to Ban Critical Race Theory in Schools," The Pew Charitable Trusts: *Stateline*, June 14, 2021, www.pewtrusts.

org/en/research-and-analysis/blogs/stateline/2021/06/14/gop-lawmakers-intensify-effort-to-ban-critical-race-theory-in-schools.

131. John McWhorter, "If It's Not Critical Race Theory, It's Critical Race Theory-lite," *New York Times*, November 9, 2021, www.nytimes.com/2021/11/09/opinion/critical-race-theory.html.

132. Anne Case and Angus Deaton, *Deaths of Despair and the Future of Capitalism* (Princeton, NJ: Princeton University Press, 2020), 4. Case and Deaton define the working-age population as the 171 million Americans between the ages of 25 and 64, according to U.S. Census Bureau data from 2018.

133. Ibid.

134. Hitchens, "The Perils of Identity Politics."

135. Hitchens, *Unacknowledged Legislation*, xiii.

136. Nikole Hannah-Jones, "Our democracy's founding ideals were false when they were written. Black Americans have fought to make them true," *New York Times* 1619 Project, August 14, 2019, www.nytimes.com/interactive/2019/08/14/magazine/black-history-american-democracy.html.

137. Robby Soave, "1619 Project Author Nikole Hannah-Jones Now Says She Never Implied That Year Was America's True Founding," *Reason*, September 21, 2020, reason.com/2020/09/21/1619-project-author-nikole-hannah-jones-america-founding-1776/.

138. Jake Silverstein, "On Recent Criticism of The 1619 Project," *New York Times*, October 16, 2020, www.nytimes.com/2020/10/16/magazine/criticism-1619-project.html.

139. Hannah-Jones, "Our democracy's founding ideals were false when they were written. Black Americans have fought to make them true."

140. Robby Soave, "Yes, the 1619 Project Actually Suggests That Year Was America's True Founding, and Nikole Hannah-Jones Admits It," *Reason*, September 23, 2020, reason.com/2020/09/23/1619-project-nikole-hannah-jones-1776-founding-race-new-york-times/.

141. Lisa Grace Lednicer, "Four hundred years of harsh history delivered in 8,000 unflinching words," interview with Nikole Hannah-Jones, *Nieman News*, Nieman Foundation at Harvard, January 17, 2020, nieman.harvard.edu/stories/four-hundred-years-of-harsh-history-carried-through-8000-elegant-words/. Hannah-Jones told the interviewer: "I certainly expected there'd be conservative pushback to this reframing of this idea that 1619 is our true founding."

142. Silverstein, "On Recent Criticism of The 1619 Project."

143. David W. Blight, introduction to "Teaching Hard History," Kate Shuster, Southern Poverty Law Center, 8, www.splcenter.org/sites/default/files/tt_hard_history_american_slavery.pdf.

144. Adam Serwer, "The Fight Over the 1619 Project Is Not About the Facts," *Atlantic*, December 23, 2019, www.theatlantic.com/ideas/archive/2019/12/historians-clash-1619-project/604093/.

145. Hannah-Jones, "Our democracy's founding ideals were false when they were written. Black Americans have fought to make them true."

146. Ibid.

147. Martin Luther King, Jr., "Letter from Birmingham Jail," April 16, 1963, kinginstitute.stanford.edu/sites/mlk/files/letterfrombirmingham_wwcw_0.pdf.

148. Ibid.

149. Ibid.

150. Ibid.

151. Ibid.

152. Hannah-Jones, "Our democracy's founding ideals were false when they were written. Black Americans have fought to make them true."

153. Ibid.

154. Ibid.

155. Serwer, "The Fight Over the 1619 Project Is Not About the Facts."

156. Trump, "Remarks by President Trump at the White House Conference on American History."

157. Ibid.

158. Benjamin Rush, *A memorial containing travels through life or sundry incidents in the life of Dr. Benjamin Rush, born Dec. 24, 1745 (old style) died April 19, 1813*, edited by Louis Alexander Biddle, The Library of Congress, 1905, 84-85, archive.org/details/memorialcontaini00rush/page/84/mode/2up?q=paine. Rush writes that Paine "readily assented to the proposal" to write a pamphlet in favor of American independence, "and from time to time he called at my house, and read to me every chapter of the proposed pamphlet as he composed it....When Mr. Paine had finished his pamphlet, I advised him to shew [sic] it to Dr. Franklin, Mr. Rittenhouse, and Mr. Samuel Adams, all of whom I knew were decided friends to American independence. I mention these facts to refute a report that Mr. Paine was assisted in composing his pamphlet by one or more of the above gentlemen. They never saw it until it was written and then only by my advice. I gave it at his request the title of 'Common Sense'."

159. James V. Lynch, "The Limits of Revolutionary Radicalism: Tom Paine and Slavery," *The Pennsylvania Magazine of History and Biography*, July 1999, 194, www.jstor.org/stable/20093287.

160. Christopher Hitchens, *Thomas Paine's Rights of Man* (New York: Grove Press, 2006), 28.

161. Christopher Hitchens, "The Man Who Ended Slavery," *Atlantic*, May 2005, www.theatlantic.com/magazine/archive/2005/05/the-man-who-ended-slavery/303915/.

162. Ibid.

163. Christopher Hitchens, *Thomas Jefferson: Author of America* (New York: HarperCollins, 2005), 188.

164. Ibid., 187–188.

165. Ibid., xii.

166. Annette Gordon-Reed, *Thomas Jefferson and Sally Hemings: An American Controversy* (Charlottesville, VA: University of Virginia Press, 1997).

167. Annette Gordon-Reed, *The Hemingses of Monticello: An American Family* (New York: W. W. Norton, 2008).

168. Hitchens, *Thomas Jefferson: Author of America*, 3.

169. Ibid., 5.

170. Julian Boyd, *The Papers of Thomas Jefferson*, (Princeton, NJ: Princeton University Press, 1950), Vol. 1: 1760 to 1776, 426.

171. Ibid.

172. Hitchens, *Thomas Jefferson: Author of America*, 28.

173. Ibid.

174. Hitchens, "Reparations for Slavery" debate, 53:58.

175. Hitchens, *Thomas Jefferson: Author of America*, xiv.

176. Annette Gordon-Reed, "The Road to Monticello," *Slate*, December 17, 2011, slate.com/news-and-politics/2011/12/christopher-hitchens-death-annette-gordon-reed-on-his-love-of-thomas-jefferson.html.

177. Ibid.

178. Annette Gordon-Reed (@agordonreed), "I dissent from this part. The United States of America was founded in 1776, or when the Americans could definitely hold the territory," Twitter, September 12, 2019, twitter.com/agordonreed/status/1172232168954839041.

179. Annette Gordon-Reed (@agordonreed), "1619 is an extremely important date to remember. It begins the Anglo American experience with slavery. Everyone, children and adults, should know about that," Twitter, September 12, 2019, twitter.com/agordonreed/status/1172243579663765505.

180. Annette Gordon-Reed, "In Depth with Annette Gordon-Reed," C-SPAN Book TV recording, 2:48, July 4, 2021, www.c-span.org/video/?511684-1/depth-annette-gordon-reed.

181. Ibid.

182. Hitchens, *Thomas Jefferson: Author of America*, 26.

183. Hitchens, *Letters to a Young Contrarian*, 138.

184. Christopher Hitchens, "Socialism Versus Capitalism," C-SPAN recording, 32:46, November 11, 1986, www.c-span.org/video/?150777-1/socialism-versus-capitalism.

185. Ibid., 34:13.

186. Ibid., 32.55.

187. Hitchens, *Letters to a Young Contrarian*, 99.

188. Bayard Rustin, "The Failure of Black Separatism," *Harper's Magazine*, January 1970, platypus1917.org/wp-content/uploads/archive/rgroups/2008-09/rustinbayard_blackseparatismfailure1970.pdf.

189. Hitchens, *Letters to a Young Contrarian*, 108.

190. Ibid., 110.

191. Hitchens, *God Is Not Great*, 8–9.

192. Peter Singer, *The Expanding Circle: Ethics, Evolution, and Moral Progress* (New York: Farrar, Straus & Giroux, 1981).

193. Hitchens, *Letters to a Young Contrarian*, 107.

194. Ibid.

195. Ibid., 109

196. Christopher Hitchens, "The Perils of Partition," *Atlantic*, March 2003, www.theatlantic.com/magazine/archive/2003/03/the-perils-of-partition/302686/.

197. Christopher Hitchens, "Malcolm X, The Movie: Cinema as History," C-SPAN 2 recording, 1:45:32, March 1, 1993, www.c-span.org/video/?38333-1/malcolm-x-movie-cinema-history&playEvent.

198. Christopher Hitchens, "Red Rosa," *Atlantic*, June 2011, www.theatlantic.com/magazine/archive/2011/06/red-rosa/308500/.

199. Ibid.

200. Hitchens, *Hitch-22*, 384.

201. Christopher Hitchens, "Daniel Pearl Memorial Lecture," UCLA Burkle Center for International Relations, 41:35, March 3, 2010, www.international.ucla.edu/burkle/multimedia/114126.

202. Hitchens, *Letters to a Young Contrarian*, 64.

203. Hitchens, *God Is Not Great*, 64.

204. Francis Fukuyama, *The Origins of Political Order: From Prehuman Times to the French Revolution* (New York: Farrar, Straus & Giroux, 2011), 78.

3 One Cannot Be Just a Little Bit Heretical

1. Martin Amis, *Koba the Dread: Laugher and the Twenty Million* (New York: Vintage, 2003), 245, first published by Talk Miramax Books (New York) in 2002.

2. Ibid., 248.

3. Ibid.

4. Christopher Hitchens, "Lightness at Midnight," *Atlantic*, September 2002, www.theatlantic.com/magazine/archive/2002/09/lightness-at-midnight/376642/.

5. Arthur Koestler, *Darkness at Noon* (New York: Macmillan, 1940).

6. Amis, *Koba the Dread*, 257.

7. Hitchens, "Lightness at Midnight."

8. Ibid.

9. Christopher Hitchens, "Don't. Be. Silly," *Guardian*, September 4, 2002, www.theguardian.com/books/2002/sep/04/history.highereducation.

10. George Orwell, "Burnham's View of the Contemporary World Struggle," *New Leader*, March 29, 1947.

11. Amis, *Koba the Dread*, 47.

12. Ian McEwan, "Remembering Christopher Hitchens," Charlie Rose, 14:51, April 13, 2012, charlierose.com/videos/14685.

13. Christopher Hitchens, "No, Prime Minister," *Vanity Fair*, July 6, 2009, www.vanityfair.com/news/2009/08/hitchens200908.

14. Christopher Hitchens, "Long Live Labor," *Slate*, April 25, 2005, slate.com/news-and-politics/2005/04/long-live-labor.html.

15. Christopher Hitchens, "Heaven on Earth: The Rise and Fall of Socialism," PBS, 2005, web.archive.org/web/20060612210516/http://www.pbs.org/heavenonearth/interviews_hitchens.html.

16. Hitchens, interview with *The Progressive Magazine*.

17. Hitchens, "Red Rosa."

18. Ibid.

19. Christopher Hitchens, "Trotsky with Hitchens and Service," Uncommon Knowledge with Peter Robinson, Stanford University Hoover Institution, August 10, 2009, www.hoover.org/sites/default/files/documents/uk-transcript-hitchens-service.pdf, www.hoover.org/research/trotsky-hitchens-and-service.

20. Hitchens, interview with *The Progressive Magazine*.

21. Ibid.

22. Hitchens, "Don't. Be. Silly."

23. Amis, *Koba the Dread*, 250.

24. Ibid.

25. Ibid., 47.

26. Hitchens, *Letters to a Young Contrarian*, xiii.

27. Christopher Hitchens, "Paxman Meets Hitchens: A Newsnight Special," *BBC Newsnight*, 18:47, November 2010, www.bbc.co.uk/programmes/b00wkrbk, www.youtube.com/watch?v=LIVEsa2g4ag.

28. Paul Berman, *A Tale of Two Utopias: The Political Journey of the Generation* of 1968 (New York: W. W. Norton, 1996), 14.

29. Berman, *A Tale of Two Utopias*, 13–14.

30. Hitchens, *Hitch-22*, 98.

31. Nicholas Kulish, "Leszek Kolakowski, Polish Philosopher, Dies at 81," *New York Times*, July 20, 2009, www.nytimes.com/2009/07/21/world/europe/21kolakowski. html.

32. "Poland's Andrzej Duda apologises to Jews expelled in 1968," *BBC News*, March 8, 2018, www.bbc.com/news/world-europe-43330963.

33. Leszek Kołakowski, *Main Currents of Marxism: Its Rise, Growth, and Dissolution* (New York: Oxford University Press, 1978), first published by Institut Littéraire in Paris (1976).

34. Leszek Kołakowski, *Main Currents of Marxism, The Founders, The Golden Age, The Breakdown* (New York: W. W. Norton, 2005), vi.

35. Hitchens, *Hitch-22*, 122.

36. Ibid., 123.

37. Christopher Hitchens, "A Sense of Historical Irony," *Slate*, July 20, 2009, slate. com/news-and-politics/2009/07/leszek-kolakowski-1927-2009.html.

38. Hitchens, *Conversations with History*, 37:37.

39. Ibid., 38:30.

40. Ibid., 38:00.

41. Christopher Hitchens, "Free Radical," interview by Rhys Southan, *Reason*, November 2001, reason.com/2001/11/01/free-radical-2/.

42. Hitchens, "Heaven on Earth: The Rise and Fall of Socialism."

43. Ibid.

44. Hitchens, *Letters to a Young Contrarian*, 96.

45. Martin Amis, "Remembering Christopher Hitchens," Charlie Rose, 6:07.

46. James Fenton, "Remembering Christopher Hitchens," Charlie Rose, 12:34.

47. Christopher Hitchens, "Why Bosnia matters," *London Review of Books*, September 10, 1992, www.lrb.co.uk/the-paper/v14/n17/christopher-hitchens/why-bosnia-matters.

48. Ibid.

49. Elaine Sciolino, "Clinton Urges Stronger U.S. Stand On Enforcing Bosnia Flight Ban," *New York Times*, December 12, 1992, www.nytimes.com/1992/12/12/world/clinton-urges-stronger-us-stand-on-enforcing-bosnia-flight-ban.html.

50. Ivo H. Daalder, *Getting to Dayton: The Making of America's Bosnia Policy* (Washington, DC: Brookings Institution Press, 1999), 11-16.

51. George Packer, *Our Man: Richard Holbrooke and the End of the American Century* (New York: Knopf, 2019), 267-268.

52. Daalder, *Getting to Dayton*, 17–18.

53. Craig R. Whitney, "NATO's Leadership Gap; Washington's Seeming Confusion on Bosnia Throws Alliance Into Crisis of Relevance," *New York Times*, May 29, 1993, www.nytimes.com/1993/05/29/world/nato-s-leadership-gap-washington-s-

seeming-confusion-bosnia-throws-alliance-into.html.

54. Christopher Hitchens, "Never Trust Imperialists," *Boston Review*, December 2, 1993, bostonreview.net/articles/hitchens-never-trust-imperialists/.

55. Christopher Hitchens, "Events in the News," C-SPAN recording, February 14, 1994, 1:15, www.c-span.org/video/?54546-1/events-news.

56. Hitchens, "Never Trust Imperialists." Hitchens's reassessment of American interventionism may have begun even sooner. In *Hitch-22*, he recalls riding in a jeep with two Kurdish *peshmerga* soldiers who had taped a photograph of George H.W. Bush to the windshield. "After a while," Hitchens writes, "I was moved to ask if they felt they had to do this. (I think I may have wondered what I would say if we ran into any smart-ass reporter I knew.) The straightness of their answer shamed the deviousness of my question. 'Without your Mr. Bush,' they said, 'we think we and our families would all be dead.' I didn't have to look very closely at my surroundings to see, and to appreciate, the blunt truth of this." They were referring to a no-fly zone that had been established over northern Iraq by the United States and its allies to prevent Saddam Hussein from continuing to slaughter the Kurds following an uprising which took place after the Gulf War.

57. Christopher Hitchens, "Why Bosnia Matters," Alternative Radio, March 4, 1994, www.alternativeradio.org/products/hitc002/.

58. Ibid.

59. Ibid.

60. Christopher Hitchens, "Military Intervention in Haiti or Bosnia," C-SPAN 2 recording, 25:58, March 29, 1994, www.c-span.org/video/?55700-1/military-intervention-haiti-bosnia.

61. Ibid., 33:06.

62. Ibid.

63. Ibid., 36:10.

64. Hitchens, "Never Trust Imperialists."

65. Ibid.

66. Ian Parker, "He Knew He Was Right," *New Yorker*, October 8, 2006, www.newyorker.com/magazine/2006/10/16/he-knew-he-was-right-2.

67. Hitchens, "Never Trust Imperialists."

68. Seymour, *Unhitched*, xiii.

69. Ian McEwan, "Remembering Christopher Hitchens," 15:08.

70. Christopher Hitchens, *Arguably: Essays* (New York: Twelve, 2011), xvii-xviii.

71. Ibid.

72. Patrick Cockburn, "Christopher Hitchens made a cogent case for war—but he was still wrong," *The Independent*, April 28, 2012, www.independent.co.uk/voices/commentators/patrick-cockburn-christopher-hitchens-made-a-cogent-case-for-war-but-he-was-still-wrong-7687385.html.

73. Hitchens, "Never Trust Imperialists."

74. Paul Berman, *Power and the Idealists: Or, the Passion of Joschka Fischer and Its Aftermath* (New York: W. W. Norton, 2007), first published by Soft Skull Press (New York) in 2005.

75. Ibid., 259. For a more specific discussion of how these interventionist concepts influenced U.S. foreign policy—as well as a joint review of Packer's *Our Man* and Berman's *Power and the Idealists*—see my essay published in *Quillette*: "Holbrooke and the 68ers," February 11, 2020, quillette.com/2020/02/11/holbrooke-and-the-68ers/.

76. Ibid., 69.

77. Vo Van Ai, "Isle of Light: A Look Back at the Boat People and the European Left," *World Affairs*, March-April 2014, 45, www.jstor.org/stable/43555090.

78. Ibid., 40.

79. Ibid.

80. Ibid., 40–41.

81. Colin Gordon, "The drowned and the saved: Foucault's texts on migration and solidarity," *openDemocracy*, November 13, 2015, www.opendemocracy.net/en/can-europe-make-it/drowned-and-saved-foucaults-texts-on-migration-and-solidarity/.

82. Ai, "Isle of Light."

83. Berman, *Power and the Idealists*.

84. Hortense Goulard, "Danny the Red, still talking about a revolution," *Politico*, September 7, 2016, www.politico.eu/article/daniel-cohn-bendit-mep-libertarian-interview/.

85. "Secretary-General appoints Bernard Kouchner (France) as his Special Representative for United Nations Mission in Kosovo," statement by the spokesman for UN Secretary-General Kofi Annan, July 2, 1999, digitallibrary.un.org/record/1489277?ln=en.

86. Joschka Fischer, speech at the Green Party Congress in Bielefeld, May 13, 1999, ghdi.ghi-dc.org/docpage.cfm?docpage_id=4440.

87. Wolfgang-Uwe Friedrich, "The Legacy of Kosovo: German Politics and Policies in the Balkans," the American Institute for Contemporary German Studies, Johns Hopkins University, 2000, 8, www.aicgs.org/site/wp-content/uploads/2011/11/legacy_of_kosovo.pdf.

88. Ibid., 19.

89. Andrew Nagorski, "The Paint Attack," *Newsweek*, May 23, 1999, www.newsweek.com/paint-attack-166840.

90. Ian Traynor, "Greens back Nato amid uproar," *Guardian*, May 13, 1999, www.theguardian.com/world/1999/may/14/greenpolitics.

91. Friedrich, "The Legacy of Kosovo," 8.

92. Roger Cohen, "Half a Century After Hitler, German Jets Join the Attack," *New York Times*, March 26, 1999, archive.nytimes.com/www.nytimes.com/library/world/europe/032699kosovo-germany.html.

93. Traynor, "Greens back Nato amid uproar."

94. Fischer, speech at the Green Party Congress in Bielefeld.

95. Roger Cohen, "A Generation of German Pacifists Finds Itself at Odds Over the Kosovo Air War," *New York Times*, May 16, 1999, www.nytimes.com/1999/05/16/world/crisis-balkans-germany-generation-german-pacifists-finds-itself-odds-over-kosovo.html.

96. Hans Von Der Burchard, "From doves to über-hawks: Ukraine war recasts Germany's Greens," *Politico*, April 22, 2022, www.politico.eu/article/ukraine-war-recasts-germany-green-party-russia/.

97. Ibid.

98. Markus Berg, "The new darling of the nation," *Bild*, ZDF Politbarometer, April 8, 2022, www.bild.de/politik/inland/politik-inland/habeck-hammer-im-politbarometer-der-neue-liebling-der-nation-79711098.bild.html.

99. Anton Hofreiter, "Hofreiter warns of 'Third World War,'" ZDF Morning Magazine, April 20, 2022, www.zdf.de/nachrichten/zdf-morgenmagazin/deutsche-waffenlieferungen-lasst-uns-das-einfach-tun-sagt-anton-hofreiter-100.html.

100. Kofi Annan, "Secretary-General presents his Annual Report to the General Assembly," September 20, 1999, www.un.org/sg/en/content/sg/speeches/1999-09-20/secretary-general-presents-his-annual-report-general-assembly.

101. Resolution 60/1, adopted by the General Assembly of the United Nations on September 16, 2005, www.un.org/en/development/desa/population/migration/general-assembly/docs/globalcompact/A_RES_60_1.pdf.

102. Kofi Annan, "'We the Peoples': The Role of the United Nations in the 21st Century" (New York: UN Department of Public Information, 2000), United Nations Digital Library, digitallibrary.un.org/record/413745.

103. Hitchens, *Letters to a Young Contrarian*, 129.

104. Ibid., 128.

105. Hitchens, *Hitch-22*, 413.

106. Hitchens, "Never Trust Imperialists."

107. Ibid.

108. Ibid.

109. Hitchens, *Hitch-22*, 419.

110. Ibid.

111. Hitchens, *For the Sake of Argument*, xii.

112. Ibid., xi.

113. Ibid., xiii.

114. Christopher Hitchens, "For the Sake of Argument," C-SPAN Booknotes recording, 7:56, September 1, 1993, www.c-span.org/video/?51559-1/for-sake-argument.

115. Ibid., 8:27.

116. Dick Morris, PBS Frontline, interview conducted by Chris Bury, June 2000, www.pbs.org/wgbh/pages/frontline/shows/clinton/interviews/morris.html.

117. Christopher Hitchens, *No One Left to Lie To: The Triangulations of William Jefferson Clinton* (New York: Verso, 1999).

118. Christopher Hitchens, "Events in the News," C-SPAN recording, 15:53, August 23, 1993, www.c-span.org/video/?49150-1/events-news.

119. Hitchens, interview with *The Progressive Magazine*.

120. Ibid.

121. General election results, 1 May 1997, Staff of the House of Commons Social and General Statistics Section, February 1999, www.parliament.uk/globalassets/documents/commons-information-office/m15.pdf.

122. Christopher Hitchens, "Almost Noble," *Atlantic*, October 2010, www.theatlantic.com/magazine/archive/2010/10/almost-noble/308211/.

123. Christopher Hitchens, "The Future of Socialism," PBS Think Tank with Ben Wattenberg, July 7, 2005, www.pbs.org/thinktank/transcript1193.html.

124. Ibid.

125. Ibid.

126. Hitchens, interview with *The Progressive Magazine*.

127. Christopher Hitchens, "Hitchens: Clinton could sell out Blair," interview conducted by Edward Main, *BBC News*, June 3, 1999, news.bbc.co.uk/2/hi/uk_news/politics/354470.stm.

128. Ibid.

129. Hitchens, "Almost Noble."

130. Ibid.

131. Christopher Hitchens, "A friend in need," *Guardian*, April 8, 2007, www.theguardian.com/politics/2007/apr/08/tonyblair.labour9.

132. Tony Blair, "Doctrine of International Community," speech to The Economic Club of Chicago, April 22, 1999.

133. Ibid.

134. Ibid.

135. Ibid.

136. Ibid.

137. David H. Ucko, "When Intervention Works: The Instructive Case of Sierra Leone," *War on the Rocks* (adapted from a longer article in Journal for Strategic Studies), August 31, 2016, warontherocks.com/2016/08/when-intervention-works-the-instructive-case-of-sierra-leone/, www.tandfonline.com/doi/pdf/10.1080/01402390.2015.1110695.

138. Hitchens, "Long Live Labor."

139. Hitchens, "Almost Noble."

140. Ibid.

141. Blair, "Doctrine of International Community."

142. Christopher Hitchens, "An Anglosphere Future," *City Journal*, fall 2007, www.city-journal.org/html/anglosphere-future-13044.html.

143. John Rodden, "Fellow Contrarians? Christopher Hitchens and George Orwell," *The Kenyon Review*, Winter 2006, 144, www.jstor.org/stable/4338861.

144. David Carr, "The Nation and a Longtime Columnist Are Parting Ways," *New York Times*, September 26, 2002, www.nytimes.com/2002/09/26/business/the-nation-and-a-longtime-columnist-are-parting-ways.html.

145. Christopher Hitchens, "Taking Sides," *Nation*, September 26, 2002, www.thenation.com/article/archive/taking-sides/.

146. Christopher Hitchens, "Against Rationalization," *Nation*, September 20, 2001, www.thenation.com/article/politics/against-rationalization/.

147. Christopher Hitchens, "Role of the U.S. in the World," C-SPAN recording, 8:15, October 8, 2005, www.c-span.org/video/?188655-9/role-us-world.

148. Salman Rushdie, "Christopher Hitchens, 1949–2011," *Vanity Fair*, January 6, 2012, www.vanityfair.com/culture/2012/02/rushdie-on-hitchens-201202.

149. Ibid.

150. Glenn Greenwald, "Christopher Hitchens and the protocol for public figure deaths," *Salon*, December 17, 2011, www.salon.com/2011/12/17/christohper_hitchens_and_the_protocol_for_public_figure_deaths/.

151. Glenn Greenwald, "In Solidarity With a Free Press: Some More Blasphemous Cartoons," *The Intercept*, January 9, 2015, theintercept.com/2015/01/09/solidarity-charlie-hebdo-cartoons/.

152. Greenwald, "Christopher Hitchens and the protocol for public figure deaths."

153. Perrin, "Obituary for a Former Contrarian."

154. Ibid.

155. Chris Hedges, "The Dangerous Atheism of Christopher Hitchens and Sam Harris," *AlterNet*, March 22, 2008, www.alternet.org/2008/03/the_dangerous_atheism_of_christopher_hitchens_and_sam_harris/.

156. Hitchens, "Why Bosnia Matters."

157. Ibid.

158. Hitchens, *Letters to a Young Contrarian*, 130.

159. Christopher Hitchens, "Letters to a Young Contrarian," C-SPAN Washington Journal recording, 59:03, November 11, 2001, www.c-span.org/video/?167249-3/letters-young-contrarian.

160. Samuel P. Huntington, "The Clash of Civilizations?" *Foreign Affairs*, Summer 1993, www.jstor.org/stable/20045621.

161. Hitchens, "Letters to a Young Contrarian," interview on C-SPAN Washington Journal.

162. Christopher Hitchens, "Facing the Islamist Menace," City Journal, Winter 2007, www.city-journal.org/html/facing-islamist-menace-12993.html.

163. Christopher Hitchens, "Saving Islam from bin Laden," The Age, September 5, 2002, www.theage.com.au/national/saving-islam-from-bin-laden-20020905-gduk66.html.

164. Christopher Hitchens, "So Long, Fellow Travelers," Washington Post, October 20, 2002, www.washingtonpost.com/archive/opinions/2002/10/20/so-long-fellow-travelers/f8a66a1c-3f65-4410-8290-d1581712a1fb/.

165. Hitchens, "Never Trust Imperialists."

166. "Endless Torment: The 1991 Uprising in Iraq And Its Aftermath," Human Rights Watch, June 1992, www.hrw.org/reports/1992/Iraq926.htm.

167. "Genocide in Iraq: The Anfal Campaign Against the Kurds," Human Rights Watch, July 1993, www.hrw.org/reports/1993/iraqanfal/ANFALINT.htm.

168. Joost R. Hiltermann, A Poisonous Affair: America, Iraq, and the Gassing of Halabja (New York: Cambridge University Press, 2007), 135-138. Here's how Hiltermann summarizes the state of U.S. intelligence on the Anfal genocide on page 138: "...the reason for weak US knowledge of Anfal and zero intervention, even at the diplomatic level, may have been Washington's preoccupation with the southern front, as well as its strong support for the Iraqi war effort. The Kurds, after all, were Iran's allies, and whatever the Iraqi regime was doing to them Washington considered an internal matter. Aware that it had a free hand, Iraq disposed of its internal problem once and for all by using gas to scare villagers into its arms. At least it must have thought it had fixed this nagging question for good. If the 1991 Gulf War and its aftermath had not given the Kurdish national movement a new lease on life, Kurdistan would have remained a wasteland, Halabja forgotten, and Anfal concealed by layers of desert sand."

169. Hitchens, "So Long, Fellow Travelers."

170. Christopher Hitchens, "U.S. Imperialism Or A Just Response To Terror? A Debate Between Christopher Hitchens And Tariq Ali," Pacifica National Programming, April 17, 2002, www.pacificaradioarchives.org/recording/pz0500.

171. Ibid.

172. Ibid.

173. Barham Salih (@BarhamSalih), "So saddened for death of Christopher Hitchens; mesmerizing intellect, tenacious moral warrior. Kurds lost [a] good friend; will miss him so v much," Twitter, December 16, 2011, twitter.com/BarhamSalih/status/147570667229954048.

174. Christopher Hitchens, "Appointment in Samarra?" Nation, September 12, 2002, www.thenation.com/article/archive/appointment-samarra/.

175. Hitchens, "Military Intervention in Haiti or Bosnia," C-SPAN 2 recording, 30:16.

176. Ibid., 31:04.

177. Hitchens, "U.S. Imperialism Or A Just Response To Terror? A Debate Between Christopher Hitchens And Tariq Ali."

178. Richard Seymour, "The Genocidal Imagination of Christopher Hitchens," *Monthly Review*, November 26, 2005, mronline.org/2005/11/26/the-genocidal-imagination-of-christopher-hitchens/.

179. Ibid.

180. Seymour, *Unhitched*, 12.

181. Ibid., 29

182. Ibid.

183. Ibid.

184. Ibid.

185. Carr, "The Nation and a Longtime Columnist Are Parting Ways."

186. Hitchens, ACLU lawsuit statement, 2006.

187. Hitchens, "Believe Me, It's Torture."

188. Hitchens, *Hitch-22*, 381–384.

189. Christopher Hitchens, "Bad Timing," *Slate*, January 5, 2009, slate.com/news-and-politics/2009/01/gaza-could-have-been-a-model-of-the-future-palestinian-state.html.

190. Christopher Hitchens, "Scenes from an Execution," *Vanity Fair*, January 1998, archive.vanityfair.com/article/share/3472d8c9-8efa-4989-b3da-72c7922cf70a.

191. Hitchens, *Hitch-22*, 68–69.

192. Christopher Hitchens, conversation with David Frum, C-SPAN Washington Journal recording, 1:29:40, December 11, 1996 www.c-span.org/video/?77242-1/washington-journal-wednesday.

193. Hitchens, "Reparations for Slavery" debate.

194. Hitchens, conversation with David Frum, 1:54:44.

195. Hitchens, "Free Radical," interview by Rhys Southan.

196. Hitchens, "Against Rationalization."

197. Tad Friend, "Oliver Stone's Chaos Theory," *New Yorker*, October 14, 2001, www.newyorker.com/magazine/2001/10/22/oliver-stones-chaos-theory.

198. Noam Chomsky, *9-11* (New York: Seven Stories Press, 2001).

199. Hitchens, "Stranger in a Strange Land."

200. George Scialabba, "Hitchens Distorts Noam Chomsky," Guernica, May 11, 2011, www.cfr.org/backgrounder/saudi-arabia-withdrawl-us-forces.

201. Ibid.

202. Sharon Otterman, "Saudi Arabia: Withdrawal of U.S. Forces," Council on Foreign Relations, February 7, 2005, www.cfr.org/backgrounder/saudi-arabia-with-

drawl-us-forces.

203. Seth Mydans, "In East Timor, Decisive Vote For a Break From Indonesia," *New York Times*, September 4, 1999, www.nytimes.com/1999/09/04/world/in-east-timor-decisive-vote-for-a-break-from-indonesia.html.

204. Richard C. Paddock, "At Site of Bali Bombings, a Fight Brews Over Money and Memorials," *New York Times*, May 6, 2019, www.nytimes.com/2019/05/06/world/asia/indonesia-bali-bombings-memorial.html.

205. David Teather and Julian Borger, "Bin Laden tape praises Bali attack," *Guardian*, November 12, 2002, www.theguardian.com/world/2002/nov/13/indonesia.alqaida.

206. "Bali attack 'targeted Australians,'" *BBC News*, February 10, 2003, news.bbc.co.uk/2/hi/asia-pacific/2743679.stm.

207. "Bin Laden's Statement," *New York Times*, November 3, 2001, www.nytimes.com/2001/11/03/international/bin-ladens-statement.html.

208. Christopher Hitchens, "Why Ask Why?" *Slate*, October 3, 2005, slate.com/news-and-politics/2005/10/don-t-bother-looking-for-explanations-for-terrorist-attacks.html.

209. "In-depth with Christopher Hitchens," C-SPAN 2 Book TV recording, 48:04, September 2, 2007, www.c-span.org/video/?198800-1/depth-christopher-hitchens.

210. Scialabba, "Hitchens Distorts Noam Chomsky."

211. George Galloway, "Iraq War Debate," C-SPAN 2 Book TV recording, 48:08, September 14, 2005.

212. Bruckner, *The Tyranny of Guilt*.

213. Hitchens, "Against Rationalization."

214. Christopher Hitchens, "Multicultural Masochism," *Slate*, November 23, 2009, slate.com/news-and-politics/2009/11/the-war-on-terrorism-didn-t-cause-the-fort-hood-shootings.html.

215. Susan Sontag, "Tuesday, and After: New Yorker writers respond to 9/11," *New Yorker*, September 16, 2001, www.newyorker.com/magazine/2001/09/24/tuesday-and-after-talk-of-the-town.

216. Maral Shamloo, "Chomsky Discusses Terrorism," *The Tech*, October 19, 2001, tech.mit.edu/V121/N52/52chomsky.52n.html.

217. Sarah H. Wright, "Chomsky criticizes US violence," *MIT News*, October 24, 2001 (a version of the article also appeared in MIT Tech Talk on the same day), news.mit.edu/2001/chomsky-1024.

218. "On Russia's Invasion of Ukraine," statement by the Democratic Socialists of America, February 26, 2022, www.dsausa.org/statements/on-russias-invasion-of-ukraine/.

219. Max Blumenthal, "What the Mainstream Media Gets Wrong about Syria," interview conducted by Robert Wright for Bloggingheads.tv, October 16, 2019, bloggingheads.tv/videos/57520.

220. Max Blumenthal, "Was bombing of Mariupol theater staged by Ukrainian Azov extremists to trigger NATO intervention?" *The Grayzone*, March 18, 2022, thegrayzone.com/2022/03/18/bombing-mariupol-theater-ukrainian-azov-nato-intervention/.

221. Benjamin Norton (@BenjaminNorton), "These are the Western media's and NATO's favorite angelic 'peaceful protesters' in Russia: fanatical supporters of far-right fringe opposition figure Navalny who brutally beat up counter-protesters who dare to hold up signs. This is NATO's hope for Russia's future," Twitter, January 23, 2021, twitter.com/BenjaminNorton/status/1352976384365355009. The video cited in the tweet was removed, but it depicted several protesters assaulting counter-protesters.

222. Benjamin Norton (@BenjaminNorton), "The US/NATO are attempting a 'color revolution' to overthrow the government in Belarus, the only remaining ex-Soviet state that still has socialistic policies and state control over the economy. Stratfor, 'the Shadow CIA,' is admitting they want a neoliberal Western puppet regime," Twitter, August 7, 2020, twitter.com/benjaminnorton/status/1291737176510730242.

223. Max Blumenthal, "Hostile new cold war imperialist narrative needs factual vaccine," *Global Times*, August 5, 2020, www.globaltimes.cn/content/1196790.shtml.

224. Nick Cohen, *What's Left? How the Left Lost its Way* (London: Harper Perennial, 2007), 255, first published by Fourth Estate.

225. Ibid., 273.

226. Ibid.

227. Ibid., 274.

228. Noam Chomsky, "Vietnam and the Intellectuals," interview conducted by William F. Buckley Jr., Firing Line, April 3, 1969, digitalcollections.hoover.org/objects/6077.

229. Noam Chomsky, *On Power and Ideology: The Managua Lectures* (Chicago: Haymarket Books, 2015), 63, first published in 1987 by South End Press (Boston).

230. Noam Chomsky, "Activism, Anarchism, and Power," interview by Harry Kreisler, *Conversations with History*, Institute of International Studies, UC Berkeley, 7:59, www.youtube.com/watch?v=8ghoXQxdk6s&t=5s.

231. George Orwell, *Homage to Catalonia* (New York: Houghton Mifflin Harcourt, 1952), first published in 1938 by Secker and Warburg (London.).

232. Hitchens, "Never Trust Imperialists."

233. Alison Des Forges, *Leave None to Tell the Story: Genocide in Rwanda* (New York: Human Rights Watch, 1999), 12, www.hrw.org/sites/default/files/media_2020/12/rwanda-leave-none-to-tell-the-story.pdf.

234. Bill Clinton, interview for "Erin Burnett Outfront," CNN, July 19, 2012, www.cnn.com/videos/bestoftv/2012/07/19/exp-erin-bill-clinton-rwanda-genocide.cnn, transcripts.cnn.com/show/ebo/date/2012-07-19/segment/01.

235. Christopher Hitchens, "Realism in Darfur," *Slate*, November 7, 2005, slate.com/news-and-politics/2005/11/what-realism-has-wrought-in-africa.html.

236. Nicholas D. Kristof, "The Secret Genocide Archive," *New York Times*, Febru-

ary 23, 2005, www.nytimes.com/2005/02/23/opinion/the-secret-genocide-archive.html. Kristof published a series of columns about Darfur in the months that followed, for which he won the 2006 Pulitzer Prize in Commentary. The columns can be found here: www.pulitzer.org/winners/nicholas-d-kristof.

237.   Hitchens, "Never Trust Imperialists."

238.   "An Open Letter to the United Nations, President Clinton, and the Congress," *New York Review of Books*, March 4, 1993, www.nybooks.com/articles/1993/03/04/an-open-letter-to-the-united-nations-president-cli/.

239.   Christopher Hitchens, "Stranger in a Strange Land," *Atlantic*, December 2001, www.theatlantic.com/magazine/archive/2001/12/stranger-in-a-strange-land/302349/.

240.   Christopher Hitchens and Noam Chomsky, "The 'Single Standard' in Kosovo," *Nation*, December 15, 1999, www.thenation.com/article/archive/single-standard-kosovo/.

241.   Hitchens, *Hitch-22*, 414.

242.   Ibid., 412.

243.   André Gide, Richard Wright, Ignazio Silone, Stephen Spender, Arthur Koestler, and Louis Fischer, *The God that Failed* (New York: Columbia University Press, 2001), first published in 1950 by Hamilton (London).

244.   Arthur Koestler, *The God that Failed*, 74.

245.   Hitchens, *Hitch-22*, 415.

246.   Ibid.

247.   Ibid., 412.

248.   Kylie MacLellan, "Labour's Corbyn, who voted 'No' in 1975, raises Brexit fears," *Reuters*, September 11, 2015, www.reuters.com/article/uk-britain-politics-labour-corbyn/labours-corbyn-who-voted-no-in-1975-raises-brexit-fears idUKKC-N0RB1IK20150911.

249.   Ibid.

250.   Elizabeth Piper, "Jeremy Corbyn, Britain's unlikely EU warrior, makes last stand on Brexit," *Reuters*, September 9, 2019, www.reuters.com/investigates/special-report/britain-eu-corbyn/.

251.   Treaty of Lisbon amending the Treaty on European Union and the Treaty establishing the European Community, December 13, 2007, eur-lex.europa.eu/legal-content/EN/TXT/?uri=CELEX:12007L/TXT.

252.   Benjamin Kentish, "Jeremy Corbyn warned of 'European empire' and said EU treaty would create 'a military Frankenstein,'" *The Independent*, February 6, 2019, www.independent.co.uk/news/uk/politics/jeremy-corbyn-brexit-eu-lisbon-treaty-europe-empire-military-video-a8766421.html.

253.   Ibid.

254.   Patrick Worrall, "Corbyn did call for NATO to disband—but it's Labour policy to stay in," Channel 4 News, October 17, 2019, www.channel4.com/news/fact-

check/factcheck-corbyn-did-call-for-nato-to-disband-but-its-labour-policy-to-stay-in.

255. "Jeremy Corbyn was wrong on Nato, says Sir Keir Starmer," *BBC News*, February 10, 2022, www.bbc.com/news/uk-politics-60333340.

256. Jeremy Corbyn, "No War in Ukraine: Stop NATO Expansion," panel discussion published by the Stop the War Coalition, February 10, 2022, www.stopwar.org.uk/article/watch-no-war-in-ukraine-stop-nato-expansion/.

257. Francis Wheen, "Why we are right to bomb the Serbs," *Guardian*, April 6, 1999, www.theguardian.com/theguardian/1999/apr/07/features11.g24.

258. Marko Attila Hoare, "Arnesa Buljusmic-Kustura's 'woke' excuses for Jeremy Corbyn's Balkan genocide revisionism," *Greater Surbiton*, June 13, 2020, greatersurbiton.wordpress.com/2020/06/13/arnesa-buljusmic-kusturas-woke-excuses-for-jeremy-corbyns-balkan-genocide-revisionism/.

259. John Pilger, "How Silent are the Humanitarian Invaders of Kosovo?" *New Statesman*, December 8, 2004, johnpilger.com/articles/reminders-of-kosovo.

260. "John Pilger and Kosovo," Early Day Motion, UK Parliament, tabled on December 14, 2004, edm.parliament.uk/early-day-motion/26919.

261. Jeremy Corbyn, "Welcome To The Nato-Fest," *Morning Star*, August 28, 2014, web.archive.org/web/20140901094632/morningstaronline.co.uk/a-3235-Welcome-to-the-Nato-fest/#.VARArmr7Q6g.

262. Berman, *Power and the Idealists*, 64.

263. Ibid., 81.

264. Ibid., 82.

265. Ibid., 85.

266. Ibid., 86.

267. Ibid.

268. Ibid.

269. Ibid., 87

270. Ibid.

271. Hitchens, *Hitch-22* audiobook interview (Chapter 25), 5:43.

272. Hitchens, *Letters to a Young Contrarian*, 130-131.

273. Ibid., 136.

274. Ibid.

275. Oscar Wilde, "The Soul of Man Under Socialism," *Fortnightly Review*, February 1891.

276. Hitchens, *Hitch-22*, 420.

277. Ibid.

278. Hitchens, *Letters to a Young Contrarian*, 36.

279. Berman, *Power and the Idealists*, 102.

280. Ibid., 104.

281. Ibid., 105.

282. Hitchens, "Why Bosnia Matters."

283. Hitchens, *Letters to a Young Contrarian*, 133.

284. Hitchens, *Letters to a Young Contrarian*, 136.

285. Christopher Hitchens, "The Euro," *Foreign Policy Magazine*, October 20, 2009, foreignpolicy.com/2009/10/20/the-euro/.

286. Christopher Hitchens, "Is the Euro Doomed?" *Slate*, April 26, 2010, slate.com/news-and-politics/2010/04/is-the-euro-doomed-to-be-just-one-european-currency-among-many.html.

287. Ibid.

288. Ibid.

289. Ibid.

290. "European Commission statement on the judgment of the European Court of Justice on Poland's Ordinary Courts law," European Commission press release, November 5, 2019, ec.europa.eu/commission/presscorner/detail/es/statement_19_6225.

291. Steven Erlanger and Monika Pronczuk, "Poland Escalates Fight With Europe Over the Rule of Law," *New York Times*, July 15, 2021, www.nytimes.com/2021/07/15/world/europe/poland-hungary-europe.html.

292. "Most Poles want Warsaw to back down in EU dispute," EUobserver, October 27, 2021, euobserver.com/tickers/153347.

293. Peter Hitchens, "The late Christopher Hitchens attacks the EU! Or Does He?" *The Daily Mail*, July 11, 2014, hitchensblog.mailonsunday.co.uk/2014/07/the-late-christopher-hitchens-attacks-the-eu-or-does-he-.html.

294. George Orwell, "Toward European Unity," *Partisan Review*, Summer 1947.

295. Ibid.

296. Hitchens, *Hitch-22*, 419.

297. Hitchens, *Letters to a Young Contrarian*, 32.

298. Ibid., 138.

299. Christopher Hitchens, "Beautiful behemoth," *Guardian*, November 8, 1999, www.theguardian.com/world/1999/nov/08/usa.features113.

300. "Americans' Trust in Government Remains Low," Gallup, September 30, 2021, news.gallup.com/poll/355124/americans-trust-government-remains-low.aspx.

301. Orwell, "The Freedom of the press."

302. Christopher Hitchens, "The Lessons of 1989," *Slate*, November 8, 2009, slate.com/news-and-politics/2009/11/the-lessons-of-1989.html.

303. Hitchens, *Hitch-22*, 89.

304. G.W.F. Hegel, *Elements of the Philosophy of Right*, (Cambridge: Cambridge University Press, 1991), edited by Allen W. Wood, translated by H.B. Nisbet, 23, first published in 1821.

305. Hitchens, *Conversations with History*, 13:09.

306. James Atlas, "What is Fukuyama Saying? And To Whom is He Saying It?" *New York Times*, October 22, 1989, www.nytimes.com/1989/10/22/magazine/what-is-fukuyama-saying-and-to-whom-is-he-saying-it-723189.html.

307. Hitchens, *Letters to a Young Contrarian*, 136–137.

4 Iraq

1. Thom Shanker, Michael S. Schmidt and Robert F. Worth, "In Baghdad, Panetta Leads Uneasy Moment of Closure," *New York Times*, December 15, 2011, www.nytimes.com/2011/12/16/world/middleeast/panetta-in-baghdad-for-iraq-military-handover-ceremony.html.

2. Michael Calderone, "Christopher Hitchens, Despite Criticism And Casualties, Defended Iraq War To The End," *HuffPost*, December 16, 2011, www.huffpost.com/entry/christopher-hitchens-dead-iraq-war_n_1154152.

3. "The struggle against bullshit," *Economist*, December 16, 2011, www.economist.com/democracy-in-america/2011/12/16/the-struggle-against-bullshit.

4. John Cook, "Christopher Hitchens' Unforgivable Mistake," Gawker, December 16, 2011, www.gawker.com/5868761/christopher-hitchens-unforgivable-mistake.

5. Christopher Hitchens, "Why I'm voting for Bush (but only just)," *Guardian*, October 31, 2004, www.theguardian.com/world/2004/oct/31/uselections2004.comment2.

6. Christopher Hitchens, "Taking Sides," *Nation*, September 26, 2002, www.thenation.com/article/archive/taking-sides/.

7. Christopher Hitchens, "American Power and the Crisis Over Iraq," C-SPAN recording, 58:50, March 15, 2003, www.c-span.org/video/?175524-1/american-power-crisis-iraq.

8. Ibid.

9. Wolf Blitzer, "Search for the 'smoking gun,'" CNN, January 10, 2003, www.cnn.com/2003/US/01/10/wbr.smoking.gun/.

10. Christopher Hitchens, "A War to Be Proud Of," the *Washington Examiner*, first published in *The Weekly Standard*, September 5, 2005, www.washingtonexaminer.com/weekly-standard/a-war-to-be-proud-of, article reprinted in *Christopher Hitchens and His Critics*, 152–160.

11. Christopher Hitchens, "Second Thinking," *Slate*, April 19, 2004, slate.com/news-and-politics/2004/04/what-i-got-wrong-about-iraq.html.

12. Christopher Hitchens, "So, Mr. Hitchens, Weren't You Wrong About Iraq?"

Slate, March 19, 2007, slate.com/news-and-politics/2007/03/so-mr-hitchens-weren-t-you-wrong-about-iraq.html.

13. Christopher Hitchens, "Restating the Case for War," *Slate*, November 5, 2003, slate.com/news-and-politics/2003/11/restating-the-case-for-intervention-in-iraq.html.

14. United Nations Special Commission (UNSCOM), list of key documents and resolutions, www.un.org/depts/unscom/unscmdoc.htm.

15. Christopher Hitchens, "I Wanted It to Rain on Their Parade," *The Mirror*, February 18, 2003, article reprinted in *Christopher Hitchens and His Critics,* 109.

16. Christopher Hitchens, "Clarke's Progress," *Slate*, March 29, 2004, slate.com/news-and-politics/2004/03/clarke-s-progress.html.

17. Christopher Hitchens, "How Should We Use Our Power? Iraq and the War on Terror," debate with Mark Danner, hosted by the UC Berkeley Graduate School of Journalism, January 28, 2003, markdanner.com/2003/01/28/danner-vs-hitchens-how-should-we-use-our-power-iraq-and-the-war-on-terror/.

18. Ibid.

19. Christopher Hitchens, "Ha ha ha to the pacifists," *Guardian*, November 13, 2001, www.theguardian.com/world/2001/nov/14/afghanistan.terrorism1.

20. Christopher Hitchens, "The Ends of War," *Nation*, November 29, 2001, www.thenation.com/article/archive/ends-war/.

21. Christopher Hitchens, "The Literal Left," *Slate*, December 4, 2003, slate.com/news-and-politics/2003/12/the-literal-left.html.

22. Cockburn, "Christopher Hitchens made a cogent case for war—but he was still wrong."

23. Ibid.

24. Hitchens, "A War to Be Proud Of."

25. Parker, "He Knew He Was Right."

26. Hitchens, "An Anglosphere Future."

27. Hitchens, *Hitch-22*, 185.

28. Hitchens, *Letters to a Young Contrarian*, 135.

29. Ibid.

30. Hitchens, interview with *The Progressive Magazine*.

31. Peter Maass, "It's Risky to Talk Tough on Kosovo," *New York Times*, March 10, 1998, www.nytimes.com/1998/03/10/opinion/it-s-risky-to-talk-tough-on-kosovo.html.

32. Michael R. Gordon, "Powell Delivers a Resounding No On Using Limited Force in Bosnia," New York Times, September 28, 1992, www.nytimes.com/1992/09/28/world/powell-delivers-a-resounding-no-on-using-limited-force-in-bosnia.html.

33. Michael R. Gordon, "Bush Would Stop U.S. Peacekeeping In Balkan Fights," *New York Times*, October 21, 2000, www.nytimes.com/2000/10/21/us/the-

2000-campaign-the-military-bush-would-stop-us-peacekeeping-in-balkan-fights.
html#:~:text=%27%27Carrying%20out%20civil%20administration%20and,%27%27.

34. Ibid.

35. George Packer, *The Assassins' Gate: America In Iraq* (New York: Farrar, Straus and Giroux, 2005), 57.

36. Daniel Cohn-Bendit and Richard Perle, "Blessed Are the Warmakers?" *Foreign Policy Magazine*, May 1, 2003, foreignpolicy.com/2003/05/01/blessed-are-the-warmakers/.

37. Ibid.

38. Hitchens, *Hitch-22*, 410.

39. Christopher Hitchens, "That Bleeding Heart Wolfowitz," *Slate*, March 22, 2005, slate.com/news-and-politics/2005/03/that-bleeding-heart-paul-wolfowitz.html.

40. Ibid.

41. Christopher Hitchens, "The Axis of Evil," speech at the Center for American Studies, the University of Western Ontario, April 9, 2005, www.tvo.org/transcript/907589/christopher-hitchens-on-the-axis-of-evil.

42. Hitchens, "So Long, Fellow Travelers."

43. Ibid.

44. Ibid.

45. Pierre Razoux, *The Iran-Iraq War* (Cambridge, MA: Harvard University Press, 2015), 471.

46. Kevin M. Woods, Williamson Murray, and Thomas Holaday, *Saddam's War: An Iraqi Military Perspective of the Iran-Iraq War* (Washington, DC: National Defense University Press, 2009), 6.

47. Ibid., 11.

48. Williamson Murray and Kevin M. Woods, *The Iran–Iraq War: A Military and Strategic History* (Cambridge: Cambridge University Press, 2014), 1-2.

49. Anthony H. Cordesman and Abraham Wagner, *Lessons of Modern War—Volume II: The Iran-Iraq War*, Chapter 6, 4-6, csis-website-prod.s3.amazonaws.com/s3fs-public/legacy_files/files/media/csis/pubs/9005lessonsiraniraqii-chap06.pdf.

50. Hiltermann, *A Poisonous Affair*, 26–37.

51. Ibid., 37–65.

52. Christopher Hitchens, "Why We Are Stuck in the Sand," *Harper's Magazine*, January 1991, harpers.org/archive/1991/01/why-we-are-stuck-in-the-sand/.

53. Ibid.

54. Stephen Walt, *The Hell of Good Intentions: America's Foreign Policy Elite and the Decline of U.S. Primacy* (New York: Farrar, Straus and Giroux, 2018), 265.

55. Ibid., 266.

56. Ranj Alaaldin, "How the Iran-Iraq war will shape the region for decades to come," The Brookings Institution, October 9, 2020, www.brookings.edu/blog/order-from-chaos/2020/10/09/how-the-iran-iraq-war-will-shape-the-region-for-decades-to-come/.

57. Ibid.

58. Donald J. Trump, "Remarks by President Trump on Iran," January 8, 2020, trumpwhitehouse.archives.gov/briefings-statements/remarks-president-trump-iran/.

59. "A Conversation with Christopher Hitchens," interview conducted by James Kirchick, *Radio Free Europe / Radio Liberty*, December 7, 2010, www.rferl.org/a/transcript_conversation_with_christopher_hitchens/2244720.html%5C.

60. Hiltermann, *A Poisonous Affair*.

61. "Genocide in Iraq: The Anfal Campaign Against the Kurds," Human Rights Watch, July 1993, www.hrw.org/reports/1993/iraqanfal/ANFALINT.htm.

62. Ibid.

63. Ibid.

64. Ibid.

65. "Who Was Ali Hassan Al-Majid ('Chemical Ali')?" Human Rights Watch, April 6, 2003, www.hrw.org/news/2003/04/06/who-was-ali-hassan-al-majid-chemical-ali.

66. Hiltermann, *A Poisonous Affair*, 26–37.

67. Ibid., 14.

68. Ibid., xii.

69. "Genocide in Iraq: The Anfal Campaign Against the Kurds," Human Rights Watch.

70. Hiltermann, *A Poisonous Affair*, 183-206.

71. Ibid., 204.

72. Ibid., 201

73. Ibid., 16

74. George H.W. Bush, "Excerpts From 2 Statements by Bush on Iraq's Proposal for Ending Conflict," *Reuters*, reprinted in *New York Times*, February 16, 1991, www.nytimes.com/1991/02/16/world/war-gulf-bush-statement-excerpts-2-statements-bush-iraq-s-proposal-for-ending.html.

75. Ibid.

76. Kenneth M. Pollack, *The Threatening Storm: The Case for Invading Iraq* (New York: Random House, 2002), 48.

77. "Endless Torment: The 1991 Uprising in Iraq And Its Aftermath," Human Rights Watch.

78. R. Jeffrey Smith, "Administration Officials Still Debate Targeting Iraqi Copters Hitting Rebels," *Washington Post*, March 30, 1991, www.washingtonpost.com/ar-

chive/politics/1991/03/30/administration-officials-still-debate-targeting-iraqi-copters-hitting-rebels/6c16ea1d-c7c2-49a6-b2aa-0961b1be62a7/.

79. George H.W. Bush and Brent Scowcroft, *A World Transformed* (New York: Vintage, 1998), 472.

80. Laurie Mylroie, "Iraq's Real Coup," *Washington Post*, June 28, 1992, www.washingtonpost.com/archive/opinions/1992/06/28/iraqs-real-coup/75e6570a-5158-426c-b2d8-1382807a2014/.

81. Ibid.

82. Ibid.

83. Ibid.

84. Smith, "Administration Officials Still Debate Targeting Iraqi Copters Hitting Rebels."

85. Ibid.

86. Christopher Hitchens, "Saddam's Long Good-Bye," *Vanity Fair*, June 1, 2003, www.vanityfair.com/news/2003/06/saddam-200306.

87. Pollack, *The Threatening Storm*, 50.

88. Ibid., 51

89. Hitchens, "Saddam's Long Good-Bye."

90. Ibid.

91. Christopher Hitchens, *A Long Short War: The Postponed Liberation of Iraq* (New York: Plume, 2003).

92. Hitchens, "A War to Be Proud Of."

93. Christopher Hitchens, "Fighting Words," *Slate*, October 3, 2007, slate.com/news-and-politics/2007/10/the-article-that-inspired-a-young-man-to-enlist.html.

94. Hitchens, "A War to Be Proud Of."

95. Hitchens, "So, Mr. Hitchens, Weren't You Wrong About Iraq?"

96. Mary Anne Weaver, "The Short, Violent Life of Abu Musab al-Zarqawi," *Atlantic*, Summer 2006, www.theatlantic.com/magazine/archive/2006/07/the-short-violent-life-of-abu-musab-al-zarqawi/304983/.

97. Kanan Makiya, *Republic of Fear: The Politics of Modern Iraq* (Berkeley, CA: University of California Press, 1998), xxx-xxxi, first published under the pseudonym Samir al-Khalil in 1989.

98. Ibid., xv.

99. Ibid.

100. Ibid.

101. Christopher Hitchens, "A Hell of a Country," *Slate*, April 23, 2007, slate.com/news-and-politics/2007/04/ali-allawi-s-new-memoir-shows-iraq-s-collapse-was-inevitable.html.

102. Ibid.

103. Youssef M. Ibrahim, "Iraq Is Near Economic Ruin But Hussein Appears Secure," *New York Times*, October 25, 1994, www.nytimes.com/1994/10/25/world/baghdad-s-burden-special-report-iraq-near-economic-ruin-but-hussein-appears.html.

104. Ibid.

105. Ibid.

106. David B. Ottaway, "Gulf Arabs Place Reins on Iraq While Filling Its War Chest," *Washington Post*, December 21, 1981, www.washingtonpost.com/archive/politics/1981/12/21/gulf-arabs-place-reins-on-iraq-while-filling-its-war-chest/f99361f1-f9b8-47d2-9c97-f7058c3dc83d/.

107. Makiya, *Republic of Fear*, xx.

108. Ibrahim, "Iraq Is Near Economic Ruin But Hussein Appears Secure."

109. Makiya, *Republic of Fear*, xvi-xvii.

110. Hitchens, "Restating the Case for War."

111. Michael R. Gordon and Bernard E. Trainor, "How Iraq Escaped to Threaten Kuwait Again," *New York Times*, October 23, 1994, www.nytimes.com/1994/10/23/world/middleeast/how-iraq-escaped-to-threaten-kuwait-again.html.

112. Christopher Hitchens, "Weapons of Mass Distraction," *Vanity Fair*, March 1999, archive.vanityfair.com/article/1999/3/weapons-of-mass-distraction.

113. Ibid.

114. Makiya, *Republic of Fear*, xvii.

115. Ibid., xix.

116. Ibid.

117. Resolution 688, adopted by the United Nations Security Council on April 5, 1991, digitallibrary.un.org/record/110659?ln=en#record-files-collapse-header.

118. Ibid.

119. Makiya, *Republic of Fear*, xxii.

120. Bernard Kouchner, "The Changing Role of Humanitarianism: A Study Guide to the Work of Bernard Kouchner," Morgenthau Lectures, Carnegie Council for Ethics in International Affairs, September 22, 2004, www.carnegiecouncil.org/media/series/morgenthau/morgenthau-lectures-1981-2006-the-changing-role-of-humanitarianism-a-study-guide-to-the-work-of-bernard-kouchner#3.

121. Clifford Krauss, "U.S. Will Airdrop Food and Clothes to Kurds in Iraq," *New York Times*, April 6, 1991, www.nytimes.com/1991/04/06/world/after-the-war-us-will-airdrop-food-and-clothes-to-kurds-in-iraq.html.

122. Hitchens, "A War to Be Proud Of."

123. Blair, "Doctrine of International Community" (italics added).

124. Ibid.

125. Tony Blair, address reflecting on the "Doctrine of International Community," April 2009, transcript printed in the Yale Journal of International Affairs (Spring/Summer 2009), edisciplinas.usp.br/pluginfile.php/5058109/mod_resource/content/1/The%20doctrine%20of%20the%20international%20community.pdf.

126. Ibid.

127. Ibid.

128. Ibid.

129. Hitchens, "A War to Be Proud Of."

130. Resolution 678, adopted by the United Nations Security Council on November 29, 1990, unscr.com/en/resolutions/doc/678.

131. Resolution 687, adopted by the United Nations Security Council on April 3, 1991, www.un.org/Depts/unmovic/documents/687.pdf.

132. Resolution 1441, adopted by the United Nations Security Council on November 8, 2002, www.un.org/Depts/unmovic/documents/1441.pdf.

133. Hitchens, "A War to Be Proud Of."

134. Christopher Hitchens, "From Srebrenica to Baghdad," *Slate*, July 11, 2005, slate.com/news-and-politics/2005/07/what-the-genocide-taught-us-about-intervention.html.

135. Hitchens, "Realism in Darfur."

136. Annan, "'We the Peoples': The Role of the United Nations in the 21st Century."

137. Patrick E. Tyler, "Annan Says Iraq War Was 'Illegal,'" *New York Times*, September 16, 2004, www.nytimes.com/2004/09/16/international/annan-says-iraq-war-was-illegal.html.

138. Cohn-Bendit and Perle, "Blessed Are the Warmakers?"

139. "Iraq," Gallup Historical Trends, polling regularly conducted from March 2003 to August 2019, news.gallup.com/poll/1633/iraq.aspx.

140. Barack Obama, "Remarks by the President in Address to the Nation on Syria," September 10, 2013, obamawhitehouse.archives.gov/the-press-office/2013/09/10/remarks-president-address-nation-syria.

141. Ibid.

142. Barack Obama, "Remarks by the President to the White House Press Corps," August 20, 2012, obamawhitehouse.archives.gov/the-press-office/2012/08/20/remarks-president-white-house-press-corps.

143. "Attacks on Ghouta: Analysis of Alleged Use of Chemical Weapons in Syria," Human Rights Watch, September 10, 2013, www.hrw.org/report/2013/09/10/attacks-ghouta/analysis-alleged-use-chemical-weapons-syria.

144. Barack Obama, "Remarks by the President in Address to the Nation on Syria," September 10, 2013, obamawhitehouse.archives.gov/the-press-office/2013/09/10/remarks-president-address-nation-syria.

145. Ibid.

146. "Death by Chemicals: The Syrian Government's Widespread and Systematic Use of Chemical Weapons," Human Rights Watch, May 1, 2017, www.hrw.org/report/2017/05/01/death-chemicals/syrian-governments-widespread-and-systematic-use-chemical-weapons.

147. Obama, "Remarks by the President in Address to the Nation on Syria."

148. Ibid.

149. "Death of a Dictator: Bloody Vengeance in Sirte," Human Rights Watch, October 16, 2012, www.hrw.org/report/2012/10/16/death-dictator/bloody-vengeance-sirte#.

150. Mariam Fam, "Qaddafi's Son Warns of 'Rivers of Blood,' Calls For Dialogue," *Bloomberg*, February 20, 2011, www.bloomberg.com/news/articles/2011-02-20/libyan-revolt-widens-as-attacks-on-protesters-draw-condemnation#xj4y7vzkg.

151. Resolution 1973, adopted by the United Nations Security Council on March 17, 2011, documents-dds-ny.un.org/doc/UNDOC/GEN/N11/268/39/PDF/N1126839.pdf?OpenElement.

152. Resolution 2016, adopted by the United Nations Security Council on October 27, 2011, documents-dds-ny.un.org/doc/UNDOC/GEN/N11/567/10/PDF/N1156710.pdf?OpenElement.

153. "Libya's Mustafa Abdul Jalil asks Nato to stay longer," *BBC News*, October 26, 2011, www.bbc.com/news/world-africa-15459473.

154. Barack Obama, "The Obama Doctrine," interview conducted by Jeffrey Goldberg, *Atlantic*, April 2016, www.theatlantic.com/magazine/archive/2016/04/the-obama-doctrine/471525/.

155. Barack Obama, "President Barack Obama on 'Fox News Sunday,'" interview conducted by Chris Wallace, Fox News, April 10, 2016, www.foxnews.com/transcript/exclusive-president-barack-obama-on-fox-news-sunday.

156. "Barack Obama says Libya was 'worst mistake' of his presidency," *Guardian*, April 11, 2016, www.theguardian.com/us-news/2016/apr/12/barack-obama-says-libya-was-worst-mistake-of-his-presidency.

157. Scott Shane and Jo Becker, "A New Libya, With 'Very Little Time Left,'" *New York Times*, February 27, 2016, www.nytimes.com/2016/02/28/us/politics/libya-isis-hillary-clinton.html.

158. Hitchens, "Never Trust Imperialists."

159. Christopher Hitchens, "Don't Let Qaddafi Win," *Slate*, March 14, 2011, slate.com/news-and-politics/2011/03/obama-libya-policy-doing-nothing-is-not-an-option.html.

160. Ibid.

161. Ibid.

162. Christopher Hitchens, "Go After Qaddafi," *Slate*, April 25, 2011, slate.com/news-and-politics/2011/04/war-in-libya-america-needs-an-entrance-strategy-not-an-

exit-strategy.html.

163. Barack Obama, David Cameron, and Nicolas Sarkozy, "Libya's Pathway to Peace," *New York Times*, April 14, 2011, www.nytimes.com/2011/04/15/opinion/15iht-edlibya15.html.

164. Ibid.

165. Ibid.

166. Helene Cooper and Steven Lee Myers, "Obama Takes Hard Line With Libya After Shift by Clinton," *New York Times*, March 18, 2011, www.nytimes.com/2011/03/19/world/africa/19policy.html?pagewanted=all.

167. Hitchens, "Go After Qaddafi."

168. Ibid.

169. Ibid.

170. Christopher Hitchens, "The Crimes of Col. Qaddafi," *Slate*, August 25, 2011, slate.com/news-and-politics/2011/08/libya-muammar-qaddafi-s-hideous-crimes-must-not-be-forgotten.html.

171. Ibid.

172. Ibid.

173. Ibid.

174. Richard Leiby and Muhammad Mansour, "Arab League asks U.N. for no-fly zone over Libya," *Washington Post*, March 12, 2011, www.washingtonpost.com/world/arab-league-asks-un-for-no-fly-zone-over-libya/2011/03/12/ABoie0R_story.html.

175. Hitchens, "Don't Let Qaddafi Win."

176. Tim Arango, "Ready or Not, Iraq Ascends to Take Helm of Arab Bloc," *New York Times*, March 23, 2011, www.nytimes.com/2011/03/24/world/middleeast/24iraq.html.

177. Christopher Hitchens, "The Iraq Effect," *Slate*, March 28, 2011, slate.com/news-and-politics/2011/03/if-saddam-hussein-were-still-in-power-the-uprisings-in-egypt-tunisia-and-libya-could-never-have-happened.html.

178. Arango, "Ready or Not, Iraq Ascends to Take Helm of Arab Bloc."

179. Hitchens, "The Iraq Effect."

180. Hitchens, "The Crimes of Col. Qaddafi."

181. Data published by the United Nations High Commissioner for Refugees, March 15, 2021, www.unhcr.org/en-us/syria-emergency.html.

182. "Syria: 'The tragedy is deepening' as UN figures reveal nearly 5 million children have known nothing but war," UN News, March 14, 2020, news.un.org/en/story/2020/03/1059471.

183. Report of the Independent International Commission of Inquiry on the Syrian Arab Republic, United Nations Human Rights Council, January 28, 2020, documents-dds-ny.un.org/doc/UNDOC/GEN/G20/022/08/PDF/G2002208.pdf?OpenElement.

184. Report of the Independent International Commission of Inquiry on the Syrian Arab Republic, United Nations Human Rights Council, July 2, 2020, www.ohchr.org/en/press-releases/2020/07/rampant-human-rights-violations-and-war-crimes-war-torn-idlib-faces-pandemic?LangID=E&NewsID=26044.

185. Christopher Hitchens, "Iraq Flexes Arab Muscle," *New Statesman*, April 2, 1976.

186. Christopher Hitchens, "Don't Hang Saddam," *Slate*, November 6, 2006, slate.com/news-and-politics/2006/11/don-t-hang-saddam.html.

187. Dennis Perrin, "Youthful Indiscretions," *HuffPost*, July 10, 2007, www.huffpost.com/entry/youthful-indiscretions_1_b_55592.

188. Richard Seymour, "The late Christopher Hitchens," *International Socialism*, March 27, 2012, isj.org.uk/the-late-christopher-hitchens/.

189. Hitchens, *Hitch-22*, 282.

190. Hitchens, "Iraq Flexes Arab Muscle."

191. Ibid.

192. Ibid.

193. Ibid.

194. Hitchens, *Hitch-22*, 285–286.

195. Hitchens, "Taking Sides."

196. Hitchens, *Hitch-22*, 288–292.

197. Elaine Sciolino and Michael R. Gordon, "U.S. Gave Iraq Little Reason Not to Mount Kuwait Assault," *New York Times*, September 23, 1990, www.nytimes.com/1990/09/23/world/confrontation-in-the-gulf-us-gave-iraq-little-reason-not-to-mount-kuwait-assault.html.

198. Hitchens, *Hitch-22.*, 297.

199. George W. Bush, "Remarks by the President at the 20th Anniversary of the National Endowment for Democracy," November 6, 2003, georgewbush-whitehouse.archives.gov/news/releases/2003/11/20031106-2.html#:~:text=Sixty%20years%20of%20Western%20nations,at%20the%20expense%20of%20liberty..

200. Ibid.

201. Ibid.

202. Karl Rove, "The President's Apology Tour," *Wall Street Journal*, April 23, 2009, www.wsj.com/articles/SB124044156269345357.

203. Barack Obama, "A New Beginning, Remarks by the President at Cairo University," June 4, 2009, obamawhitehouse.archives.gov/the-press-office/remarks-president-cairo-university-6-04-09.

204. Hitchens, "American Power and the Crisis Over Iraq," 1:27:51.

205. Ibid., 1:27:33.

206. John Mearsheimer, "Why We Will Soon Miss The Cold War," *Atlantic*, Au-

gust 1990, www.mearsheimer.com/wp-content/uploads/2019/07/A0014.pdf.

207. Ibid.

208. Ibid.

209. Ibid.

210. Walt, *The Hell of Good Intentions*.

211. Hitchens, "Why We Are Stuck in the Sand."

212. Ibid.

213. Christopher Hitchens, "Overstating Jewish Power," *Slate*, March 27, 2006, slate.com/news-and-politics/2006/03/exaggerating-the-strength-of-the-israeli-lobby. html.

214. Stephen Walt and John Mearsheimer, "The Israel Lobby," *London Review of Books*, March 23, 2006, www.lrb.co.uk/the-paper/v28/n06/john-mearsheimer/the-israel-lobby.

215. Stephen Walt and John Mearsheimer, *The Israel Lobby and U.S. Foreign Policy* (New York: Farrar, Straus and Giroux, 2007).

216. Hitchens, "Overstating Jewish Power."

217. Stephen Walt and John Mearsheimer, "The Case for Offshore Balancing," *Foreign Affairs*, Summer 2016, www.mearsheimer.com/wp-content/uploads/2019/04/ Offshore-Balancing.pdf.

218. Hitchens, "The Axis of Evil," speech at the Center for American Studies.

219. Max van der Stoel, "Report on the situation of human rights in Iraq," United Nations Commission on Human Rights, 4, February 25, 1994, digitallibrary.un.org/ record/226418?ln=en.

220. Makiya, *Republic of Fear*, xiii.

221. Van der Stoel, "Report on the situation of human rights in Iraq," 37.

222. Ibid., 61.

223. Ibid.

224. Hitchens, "The Axis of Evil," speech at the Center for American Studies.

225. Samantha Power, *"A Problem from Hell": America and the Age of Genocide* (New York: Basic Books, 2013), first published by Basic Books in 2002.

226. Ibid., 233.

227. Ibid., 231.

228. Ibid., 233.

229. Christopher Hitchens, "'Evil,'" *Slate*, December 31, 2002, slate.com/news-and-politics/2002/12/the-necessity-of-evil.html.

230. Ibid.

231. *Associated Press*, "Gulf Found to Recover From War's Oil Spill," reprinted in

New York Times, March 18, 1993, www.nytimes.com/1993/03/18/world/gulf-found-to-recover-from-war-s-oil-spill.html.

232. Christopher Hitchens, "Christopher Hitchens Responds," *Slate*, September 26, 2006, slate.com/news-and-politics/2006/09/christopher-hitchens-responds-to-david-corn.html.

233. Vladimir Putin, "A Plea for Caution From Russia," *New York Times*, September 11, 2013, www.nytimes.com/2013/09/12/opinion/putin-plea-for-caution-from-russia-on-syria.html.

234. Ibid.

235. "Russia/Syria: War Crimes in Month of Bombing Aleppo," Human Rights Watch, December 1, 2016, www.hrw.org/news/2016/12/01/russia/syria-war-crimes-month-bombing-aleppo.

236. "Russia Backs Syria in Unlawful Attacks on Eastern Ghouta," Human Rights Watch, March 18, 2018, www.hrw.org/news/2018/03/18/russia-backs-syria-unlawful-attacks-eastern-ghouta.

237. "'Targeting Life in Idlib,'" Human Rights Watch, October 15, 2020, www.hrw.org/report/2020/10/15/targeting-life-idlib/syrian-and-russian-strikes-civilian-infrastructure.

238. Putin, "A Plea for Caution From Russia."

239. Michelle Nichols, "Russia, backed by China, casts 14th U.N. veto on Syria to block cross-border aid," *Reuters*, December 20, 2019, www.reuters.com/article/us-syria-security-un/russia-backed-by-china-casts-14th-u-n-veto-on-syria-to-block-cross-border-aid-idUSKBN1YO23V.

240. Putin, "A Plea for Caution From Russia."

241. Ibid.

242. "Putin Signs Law Allowing Expansion Of Russian Naval Facility In Syria," *Radio Free Europe / Radio Liberty*, December 29, 2017, www.rferl.org/a/putin-signs-law-syria-tartus-naval-facility/28946167.html.

243. Christopher Hitchens, "Cause and Effect," *Slate*, July 5, 2006, slate.com/news-and-politics/2006/07/stop-blaming-the-good-guys-in-iraq.html.

244. Putin, "A Plea for Caution From Russia."

245. Christopher Hitchens, "South Ossetia Isn't Kosovo," *Slate*, August 18, 2008, slate.com/news-and-politics/2008/08/the-comparison-between-south-ossetia-and-kosovo-is-bunk.html.

246. Michelle Nichols, "Russia, China veto Syria aid via Turkey for second time this week," *Reuters*, July 10, 2020, www.reuters.com/article/uk-syria-security-un-idUKKBN24B2O0.

247. Austin Ramzy and Mike Ives, "Hong Kong Protests, One Year Later," *New York Times*, June 9, 2020, www.nytimes.com/2020/06/09/world/asia/hong-kong-protests-one-year-later.html.

248. Lexi Lonas, "China accuses US of interfering in Hong Kong 100 times,"

The Hill, September 24, 2021, thehill.com/policy/international/china/573845-china-blames-us-of-interfering-in-hong-kong-100-times/.

249. Anton Troianovski, Andrew E. Kramer, Ivan Nechepurenko, and Andrew Higgins, "Russia Protesters Defy Vast Police Operation as Signs of Kremlin Anxiety Mount," *New York Times*, January 31, 2021, www.nytimes.com/2021/01/31/world/europe/russia-protests-navalny-live-updates.html.

250. Guy Faulconbridge, "More than 4,300 detained at anti-war protests in Russia," *Reuters*, March 7, 2022, www.reuters.com/world/europe/more-than-64-people-detained-anti-war-protests-russia-protest-monitor-2022-03-06/.

251. Anton Troianovski and Valeriya Safronova, "Aleksei Navalny, Fiery Putin Critic, Is Handed a New, 9-Year Prison Sentence," *New York Times*, March 22, 2022, www.nytimes.com/2022/03/22/world/europe/russia-navalny-prison.html.

252. "A Conversation with Christopher Hitchens," interview conducted by James Kirchick.

253. Hitchens, "Don't Hang Saddam."

254. Christopher Hitchens, "News Review," C-SPAN Washington Journal recording, 1:50, January 22, 2001, www.c-span.org/video/?162054-2/news-review.

255. Christopher Hitchens, *The Trial of Henry Kissinger* (New York: Verso, 2001), x.

256. Ibid.

257. Ibid., xi.

258. Ibid.

259. Ibid.

260. Hitchens, *Conversations with History*, 47:20.

261. Ibid., 47:56.

262. Christopher Hitchens, "The Case Against Henry Kissinger," *Harper's Magazine*, February 2001, harpers.org/archive/2001/02/the-case-against-henry-kissinger-part-one/.

263. Hitchens, "News Review," C-SPAN Washington Journal recording, 23:34.

264. Ibid., 25:51.

265. Ibid., 11:55.

266. Maggie Farley, "Sudan Inclined to Reject U.N. Peacekeeping Offer," *The Los Angeles Times*, June 7, 2006, www.latimes.com/archives/la-xpm-2006-jun-07-fg-sudan7-story.html.

267. Hitchens, "Realism in Darfur."

268. "The Prosecutor v. Omar Hassan Ahmad Al Bashir," International Criminal Court arrest warrants issued on March 4, 2009 and July 12, 2010, www.icc-cpi.int/darfur/albashir.

269. Hitchens, *The Trial of Henry Kissinger*, ix.

270. Hitchens, "Why We Are Stuck in the Sand."

271. Ibid.

272. "A Conversation with Christopher Hitchens," interview conducted by James Kirchick.

273. Ibid.

274. Ibid.

275. Hitchens, *God Is Not Great*, 153.

276. George Scialabba, "Farewell, Hitch," *n+1*, Winter 2005, www.nplusonemag.com/issue-2/reviews/farewell-hitch/.

277. David Corn, "Sorry, Hitch—You're Wrong About Niger," *Slate*, September 26, 2006, slate.com/news-and-politics/2006/09/david-corn-takes-on-christopher-hitchens.html.

278. Hitchens, "Christopher Hitchens Responds."

5 The Enemy

1. Orwell, "Toward European Unity."

2. Ibid.

3. George Orwell, "You and the Atom Bomb," *Tribune*, October 19, 1945.

4. Jason Cowley, "Christopher Hitchens, the enemy of the totalitarian," *New Statesman*, December 16, 2011, www.newstatesman.com/politics/2011/12/christopher-hitchens-enemy-totalitarian.

5. Parker, "He Knew He Was Right."

6. Stephen Walt, "Deaths in the Family," *Foreign Policy Magazine*, December 19, 2011, foreignpolicy.com/2011/12/19/deaths-in-the-family/.

7. Hitchens, *Letters to a Young Contrarian*, 64.

8. Ibid., 103.

9. Hitchens, *Hitch-22*, 192.

10. Hitchens, *Hitch-22* audiobook interview, 4:05.

11. Walt, "Deaths in the Family."

12. Heinrich August Winkler, *The Age of Catastrophe: A History of the West, 1914–1945* (New Haven: Yale University Press, 2015), 335.

13. McEwan, "Remembering Christopher Hitchens."

14. Christopher Hitchens, interviewed by Margaret Throsby, *ABC Classic*, May 2010.

15. Christopher Hitchens, "On Becoming American," *Atlantic*, May 2005, www.theatlantic.com/magazine/archive/2005/05/on-becoming-american/303889/.

16. Christopher Hitchens, "An empire after all," *Salon*, October 16, 1999, www.salon.com/1999/10/16/buchanan_5/.

17. Tim Alberta, "'The Ideas Made It, But I Didn't,'" *Politico Magazine*, May-June 2017, www.politico.com/magazine/story/2017/04/22/pat-buchanan-trump-president-history-profile-215042/.

18. Charles Lindbergh, speech about World War II in Des Moines, IA, September 11, 1941, www.cfr.org/blog/twe-remembers-charles-lindberghs-des-moines-speech.

19. Ibid.

20. Pat Buchanan, "Pat Buchanan On 'America First' Under Trump," interview conducted by Lourdes Garcia-Navarro, NPR, January 22, 2017, www.npr.org/2017/01/22/511048811/pat-buchanan-on-america-first-under-trump.

21. Alberta, "'The Ideas Made It, But I Didn't.'"

22. Nancy A. Youssef, Vivian Salama, and Michael C. Bender, "Trump, Awaiting Egyptian Counterpart at Summit, Called Out for 'My Favorite Dictator,'" *Wall Street Journal*, September 13, 2019, www.wsj.com/articles/trump-awaiting-egyptian-counter-part-at-summit-called-out-for-my-favorite-dictator-11568403645.

23. "All According to Plan: The Rab'a Massacre and Mass Killings of Protesters in Egypt," Human Rights Watch, August 12, 2014, www.hrw.org/report/2014/08/12/all-according-plan/raba-massacre-and-mass-killings-protesters-egypt.

24. Brett Samuels, "Trump praises Turkey's Erdoğan after US announces ceasefire deal," *The Hill*, October 17, 2019, thehill.com/homenews/administration/466334-trump-praises-turkeys-erdogan-after-us-announces-ceasefire-deal/.

25. John Bolton, "John Bolton: The Scandal of Trump's China Policy," *Wall Street Journal*, June 17, 2020, www.wsj.com/articles/john-bolton-the-scandal-of-trumps-china-policy-11592419564.

26. Brett Samuels, "Trump ramps up rhetoric on media, calls press 'the enemy of the people,'" *The Hill*, April 5, 2019, thehill.com/homenews/administration/437610-trump-calls-press-the-enemy-of-the-people/.

27. Tal Kopan and Laura Jarrett, "Judge whose Mexican heritage Trump denigrated will hear deportation case," *CNN Politics*, April 20, 2017, www.cnn.com/2017/04/20/politics/juan-manuel-montes-bojorquez-judge-curiel/index.html.

28. Veronica Stracqualursi and Ryan Struyk, "President Trump's history with Judge Gonzalo Curiel," *ABC News*, April 20, 2017, abcnews.go.com/Politics/president-trumps-history-judge-gonzalo-curiel/story?id=46916250.

29. Tucker Higgins, "Trump declares without evidence that 'Criminals and unknown Middle Easterners are mixed in' with migrant caravan making its way from Honduras," CNBC, October 22, 2018, www.cnbc.com/2018/10/22/trump-says-unknown-middle-easterners-are-mixed-in-migrant-caravan.html.

30. Ted Hesson, Rebecca Morin, and Andrew Restuccia, "'Consider it a rifle': Trump says migrants throwing rocks will be treated as armed," *Politico*, November 1, 2018, www.politico.com/story/2018/11/01/trump-immigration-953569.

31. Michael D. Shear and Julie Hirschfeld Davis, "Shoot Migrants' Legs, Build

Alligator Moat: Behind Trump's Ideas for Border," *New York Times*, October 1, 2019, www.nytimes.com/2019/10/01/us/politics/trump-border-wars.html.

32. Patrick Healy and Jonathan Martin, "Donald Trump Won't Say if He'll Accept Result of Election," *New York Times*, October 19, 2016, www.nytimes.com/2016/10/20/us/politics/presidential-debate.html.

33. Aaron Blake, "Donald Trump claims none of those 3 to 5 million illegal votes were cast for him. Zero," *Washington Post*, January 26, 2017, www.washingtonpost.com/news/the-fix/wp/2017/01/25/donald-trump-claims-none-of-those-3-to-5-million-illegal-votes-were-cast-for-him-zero/.

34. Jessica Taylor, "Trump Dissolves Controversial Election Commission," NPR, January 3, 2018, www.npr.org/2018/01/03/575524512/trump-dissolves-controversial-election-commission.

35. Nicholas Riccardi, "Here's the reality behind Trump's claims about mail voting," *Associated Press*, September 30, 2020, apnews.com/article/virus-outbreak-joe-biden-election-2020-donald-trump-elections-3e8170c3348ce3719d4bc7182146b582.

36. Terrance Smith, "Trump has longstanding history of calling elections 'rigged' if he doesn't like the results," ABC News, November 11, 2020, abcnews.go.com/Politics/trump-longstanding-history-calling-elections-rigged-doesnt-results/story?id=74126926.

37. "Presidential Election Results: Biden Wins," *New York Times*, www.nytimes.com/interactive/2020/11/03/us/elections/results-president.html?action=click&pgtype=Article&state=default&module=styln-elections-2020&region=TOP_BANNER&context=election_recirc.

38. Mike DeBonis and Jacqueline Alemany, "Trump's inner circle warned him election-fraud claims were false," *Washington Post*, June 13, 2022, www.washingtonpost.com/national-security/2022/06/13/house-panel-set-examine-trumps-persistent-lies-2nd-hearing/.

39. Jim Rutenberg, Nick Corasaniti, and Alan Feuer, "Trump's Fraud Claims Died in Court, but the Myth of Stolen Elections Lives On," *New York Times*, December 26, 2020, www.nytimes.com/2020/12/26/us/politics/republicans-voter-fraud.html.

40. Trip Gabriel and Stephanie Saul, "Could State Legislatures Pick Electors to Vote for Trump? Not Likely," *New York Times*, January 5, 2021, www.nytimes.com/article/electors-vote.html.

41. Amy Gardner, "'I just want to find 11,780 votes': In extraordinary hour-long call, Trump pressures Georgia secretary of state to recalculate the vote in his favor," *Washington Post*, January 3, 2021, www.washingtonpost.com/politics/trump-raffensperger-call-georgia-vote/2021/01/03/d45acb92-4dc4-11eb-bda4-615aaefd0555_story.html.

42. Alan Feuer, Luke Broadwater, Maggie Haberman, Katie Benner, and Michael S. Schmidt, "Jan. 6: The Story So Far," *New York Times*, www.nytimes.com/interactive/2022/us/politics/jan-6-timeline.html.

43. Ibid.

44. Ibid.

45.   Marissa J. Lang and Razzan Nakhlawi, "Identifying far-right symbols that appeared at the U.S. Capitol riot," *Washington Post*, January 15, 2021, www.washingtonpost. com/nation/interactive/2021/far-right-symbols-capitol-riot/.

46.   Maria Cramer, "Confederate Flag an Unnerving Sight in Capitol," *New York Times*, January 9, 2021, www.nytimes.com/2021/01/09/us/politics/confederate-flag-capitol.html.

47.   "Inside the Capitol Riot: An Exclusive Video Investigation," *New York Times*, June 30, 2021, www.nytimes.com/2021/06/30/us/jan-6-capitol-attack-takeaways.html.

48.   Jessica Taylor, "Trump Calls For 'Total And Complete Shutdown Of Muslims Entering' U.S.," NPR, December 7, 2015, www.npr.org/2015/12/07/458836388/trump-calls-for-total-and-complete-shutdown-of-muslims-entering-u-s.

49.   Abby Phillip and Abigail Hauslohner, "Trump on the future of proposed Muslim ban, registry: 'You know my plans,'" *Washington Post*, www.washingtonpost. com/news/post-politics/wp/2016/12/21/trump-on-the-future-of-proposed-muslim-ban-registry-you-know-my-plans/.

50.   Jeremy Diamond, "Trump doubles down on calls for mosque surveillance," CNN, June 15, 2016, www.cnn.com/2016/06/15/politics/donald-trump-muslims-mosque-surveillance.

51.   Rukmini Callimachi, "Was Orlando Shooter Really Acting for ISIS? For ISIS, It's All the Same," *New York Times*, June 12, 2016, www.nytimes.com/2016/06/13/us/orlando-omar-mateen-isis.html.

52.   Jonathan Martin, "Donald Trump Seizes on Orlando Shooting and Repeats Call for Temporary Ban on Muslim Migration," *New York Times*, June 12, 2016, www.nytimes.com/2016/06/13/us/politics/trump-clinton-sanders-shooting-reaction.html.

53.   Janet Hook, "Trump Reaffirms Support for 'Worse Than Waterboarding,'" *Wall Street Journal*, www.wsj.com/articles/BL-WB-60985.

54.   Matt Johnson, "Christopher Hitchens Would Never Have Backed Trump," *Splice Today*, February 19, 2018, www.splicetoday.com/politics-and-media/christopher-hitchens-would-never-have-backed-trump. Yglesias posted the tweet referenced here in December 2017, but later deleted it.

55.   Matt Johnson (@mattjj89), Twitter, February 20, 2018, twitter.com/mattjj89/ status/966093823066738688. When I asked Yglesias why he believed Hitchens would have been a Trump supporter, he replied, "Misogyny, dislike of Muslims, and passion for annoying liberals." You'll find our exchange at the link above.

56.   Hitchens, "Facing the Islamist Menace."

57.   Hitchens, "Against Rationalization."

58.   "A Conversation with Christopher Hitchens," interview conducted by James Kirchick.

59.   Christopher Hitchens, "Death of a Madman," *Slate*, May 2, 2011, slate.com/ news-and-politics/2011/05/osama-bin-laden-s-legacy-it-will-depend-in-part-on-what-obama-does-next.html.

60.   Charles Lister, "Jihadi Rivalry: The Islamic State Challenges al-Qaida,"

Brookings Institution, January 2016, www.brookings.edu/wp-content/uploads/2016/07/en-jihadi-rivalry.pdf.

61. Christopher Hitchens, "The War Within Islam," *Slate*, February 19, 2007, slate.com/news-and-politics/2007/02/the-war-within-islam.html.

62. Ibid.

63. Ibid.

64. Hitchens, "Facing the Islamist Menace."

65. Christopher Hitchens, "Saving Islam from bin Laden," *The Age*, September 5, 2002, www.theage.com.au/national/saving-islam-from-bin-laden-20020905-gduk66.html.

66. Ibid.

67. Christopher Hitchens, "It's a good time for war," *The Boston Globe*, September 8, 2002, archive.boston.com/news/packages/sept11/anniversary/globe_stories/090802_hitchens_entire.htm.

68. Ibid.

69. Hitchens, "Facing the Islamist Menace."

70. "Europe's Growing Muslim Population," Pew Research Center, November 29, 2017, www.pewresearch.org/religion/2017/11/29/europes-growing-muslim-population/.

71. Christopher Hitchens, "A French Quarrel," *Atlantic*, November 2006, www.theatlantic.com/magazine/archive/2006/11/a-french-quarrel/305276/.

72. Hitchens, "Facing the Islamist Menace."

73. Ibid.

74. Ibid.

75. Hitchens, *Letters to a Young Contrarian*, 138.

76. Rich Lowry, *The Case for Nationalism: How It Made Us Powerful, United, and Free* (New York: HarperCollins, 2019).

77. Yoram Hazony, *The Virtue of Nationalism* (New York: Basic Books, 2018), 11.

78. "Freedom in the World 2020: Hungary," Freedom House, freedomhouse.org/country/hungary/freedom-world/2020.

79. "FIDESZ membership suspended after EPP Political Assembly," European People's Party Press Department, March 20, 2019, www.epp.eu/press-releases/fidesz-membership-suspended-after-epp-political-assembly/.

80. Nikolaus Blome, Christian Stenzel, and Daniel Biskup, "You wanted the migrants, we didn't!" *Bild*, January 7, 2018, www.bild.de/politik/ausland/viktor-orban/orban-interview-54403736,view=conversionToLogin.bild.html.

81. "Europe's Growing Muslim Population," Pew Research Center.

82. Dorothy Manevich, "Hungarians share Europe's embrace of democratic principles but are less tolerant of refugees, minorities," Pew Research Center, September

30, 2016, www.pewresearch.org/fact-tank/2016/09/30/hungarians-share-europes-embrace-of-democratic-principles-but-are-less-tolerant-of-refugees-minorities/.

83. "Hungarian prime minister says migrants are 'poison' and 'not needed,'" *Guardian*, *Reuters*, and *Agence France-Presse*, published in the *Guardian*, July 26, 2016, www.theguardian.com/world/2016/jul/26/hungarian-prime-minister-viktor-orban-praises-donald-trump.

84. Matthew Kaminski, "'All the terrorists are migrants,'" *Politico*, November 23, 2015, www.politico.eu/article/viktor-orban-interview-terrorists-migrants-eu-russia-putin-borders-schengen/.

85. Maciej Kisilowski, "Poland's 'overnight court' breaks all the rules," *Politico*, December 8, 2015, www.politico.eu/article/law-vs-justice-poland-constitution-judges/.

86. Zosia Wanat, "Poland's 'Russian roulette' with the EU," *Politico*, October 21, 2021, www.politico.eu/article/poland-rule-of-law-judicial-system-eu-pis-jaroslaw-kaczynski/.

87. "Freedom in the World 2021: Poland," Freedom House, freedomhouse.org/country/poland/freedom-world/2021.

88. Ibid.

89. Jan Cienski, "Migrants carry 'parasites and protozoa,' warns Polish opposition leader," *Politico*, October 14, 2015, www.politico.eu/article/migrants-asylum-poland-kaczynski-election/.

90. Ibid.

91. Andrew Higgins, Anatol Magdziarz, and Monika Pronczuk, "Poland's Top Court Rules Its Constitution Trumps E.U. Law," *New York Times*, October 7, 2021, www.nytimes.com/2021/10/07/world/europe/poland-eu-law-constitution.html.

92. "Most Poles want Warsaw to back down in EU dispute," *EUobserver*, October 27, 2021, euobserver.com/tickers/153347.

93. Andrew Higgins, "Long on Europe's Fringe, Poland Takes Center Stage as War Rages in Ukraine," *New York Times*, March 25, 2022, www.nytimes.com/2022/03/25/world/europe/poland-ukraine-russia.html.

94. Ibid.

95. Justin Spike and Vanessa Gera, "Is it a bluff? Some in Hungary and Poland talk of EU pullout," *Associated Press*, September 25, 2021, apnews.com/article/europe-poland-hungary-brexit-brussels-95779c949531b17aad909ba7d90614d0.

96. *Politico* Poll of Polls, Poland, June 13, 2022, www.politico.eu/europe-poll-of-polls/poland/.

97. *Politico* Poll of Polls, Germany, June 20, 2022, www.politico.eu/europe-poll-of-polls/germany/.

98. *Politico* Poll of Polls, Netherlands, June 13, 2022, www.politico.eu/europe-poll-of-polls/netherlands/.

99. Adam Taylor, "Geert Wilders, the champion of 'free speech' in Texas, wants to ban the Koran in Holland," *Washington Post*, May 4, 2015, www.washingtonpost.com/

news/worldviews/wp/2015/05/04/geert-wilders-the-champion-of-free-speech-in-tex-as-wants-to-ban-the-koran-in-holland/.

100. "Dutch populist Wilders calls for ban on Koran," *Reuters*, August 8, 2007, www.reuters.com/article/uk-dutch-koran/dutch-populist-wilders-calls-for-ban-on-koran-idUKL0819099220070808.

101. Roger Cohen, "Emmanuel Macron Defeats Marine Le Pen for Second Term as French President," *New York Times*, April 24, 2022, www.nytimes.com/2022/04/24/world/europe/french-election-results-macron-le-pen.html.

102. Norimitsu Onishi, Constant Méheut, and Aurelien Breeden, "A Fragmented Parliament Brings Macron Back Down to Earth," *New York Times*, June 20, 2022, www.nytimes.com/2022/06/20/world/europe/france-elections-macron-majority.html.

103. Andrew Higgins, "In the Tinderbox of Bosnia, a Serb Nationalist Lights a Match," *New York Times*, January 2, 2022, www.nytimes.com/2022/01/02/world/europe/bosnia-war-putin.html.

104. Ibid.

105. Joshua Hammer, "Bosnia on the Brink," *New York Times Magazine*, June 14, 2022, www.nytimes.com/2022/06/14/magazine/bosnia-genocide-pyramids.html.

106. Hitchens, "The Perils of Partition."

107. Christopher Hitchens, "Déjà vu all over again," *Salon*, November 11, 1996, www.salon.com/1996/11/11/news_574/.

108. Nicholas Kulish and Eugen Freund, "Jörg Haider, Austrian Rightist, Is Dead at 58," *New York Times*, October 11, 2008, www.nytimes.com/2008/10/12/world/europe/12haider.html.

109. Hitchens, "Déjà vu all over again."

110. Heather Berit Freeman, "Austria: The 1999 Parliament Elections and the European Union Members' Sanctions," *Boston College International and Comparative Law Review*, December 2002, 109-110, lawdigitalcommons.bc.edu/cgi/viewcontent.cgi?article=1162&context=iclr.

111. Hitchens, "Déjà vu all over again."

112. Ibid.

113. Ibid.

114. Hitchens, "White Fright."

115. Harriet Agnew and Anne-Sylvaine Chassany, "Le Pen steps up anti-immigration rhetoric ahead of French election," *Financial Times*, April 18, 2017, www.ft.com/content/967daaae-2412-11e7-8691-d5f7e0cd0a16.

116. Dominique Vidalon, "France's Le Pen vows to hold referendum on EU if elected," *Reuters*, September 3, 2016, www.reuters.com/article/us-france-lepen-referendum/frances-le-pen-vows-to-hold-referendum-on-eu-if-elected-idUSKCN1190HW.

117. Steven Erlanger, "A victory for Le Pen would be a debacle for the E.U.," *New York Times*, April 24, 2022, www.nytimes.com/2022/04/24/world/europe/a-victory-for-

le-pen-would-be-a-debacle-for-the-eu.html.

118. "National Conservatism" overview, the Edmund Burke Foundation, nationalconservatism.org/about/.

119. Hitchens, "On Becoming American."

120. Hitchens, *Letters to a Young Contrarian*, 103-104.

121. Donald J. Trump, inaugural address, January 20, 2017, www.politico.com/story/2017/01/full-text-donald-trump-inauguration-speech-transcript-233907.

122. Ibid.

123. George Packer, "Hillary Clinton and the Populist Revolt," *New Yorker*, October 24, 2016, www.newyorker.com/magazine/2016/10/31/hillary-clinton-and-the-populist-revolt.

124. Christopher Hitchens, "Q&A," C-SPAN recording, 11:37, April 22, 2009, www.c-span.org/video/?285444-1/qa-christopher-hitchens.

125. Christopher Hitchens, "Vote for Obama," *Slate*, October 13, 2008, slate.com/news-and-politics/2008/10/vote-obama-mccain-lacks-the-character-and-temperament-to-be-president-and-palin-is-simply-a-disgrace.html.

126. Ibid.

127. Christopher Hitchens, "Palin's Pals," *Slate*, December 7, 2009, slate.com/news-and-politics/2009/12/sarah-palin-s-brand-of-populism-is-dangerous-and-deceptive.html.

128. Ibid.

129. Ibid.

130. Christopher Hitchens, "Sarah Palin's Political Instincts," *Newsweek*, November 13, 2009, www.newsweek.com/sarah-palins-political-instincts-hitchens-77013.

131. Pat Buchanan, "Hardball with Chris Matthews," NBC, August 29, 2008, www.nbcnews.com/id/wbna26514861.

132. Hitchens, "Sarah Palin's Political Instincts."

133. Christopher Hitchens, "Secular Values and Republican Virtues: Resisting The Virtual and Vicarious," *Salmagundi*, Spring-Summer 1998, 197, www.jstor.org/stable/40549314. According to a note on the first page, this essay was "presented as a public lecture at Columbia University, under the patronage of Professor Edward Said, on November 5, 1997."

134. Hitchens, *Letters to a Young Contrarian*, 72.

135. Hitchens, "Tea'd Off."

136. Ibid.

137. Noam Chomsky, "The Politics of Red Lines," *In These Times*, May 1, 2014, inthesetimes.com/article/russia-ukraine-noam-chomsky.

138. Ibid.

139. Ibid.

140. Ibid.

141. Tariq Ali, "How Vladimir Putin became evil," *Guardian*, March 28, 2014, www.theguardian.com/commentisfree/2014/mar/28/why-putin-crimea-strategy-west-villain.

142. Svetlana Savranskaya and Tom Blanton, "NATO Expansion: What Gorbachev Heard," National Security Archive at George Washington University, Briefing Book no. 613, Dec 12, 2017, nsarchive.gwu.edu/briefing-book/russia-programs/2017-12-12/nato-expansion-what-gorbachev-heard-western-leaders-early.

143. "Ukraine's president signs anti-protest bill into law," BBC News, January 17, 2014, www.bbc.com/news/world-europe-25771595.

144. Andrew E. Kramer and Andrew Higgins, "Ukraine's Forces Escalate Attacks Against Protesters," *New York Times*, February 20, 2014, www.nytimes.com/2014/02/21/world/europe/ukraine.html.

145. Ibid.

146. William Booth, "Ukraine's parliament votes to oust president; former prime minister is freed from prison," *Washington Post*, February 22, 2014, www.washingtonpost.com/world/europe/ukraines-yanukovych-missing-as-protesters-take-control-of-presidential-residence-in-kiev/2014/02/22/802f7c6c-9bd2-11e3-ad71-e03637a299c0_story.html.

147. Adam Taylor, "Ukrainians keep pulling down Soviet statues. Now Russia is getting angry," *Washington Post*, February 25, 2014, www.washingtonpost.com/news/worldviews/wp/2014/02/25/ukrainians-keep-pulling-down-soviet-statues-now-russia-is-getting-angry/.

148. John Paul Rathbone, Sam Jones, and Daniel Dombey, "Military briefing: why Russia is deploying more troops to Ukraine," *Financial Times*, March 17, 2022, www.ft.com/content/d721718e-37cd-4113-8c2f-489f930991fb.

149. Julian E. Barnes, Michael Crowley, and Eric Schmitt, "Russia Positioning Helicopters, in Possible Sign of Ukraine Plans," *New York Times*, January 10, 2022, www.nytimes.com/2022/01/10/us/politics/russia-ukraine-helicopters.html.

150. Vladimir Putin, "On the Historical Unity of Russians and Ukrainians," Kremlin News, July 12, 2021, en.kremlin.ru/events/president/news/66181.

151. Vladimir Putin, address on February 21, 2022, en.kremlin.ru/events/president/news/67828.

152. "On Russia's Invasion of Ukraine," statement by the Democratic Socialists of America, February 26, 2022, www.dsausa.org/statements/on-russias-invasion-of-ukraine/.

153. Michael Tracey (@mtracey), "FOX NEWS host Harris Faulkner turns to Condoleezza Rice this morning and says, 'When you invade a sovereign nation, that is a war crime'—Rice nods in solemn agreement. Just incredible. Establishment factions are going all-out leveraging this to whitewash their own past actions," Twitter, February 27, 2022, twitter.com/mtracey/status/1498026998265909250.

154. Glenn Greenwald (@ggreenwald), "This is, without exaggeration, one of the

most amazing things I've ever seen on television, and tells you all you need to know about the state of mainstream US discourse and the implicit premises on which it's based," Twitter, February 27, 2022, twitter.com/ggreenwald/status/1498060937605046272. Greenwald was referring to the same interview as Tracey.

155. "A Conversation with Christopher Hitchens," interview conducted by James Kirchick.

156. Ibid.

157. Vladimir Putin, address on March 18, 2014, en.kremlin.ru/events/president/news/20603.

158. Andrew Osborn, "Putin, before vote, says he'd reverse Soviet collapse if he could: agencies," *Reuters*, March 2, 2018, www.rcuters.com/article/us-russia-election-putin/putin-before-vote-says-hed-reverse-soviet-collapse-if-he-could-agencies-idUSKCN1GE2TF.

159. Putin, address on March 18, 2014.

160. Hitchens, "The Axis of Evil," speech at the Center for American Studies, the University of Western Ontario.

161. Hitchens, "South Ossetia Isn't Kosovo."

162. "A Conversation with Christopher Hitchens," interview conducted by James Kirchick.

163. Christopher Hitchens, "Bons Mots and Bêtes Noires," *New York Times*, September 19, 2008, www.nytimes.com/2008/09/21/books/review/Hitchens-t.html.

164. Hitchens, "South Ossetia Isn't Kosovo."

165. Nandita Bose and Steve Holland, "U.S. offers assurances to Sweden, Finland over NATO application," *Reuters*, May 5, 2022, www.reuters.com/world/europe/us-offers-assurances-sweden-finland-over-nato-application-2022-05-05/.

166. Hitchens, "South Ossetia Isn't Kosovo."

167. Maria Kiselyova, "Putin orders Russian forces to 'perform peacekeeping functions' in eastern Ukraine's breakaway regions," *Reuters*, February 22, 2022, www.reuters.com/world/europe/putin-orders-russian-peacekeepers-eastern-ukraines-two-breakaway-regions-2022-02-21/.

168. Putin, address on February 21, 2022.

169. Anton Troianovski, "Why Vladimir Putin Invokes Nazis to Justify His Invasion of Ukraine," March 17, 2022, www.nytimes.com/2022/03/17/world/europe/ukraine-putin-nazis.html.

170. "Ukraine election: Comedian Zelensky wins presidency by landslide," *BBC News*, April 22, 2019, www.bbc.com/news/world-europe-48007487.

171. Hitchens, "South Ossetia Isn't Kosovo."

172. Higgins, "In the Tinderbox of Bosnia, a Serb Nationalist Lights a Match."

173. Lionel Barber and Henry Foy, "Vladimir Putin says liberalism has 'become obsolete,'" *Financial Times*, June 27, 2019, www.ft.com/content/670039ec-98f3-11e9-

9573-ee5cbb98ed36.

174. Gabriela Baczynska and John Chalmers, "Hungary's Orban says EU should reverse Russia sanctions, not push Cyprus on Belarus," *Reuters*, September 25, 2020, www.reuters.com/article/uk-hungary-orban-russia-belarus-idUKKCN26G2HR.

175. David Brennan, "Viktor Orban About To Make West's Putin Problem Worse, Opponent Warns," *Newsweek*, April 12, 2022, www.newsweek.com/viktor-orban-hungary-russia-ukraine-eu-us-1697264.

176. Leonie Kijewski, "Orbán: Oil sanctions plan is 'nuclear bomb' for Hungarian economy," *Politico*, May 6, 2022, www.politico.eu/article/orban-commissions-sanction-plans-a-nuclear-bomb-for-economy/.

177. Suzanne Daley and Maïa de la Baume, "French Far Right Gets Helping Hand With Russian Loan," *New York Times*, December 1, 2014, www.nytimes.com/2014/12/02/world/europe/french-far-right-gets-helping-hand-with-russian-loan-.html.

178. Joseph Gedeon and Kyle Chency, "Trump calls Putin 'genius' and 'savvy' for Ukraine invasion," *Politico*, February 23, 2022, www.politico.com/news/2022/02/23/trump-putin-ukraine-invasion-00010923.

179. Lindsey German, "Ten Things to Remember About the Crisis in Ukraine and Crimea," Stop the War Coalition, March 3, 2014, www.stopwar.org.uk/article/10-things-to-remember-about-the-crisis-in-ukraine-and-crimea-2/.

180. Ibid.

181. Putin, address on March 18, 2014.

182. German, "Ten Things to Remember About the Crisis in Ukraine and Crimea."

183. Putin, address on March 18, 2014.

184. German, "Ten Things to Remember About the Crisis in Ukraine and Crimea."

185. Putin, address on March 18, 2014.

186. German, "Ten Things to Remember About the Crisis in Ukraine and Crimea."

187. "Statement on Ukraine," Stop the War Coalition, February 22, 2022, www.stopwar.org.uk/article/stop-the-war-statement-on-ukraine-22-02-22/.

188. Pat Buchanan, "When did Ukraine become a 'critical ally'?" *The Joplin Globe*, November 18, 2019, www.joplinglobe.com/opinion/columns/patrick-buchanan-when-did-ukraine-become-a-critical-ally/article_4c468ec5-bb81-534c-af1d-7fcfbbad881f.html. This was a syndicated column, so it can be found in many U.S. newspapers if the above link is broken.

189. Ibid.

190. Pat Buchanan, *A Republic, Not An Empire: Reclaiming America's Destiny* (Washington, DC: Regnery Publishing, 1999).

191. Christopher Hitchens, "An empire after all," *Salon*, October 16, 1999, www.salon.com/1999/10/16/buchanan_5/.

192. "Away from the Abyss," open letter published in *Compact*, March 31, 2022, compactmag.com/article/away-from-the-abyss. The letter also contained the following warning: "President Biden recently described the confrontation with Moscow as a long war 'between democracy and autocracy.' Similarly grandiose rhetoric ensnared the West in the quicksand of the Middle East after 9/11, costing hundreds of thousands of lives and untold treasure." This is another reminder that the wars in Afghanistan and Iraq will continue to be invoked by those who wish to avoid necessary confrontations with dictatorships that are expressly hostile toward the values and goals of liberal democracies around the world.

193. Hitchens, "An empire after all."

194. Aaron Rupar, "Tucker Carlson's defense of Russia takes 'America First' to its logical conclusion," *Vox*, November 26, 2019, www.vox.com/2019/11/26/20983778/tucker-carlson-rooting-for-russia-ukraine-invasion-america-first.

195. Eric Bradner and David Wright, "Trump says Putin is 'not going to go into Ukraine,' despite Crimea," CNN, August 1, 2016, www.cnn.com/2016/07/31/politics/donald-trump-russia-ukraine-crimea-putin/index.html.

196. Aaron Blake, "Trump's Montenegro comments make it abundantly clear he doesn't understand NATO," *Washington Post*, July 18, 2018, www.washingtonpost.com/news/the-fix/wp/2018/07/18/trump-makes-it-abundantly-clear-he-doesnt-know-how-nato-works/.

197. Ibid.

198. Julian E. Barnes and Helene Cooper, "Trump Discussed Pulling U.S. From NATO, Aides Say Amid New Concerns Over Russia," *New York Times*, January 14, 2019, www.nytimes.com/2019/01/14/us/politics/nato-president-trump.html.

199. John Mearsheimer, "Why the Ukraine Crisis Is the West's Fault," *Foreign Affairs*, September-October 2014, 77, www.jstor.org/stable/24483306.

200. Philip Hamilton, "Professor Stephen Walt on the Crisis in Ukraine," Boston Global Forum, March 25, 2014, bostonglobalforum.org/news-and-events/events/professor-stephen-walt-on-the-crisis-in-ukraine/.

201. Stephen Walt, "Liberal Illusions Caused the Ukraine Crisis," *Foreign Policy*, January 19, 2022, foreignpolicy.com/2022/01/19/ukraine-russia-nato-crisis-liberal-illusions/.

202. Christine Huang and Jeremiah Cha, "Russia and Putin receive low ratings globally," Pew Research Center, February 7, 2020, www.pewresearch.org/fact-tank/2020/02/07/russia-and-putin-receive-low-ratings-globally/.

203. Elisabeth Rosenthal, "Liberal Leader From Ukraine Was Poisoned," *New York Times*, December 12, 2004, www.nytimes.com/2004/12/12/world/europe/liberal-leader-from-ukraine-was-poisoned.html.

204. "Viktor Yushchenko: Ukraine's ex-president on being poisoned," *BBC News*, April 2, 2018, www.bbc.com/news/av/world-europe-43611547.

205. Hitchens, "The Axis of Evil," speech at the Center for American Studies, the University of Western Ontario.

206. "Russia won't extradite Ukrainian official," UPI, July 16, 2008, www.upi.com/Top_News/2008/07/16/Russia-wont-extradite-Ukrainian-official/35661216236749/?st_rec=81601095788376&u3L=1.

207. Anton Troianovski, "As Evidence Mounts that Navalny Was Poisoned by State, Russians Just Sigh," New York Times, December 23, 2020, www.nytimes.com/2020/12/23/world/europe/russia-navalny-poisoning.html.

208. Anton Troianovski, Andrew E. Kramer, and Andrew Higgins, "In Aleksei Navalny Protests, Russia Faces Biggest Dissent in Years," New York Times, January 23, 2021, www.nytimes.com/2021/01/23/world/europe/navalny-protests-russia.html.

209. Gabrielle Tétrault-Farber, "Some Russians gear up for sub-zero rally for Kremlin critic Navalny," Reuters, January 29, 2021, www.reuters.com/article/us-russia-politics-navalny-yakutsk/some-russians-gear-up-for-sub-zero-rally-for-kremlin-critic-navalny-idUSKBN29Y1VK.

210. Troianovski, "As Evidence Mounts that Navalny Was Poisoned by State, Russians Just Sigh."

211. Max Blumenthal (@MaxBlumenthal), "This is a tactic the CIA tried unsuccessfully in Venezuela. Incidentally, both Leonid Volkov and Navalny were fellows at Yale's Maurice 'Hank' Greenberg program. While overseeing AIG's illicit practices, Greenberg reportedly sponsored CIA activity around the globe," Twitter, February 1, 2021, twitter.com/i/web/status/1356418789060059138.

212. Benjamin Norton (@BenjaminNorton), "These are the Western media's and NATO's favorite angelic 'peaceful protesters' in Russia: fanatical supporters of far-right fringe opposition figure Navalny who brutally beat up counter-protesters who dare to hold up signs. This is NATO's hope for Russia's future," Twitter, January 23, 2021, twitter.com/BenjaminNorton/status/1352976384365355009. As noted above, the video cited in the tweet was removed, but it depicted several protesters assaulting counter-protesters.

213. Max Blumenthal, "Is the US backing neo-Nazis in Ukraine?" Salon, February 25, 2014, www.salon.com/2014/02/25/is_the_us_backing_neo_nazis_in_ukraine_partner/.

214. Max Blumenthal, "Was bombing of Mariupol theater staged by Ukrainian Azov extremists to trigger NATO intervention?" The Grayzone, March 18, 2022, thegrayzone.com/2022/03/18/bombing-mariupol-theater-ukrainian-azov-nato-intervention/.

215. Andrei Makhovsky and Vasily Fedosenko, "'We don't need war': Belarus releases detainees in bid to quell protests," Reuters, August 13, 2020, www.reuters.com/article/us-belarus-election/we-dont-need-war-belarus-releases-detainees-in-bid-to-quell-protests-idUSKCN25925Z.

216. Benjamin Norton (@BenjaminNorton), "The US/NATO are attempting a 'color revolution' to overthrow the government in Belarus, the only remaining ex-Soviet state that still has socialist policies and state control over the economy ... Stratfor, 'the Shadow CIA,' is admitting they want a neoliberal Western puppet regime," Twitter, August 7, 2020, twitter.com/benjaminnorton/status/1294337278404329473?lang=en.

217. Max Blumenthal, "Hostile new cold war imperialist narrative needs factual vaccine," *Global Times*, August 5, 2020, www.globaltimes.cn/content/1196790.shtml.

218. Max Blumenthal (@MaxBlumenthal), "One of the most revealing moments of #impeachment trial was @JoaquinCastrotx defending the rioters that attacked Hong Kong's legislature as 'pro-democracy protesters.' Castro basically admitted the US supports mobs that ransack the gov't buildings of foreign 'adversaries,'"Twitter, February 13, 2021, mobile.twitter.com/MaxBlumenthal/status/1360676175622922240.

219. Max Blumenthal (@MaxBlumenthal), "Hong Kong protesters claim to fight for 'self-determination,' but movement leaders have joined w/ regime change hardliners in Washington to form a new lobbying operation. @ajitxsingh on how HK protests are subordinating the city to Washington's agenda: thegrayzone.com/2019/11/22/hong-kong-opposition-unites-washington-hardliners/," Twitter, November 22, 2019, twitter.com/maxblumenthal/status/1198039533788504064.

220. Blumenthal, "Hostile new cold war imperialist narrative needs factual vaccine."

221. Max Blumenthal, interview with Massachusetts Peace Action, March 23, 2021, masspeaceaction.org/event/the-us-accusation-of-genocide-in-china-with-max-blumenthal-and-zhun-xu/, www.youtube.com/watch?v=7hgAznkTcHQ&t=0s.

222. Pat Buchanan, "Why the Authoritarian Right Is Rising," personal website, April 20, 2018, buchanan.org/blog/why-the-authoritarian-right-is-rising-129153.

223. Ibid.

224. Hitchens, "Secular Values and Republican Virtues: Resisting The Virtual and Vicarious," 201.

225. Ibid.

226. Ibid., 201–203.

227. Ibid., 203.

228. Julian E. Barnes and Helene Cooper, "Trump Discussed Pulling U.S. From NATO, Aides Say Amid New Concerns Over Russia," *New York Times*, January 14, 2019, www.nytimes.com/2019/01/14/us/politics/nato-president-trump.html.

229. Trump, inaugural address, January 20, 2017.

230. Ibid.

231. Ibid.

232. Stephanie Condon, "Donald Trump: Japan, South Korea might need nuclear weapons," *CBS News*, March 29, 2016, www.cbsnews.com/news/donald-trump-japan-south-korea-might-need-nuclear-weapons/.

233. Hitchens, "Secular Values and Republican Virtues: Resisting The Virtual and Vicarious," 203.

234. Chomsky, *On Power and Ideology: The Managua Lectures*.

235. Tom Jones, "And the most-watched cable news show ever is . . ." Poynter, July 1, 2020, www.poynter.org/newsletters/2020/and-the-most-watched-cable-news-show-

ever-is/.

236. Tucker Carlson, interviewed by Gavin McInnes on the Free Speech Podcast, April 2, 2015, play.acast.com/s/freespeech/tag%3Asoundcloud%2C2010%3Atracks%2F198935778.

237. Glenn Greenwald, "Should the Populist Left Work With the Populist Right Where They Have Common Ground, or Shun Them?" *The Intercept*, June 25 2020, theintercept.com/2020/06/25/should-the-populist-left-work-with-the-populist-right-where-they-have-common-ground-or-shun-them/.

238. Eugene Scott, "Donald Trump: 'Had we taken the oil, you wouldn't have ISIS,'" CNN, January 26, 2017, www.cnn.com/2017/01/26/politics/trump-oil-isis-iraq/index.html.

239. Janet Hook, "Trump Reaffirms Support for 'Worse Than Waterboarding,'" *Wall Street Journal*, February 7, 2016, www.wsj.com/articles/BL-WB-60985.

240. Adam Taylor, "Trump said he would 'take out' the families of ISIS fighters. Did an airstrike in Syria do just that?" *Washington Post*, May 27, 2017, www.washingtonpost.com/news/worldviews/wp/2017/05/27/trump-said-he-would-take-out-the-families-of-isis-fighters-did-an-airstrike-in-syria-do-just-that/.

241. Steve Holland, "Trump to West Point grads: 'We are ending the era of endless wars,'" *Reuters*, June 13, 2020, www.reuters.com/article/us-usa-trump-wars/trump-to-west-point-grads-we-are-ending-the-era-of-endless-wars-idUSKBN23K0PR.

242. Mark Landler and Peter Baker, "Trump Vetoes Measure to Force End to U.S. Involvement in Yemen War," *New York Times*, April 16, 2019, www.nytimes.com/2019/04/16/us/politics/trump-veto-yemen.html.

243. Helene Cooper, Thomas Gibbons-Neff, and Ben Hubbard, "U.S., Britain and France Strike Syria Over Suspected Chemical Weapons Attack," *New York Times*, April 13, 2018, www.nytimes.com/2018/04/13/world/middleeast/trump-strikes-syria-attack.html.

244. Glenn Greenwald, interviewed on Tucker Carlson Tonight, Fox News, April 10, 2018, www.youtube.com/watch?v=V-yba3R6IBY.

245. Ibid.

246. Glenn Greenwald, interviewed on Tucker Carlson Tonight, Fox News, February 24, 2022, www.foxnews.com/media/glenn-greenwald-america-stop-russia-ukraine-war.

247. Glenn Greenwald (@ggreenwald), "Some have speculated that the US goal isn't to protect Ukrainians—that's the pretext—but rather sacrifice Ukraine by turning it into Syria or Afghanistan where war rages for years and destroys the country, bogging down Russia. No proof, but US actions consistent with that," Twitter, March 5, 2022, twitter.com/ggreenwald/status/1500196362209615875.

248. Tucker Carlson Tonight, Fox News, March 21, 2022, www.youtube.com/watch?v=oifqp1bJp8Y.

249. Tucker Carlson (@TuckerCarlson), "Ukraine isn't a democracy. It's a State Department client state," Twitter, February 23, 2022, twitter.com/tuckercarlson/status/1

496668655727349763?lang=en.

250. Rowena Mason, "Labour membership falls slightly but remains above 500,000," *Guardian*, August 8, 2019, www.theguardian.com/politics/2019/aug/08/labour-membership-falls-slightly-but-remains-about-500000.

251. Allison McCann, Lauren Leatherby, and Blacki Migliozzi, "U.K. Election Results Map: How Conservatives Won in a Landslide," *New York Times*, December 13, 2019, www.nytimes.com/interactive/2019/12/13/world/europe/uk-general-election-results.html.

252. Jeremy Corbyn approval rating, YouGov, December 22, 2019, yougov.co.uk/topics/politics/trackers/jeremy-corbyn-approval-rating.

253. "Investigation into antisemitism in the Labour Party," Equality and Human Rights Commission, October 2020, www.equalityhumanrights.com/sites/default/files/investigation-into-antisemitism-in-the-labour-party.pdf.

254. Heather Stewart, "Corbyn in antisemitism row after backing artist behind 'offensive' mural," *Guardian*, March 23, 2018, www.theguardian.com/politics/2018/mar/23/corbyn-criticised-after-backing-artist-behind-antisemitic-mural.

255. Allison Keyes, "Destroyed By Rockefellers, Mural Trespassed On Political Vision," *NPR Weekend Edition Sunday*, March 9, 2014, www.npr.org/2014/03/09/287745199/destroyed-by-rockefellers-mural-trespassed-on-political-vision.

256. Jessica Elgot, "Labour expels Jackie Walker for leaked antisemitism remarks," *Guardian*, March 27, 2019, www.theguardian.com/politics/2019/mar/27/labour-expels-jackie-walker-for-leaked-antisemitism-comments.

257. "Labour suspends activist over alleged anti-Semitic comments," *BBC News*, May 5, 2016, www.bbc.com/news/uk-england-kent-36203911.

258. Rajeev Syal, "Jeremy Corbyn says he regrets calling Hamas and Hezbollah 'friends,'" *Guardian*, July 4, 2016, www.theguardian.com/politics/2016/jul/04/jeremy-corbyn-says-he-regrets-calling-hamas-and-hezbollah-friends.

259. Daniella Peled, "Why I Found a London Play Framing Jews as a KKK-style Lynch Mob Strangely Touching," *Haaretz*, October 5, 2017, www.haaretz.com/opinion/2017-10-05/ty-article/the-london-play-framing-jews-as-the-revamped-kkk/0000017f-e4a6-d568-ad7f-f7ef7bef0000.

260. Christopher Hitchens, Daniel Pearl Memorial Lecture at UCLA, March 3, 2010, 25:47, www.international.ucla.edu/burkle/multimedia/114126.

261. Ibid., 26:00.

262. Jeremy Corbyn, "Why I'm Stepping Down as Chair of the Stop the War Coalition," Stop the War Coalition website, September 20, 2015, www.stopwar.org.uk/article/jeremy-corbyn-statement-to-the-stop-the-war-conference-19-september-2015/.

263. Matt Dathan, "Jeremy Corbyn faces prospect of resignations after Stop the War says Paris 'reaped whirlwind of Western extremism,'" *The Independent*, November 17, 2015, www.independent.co.uk/news/uk/politics/jeremy-corbyn-faces-prospect-of-resignations-after-stop-the-war-says-paris-reaped-whirlwind-of-western-extremism-a6737621.html.

264. Nicholas Watt, "Corbyn rejects call to pull out of Stop the War fundraising event," *Guardian*, December 6, 2015, www.theguardian.com/politics/2015/dec/06/corbyn-stop-the-war-fundraiser.

265. John Rees, speech at a Stop the War Coalition meeting, March 30, 2009, www.youtube.com/watch?v=8VZKwdrquLA.

266. Jeremy Corbyn, speech at a Stop the War Coalition meeting, March 30, 2009, www.youtube.com/watch?v=FQLKpY3NdeA.

267. Ibid.

268. Rees, speech at a Stop the War Coalition meeting.

269. Corbyn, speech at a Stop the War Coalition meeting.

270. Hamas, "The Covenant of the Islamic Resistance Movement," August 18, 1988, avalon.law.yale.edu/20th_century/hamas.asp.

271. Ibid.

272. Ibid.

273. Ibid.

274. Ibid.

275. Hitchens, *God Is Not Great*, 24.

276. Ibid.

277. Corbyn, speech at a Stop the War Coalition meeting.

278. Hitchens, *God Is Not Great*, 19-20.

279. Hitchens, "The Swastika and the Cedar."

280. Christopher Hitchens, "Hezbollah's Progress," *Slate*, October 18, 2010, slate.com/news-and-politics/2010/10/how-hezbollah-became-lebanon-s-most-powerful-faction.html.

281. "Muslim Publics Divided on Hamas and Hezbollah," Pew Research Center, December 2, 2010, www.pewresearch.org/global/2010/12/02/muslims-around-the-world-divided-on-hamas-and-hezbollah/. This report found that 94 percent of Shia had a favorable view of Hezbollah in Lebanon—a proportion that collapsed to 12 percent among Sunni.

282. Hitchens, "Hezbollah's Progress."

283. Christopher Hitchens, "Suicide Voters," *Slate*, January 30, 2006, slate.com/news-and-politics/2006/01/how-hamas-dooms-palestine.html.

284. Sue Surkes, "Corbyn defends £20,000 payment for Iranian TV appearances," *The Times of Israel*, September 1, 2016, www.timesofisrael.com/corbyn-defends-payment-for-5-iranian-tv-appearances/.

285. Hitchens, "Suicide Voters."

286. Ibid.

287. Christopher Hitchens, "On Not Knowing the Half of It: My Jewish Self:

Homage to Telegraphist Jacobs," *Grand Street*, Summer 1988, 131, www.jstor.org/stable/25007142.

288. Hitchens, *Hitch-22*, 383.

289. Christopher Hitchens, "Can Israel Survive for Another 60 Years?" *Slate*, May 12, 2008, slate.com/news-and-politics/2008/05/can-israel-survive-for-another-60-years.html.

290. Ibid.

291. Ben Burgis, *Christopher Hitchens: What He Got Right, How He Went Wrong, and Why He Still Matters* (Alresford, Hampshire, UK: Zero Books, 2021), 136.

292. George Orwell, letter to Noel Willmett, May 18, 1944, published in *George Orwell: A Life in Letters* (New York: Liveright, 2013), edited by Peter Davison, 232, first published in 2010.

293. Ibid.

294. Ibid.

295. Ibid.

296. Ibid., 233.

297. Hitchens, "The Axis of Evil," speech at the Center for American Studies, the University of Western Ontario.

298. Christopher Hitchens, "In the bright autumn of my senescence," *London Review of Books*, January 6, 1994, www.lrb.co.uk/the-paper/v16/n01/christopher-hitchens/in-the-bright-autumn-of-my-senescence.

299. Hitchens, "Why Bosnia matters."

300. Hitchens, "The Axis of Evil."

301. Paul Berman, *Terror and Liberalism* (New York: W.W. Norton, 2003).

302. Paul Berman, *The Flight of the Intellectuals: The Controversy Over Islamism and the Press* (New York: Melville House, 2011).

303. Christopher Hitchens, "Iraq's Budget Surplus Scandal," *Slate*, August 10, 2008, slate.com/news-and-politics/2008/08/why-do-we-have-such-a-hard-time-hearing-good-news-from-baghdad.html.

304. Hitchens, *Thomas Paine's Rights of Man*, 8.

6 The Highest Form of Patriotism

1. Christopher Hitchens, "What Is Patriotism?" *Nation*, July 1991. Reprinted in *And Yet: Essays* (New York: Simon & Schuster, 2015), 321.

2. Hitchens, "On Becoming American."

3. Thomas Jefferson, letter to Roger Weightman, June 24, 1826, www.loc.gov/exhibits/jefferson/214.html.

4. Christopher Hitchens, "The Export of Democracy," *Wall Street Journal*, July 12, 2005, www.wsj.com/articles/SB112113100274182982.

5. Steven Pinker, *Enlightenment Now: The Case for Reason, Science, Humanism, and Progress* (New York: Viking, 2018), 28.

6. Packer, "The Enemies of Writing."

7. Hitchens, "On Becoming American."

8. Hitchens, interview with *The Progressive Magazine*.

9. Christopher Hitchens, "What I Don't See at the Revolution," *Vanity Fair*, March 7, 2011, www.vanityfair.com/news/2011/04/hitchens-201104.

10. Ibid.

11. Bastian Herre and Max Roser, "Democracy," *Our World In Data*, 2013, ourworldindata.org/democracy.

12. "A Conversation with Christopher Hitchens," interview conducted by James Kirchick.

13. Ibid.

14. Stephen Kotkin, *Armageddon Averted: The Soviet Collapse, 1970-2000* (New York: Oxford University Press, 2001).

15. Berman, *Power and the Idealists*, 105.

16. Robert Wright, *Nonzero: The Logic of Human Destiny* (New York: Vintage, 2000), 216.

17. Pinker, *Enlightenment Now*, 157-158.

18. Ibid., 164.

19. Christopher Hitchens, "How neoconservatives perish," *Harper's Magazine*, July 1990, harpers.org/archive/1990/07/how-neoconservatives-perish/. Reprinted in *For the Sake of Argument* (London: Atlantic Books, 2021), 178–189.

20. Christopher Hitchens, "Imperialism," *Slate*, December 10, 2002, slate.com/news-and-politics/2002/12/american-imperialism-then-and-now.html.

21. Hitchens, "How neoconservatives perish," *For the Sake of Argument*, 178.

22. Ibid., 186.

23. Ibid.

24. Hitchens, "Imperialism."

25. Hitchens, "She's No Fundamentalist."

26. Hitchens, "What Is Patriotism?"

27. Hitchens, "Don't. Be. Silly."

28. Fatos Bytyci, "Kosovo parliament urges government to start NATO membership bid," *Reuters*, March 3, 2022, www.reuters.com/world/europe/kosovo-parliament-urges-government-start-nato-membership-bid-2022-03-03/.

29. "EU Referendum: Boris Johnson stands by Hitler EU comparison," *BBC News*, May 16, 2016, www.bbc.com/news/uk-politics-eu-referendum-36295208.

30. Naomi Adedokun, "Nigel Farage attacks Guy Verhofstadt after chief Eurocrat 'called for European Empire,'" *Daily Express*, September 17, 2019, www.express.co.uk/news/uk/1178957/Brexit-News-Nigel-Farage-latest-LBC-EU-Andrew-Adonis-Twitter-Guy-Verhofstadt.

31. Nick Cohen, "Why are Labour's leaders so quiet on Europe? Maybe it's the lure of disaster," *The Observer*, December 16, 2018, www.theguardian.com/commentisfree/2018/dec/16/why-are-labour-party-leaders-so-quiet-on-europe---maybe-it-is-the-lure-of-disaster.

32. Tony Benn, address at the Oxford Union, February 7, 2013, www.youtube.com/watch?v=DFlrA01OOqs&t=0s.

33. Christopher Hitchens, "'Wicked Or Merely Stupid?' Tony Benn and the Orwell Question," *Mother Jones*, March 14, 2014, www.motherjones.com/politics/2014/03/christopher-hitchens-1981-profile-anthony-benn/.

34. George Galloway, address at a Grassroots Out rally, February 19, 2016, www.youtube.com/watch?v=S8cF93B58Vw.

35. Ibid.

36. Hitchens, "The Perils of Partition."

37. Hitchens, *Hitch-22*, 239.

38. Christopher Hitchens, "The Abolition of Britain," a debate with Peter Hitchens, C-SPAN2 Book TV recording, October 14, 1999, www.c-span.org/video/?153240-1/the-abolition-britain.

39. Ibid., 44:16.

40. Ibid., 44:52.

41. Ibid., 46:09.

42. Ibid., 45:29.

43. "Hungary voters approve EU membership," UPI, April 12, 2003, www.upi.com/Defense-News/2003/04/12/Hungary-voters-approve-EU-membership/71051050185906/.

44. Gergely Szakacs, "Hungary will not veto EU sanctions on Russia—Orban," *Reuters*, March 3, 2022, www.reuters.com/world/europe/hungary-will-not-veto-eu-sanctions-russia-orban-2022-03-03/.

45. Hitchens, "The Abolition of Britain," a debate with Peter Hitchens, 46:11.

46. Sumantra Maitra, "'The EU is Essentially a German Empire': Peter Hitchens on Geopolitics and the Future of Europe," *Quillette*, May 19, 2017, quillette.com/2017/05/19/eu-essentially-german-empire-peter-hitchens-geopolitics-future-europe/.

47. Christopher Hitchens, "The Wartime Toll on Germany," *Atlantic*, January/February 2003, www.theatlantic.com/magazine/archive/2003/01/the-wartime-toll-on-germany/302661/.

48. Hitchens, *Hitch-22*, 202.

49. Hitchens, "The Euro," *Foreign Policy Magazine*.

50. Ibid.

51. Hitchens, "An Anglosphere Future."

52. Hitchens, "Free Radical," interview by Rhys Southan.

53. Ibid.

54. Hitchens, *Letters to a Young Contrarian*, 136.

55. Hitchens, *Conversations with History*, 44:27.

56. Stephen Kotkin, lecture at the Institute for Human Sciences in Vienna, 1:03:15, April 26, 2017, www.youtube.com/watch?v=7pUZK_J6cL0&t=3881s.

57. George Galloway, address at a Grassroots Out rally.

58. Bruckner, *The Tyranny of Guilt*, 202.

59. Christopher Hitchens, "Kosovo on Hold," *The Nation*, March 30, 2000, www.thenation.com/article/archive/kosovo-hold/.

60. "A Conversation with Christopher Hitchens," interview conducted by James Kirchick.

61. Hitchens, "Never Trust Imperialists."

62. Christopher Hitchens, "The Struggle of the Kurds," *National Geographic*, August 1992.

63. Hitchens, "Appointment in Samarra?"

64. "A Conversation with Christopher Hitchens," interview conducted by James Kirchick.

65. Christopher Hitchens, "Guerrillas in the Mist," *Slate*, January 2, 2004, slate.com/news-and-politics/2004/01/why-the-war-in-iraq-is-nothing-like-the-battle-of-algiers.html.

66. Christopher Hitchens, "My Ideal War," *Slate*, March 20, 2006, slate.com/news-and-politics/2006/03/what-the-world-should-have-done-after-sept-12-2002.html.

67. Christopher Hitchens, review of *Kurdistan: In the Shadow of History* by Susan Meiselas, *The Los Angeles Times*, December 7, 1997, www.latimes.com/archives/la-xpm-1997-dec-07-bk-61392-story.html.

68. Christopher Hitchens, "Holiday in Iraq," *Vanity Fair*, March 12, 2007, www.vanityfair.com/news/2007/04/hitchens200704.

69. David Zucchino, "As Kurds Celebrate Independence Vote, Neighbors Threaten Military Action," *New York Times*, September 25, 2017, www.nytimes.com/2017/09/25/world/middleeast/kurds-referendum.html.

70. Qubad Talabani (@qubadjt), "If only Christopher could have been with us today, wearing his Kurdistan flag lapel pin, cheering us on as we voted yes to Independance [sic]," Twitter, September 25, 2017, twitter.com/qubadjt/status/912419938631024640.

71. Tamer El-Ghobashy and Kareem Fahim, "Iraqi Kurds vote in favor of independence as crisis escalates," *Washington Post*, September 27, 2017, www.washingtonpost.com/world/iraqi-parliament-authorizes-troops-deployed-to-contested-city-as-kurdish-independence-crisis-escalates-/2017/09/27/845d7220-a381-11e7-8c37-e1d99ad6aa22_story.html.

72. Maher Chmaytelli and Raya Jalabi, "Iraqi forces complete Kirkuk province takeover after clashes with Kurds," *Reuters*, October 20, 2017, www.reuters.com/article/us-mideast-crisis-iraq-kurds-clash/iraqi-forces-complete-kirkuk-province-takeover-after-clashes-with-kurds-idUSKBN1CP0PT.

73. Loveday Morris, "How the Kurdish independence referendum backfired spectacularly," *Washington Post*, October 20, 2017, www.washingtonpost.com/world/how-the-kurdish-independence-referendum-backfired-/2017/10/20/3010c820-b371-11e7-9b93-b97043e57a22_story.html.

74. Ibid.

75. Hitchens, "Holiday in Iraq."

76. Hitchens, *Thomas Paine's Rights of Man*.

77. Hitchens, "Holiday in Iraq."

78. Christopher Hitchens, introduction to *When the Borders Bleed: The Struggle of the Kurds by Ed Kashi* (New York: Pantheon, 1994). Reprinted in Hitchens's *Love, Poverty, and War: Journeys and Essays* (New York: Nation Books, 2004), 360.

79. Ibid., 361.

80. Christopher Hitchens, "A People Betrayed," *Washington Post*, July 20, 1997, www.washingtonpost.com/archive/entertainment/books/1997/07/20/a-people-betrayed/0108103f-062b-49c9-a27c-e518733166c7/.

81. Ibid.

82. Ibid.

83. Noam Chomsky, interviewed by Jeremy Scahill on the *Intercepted* podcast, September 26, 2018, theintercept.com/2018/09/26/trump-united-nations-noam-chomsky/.

84. Ibid.

85. Ibid.

86. Ben Hubbard and Eric Schmitt, "Assad Forces Surge Forward in Syria as U.S. Pulls Back," *New York Times*, October 14, 2019, www.nytimes.com/2019/10/14/world/europe/syria-us-assad-kurds-turkey.html.

87. Hitchens, "The Perils of Partition."

88. Ibid.

89. Christopher Hitchens, "The Narcissism of the Small Difference," *Slate*, June 28, 2010, slate.com/news-and-politics/2010/06/in-ethno-national-conflicts-it-really-is-the-little-things-that-tick-people-off.html.

90. Hitchens, *God Is Not Great*, 36.

91. Hitchens, "The Perils of Partition."

92. Packer, *Our Man*, 268.

93. Rand Paul, interviewed by Chuck Todd on NBC's *Meet the Press*, October 13, 2019, www.youtube.com/watch?v=lp9r6NCgVe0.

94. David Weigel, "Rand Paul tells veterans why America should avoid wars in the Middle East," *Washington Post*, July 28, 2015, www.washingtonpost.com/news/post-politics/wp/2015/07/28/rand-paul-tells-veterans-why-america-should-avoid-wars-in-the-middle-east/.

95. Hitchens, "The Perils of Partition."

96. Ibid.

97. Hitchens, "Why Bosnia Matters."

98. Christopher Hitchens, "Which Iraq War Do You Want To End?" *Slate*, August 27, 2007, slate.com/news-and-politics/2007/08/we-re-fighting-at-least-three-wars-in-iraq-do-you-want-to-end-them-all.html.

99. Hitchens, "Iraq War Debate," C-SPAN 2 Book TV recording, 11:46, September 14, 2005.

100. Christine McCaffray van den Toorn, "Was Iraq's recent election a democratic success? Depends whom you ask," *Washington Post*, May 23, 2018, www.washingtonpost.com/news/monkey-cage/wp/2018/05/23/was-iraqs-recent-election-a-democratic-success-depends-who-you-ask/.

101. Hitchens, "Facing the Islamist Menace."

102. Hitchens, "A People Betrayed."

103. Kanan Makiya, "The Politics of Betrayal," *New York Review of Books*, October 17, 1996, www.nybooks.com/articles/1996/10/17/the-politics-of-betrayal/.

104. Christopher Hitchens, "Are Elections Democratic?" *Slate*, January 3, 2006, slate.com/news-and-politics/2006/01/why-is-the-anti-war-camp-so-ambivalent-about-democracy.html.

105. John Davison and Ahmed Rasheed, "In Iraq, an old U.S. foe grows his political power," *Reuters*, June 29, 2021, www.reuters.com/investigates/special-report/iraq-cleric/.

106. Hitchens, "Are Elections Democratic?"

107. Ibid.

108. Hitchens, "What I Don't See at the Revolution."

109. Ibid.

110. Ibid.

111. Ibid.

112. Ibid.

113. "All According to Plan: The Rab'a Massacre and Mass Killings of Protesters in Egypt," Human Rights Watch.

114. Hitchens, "What I Don't See at the Revolution."

115. Ibid.

116. Ibid.

117. Hitchens, *Arguably: Essays*, xvii.

118. Ibid., xvii–xviii.

119. Ibid., xvi.

120. Christopher Hitchens, "The Shame Factor," *Slate*, January 31, 2011, slate.com/news-and-politics/2011/01/egyptian-protests-shame-drives-people-to-the-streets.html.

121. Christopher Hitchens, "Iran's Waiting Game," *Vanity Fair*, July 2005, www.vanityfair.com/news/2005/07/hitchens-200507.

122. Christopher Hitchens, "Don't Call What Happened in Iran Last Week an Election," *Slate*, June 14, 2009, slate.com/news-and-politics/2009/06/don-t-call-what-happened-in-iran-last-week-an-election.html.

123. Farnaz Fassihi, "Iran Clears Way for Hard-line Judiciary Chief to Become President," *New York Times*, May 28, 2021, www.nytimes.com/2021/05/28/world/middleeast/iran-election-khamenei-raisi.html.

124. Hitchens, "The Shame Factor."

125. David D. Kirkpatrick, "Gaining Power in Parliament, Islamists Block a Cairo Protest," *New York Times*, January 31, 2012, www.nytimes.com/2012/02/01/world/middleeast/muslim-brotherhood-blocks-protest-in-egypt.html.

126. David D. Kirkpatrick, "Named Egypt's Winner, Islamist Makes History," *New York Times*, June 24, 2012, www.nytimes.com/2012/06/25/world/middleeast/mohamed-morsi-of-muslim-brotherhood-declared-as-egypts-president.html.

127. Hitchens, *Arguably: Essays*, xvi-xvii.

128. Hitchens, "The Shame Factor."

129. Christopher Hitchens, interviewed by Jamie Glazov for *Frontpage*, December 10, 2003, reprinted in *Christopher Hitchens and His Critics*, 205.

130. Christopher Hitchens, "Did We Take a Wrong Turn in Afghanistan?" *Slate*, July 16, 2009, slate.com/news-and-politics/2009/07/we-took-some-wrong-turns-in-afghanistan-but-it-s-too-early-for-despair.html.

131. "A Conversation with Christopher Hitchens," interview conducted by James Kirchick.

132. Aneurin Bevan, debate in the House of Commons on March 19, 1959, hansard.parliament.uk/Commons/1959-03-19/debates/e972ca63-9370-410c-9982-b53762e60fdf/Cyprus.

133. Hitchens, "Did We Take a Wrong Turn in Afghanistan?"

134. Heidi M. Peters, "Department of Defense Contractor and Troop Levels in Afghanistan and Iraq: 2007-2020," *Congressional Research Service*, February 22, 2021,

sgp.fas.org/crs/natsec/R44116.pdf.

135. Christina Goldbaum, Sharif Hassan, and Fahim Abed, "Afghanistan Collapse Accelerates as the Taliban Capture 3 Vital Cities," *New York Times*, August 12, 2021, www.nytimes.com/2021/08/12/world/asia/kandahar-afghanistan-taliban.html.

136. "A Conversation with Christopher Hitchens," interview conducted by James Kirchick.

137. Ibid.

138. David Zucchino, "Afghan Women Who Once Presided Over Abuse Cases Now Fear for Their Lives," *New York Times*, October 20, 2021, www.nytimes.com/2021/10/21/world/asia/afghan-judges-women-taliban.html.

139. Matthieu Aikins, Salman Masood, and Marc Santora, "As Taliban Crush Dissent, New Leaders Face Cascading Challenges," *New York Times*, September 8, 2021, www.nytimes.com/2021/09/08/world/asia/taliban-protests-pakistan.html?searchResultPosition=5.

140. Zucchino, "Afghan Women Who Once Presided Over Abuse Cases Now Fear for Their Lives."

141. David Zucchino and Safiullah Padshah, "Taliban Impose Head-to-Toe Coverings for Women," *New York Times*, May 7, 2022, www.nytimes.com/2022/05/07/world/asia/taliban-afghanistan-burqa.html.

142. Joe Biden, "Remarks by President Biden on the Drawdown of U.S. Forces in Afghanistan," July 8, 2021, www.whitehouse.gov/briefing-room/speeches-remarks/2021/07/08/remarks-by-president-biden-on-the-drawdown-of-u-s-forces-in-afghanistan/.

143. Ibid.

144. Peter Slevin, "Biden Says U.S. Role Needed In Afghan Peacekeeping Force," *Washington Post*, February 5, 2002, www.washingtonpost.com/archive/politics/2002/02/05/biden-says-us-role-needed-in-afghan-peacekeeping-force/66907bcb-eb74-47cc-b6af-00e4f0387acf/.

145. "Agreement for Bringing Peace to Afghanistan between the Islamic Emirate of Afghanistan which is not recognized by the United States as a state and is known as the Taliban and the United States of America," February 29, 2020, www.state.gov/wp-content/uploads/2020/02/Agreement-For-Bringing-Peace-to-Afghanistan-02.29.20.pdf.

146. Remarks by President Biden on the Drawdown of U.S. Forces in Afghanistan.

147. Jeremy Scahill, "Why Biden Is Right to Leave Afghanistan," *New York Times*, May 20, 2021, www.nytimes.com/2021/05/20/opinion/biden-afghanistan-war.html.

148. Hitchens, "Against Rationalization."

149. Female primary school enrollment, UNESCO Institute for Statistics, data as of June 2022, data.worldbank.org/indicator/SE.PRM.ENRR.FE?locations=AF.

150. United Nations Human Development Report 2020, Afghanistan country

profile, hdr.undp.org/sites/default/files/Country-Profiles/AFG.pdf.

151. Ibid.

152. David Zucchino and Safiullah Padshah, "Taliban Impose Head-to-Toe Coverings for Women."

153. Greg Jaffe, "The war in Afghanistan shattered Joe Biden's faith in American military power," *Washington Post*, February 18, 2020, www.washingtonpost.com/politics/2020/02/18/biden-afghanistan-military-power/.

154. Christopher Hitchens, "Afghanistan's Dangerous Bet," *Vanity Fair*, December 3, 2007, www.vanityfair.com/news/2004/11/hitchens200411.

155. Kara Fox, Kareem Khadder, Nilly Kohzad, and Zixu Wang, "Afghanistan is now one of very few countries with no women in top government ranks," CNN, September 10, 2021, www.cnn.com/2021/09/09/asia/taliban-government-women-global-comparison-intl/index.html.

156. Ibid.

157. Burgis, *Christopher Hitchens: What He Got Right, How He Went Wrong, and Why He Still Matters*, 57-58.

158. Farnaz Fassihi, "A 17-year-old Afghan soccer player died falling from a U.S. evacuation plane," *New York Times*, August 19, 2021, www.nytimes.com/2021/08/19/world/asia/zaki-anwari-dead.html.

159. Hitchens, "Did We Take a Wrong Turn in Afghanistan?"

160. Trends in Maternal Mortality: 2000 to 2017, World Health Organization, 2019, data.worldbank.org/indicator/SH.STA.MMRT?end=2017&locations=AF&start=2000.

161. Burgis, *Christopher Hitchens: What He Got Right, How He Went Wrong, and Why He Still Matters*, 60.

162. Walzer, *A Foreign Policy for the Left*, 3.

163. Christopher Hitchens, "U.S. Imperialism Or A Just Response To Terror?—A Debate Between Christopher Hitchens And Tariq Ali," *Pacifica National Programming*, April 17, 2002, www.pacificaradioarchives.org/recording/pz0500.

164. Joe Biden, "Democratic Perspective on World Affairs," C-SPAN recording, 16:15, www.c-span.org/video/?193498-1/democratic-perspective-world-affairs.

165. "A Conversation with Christopher Hitchens," interview conducted by James Kirchick.

166. Hitchens, *God Is Not Great*, 31.

167. Christopher Hitchens, afterword to *Christopher Hitchens and His Critics*, 331.

168. Hitchens, "Imperialism."

169. "Afghanistan situation," UNHCR operational data portal, May 31, 2022, data.unhcr.org/en/situations/afghanistan.

170. Christina Goldbaum and Fatima Faizi, "As Fears Grip Afghanistan, Hun-

dreds of Thousands Flee," *New York Times*, July 31, 2021, www.nytimes.com/2021/07/31/world/asia/afghanistan-migration-taliban.html?smtyp=cur&smid=tw-nytimes.

171. George Orwell, "England Your England," first essay in *The Lion and the Unicorn: Socialism and the English Genius* (London: Searchlight Books, 1941), www.orwellfoundation.com/the-orwell-foundation/orwell/essays-and-other-works/the-lion-and-the-unicorn-socialism-and-the-english-genius/.

172. Peter Singer, *The Expanding Circle: Ethics, Evolution, and Moral Progress* (Princeton, NJ: Princeton University Press, 2011), 120. First published in 1981 by Farrar, Straus & Giroux (New York).

173. Hitchens, *Arguably: Essays*, xviii.

174. Christopher Hitchens, "In God They Trust," *Slate*, November 21, 2011, slate.com/news-and-politics/2011/11/how-the-conservative-belief-in-american-exceptionalism-has-become-a-matter-of-faith.html.

175. Ibid.

176. Hitchens, *Hitch-22*, 418.

177. Ibid.

178. Francis Fukuyama, "The End of History?" *National Interest*, Summer 1989, www.jstor.org/stable/24027184.

179. Patrick E. Tyler, "Bush's Arms Plan: 'Dr. Strangelove' No More; And for the B-52's [sic], the Alert Is Finally Over," *New York Times*, September 29, 1991, timesmachine.nytimes.com/timesmachine/1991/09/29/895491.html?pageNumber=11.

180. Hans M. Kristensen, Robert S. Norris, and Matt Korda, "Estimated Global Nuclear Warhead Inventories: 1945-2020," Federation of American Scientists, June 2020, www.armscontrol.org/sites/default/files/images/Factsheets/WarheadInventories_1945-2020.png.

181. Steven Erlanger and Michael D. Shear, "NATO formally invites Finland and Sweden to join the alliance," *New York Times*, June 29, 2022, www.nytimes.com/2022/06/29/world/europe/nato-sweden-finland.html.

182. Max Roser, "Economic Growth," *Our World In Data*, 2013, ourworldindata.org/economic-growth.

183. Max Roser and Esteban Ortiz-Ospina, "Global Extreme Poverty," *Our World in Data*, 2013, ourworldindata.org/extreme-poverty.

184. Herre and Roser, "Democracy," *Our World In Data*.

185. Pinker, *Enlightenment Now*, 39.

186. Fintan Smith, "With the transition period almost over, by 51% to 40% Britons think we were wrong to vote to leave," YouGov, December 22, 2020, yougov.co.uk/topics/politics/articles-reports/2020/12/22/transition-period-almost-over-51-40-britons-think-.

187. Glenn Greenwald, "Brexit Is Only the Latest Proof of the Insularity and Failure of Western Establishment Institutions," *The Intercept*, June 25, 2016, theintercept.com/2016/06/25/brexit-is-only-the-latest-proof-of-the-insularity-and-failure-of-

western-establishment-institutions/.

188. Hitchens, *Letters to a Young Contrarian*, 109.

189. Ibid., 108.

190. Christopher Hitchens, introduction to *Animal Farm* by George Orwell (New York: Penguin, 2010), reprinted in Hitchens's *Arguably: Essays*, 234-235. *Animal Farm* was first published in 1945 by Secker and Warburg (London).

191. Christopher Hitchens, "American Power and the War in Iraq Panel," C-SPAN 2 Book TV recording, 13:07, April 26, 2003, www.c-span.org/video/?176342-5/american-power-war-iraq-panel.

7 America

1. "Liberalism," *Stanford Encyclopedia of Philosophy*, published November 28, 1996, substantive revision February 22, 2022, plato.stanford.edu/entries/liberalism/#Con.

2. Ibid.

3. Ibid.

4. Ibid.

5. George Orwell, "Charles Dickens," *Inside the Whale*, March 11, 1940, www.orwellfoundation.com/the-orwell-foundation/orwell/essays-and-other-works/charles-dickens/.

6. Packer, "The Enemies of Writing."

7. Amis, "The Boy Can't Help It," interview by Meryl Gordon, *New York Magazine*.

8. Hitchens, *Letters to a Young Contrarian*, 99.

9. Burgis, *Christopher Hitchens: What He Got Right, How He Went Wrong, and Why He Still Matters*, 137.

10. Jane Mayer, "Hitch," *New Yorker*, December 16, 2011, www.newyorker.com/news/news-desk/hitch.

11. D.J. Taylor, *Orwell: The Life* (New York: Henry Holt & Company, 2003), 9.

12. Hitchens, *Conversations with History*, 6:21.

13. Hitchens, *Letters to a Young Contrarian*, 2.

14. Christopher Hitchens, "The You Decade," *Slate*, April 9, 2007, slate.com/news-and-politics/2007/04/welcome-to-the-you-decade.html.

15. Martin Amis, "Authors on Christopher Hitchens' Mortality," C-SPAN 2 Book TV recording, 10:44, November 17, 2012, www.c-span.org/video/?309425-11/authors-christopher-hitchens-mortality&start=1266#!.

16. Salman Rushdie, "Remembering Christopher Hitchens," Charlie Rose, 22:51, charlierose.com/videos/14685.

17. Salman Rushdie, "Christopher Hitchens, 1949—2011," *Vanity Fair*, January 6, 2012, www.vanityfair.com/culture/2012/02/rushdie-on-hitchens-201202.

18. Hitchens, *Hitch-22*, 186.

19. Ibid.

20. Ibid., 186-187.

21. Christopher Hitchens, "The Future of Socialism," *Think Tank with Ben Wattenberg* on PBS, July 7, 2005, www.pbs.org/thinktank/transcript1193.html.

22. Christopher Hitchens, "The Revenge of Karl Marx," *Atlantic*, April 2009, www.theatlantic.com/magazine/archive/2009/04/the-revenge-of-karl-marx/307317/.

23. "The 25 Most Influential Liberals In The U.S. Media," *Forbes*, January 29, 2009, www.forbes.com/2009/01/22/influential-media-obama-oped-cx_tv_ee_hra_0122liberal_slide.html?sh=5a0231d2624c.

24. Christopher Hitchens, "For the Sake of Argument," C-SPAN Booknotes recording, 44:55.

25. Hitchens, *Hitch-22*, 411.

26. Ibid., 186.

27. Hitchens, *Letters to a Young Contrarian*, 97.

28. Ibid., 100.

29. Ibid.

30. Lionel Trilling, "George Orwell and the Politics of Truth," *Commentary*, March 1952, www.commentary.org/articles/lionel-trilling/george-orwell-and-the-politics-of-truthportrait-of-the-intellectual-as-a-man-of-virtue/.

31. George Orwell, letter to the Duchess of Atholl, November 15, 1945, *The Collected Essays, Journalism and Letters of George Orwell, Volume IV: In Front of Your Nose*, edited by Sonia Orwell and Ian Angus (London: Seckcr & Warburg, 1968), 30.

32. Hitchens, *Why Orwell Matters*, 211.

33. Hitchens, *Hitch-22*, 190.

34. Ibid., 192.

35. Ibid., 420.

36. Ibid.

37. Hitchens, "The Future of Socialism," *Think Tank with Ben Wattenberg*.

38. Hitchens, *Arguably: Essays*, xviii.

39. "Getting off the train," *The Economist*, February 4, 2016, www.economist.com/special-report/2016/02/04/getting-off-the-train.

40. Caroline Kelly, "Ocasio-Cortez compares migrant detention facilities to concentration camps," *CNN Politics*, June 18, 2019, www.cnn.com/2019/06/18/politics/alexandria-ocasio-cortez-concentration-camps-migrants-detention/index.html.

41. Hitchens, *Hitch-22*, 165.

42. Hitchens, "What Is Patriotism?"

43. Hitchens, "On Becoming American."

44. Ibid.

Index

About the Author

Matt Johnson is a writer and editor. You'll find his work in *Haaretz, The Bulwark, Quillette, American Purpose, Stanford Social Innovation Review, South China Morning Post, New Eastern Europe, RealClearDefense, Arc Digital, Areo Magazine, The Kansas City Star,* and many other outlets. He also writes for the Foundation Against Intolerance and Racism (FAIR) and Counterweight.